D0513907

THE LIFE

OF

JOHN DRYDEN

by

SIR WALTER SCOTT

Edited with an introduction by
Bernard Kreissman

UNIVERSITY OF NEBRASKA PRESS · LINCOLN

Publishers on the Plains

UNP

The text of *The Life of Dryden* is reproduced from Volume I of the Miscellaneous Prose Works of Sir Walter Scott, Bart., published by Robert Cadell, Edinburgh, 1834.

Library of Congress Catalog Card Number 63–8121

Manufactured in the United States of America

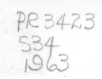

Contents

INTRODUCTION

Writing to his friend William Erskine in 1796, Sir Walter Scott noted that many apologies for publication "are in fact no apologies at all—Either the things are worthy the attention of the public or they are not, in the one case an apology would be superfluous in the other impertinent." However, as the scores of critical prefaces which he later wrote indicate, he knew the value of an explicatory introduction, and he would agree that in presenting a biography containing many notably incorrect facts, an explanation is not only in order, it is indispensable.

When Scott set out to write the life of Dryden in 1805, he had before him Samuel Johnson's criticism of Dryden's poetry and the biographical material collected by Edmond Malone, the greatest literary researcher of the eighteenth century. Malone spent years in his investigations of Dryden's life, sifting the fact, hint, hyperbole, and nonsense which had accreted in the century following Dryden's death, and unearthing almost as much new information as had been discovered by all previous biographers. His painstaking verification of all the accepted anecdotes about Dryden permitted him to disprove and discard a mass of apocrypha which had battened on ignorance, conjecture, and ill will. Every note and every document that Malone found was squeezed into a biography which he appended to his edition of the *Prose Works of John Dryden* (1800). Wholly unselective and put together with no thought for aesthetic construction, the biography, though a mine of information, was poorly received by the public, and a projected revised edition was never published.

Coming to the same task five years later, Scott proceeded on the assumption that the indefatigable Malone had uncovered and collected all the extant facts about the poet. It was a sensible assumption for his day, but in the century and a half since then our knowledge of Dryden has increased materially. Succeeding researchers have refined, improved on, and added to the methods originally used by Malone, and many of the points bearing on dates, places, patronage, and even canon which were accepted in the early nineteenth century are now known to be erroneous. Thus, Scott's *Dryden* should not be read for information of this kind; for such details one must refer to the scholarship of the last hundred years, or to Charles E. Ward's *Life of Dryden* (1961), which incorporates many of these findings.

Normally, such a statement is sufficiently damning to sound the knell of any ordinary biography (and it has for several contemporary Dryden biographies), but Scott's *Dryden* is no ordinary work. Despite its omissions and misstatements, it still remains a salient biography, deserving of study and worthy of the attention of the public.

ii

In the opening sentence of the *Life of John Dryden* Scott declared that the book "may be said to comprehend a history of the literature of England and its changes, during nearly half a century"—a bold claim, yet students of Dryden will find this statement no more than the truth, and reason enough for their rediscovery of the biography. A purist in matters of definition might object to classing the volume as a biography, for it is rather an artful blend of literary history and criticism, social history, and personal biography. Reading it, we recall that various historians have said or suggested that Scott was one of the greatest historians of the Restoration period. Certainly no other biographer of Dryden knew the period as Sir Walter knew it. Since Scott there have been some notable biographies of Dryden, among them Saintsbury's and Ward's, but the former is primarily a chronological critical account and the latter a synthesis of facts. In neither work does the period or the personality come through as they do in Scott's pages. For students and admirers of Dryden his biography still stands as the only one which exhibits Dryden as a personality within a specific historical setting.

What we have in Scott's *Dryden* is a masterful picture of the period, with literature in the foreground and the great figure of the most important man of letters of the age as the highlighted center of interest. It is true that in one major respect the picture is only partially successful: Scott was forced to fill out the portrait of his central figure with assumption and conjecture, for he had only a few known personality traits to work with. Since the research of the past hundred and fifty years has failed to turn up the kind of material which would help scholars to develop a full account of Dryden's personality and character, it may well be, as some critics contend, that a clear-cut, full-length portrait of Dryden will never be achieved. At any rate, it can safely be said that no one yet has given us a clearer view of Dryden's personality than Scott. And as compensation for his imperfect delineation of the poet, we have the magnificent panorama of Restoration social, cultural, and literary history—surely reward enough and to spare for any reader.

It can also be said that Scott has surpassed his fellow biographers not only in historical perspective, but in critical acuity. In regard to criticism only Johnson's memoir and Saintsbury's brief life may presume to stand beside the Scott biography, and Scott's book has one insurmountable critical advantage over these and all other biographies of the poet. Although his *Life of Dryden* was written so that it could be published as a separate work, it originally appeared as the introductory volume of the eighteen-volume *Works of John Dryden* (1808), which Scott edited. In this capacity it serves as a guide and a key to the criticism in the other seventeen volumes. Scott occasionally refers to the extensive criticism in these other volumes, but in nearly every case he synthesizes the general criticism for the benefit of the reader of the *Life*. Thus it may be read independently, or it may be used as a guide to the greatest single body of Dryden criticism ever written.

The superiority of Scott's work as a critic has been acknowledged by almost every Dryden editor. Noyes and Kinley in many instances reprint his notes intact, and Kinley dedicated his edition of the poetry to Sir Walter, observing that he was "still the wisest and most richly endowed of Dryden's annotators." Scott's deep obeisance in the prefatory "Advertisement" (see pages xvii–xix) to Samuel Johnson's criticism of Dryden must be discounted on the score of modesty. Of course one may find echoes of Johnson in Scott's accounts of the metaphysical poets and in his comparison of Dryden and Pope. A student will even discover evidence of Johnson's (and Boswell's) influence in the construction of Scott's biographies, although it is perhaps more apparent in the memoirs of Leyden and Swift than in the Dryden life. But Scott's criticism is at once deeper and broader than the Johnson work, and his preliminary disclaimer in favor of the Great Cham must be set aside. Today we would recognize it as a critic's duty to be conversant with important earlier work, and Scott's remarks should be taken as a respectful acknowledgment of that duty performed.

Scott's announced intention was to be the first biographer to "consider Dryden's literary productions in their succession, as actuated by, and operating upon, the taste of an age, where they had so predominant influence; and who might, at the same time, connect the life of Dryden with the history of his publications, without losing sight of the fate and character of the individual." The successful attainment of this ambitious objective produced a major work of historical criticism in the canon of literary scholarship.

iii

To students of Scott and his period the arguments for the rediscovery of all his biographical, critical, and historical writings are no less compelling than for the rediscovery of his *Life of John Dryden*. For almost a century scholars have tried to pierce the fictional veil of the Waverley novels to learn more about the ideas and personality of the man behind the book. Investigations of this kind are entirely valid, for truth lies at the base of all art, but it would also seem axiomatic that when an author has made a direct statement of his artistic, or social, or religious preferences, or declared his mind on an issue under study, his words must receive careful consideration.

Scott's convictions are to be found in abundance throughout his nonfictional prose writings, and for those in quest of his critical dicta the *Life of John Dryden*—his earliest prose work of appreciable length—is an unworked lode. Students of his novels are not sufficiently aware of the importance of this volume for almost all areas of Scott study. We may find here Scott's insistence on the relationship between audience and artist, his view of intellect as the principal quality of art, his precepts on the necessity for action in drama, his ideas of poetry as communication, and his thoughts on didacticism in art. Taken together, these general critical comments may be shown to form an organic structure approaching a unified theory of criticism. Scott himself probably would deny the existence of such a theory, not only because he felt that rules of aesthetic criticism "can apply only to the form, and never to the essence," but also because he wished to dissociate himself from the literary *poseurs* who merely talked about literature. Even more important, he felt that critical rules create a sense of prejudgment which would inhibit a fresh examination of each new work of art: one of his standard critical notes concerned the deadly effect of rules on the French drama. Nonetheless, in the *Life of John Dryden* a perceptive reader may discern Scott's own, undoubtedly unconscious, theoretical table of values.

Other facets of his personality are displayed in the biography. His Tory sympathies, class attitude, and deference to the nobility are here, as are his anti-Catholic sentiments. But we also see his honesty and sense of fair play overriding these prejudices: when he came to write of Dryden's conversion to Catholicism, despite faulty evidence which seemed to point to opportunism he gave us the first logical account of the "unbroken train of reasoning," deduced from the religious poems, which led to Dryden's adoption of the church of Rome.

The biography also affords us glimpses of the future novelist, for Scott is dealing with the period which would provide the setting for some of his finest novels. Those who study the relationship of the novels to the miscellaneous prose works will find periods, places, and historical personages overlapping in both categories. They will learn too that Scott drew upon his factual works for background information for the novels, and that he would turn to the writing of history or criticism for spiritual refreshment after the fatigue of the novel.

In his novels Scott advocates the use of "plain and forcible English," and this is perhaps the best description of the prose in the *Life of Dryden*. He detested affectation in men and in prose, and he wrote that an author should avoid "the extremes of simplicity and bombast." This precept, expounded again in the biography and in his criticism of the metaphysical poets and Lyly, is present by example on every page of *Dryden*. Except for his use of metaphor, the hallmark of his prose, Scott consciously avoided rhetorical tricks. Commenting on this aspect of his style, Lockhart, his son-in-law and biographer, noted that "metaphorical illustrations, which men born with prose in their souls hunt for painfully, and find only to murder, were to him the natural and necessary offspring and playthings of ever-teeming fancy." Fortunately, Scott did not overwork this device in the Dryden biography as he did in later prose pieces, but there are enough metaphors in evidence to show that they were indeed "natural and necessary" to his writing from the earliest works on.

To many of his readers the interpolated passages in Scott's novels are among their chief delights, but to some critics these passages and the loose ends he left dangling constitute evidence of his inability to work systematically. The point is still being debated, but whatever the final verdict may be, the *Life of Dryden* is a convincing demonstration of his ability to order and organize a mass of material. His use of parallel passages to present developments in Dryden's literary career along with the story of his private life and contemporary historical events results in a smooth, unbroken narrative flow. Summaries of Dryden's activities and syntheses of his philosophy are interpolated into the historical account without disturbing its flow. Prior to Scott, no biographer had attempted to gather together the ideas Dryden scattered throughout his work. Scott's extensive study of the poet and of the thought of his time gave him a wide spectrum of sources from which to draw for his remarkably effective condensations of Dryden's arguments. These philosophical syntheses in themselves attest to Scott's ability to order his work, to the brilliance of his mind, and to the depth of his knowledge.

It is unfortunate for Scott's reputation as a biographer that he himself is the subject of Lockhart's *Life*—the one work in the history of biography as a literary form which may be placed beside Boswell's *Johnson*. All biographical works which came between these two giants must stand in their shade, but—as Professor James M. Osborn and several historians of biography have noted—Scott's *Life of John Dryden* also advanced the art of biography. The clear perspective of time—the faithful representation of a past period and the lucid description of an older social setting superimposed on the life of a figure of the past—was first achieved in this volume. Here, too, Scott's work has not received its due; but perhaps that point has been sufficiently elaborated. It merely remains to say that the common reader will enjoy Scott's *Life of Dryden* as much as the student can profit by it.

iv

Scott published his multi-volume edition of the *Works of John Dryden* in 1808. A second, slightly revised edition was issued in 1821, and the set was re-edited by George Saintsbury between 1882 and 1893. The *Life of John Dryden,* originally Volume I of the *Works,* was published separately in 1808 and 1826; and in 1834 it was edited by John Gibson Lockhart for publication as the first volume of a collection of Scott's miscellaneous prose.

The text of the present edition is reproduced from the 1834 edition, which was preferred to Saintsbury's because of the contemporary notes Lockhart included. Lockhart's notes are to be found at the foot of the page, enclosed in brackets. Scott's original notes are also at the foot of the page, unenclosed. The present editor's note, restricted to points of clarification and to essential corrections, begin on page 455. They are indexed by page and line, but *not* by superior numbers in the text. References in the text to the *Works of Dryden* are to the second (1821) edition.

BERNARD KREISSMAN

City College, New York

THE LIFE OF JOHN DRYDEN

Editor should rival the criticism of Johnson, or produce facts which had escaped the accuracy of Malone. While, however, he has availed himself of the labours of both, particularly of the latter, whose industry has removed the cloud which so long hung over the events of Dryden's life, he has endeavoured to take a different and more enlarged view of the subject than that which his predecessors have presented. The general critical view of Dryden's works being sketched by Johnson with unequalled felicity, and the incidents of his life accurately discussed and ascertained by Malone, something seemed to remain for him who should consider these literary productions in their succession, as actuated by, and operating upon, the taste of an age, where they had so predominant influence; and who might, at the same time, connect the life of Dryden with the history of his publications, without losing sight of the fate and character of the individual. How far this end has been attained, is not for the Editor to guess, especially when, as usual at the close of a work, he finds he is possessed of double the information he had when he commenced it. The kindness of Mr Octavius Gilchrist, who undertook a jour-

ney to Northamptonshire to examine the present state of Rushton, where Dryden often
resided, and of Mr Finlay[1] of Glasgow, who
favoured the Editor with the use of some original editions, are here gratefully acknowledged.[2]

[1] [John Finlay, author of *Wallace, or the Vale of Ellerslie*,
and other poems, died in his twenty-eighth year, in 1810.]

[2] [The Biography of Dryden was not composed by any of
his contemporaries. Dr Johnson, who wrote the first authentic life of the poet, complained that nothing could be
known of Dryden beyond what casual mention and uncertain
tradition supplied.   Since that time many mistakes have been
rectified, and omissions supplied, by the diligent researches of
Malone ; and we are now probably in possession of all the
information which it is possible to produce. Sir Walter Scott
has justly founded his narrative on the facts recorded in Malone's biography ; while he has taken a more comprehensive
view of the genius and writings of the poet, and the influence
which he exercised on the Literature of the age.   When we
therefore consider the fairness and felicity of Johnson's critical disquisitions ; the truth elicited, or errors rectified by
Malone's diligence ; and the lively, interesting, and instructive narrative of Scott, we may justly consider that Dryden
has been fortunate in his biographers."—MITFORD's *Life of
Dryden*, 1832.]

THE

LIFE OF JOHN DRYDEN.

SECTION I.

*Preliminary Remarks on the Poetry of England before the
Civil Wars—The Life of Dryden from his Birth till the
Restoration—His early Poems, including the " Annus
Mirabilis."*

THE Life of Dryden may be said to comprehend a
history of the literature of England, and its changes,
during nearly half a century. While his great contemporary Milton was in silence and secrecy laying
the foundation of that immortal fame, which no
poet has so highly deserved, Dryden's labours were
ever in the eye of the public; and he maintained,
from the time of the Restoration till his death, in
1700, a decided and acknowledged superiority over
all the poets of his age. As he wrote from necessity, he was obliged to pay a certain deference to

the public opinion; for he, whose bread depends
upon the success of his volume, is compelled to
study popularity : but, on the other hand, his better judgment was often directed to improve that of
his readers; so that he alternately influenced and
stooped to the national taste of the day. If, therefore, we would know the gradual changes which
took place in our poetry during the above period,
we have only to consult the writings of an author,
who produced yearly some new performance, allowed to be most excellent in the particular style which
was fashionable for the time. It is the object of
this Memoir to connect, with the account of Dryden's life and publications, such a general view of
the literature of the time, as may enable the reader
to estimate how far the age was indebted to the
poet, and how far the poet was influenced by the
taste and manners of the age. A few preliminary
remarks on the literature of the earlier part of the
seventeenth century will form a necessary introduction to this Biographical Memoir.

When James I. ascended the throne of England,
he came to rule a court and people, as much distinguished for literature as for commerce and arms.
Shakspeare was in the zenith of his reputation,
and England possessed other poets, inferior to
Shakspeare alone ; or, indeed, the higher order of
whose plays may claim to be ranked above the inferior dramas ascribed to him. Among these we may
reckon Massinger, who approached to Shakspeare
in dignity ; Beaumont and Fletcher, who surpassed
him in drawing female characters, and those of

polite and courtly life; and Jonson, who attempted
to supply, by depth of learning, and laboured accuracy of character, the want of that flow of imagination, which nature had denied to him.[1]   Others,
who flourished in the reign of James and his son,
though little known to the general readers of the
present age even by name, had a just claim to be
distinguished from the common herd of authors.
Ford, Webster, Marston, Brome, Shirley, even
Chapman and Decker, added lustre to the stage for
which they wrote.   The drama, it is true, was the
branch of poetry most successfully cultivated; for
it afforded the most ready appeal to the public
taste.   The number of theatres then open in all
parts of the city, secured to the adventurous poet
the means of having his performance represented
upon one stage or other; and he was neither tired
nor disgusted by the difficulties, and disagreeable
observances, which must now be necessarily undergone by every candidate for dramatic laurels.[2]   But,
although during the reigns of Queen Elizabeth and

[1] [" Then Jonson came, instructed from the school,
To please in method, and invent by rule;
His studious patience and laborious art,
By regular approach assail'd the heart:
Cold Approbation gave the ling'ring bays;
For those, who durst not censure scarce could praise.
A mortal born, he met the general doom,
But left, like Egypt's kings, a lasting tomb."
DR JOHNSON.]

[2] I do not pretend to enter into the question of the effect of
the drama upon morals.   If this shall be found prejudicial,
two theatres are too many.   But, in the present woful decline of theatrical exhibition, we may be permitted to remember, that the gardener who wishes to have a rare diversity of

James I., the stage seems to have afforded the principal employment of the poets, there wanted not many who cultivated, with success, the other departments of Parnassus. It is only necessary to name Spenser, whose magic tale continues to interest us, in despite of the languor of a continued allegory; Drayton, who, though less known, possesses perhaps equal powers of poetry; Beaumont the elder, whose poem on Bosworth Field carries us back to the days of the Plantagenets; Fairfax, the translator of Tasso, the melody of whose numbers became the model of Waller; besides many others, who ornamented this era of British literature.

Notwithstanding the splendour of these great names, it must be confessed, that one common fault, in a greater or less degree, pervaded the most admired poetry of Queen Elizabeth's age. This was the fatal propensity to *false wit*; to substitute, namely, strange and unexpected connexions of sound, or of idea, for real humour, and even for the effusions of the stronger passions. It seems likely that this fashion arose at court, a sphere in which its denizens never think they move with due lustre, until they have adopted a form of expression, as well as a system of manners, different from that which is proper to mankind at large. In

---

a common flower, sows whole beds with the species; and that the monopoly granted to two huge theatres must necessarily diminish, in a complicated ratio, both the number of playwriters, and the chance of any thing very excellent being brought forward.

Elizabeth's reign, the court language was for some time formed on the plan of one Lillie, a pedantic courtier, who wrote a book, entitled " Euphues and his England, or the Anatomy of Wit ;"[1] which quality he makes to consist in the indulgence of every monstrous and overstrained conceit, that can be engendered by a strong memory and a heated brain, applied to the absurd purpose of hatching unnatural conceits.[2] It appears, that this fantastical person had a considerable share in determining the false taste of his age, which soon became so general, that the tares which sprung from it are to be found even among the choicest of the wheat. Shakspeare himself affords us too many instances of this fashionable heresy in wit ; and he, who could create new

[1] [London, 1581, 4to. See the character of Sir Piercie Shafton in the Monastery, and Sir W. Scott's Introduction to that tale, in the collective edition of the Waverley Novels, vol. xviii.]

[2] Our deserved idolatry of Shakspeare and Milton was equalled by that paid to this pedantic coxcomb in his own time. He is called, in the titlepage of his plays, (for, besides " Euphues," he wrote what he styled " Court Comedies,") " the only rare poet of that time ; the witty, comical, facetiously quick, and unparalleled John Lillie." Moreover, his editor, Mr Blount, assures us, " that he sate at Apollo's table ; that Apollo gave him a wreath of his own bays without snatching ; and that the lyre he played on had no broken strings." Besides which, we are informed, " Our nation are in his debt for a new English, which he taught them ; ' Euphues and his England ' began first that language. All our ladies were then his scholars ; and that beauty in court who could not *parle Euphuism*, was as little regarded, as she which now there speaks not French." The Satire in Cinthia's Revels is directed by Ben Jonson against this false and pedantic taste.

worlds out of his own imagination, descended to low, and often ill-timed puns and quibbles. This was not an evil to be cured by the accession of our Scottish James, whose qualifications as a punster were at least equal to his boasted *king-craft*.[1] The false taste, which had been gaining ground even in the reign of Elizabeth, now overflowed the whole kingdom with the impetuosity of a land-flood. These outrages upon language were committed without regard to time and place. They were held good arguments at the bar, though Bacon sat on the woolsack; and eloquence irresistible by the most hardened sinner, when King or Corbet were in the pulpit.[2] Where grave and learned professions set the example, the poets, it will readily be believed, ran headlong into an error, for which they could plead such respectable example. The affectation "of the word" and "of the letter," for alliteration was almost as fashionable

[1] So that learned and sapient monarch was pleased to call his skill in politics.

[2] Witness a sermon preached at St Mary's before the University of Oxford. It is true the preacher was a layman, and harangued in a gold chain, and girt with a sword, as high sheriff of the county; but his eloquence was highly applauded by the learned body whom he addressed, although it would have startled a modern audience, at least as much as the dress of the orator. " Arriving," said he, " at the Mount of St Mary's, in the stony stage where I now stand, I have brought you some fine biscuits, baked in the oven of charity, carefully conserved for the chickens of the church, the sparrows of the spirit, and the sweet swallows of salvation."—" Which way of preaching," says Anthony Wood, the reporter of the homily, " was then mostly in fashion, and commended by the generality of scholars."—*Athenæ Oxon.*, vol. i., p. 183.

as punning, seemed, in some degree, to bring back English composition to the barbarous rules of the ancient Anglo-Saxons, the merit of whose poems consisted, not in the ideas, but in the quaint arrangement of the words, and the regular recurrence of some favourite sound or letter.

This peculiar taste for twisting and playing upon words, instead of applying them to their natural and proper use, was combined with the similar extravagance of those whom Dr Johnson has entitled Metaphysical Poets. This class of authors used the same violence towards images and ideas which had formerly been applied to words; in truth, the two styles were often combined, and, even when separate, had a kindred alliance with each other. It is the business of the punster to discover and yoke together two words, which, while they have some resemblance in sound, the more exact the better, convey a totally different signification. The metaphysical poet, on the other hand, piqued himself in discovering hidden resemblances between ideas apparently the most dissimilar, and in combining, by some violent and compelled association, illustrations and allusions utterly foreign from each other. Thus did the metaphysical poet resemble the quibbler, exercising precisely the same tyranny over ideas, which the latter practised upon sounds only

Jonson gave an early example of metaphysical poetry; indeed, it was the natural resource of a mind amply stored with learning, gifted with a tenacious memory and the power of constant labour, but to which was denied that vivid perception of

what is naturally beautiful, and that happiness of
expression, which at once conveys to the reader the
idea of the poet.   These latter qualities unite in
many passages of Shakspeare, of which the reader
at once acknowledges the beauty, the justice, and
the simplicity.   But such Jonson was unequal to
produce; and he substituted the strange, forced,
and most unnatural, though ingenious analogies,
which were afterwards copied by Donne and Cowley.[1]   In reading Shakspeare, we often meet passages so congenial to our nature and feelings, that,
beautiful as they are, we can hardly help wondering
they did not occur to ourselves; in studying Jonson, we have often to marvel how his conceptions
could have occurred to any human being.   The
one is like an ancient statue, the beauty of which,
springing from the exactness of proportion, does
not always strike at first sight, but rises upon us as
we bestow time in considering it; the other is the
representation of a monster, which is at first only
surprising, and ludicrous or disgusting ever after.
When the taste for simplicity, however, is once
destroyed, it is long ere a nation recovers it; and
the metaphysical poets seem to have retained possession of the public favour from the reign of James
I. till the beginning of the civil wars silenced the
Muses.   The universities were perhaps to blame

---

[1] Look at Ben Jonson's " Ode to the Memory of Sir Lu-
cius Carey and Sir H. Morison," and at most of his pindarics
and lyrical pieces.   But Ben, when he pleased, could assume
the garb of classic simplicity; witness many of his lesser
poems.

during this period of usurpation ; for which it may be admitted in excuse, that the metaphysical poetry could only be practised by men whose minds were deeply stored with learning, and who could boldly draw upon a large fund of acquired knowledge for supplying the expenditure of far-fetched and extravagant images, which their compositions required. The book of Nature is before all men ; but when her limits are to be overstepped, the acquirement of adventitious knowledge becomes of paramount necessity ; and it was but natural that Cambridge and Oxford should prize a style of poetry, to which depth of learning was absolutely indispensable.

I have stated, that the metaphysical poetry was fashionable during the early part of Charles the First's reign. It is true, that Milton descended to upbraid that unfortunate prince, that the chosen companion of his private hours was one *William Shakspeare, a player ;* but Charles admitted less sacred poets to share his partiality. Ben Jonson supplied his court with masques, and his pageants with verses ; and, notwithstanding an ill-natured story, shared no inconsiderable portion of his bounty. [1] Donne, a leader among the metaphysical poets, with whom King James had punned and quibbled in

---

[1] In Jonson's last illness, Charles is said to have sent him ten pieces. " He sends me so miserable a donation," said the expiring satirist, " because I am poor, and live in an alley ; go back and tell him, his soul lives in an alley." Whatever be the truth of this tradition, we know, from an epigram by Jonson, that the king at one time gave him a hundred pounds ; no trifling gift for a poor bard, even in the present day.

person,[1] shared, in a remarkable degree, the good
graces of Charles I., who may therefore be supposed no enemy to his vein of poetry, although
neither his sincere piety nor his sacred office restrained him from fantastic indulgence in extravagant conceit, even upon the most solemn themes
which can be selected for poetry.[2]   Cowley, who,
with the learning and acuteness of Donne, possessed
the more poetical qualities of a fertile imagination,
and frequent happiness of expression, and who
claims the highest place of all who ever plied the
unprofitable trade of combining dissimilar and re-
pugnant ideas, was not indeed known to the king
during his prosperity; but his talents recommended

[1] " About a year after his return out of Germany, Dr Carey
was made Bishop of Exeter; and by his removal the deanry
of St Paul's being vacant, the king sent to Dr Donne, and appointed him to attend him at dinner the next day.   When
his majesty was sate down, before he had eat any meat, he
said, after his pleasant manner, ' Dr Donne, I have invited
you to dinner; and though you sit not down with me, yet I
will carve to you of a dish that I know you love well; for
knowing you love London, I do therefore make you Dean of
Paul's; and when I have dined, then do you take your beloved dish home to your study; say grace there to yourself,
and much good may it do you."—WALTON's *Life of Donne.*

[2] See his " Verses to Mr George Herbert, sent him with
one of my seals of the anchor and Christ.   A sheaf of snakes
used heretofore to be my seal, which is the crest of our poor
family."   Upon the subject of this change of device he thus
quibbles:

> " Adopted in God's family, and so
> My old coat lost, into new arms I go;
> The cross my seal, in baptism spread below,
> Does by that form into an anchor grow:
> Crosses grow anchors; bear as thou shouldst do
> Thy cross, and that cross grows an anchor too," &c.

him at the military court of Oxford, and the most
ingenious poet of the metaphysical class enjoyed
the applause of Charles before he shared the exile
of his consort Henrietta. Cleveland also was honoured with the early notice of Charles;[1] one of
the most distinguished metaphysical bards, who
afterwards exerted his talents of wit and satire
upon the royal side, and strained his imagination
for extravagant invective against the Scottish army,
who sold their king, and the parliament leaders,
who bought him. All these, and others unnecessary to mention, were read and respected at court;
being esteemed by their contemporaries, and doubtless believing themselves, the wonder of their own,
and the pattern of succeeding ages; and however
much they might differ from each other in parts
and genius, they sought the same road to poetical
fame, by starting the most unnatural images which
their imaginations could conceive, or by hunting
more common allusions through the most minute
and circumstantial particulars and ramifications.

Yet, though during the age of Charles I. the
metaphysical poets enjoyed the larger proportion
of public applause, authors were not wanting who
sought other modes of distinguishing themselves.
Milton, who must not be named in the same paragraph with others, although he had not yet meditated the sublime work which was to carry his
name to immortality, disdained, even in his lesser
compositions, the preposterous conceits and learned

---

[1] See his Life, prefixed to his Poems, 12mo. 1677.

absurdities, by which his contemporaries acquired distinction.   Some of his slighter academic prolusions are, indeed, tinged with the prevailing taste of his age, or, perhaps, were written in ridicule of it; but no circumstance in his life is more remarkable, than that " Comus," the " Monody on Lycidas," the "Allegro and Penseroso," and the "Hymn on the Nativity," are unpolluted by the metaphysical jargon and affected language which the age esteemed indispensable to poetry.   This refusal to bend to an evil so prevailing, and which held out so many temptations to a youth of learning and genius, can only be ascribed to the natural chastity of Milton's taste, improved by an earnest and eager study of the purest models of antiquity.

But besides Milton, who stood aloof and alone, there was a race of lesser poets, who endeavoured to glean the refuse of the applause reaped by Donne, Cowley, and their followers, by adopting ornaments which the latter had neglected, perhaps, because they could be attained without much labour, or abstruse learning.   The metaphysical poets, in their slipshod pindarics, had totally despised, not only smoothness and elegance, but the common rhythm of versification.   Many and long passages may be read without perceiving the least difference between them and barbarous, jingling, ill-regulated prose; and in appearance, though the lines be divided into unequal lengths, the eye and ear acknowledge little difference between them and the inscription on a tomb-stone.   In a word, not only harmony of numbers, but numbers themselves, were altogether neglected; or, if an author so far respected ancient practice as to make lines which could be scanned like verse, he had done his part, and was perfectly indifferent, although they sounded like prose. [1] But as melody will be always acceptable to the ear, some poets chose this neglected road to fame, and gained a portion of public favour, by attending to the laws of harmony, which their rivals had discarded. Waller and Denham were the first who thus distinguished themselves; but, as Johnson happily remarks, what was acquired by Denham, was inherited by Waller. Something there was in the situation of both these authors, which led them to depart from what was then the beaten path of composition. They were men of rank, wealth, and fashion, and had experienced all the interruptions to deep study, with which such elevated station is naturally attended. It was in vain for Waller, a wit, a courtier, and a politician; or for Denham, who was only distinguished at the university as a dreaming, dissipated gambler, to attempt to rival the metaphysical subtleties of Donne and Cowley, who had spent

---

[1] It is pleasing to see the natural good taste of honest old Isaac Walton struggling against that of his age. He introduces the beautiful lines, " Come live with me, and be my love," &c. as " that smooth song made by Kit Marlow, now at least fifty years ago."—" The milk-maid's mother," he adds, " sung an answer to it, which was made by Sir Walter Raleigh in his younger days. They were old-fashioned poetry, but choicely good. I think much better than *the strong lines* that are in fashion in this critical age."—*The Complete Angler,* Edit. vi., p. 65.

serious and sequestered lives in acquiring the knowledge and learning which they squandered in their
poetry.   Necessity, therefore, and perhaps a dawn-
ing of more simple taste, impelled these courtly
poets to seek another and more natural mode of
pleasing.   The melody of verse was a province
unoccupied, and Waller, forming his rhythm upon
the modulation of Fairfax, and other poets of the
maiden reign, exhibited in his very first poem
striking marks of attention to the suavity of numbers.
Denham, in his dedication to Charles II., informs
us, that the indulgence of his poetical vein had drawn
the notice, although accompanied with the gentle
censure, of Charles I., when, in 1647, he obtained
access to his person by the intercession of Hugh
Peters.   Suckling, whom Dryden has termed " a
sprightly wit, and a courtly writer," may be added
to the list of smooth and easy poets of the period,
and had the same motives as Denham and Waller
for attaching himself to that style of composition.
He was allowed to have the peculiar art of making
whatever he did become him; and it cannot be
doubted, that his light and airy style of ballads and

---

[1] " A Poem on the danger Charles I., being Prince, escaped
in the Road at St Andero."   [Dryden himself calls " Waller
the father of our English Numbers." He says, " I mention him
for honour's sake ; and am desirous on all occasions of laying
hold on his memory ; and thereby acknowledging to the
world, that unless he had written, none of us could write."
See Pref. to Walsh's Dialogue.   Fenton says, " Waller spent
the greatest part of a summer *in correcting a poem of ten lines,*
those written in the Tasso of the Duchess of York."—See
MITFORD's *Life of Dryden,* p. 13.]

sonnets had many admirers. Upon the whole, this class of poets, although they hardly divided the popular favour with the others, were also noticed and applauded. Thus the poets of the earlier part of the seventeenth century may be divided into one class, who sacrificed both sense and sound to the exercise of extravagant, though ingenious, associations of imagery ; and a second, who, aiming to distinguish themselves by melody of versification, were satisfied with light and trivial subjects, and, too often contented with attaining smoothness of measure, neglected the more essential qualities of poetry.

The intervention of the civil wars greatly interrupted the study of poetry. The national attention was called to other objects, and those who, in the former peaceful reigns, would have perhaps distinguished themselves as poets and dramatists, were now struggling for fame in the field, or declaiming for power in the senate. The manners of the prevailing party, their fanatical detestation of every thing like elegant or literary amusement, their affected horror at stage representations, which at once silenced the theatres, and their contempt for profane learning, which degraded the universities, all operated, during the civil wars and succeeding usurpation, to check the pursuits of the poet, by withdrawing that public approbation, which is the best, and often the sole, reward of his labour. There was, at this time, a sort of interregnum in the public taste, as well as in its government. The same poets were no doubt alive who had distinguished themselves at the court of Charles : but Cowley and Denham were exiled with their sovereign ; Waller was awed into silence, by the rigour of the puritanic spirit ; and even the muse of Milton was scared from him by the clamour of religious and political controversy, and only returned like a sincere friend, to cheer the adversity of one who had neglected her during his career of worldly importance.

During this period, the most unfavourable to literature which had occurred for at least two centuries, Dryden, the subject of this Memoir, was gradually and silently imbibing those stores of learning, and cultivating that fancy, which was to do so much to further the reformation of taste and poetry. It is now time to state his descent and parentage.

The name of Dryden is local, and probably originated in the north of England, where, as well as in the neighbouring counties of Scotland, it frequently occurs, though it is not now borne by any person of distinction in those parts. David Driden, or Dryden, married the daughter of William Nicholson of Staff-hill, in the county of Cumberland, and was the great-great-grandfather of our poet. John Dryden, eldest son of David, settled in Northamptonshire, where he acquired the estate of Canons-Ashby, by marriage with Elizabeth, daughter and heiress of Sir John Cope of that county. Wood says, that John Dryden was by profession a schoolmaster, and honoured with the friendship of the great Erasmus, who

stood godfather to one of his sons.[1] He appears,
from some passages in his will, to have entertained
the puritanical principles, which, we shall presently
find, descended to his family.[2] Erasmus Driden,
his eldest son, succeeded to the estate of Canons-
Ashby, was high-sheriff of Northamptonshire in
the fortieth year of Queen Elizabeth, and was
created a knight baronet in the seventeenth of King
James I. Sir Erasmus married Frances, second
daughter and co-heiress of William Wilkes of
Hodnell, in Warwickshire, by whom he had three
sons,—first, Sir John Driden, his successor in the
title and estate of Canons-Ashby ; second, William Driden of Farndon, in Northamptonshire ;
third, Erasmus Driden of Tichmarsh, in the same
county. The last of these was the father of the
poet.

Erasmus Driden married Mary, the daughter of
the Reverend Henry Pickering, younger son of
Sir Gilbert Pickering, a person who, though in
considerable favour with James I., was a zealous
puritan, and so noted for opposition to the Catholics,
that the conspirators in the Gunpowder Treason,

---

[1] *Fasti Oxon.*, vol. i., p. 115. Considering John Dryden's
marriage with the heiress of a man of knightly rank, it seems
unlikely that he followed the profession of a schoolmaster.
But Wood could hardly be mistaken in the second circumstance, some of the family having gloried in it in his hearing.

[2] See COLLINS' *Baronetage*, vol. ii. The testator bequeaths
his soul to his Creator, with this singular expression of confidence, " the Holy Ghost assuring my spirit, that I am the
elect of God."

his own brother-in-law being one of the number,[1] had
resolved upon his individual murder, as an episode
to the main plot, determining, at the same time, so
to conduct it, as to throw the suspicion of the
destruction of the Parliament upon the puritans.[2]
These principles, we shall soon see, became hereditary in the family of Pickering.   Mr Malcne's
industry has collected little concerning our author's

[1] Robert Keies, executed 31st January, 1606, of whom Fuller, in his Church History, tells the following anecdote:—
" A few days before the fatal blow should have been given,
Keies, being at Tichmarsh, in Northamptonshire, at his brother-in-law's house, Mr Gilbert Pickering, a Protestant, he
suddenly whipped out his sword, and in merriment made
many offers therewith at the heads, necks, and sides of several
gentlemen and ladies then in his company. It was then taken
for a mere frolic, and so passed accordingly ; but afterwards,
when the treason was discovered, such as remembered his
gestures thought he practised what he intended to do when
the plot should take effect ; that is, to hack and hew, kill and
destroy, all eminent persons of a different religion from himself."—CAULFIELD's History of the Gunpowder Plot.

[2] The following curious story is told to that effect, in Caulfield's History of the Gunpowder Plot, p. 67:—" There was
a Mr Pickering of Tichmarsh-Grove, in Northamptonshire,
who was in great esteem with King James. This Mr Pickering had a horse of special note for swiftness, on which he used
to hunt with the king. A little before the blow was to be
given, Mr Keies, one of the conspirators, and brother-in-law
to Mr Pickering, borrowed this horse of him, and conveyed
him to London upon a bloody design, which was thus contrived :—Fawkes, upon the day of the fatal blow, was appointed to retire himself into St George's Fields, where this horse
was to attend him, to further his escape (as they made him
believe) as soon as the Parliament should be blown up.   It
was likewise contrived, that Mr Pickering, who was noted
for a puritan, should that morning be murdered in his bed,
and secretly conveyed away ; and also that Fawkes, as soon

maternal grandfather, excepting that he was born in 1584; named minister of Oldwinkle All-Saints in 1647; and died in 1657. From the time when he attained this preferment, it is highly probable that he had been recommended to it by the puritanical tenets which he doubtless held in common with the rest of his family.

Of the poet's father, Erasmus, we know even less than of his other relations. He acted as a justice of peace during the usurpation, and was the father of no less than fourteen children; four sons, and ten daughters. The sons were John, Erasmus, Henry, and James; the daughters, Agnes,

---

as he came into George's Fields, should be there murdered, and so mangled, that he could not be known; upon which, it was to be spread abroad, that the puritans had blown up the Parliament-house; and the better to make the world believe it, there was Mr Pickering with his choice horse ready to escape, but that stirred up some, who seeing the heinousness of the fact, and him ready to escape, in detestation of so horrible a deed, fell upon him, and hewed him to pieces; and to make it more clear, there was his horse, known to be of special speed and swiftness, ready to carry him away; and upon this rumour, a massacre should have gone through the whole land upon the puritans.

" When the contrivance of this plot was discovered by some of the conspirators, and Fawkes, who was now a prisoner in the Tower, made acquainted with it, whereas before he was made to believe by his companions, that he should be bountifully rewarded for that good service to the Catholic cause, now perceiving, that on the contrary, his death had been contrived by them, he thereupon freely confessed all that he knew concerning that horrid conspiracy, which before all the torments of the rack could not force him to do. The truth of this was attested by Mr William Perkins, who had it from Mr Clement Cotton, to whom Mr Pickering gave the above relation."

many other exercises of the same nature, in English verse, none of which are now in existence.[1]
During the last year of his residence at Westminster, the death of Henry Lord Hastings, a young
nobleman of great learning, and much beloved,
called forth no less than ninety-eight elegies, one
of which was written by our poet, then about
eighteen years old.   They were published in 1650,
under the title of " *Lachrymæ Musarum.*"

Dryden, having obtained a Westminster scholarship, was admitted to Trinity College, Cambridge, on the 11th May, 1650, his tutor being the
reverend John Templer, M.A., a man of some
learning, who wrote a Latin Treatise in confutation
of Hobbes, and a few theological tracts and single
sermons.   While at college, our author's conduct
seems not to have been uniformly regular. He was
subjected to slight punishment for contumacy to the
vice-master,[2] and seems, according to the statement
of an obscure libeller, to have been engaged in
some public and notorious dispute with a noble-

[1] " I remember," says Dryden, in a postscript to the argument of the third satire of Persius, " I translated this satire
when I was a king's scholar at Westminster school, for
Thursday night's exercise; and believe, that it, and many
other of my exercises of this nature in English verse, are still
in the hands of my learned master, the Rev. Dr Bushby."

[2] The following order is quoted, by Mr Malone, from the
Conclusion-book, in the archives of Trinity College, p. 221.—
" July 19, 1652.   Agreed, then, That Dryden be put out of
Comons, for a fortnight at least ; and that he goe not out of
the colledg, during the time aforesaid, excepting to sermons,
without express leave from the master, or vice-master; and
that, at the end of the fortnight, he read a confession of his

man's son, probably on account of the indulgence of his turn for satire.[1] He took, however, the degree of Bachelor, in January 1653–4, but neither became Master of Arts,[2] nor a fellow of the university, and certainly never retained for it much of that veneration usually paid by an English scholar to his Alma Mater. He often celebrates Oxford, but only mentions Cambridge as the contrast of the sister university in point of taste and learning:

> " Oxford to him a dearer name shall be
> Than his own mother-university:
> Thebes did his green, unknowing youth engage;
> He chooses Athens in his riper age."[3]

A preference so uncommon, in one who had studied at Cambridge, probably originated in those slight disgraces, or perhaps in some other cause of disgust, which we may now search for in vain.

In June 1654, the death of his father, Erasmus Dryden, proved a temporary interruption to our author's studies. He left the university, on this occasion, to take possession of his inheritance, con-

---

crime in the hall, at dinner-time, at the three - - - - fellowes table."—" His crime was, his disobedience to the vice-master, and his contumacy in taking his punishment inflicted by him."

[1] Shadwell, in the Medal of John Bayes,

> " At Cambridge first your scurrilous vein began,
> Where saucily you traduced a nobleman;
> Who for that crime rebuked you on the head,
> And you had been expell'd, had you not fled."

[2] He received this degree by dispensation from the Archbishop of Canterbury.

[3] Prologue to the University of Oxford, [Dryden's Works.] vol. x., p. 385.

sisting of two-thirds of a small estate near Blakesley, in Northamptonshire, worth, in all, about sixty
pounds a-year. The other third part of this small
property was bequeathed to his mother during her
life, and the property reverted to the poet after her
death in 1676. With this little patrimony our
author returned to Cambridge, where he continued
until the middle of the year 1657.

Although Dryden's residence at the university
was prolonged to the unusual space of nearly seven
years, we do not find that he distinguished himself,
during that time, by any poetical prolusions, excepting a few lines prefixed to a work, entitled, " Sion
and Parnassus ; or Epigrams on several Texts of
the Old and New Testaments," published in 1650,
by John Hoddesden.[1] Mr Malone conjectures,
that our poet would have contributed to the academic collection of verses, entitled, " Oliva Pacis,"
and published in 1654, on the peace between England and Holland, had not his father's death interfered at that period. It is probable we lose but
little by the disappearance of any occasional verses
which may have been produced by Dryden at this

---

[1] Jonathan Dryden, elected a scholar from Westminster
into Trinity College, Cambridge, in 1656, of which he became
fellow in 1662, was author of some verses in the Cambridge
Collections in 1661, on the death of the Duke of Gloucester,
and the marriage of the Princess of Orange; and in 1662, on
the marriage of Charles II., which have been imputed to our
author. An order, quoted by Mr Malone, for abatement of
the commencement-money paid at taking the Bachelor's
degree, on account of poverty, applies to Jonathan, not to John
Dryden.—MALONE, vol. i., p. 17, note.

time. The elegy on Lord Hastings, the lines prefixed to " Sion and Parnassus," and some complimentary stanzas which occur in a letter to his cousin Honor Driden,[1] would have been enough to
assure us, even without his own testimony, that
Cowley was the darling of his youth; and that he
imitated his points of wit, and quirks of epigram,
with a similar contempt for the propriety of their
application. From these poems, we learn enough
to be grateful, that Dryden was born at a later
period in his century; for had not the road to fame
been altered in consequence of the Restoration, his
extensive information and acute ingenuity would
probably have betrayed the author of the " Ode to
St Cecilia," and the father of English poetical harmony, into rivalling the metaphysical pindarics of
Donne and Cowley. The verses, to which we
allude, display their subtlety of thought, their pue-
rile extravagance of conceit, and that structure of
verse, which, as the poet himself says of Holyday's
translations, has nothing of verse in it except the
worst part of it—the rhyme, and that far from being unexceptionable. The following lines, in which

[1] [According to Mitford, p. 6, Honor was wealthy as well
as beautiful, and her poetical cousin was an unsuccessful
suitor for her hand. She died unmarried after 1707. The
verses alluded to in the text are given in Scott's Dryden, vol.
xviii., p. 86, where the Editor calls them " a woful sample
of the gallantry of the time, alternately coarse and pedantic."

" You, fairest nymph, are waxe. Oh! may you be
As well in softnesse as in puritye!
Till fate, and your own happy choice reveale
Whom you so farre shall blesse to make your seale." &c.]

the poet describes the death of Lord Hastings by
the small-pox, will be probably admitted as a justification of this censure :

> " Was there no milder way but the small-pox,
> The very filthiness of Pandora's box ?
> So many spots, like naves on Venus' soil,
> One jewel set off with so many a foil ;
> Blisters with pride swell'd, which through's flesh did
>   sprout,
> Like rose-buds, stuck i'the lily-skin about.
> Each little pimple had a tear in it,
> To wail the fault its rising did commit,
> Which, rebel-like, with its own lord at strife,
> Thus made an insurrection 'gainst his life.
> Or were these gems sent to adorn his skin,
> The cabinet of a richer soul within ?
> No comet need foretell his change drew on,
> Whose corpse might seem a constellation."

This is exactly in the tone of Bishop Corbett's invective against the same disease :

> " O thou deform'd unwoman-like disease,
> Thou plough'st up flesh and blood, and there sow'st pease ;
> And leav'st such prints on beauty that dost come,
> As clouted shoon do on a floor of loam.
> Thou that of faces honeycombs dost make,
> And of two breasts two cullenders, forsake
> Thy deadly trade ; now thou art rich, give o'er,
> And let our curses call thee forth no more." [1]

After leaving the university, our author entered
the world, supported by friends, from whose character, principles, and situation, it might have been
prophesied, with probability, that his success in
life, and his literary reputation, would have been

[1] Elegy on Lady Haddington, in Corbett's Poems, p. 121.
Gilchrist's edition.

exactly the reverse of what they actually proved.
Sir Gilbert Pickering was cousin-german to the
poet, and also to his mother ; thus standing related
to Dryden in a double connexion.[1] This gentleman was a stanch puritan, and having set out as
a reformer, ended by being a regicide, and an
abettor of the tyranny of Cromwell. He was
one of the judges of the unfortunate Charles ; and
though he did not sit in that bloody court upon
the last and fatal day, yet he seems to have con-
curred in the most violent measures of the uncon-
scientious men who did so. He had been one of
the parliamentary counsellors of state, and hesi-
tated not to be numbered among the godly and
discreet persons who assisted Cromwell as a privy
council. Moreover, he was lord chamberlain of
the Protector's court, and received the honour of
his mock peerage.

The patronage of such a person was more likely
to have elevated Dryden to the temporal greatness
and wealth acquired by the sequestrators and com-
mittee-men of that oppressive time, than to have
aided him in attaining the summits of Parnassus.
For, according to the slight records which Mr
Malone has recovered concerning Sir Gilbert
Pickering's character, it would seem, that, to the
hard, precise, fanatical contempt of every illumina-
tion, save the inward light, which he derived from

[1] Sir John Pickering, father of Sir Gilbert, married Susan,
the sister of Erasmus Dryden, the poet's father. But Mary
Pickering, the poet's mother, was niece to Sir John Pickering ;
and thus her son Sir Gilbert was *her* cousin-german also.

might reasonably hope to attain preferment. In a youth entering life under the protection of such relations, who could have anticipated the future dramatist and poet laureat, much less the advocate and martyr of prerogative and of the Stuart family, the convert and confessor of the Roman Catholic faith? In his after career, his early connexions with the puritans, and the principles of his kinsmen during the civil wars and usurpation, were often made subjects of reproach, to which he never seems to have deigned an answer.[1]

---

reserving one side aisle of it for the public service of prayers, &c. He was noted for weakness and simplicity, and never put on any business of moment, but was very furious against the clergy."

[1] In a satire called "The Protestant Poets," our author is thus contrasted with Sir Roger L'Estrange. In levelling his reproaches, the satirist was not probably very solicitous about genealogical accuracy; as, in the eighth line, I conceive Sir John Dryden to be alluded to, although he is termed our poet's grandfather, when he was in fact his uncle. Sir Erasmus Dryden was indeed a fanatic, and so was Henry Pickering, Dryden's paternal and maternal grandfather; but neither were men of mark or eminence:

> " But though he spares no waste of words or conscience,
> He wants the Tory turn of thorough nonsense,
> That thoughtless air, that makes light Hodge so jolly ;—
> Void of all weight, *he* wantons in his folly.
> Not so forced BAYES, whom sharp remorse attends,
> While his heart loaths the cause his tongue defends ;
> Hourly he acts, hourly repents the sin,
> And is all over *grandfather* within :
> By day that ill-laid spirit checks,—o'nights
> Old Pickering's ghost, a dreadful spectre, frights.
> Returns of spleen his slackened speed remit,
> And cramp his loose careers with intervals of wit :
> While, without stop at sense, or ebb of spite,
> Breaking all bars, bounding o'er wrong and right,
> Contented Roger gallops out of sight."

The death of Cromwell was the first theme of our poet's muse. Averse as the puritans were to any poetry, save that of Hopkins, of Withers, or of Wisdom, they may be reasonably supposed to have had some sympathy with Dryden's sorrow upon the death of Oliver, even although it vented itself in the profane and unprofitable shape of an elegy. But we have no means of estimating its reception with the public, if, in truth, the public long interested themselves about the memory of Cromwell, while his relations and dependents presented to them the more animated and interesting spectacle of a struggle for his usurped power. Richard, perhaps, and the immediate friends of the deceased Protector, with such of Dryden's relations as were attached to his memory, may have thought, like the Tinker in the Taming of the Shrew, that this same elegy was " marvellous good matter," but it did not probably attract much general attention. The first edition, in 1659, is extremely rare : it was reprinted, however, along with those of Sprat and Waller, in the course of the same year. After the Restoration this piece fell into a state of oblivion, from which it may be believed that the author, who had seen a new light in politics, was by no means solicitous to recall it. His political antagonist did not, however, fail to awaken its memory, when Dryden became a decided advocate for the royal prerogative, and the hereditary right of the Stuart's. During the controversies of Charles the Second's reign, in which Dryden took so decided a share, his eulogy on Cromwell was often objected to him, as a proof of inconsistence and apostasy. One passage, which plainly applies to the civil wars in general, was wrested to signify an explicit approbation of the murder of Charles the First; [1] and the whole piece was reprinted by an incensed antagonist, under the title of " An Elegy on the Usurper O. C., by the author of Absalom and Achitophel, published" (it is ironically added) " to show the loyalty and integrity of the poet,"—an odd piece of vengeance, which has perhaps never been paralleled, except in the single case of " Love in a Hollow Tree." [2] The motives of the Duchess of Marlborough, in reprinting Lord Grimestone's memorable dramatic essay, did not here apply. The elegy on Cromwell, although doubtless sufficiently faulty, contained symptoms of a regenerating taste ; and, politically considered, although a panegyric on an usurper, the topics of praise are selected with attention to truth, and are, generally speaking, such as

[1] [" Our former chiefs, like sticklers of the war,
   First sought to inflame the parties, then to poise :
The quarrel loved, but did the cause abhor ;
   And did not strike to hurt, but make a noise.
War, our consumption, was their gainful trade ;
   We inward bled, whilst they prolong'd our pain ;
He fought to end our fighting, and essay'd
   To stanch the blood by breathing of the vein."
            DRYDEN'S *Works*, vol. ix., p. 10.—Notes, *ib.*, p. 16, 17.]

[2] This piece was called in, and destroyed by the noble author ; but Sarah, Duchess of Marlborough, when opposing Lord Grimestone at an election, maliciously printed and dispersed a large impression of his smothered performance, with a frontispiece representing an elephant dancing on the slack rope.—[The republication, by our modern Radicals, of Mr Southey's juvenile piece, " Wat Tyler," had not occurred when Sir Walter Scott wrote his Life of Dryden.]

Cromwell's worst enemies could not have denied to
him.   Neither had Dryden made the errors, or
misfortunes, of the royal family, and their followers, the subject of censure or of contrast.   With
respect to them, it was hardly possible that a eulogy
on such a theme could have less offence in it.   This
was perhaps a fortunate circumstance for Dryden
at the Restoration; and it must be noticed to his
honour, that as he spared the exiled monarch in his
panegyric on the usurper, so, after the Restoration,
in his numerous writings on the side of royalty,
there is no instance of his recalling his former
praise of Cromwell.

After the frequent and rapid changes which the
government of England underwent from the death
of Cromwell, in the spring of 1660, Charles II. was
restored to the throne of his ancestors.   It may be
easily imagined, that this event, a subject in itself
highly fit for poetry, and which promised the revival of poetical pursuits, was hailed with universal
acclamation by all whose turn for verse had been
suppressed and stifled during the long reign of fanaticism.   The Restoration led the way to the revival of letters, as well as that of legal government.
With Charles, as Dryden has expressed it,

" The officious Muses came along,
  A gay, harmonious quire, like angels ever young."

It was not, however, to be expected, that an alteration of the taste which had prevailed in the days of
Charles I., was to be the immediate consequence of
the new order of things.   The muse awoke, like

the sleeping beauty of the fairy tale, in the same antiquated and absurd vestments in which she had fallen asleep twenty years before ; or if the reader will pardon another simile, the poets were like those who, after a long mourning, resume for a time their ordinary dresses, of which the fashion has in the meantime passed away. Other causes contributed to a temporary revival of the metaphysical poetry. Almost all its professors, attached to the house of Stuart, had been martyrs, or confessors at least, in its cause. Cowley, their leader, was yet alive, and returned to claim the late reward of his loyalty and his sufferings. Cleveland had died a victim to the contempt, rather than the persecution of the republicans ;[1] but this most ardent

[1] He was one of the garrison of Newark, which held out so long for Charles I., and has left a curious specimen of the wit of the time, in his controversy with a parliamentary officer, whose servant had robbed him, and taken refuge in Newark. The following is the beginning of his answer to a demand that the fugitive should be surrendered :—

" Sixthly, Beloved,

" Is it so then, that our brother and fellow-labourer in the Gospel is start aside? then this may serve for an use of instruction, not to trust in man, nor in the son of man. Did not Demas leave Paul? did not Onesimus run from his master Philemon? besides, this should teach us to employ our talent, and not to lay it up in a napkin. Had it been done among the cavaliers, it had been just; then the Israelite had spoiled the Egyptian ; but for Simeon to plunder Levi, that! that ! You see, sir, what use I make of the doctrine you sent me ; and indeed since you change style so far as to nibble at wit, you must pardon me, if, to quit scores, I pretend a little to the gift of preaching," &c. Such was the wit of Cleveland. After the complete subjugation of the royalists, he was appre-

of cavalier poets was succeeded by Wild, whose
" *Iter Boreale*," a poem on Monk's march from
Scotland, formed upon Cleveland's model, obtained
extensive popularity among the citizens of London.[1]
Dryden's good sense and natural taste perceived
the obvious defects of these, the very coarsest of
metaphysical poets; insomuch, that, in his " Essay
on Dramatic Poetry," he calls wresting and tortu-
ring one word into another, a catachresis, or Cleve-
landism, and charges Wild with being in poetry
what the French call *un mauvais buffon*.

Sprat, and a host of inferior imitators, marched
for a time in the footsteps of Cowley; delighted
probably to discover in pindaric writing, as it was

hended, having in his possession a bundle of poems and satirical songs against the republicans. He appeared before the
Commonwealth general with the dignified air of one who is
prepared to suffer for his principles. He was disappointed;
for the military judge, after a contemptuous glance at the
papers, exclaimed to Cleveland's accusers, " Is this all ye have
against him? Go, let the poor knave sell his ballads?" Such
an acquittal was more severe than any punishment. The
conscious virtue of the loyalist would have borne the latter;
but the pride of the poet could not sustain his contemptuous
dismissal; and Cleveland is said to have broken his heart in
consequence. *Biographia Britanniea*, voce *Cleveland*.

[1] " He is the very Withers of the city," says Dryden of
Wild: "they have bought more editions of his works than
would serve to lay under all their pies at the lord mayor's
Christmas. When his famous poem first came out in the year
1660, I have seen them reading it in the midst of Change
time; nay, so vehement they were at it, that they lost their
bargain by the candles' ends: but what will you say, if he
has been received amongst great persons? I can assure you
he is this day the envy of one who is lord in the art of quibbling, and who does not take it well, that any man should
intrude so far into his province."—*Works*, vol. xv., p. 298.

called, a species of poetry which required neither sound nor sense, provided only there was a sufficient stock of florid and extravagant thoughts, expressed in harsh and bombastic language.

But this style of poetry, although it was for a time revived, and indeed continued to be occasionally employed even to the end of the eighteenth century, had too slight foundation in truth and nature to maintain the exclusive pre-eminence which it had been exalted to during the reigns of the two first monarchs of the Stuart race. As Rochester profanely expressed it, Cowley's poetry was not of God, and therefore could not stand. An approaching change of public taste was hastened by the manners of the restored monarch and his courtiers. That pedantry which had dictated the excessive admiration of metaphysical conceits, was not the characteristic of the court of Charles II., as it had been of those of his grandfather and father. Lively and witty by nature, with all the acquired habits of an adventurer, whose wanderings, military and political, left him time neither for profound reflection, nor for deep study, the restored monarch's literary taste, which was by no means contemptible, was directed towards a lighter and more pleasing style of poetry than the harsh and scholastic productions of Donne and Cowley. The admirers, therefore, of this old school were confined to the ancient cavaliers, and the old courtiers of Charles I.; persons unlikely to lead the fashion in the court of a gay monarch, filled with such men as Buckingham, Rochester, Etherege, Sedley, and

Mulgrave, whose time and habits confined their
own essays to occasional verses, and satirical effusions, in which they often ridiculed the heights of
poetry. they were incapable of attaining. With
such men the class of poets, which before the civil
war held but a secondary rank, began to rise in
estimation. Waller, Suckling, and Denham, began
to assert a pre-eminence over Cowley and Donne;
the ladies, whose influence in the court of James
and Charles I. was hardly felt, and who were then
obliged to be contented with such pedantic worship
as is contained in the " Mistress" of Cowley, and
the " Epithalamion" of Donne, began now, when
their voices were listened to, and their taste consulted, to determine that their poetical lovers should
address them in strains more musical, if not more
intelligible. What is most acceptable to the fair
sex will always sway the mode of a gay court;
and the character of a smooth and easy sonnetteer
was soon considered as an indispensable requisite
to a man of wit and fashion, terms which were then
usually synonymous.

To those who still retained a partiality for that
exercise of the fancy and memory, afforded by the
metaphysical poetry, the style of satire then pre-
valent afforded opportunities of applying it. The
same depth of learning, the same extravagant
ingenuity in combining the most remote images,
and in driving casual associations to the verge of
absurdity, almost all the remarkable features which
characterised the poetry of Cowley, may be successfully traced in the satire of Hudibras. The

sublime itself borders closely on the ludicrous; but the bombast and extravagant cannot be divided from it. The turn of thought, and the peculiar kind of mental exertion, correspond in both styles of writing; and although Butler pursued the ludicrous, and Cowley aimed at the surprising, the leading features of their poetry only differ like those of the same face convulsed with laughter, or arrested in astonishment. The district of metaphysical poetry was thus invaded by the satirists, who sought weapons there to avenge the misfortunes and oppression which they had so lately sustained from the puritans; and as it is difficult in a laughing age to render serious what has been once applied to ludicrous purposes, Butler and his imitators retained quiet possession of the style which they had usurped from the grave bards of the earlier age.

A single poet, Sir William Davenant, made a meritorious, though a misguided and unsuccessful effort, to rescue poetry from becoming the mere handmaid of pleasure, or the partisan of political or personal disputes, and to restore her to her natural rank in society, as an auxiliary of religion, policy, law, and virtue. His heroic poem of " Gondibert " has, no doubt, great imperfections; but it intimates everywhere a mind above those laborious triflers, who called that poetry which was only verse; and very often exhibits a majestic, dignified, and manly simplicity, equally superior to the metaphysical school, by the doctrines of which Davenant was occasionally misled. Yet, if that author too frequently imitated their quaint affectation of uncommon sentiment and associations, he had at least the merit of couching them in stately and harmonious verse ; a quality of poetry totally neglected by the followers of Cowley. I mention Davenant here, and separate from the other poets, who were distinguished about the time of the Restoration, because I think that Dryden, to whom we are about to return, was, at that period, an admirer and imitator of " Gondibert," as we are certain that he was a personal and intimate friend of the author.[1]

With the return of the king, the fall of Dryden's political patrons was necessarily involved. Sir Gilbert Pickering, having been one of Charles' judges, was too happy to escape into obscurity, under an absolute disqualification for holding any office, political, civil, or ecclesiastical. The influence of Sir John Dryden was ended at the same time ; and thus both these relations, under whose protection Dryden entered life, and by whose influence he was probably to have been aided in

[1] [Sir Walter Scott has said elsewhere, " An Epic Poem, in elegiac stanzas, must always be tedious, because no structure of verse is more unfavourable to narration than that which peremptorily requires each sentence to be restricted, or protracted, to four lines. But the liveliness of Davenant's imagination, which Dryden has pointed out as his most striking attribute, has illuminated even the dull and dreary path which he has chosen; and perhaps few poems afford more instances of vigorous conceptions, and even felicity of expression, than the neglected · Gondibert.' "—*Note* to " The Tempest," vol. iii., p. 97.

some path to wealth or eminence, became at once incapable of assisting him; and even connexion with them was rendered, by the change of times, disgraceful, if not dangerous. Yet it may be doubted whether Dryden felt this evil in its full extent. Sterne has said of a character, that a blessing which closed his mouth, or a misfortune which opened it with a good grace, were nearly equal to him; nay, that sometimes the misfortune was the more acceptable of the two. It is possible, by a parity of reasoning, that Dryden may have felt himself rather relieved from, than deprived of, his fanatical patrons, under whose guidance he could never hope to have indulged in that career of literary pursuit, which the new order of things presented to the ambition of the youthful poet; at least, he lost no time in useless lamentation, but, now in his thirtieth year, proceeded to exert that poetical talent, which had heretofore been repressed by his own situation, and that of the country.

Dryden, left to his own exertions, hastened to testify his joyful acquiescence in the restoration of monarchy, by publishing " *Astræa Redux,*" a poem which was probably distinguished among the innumerable congratulations poured forth upon the occasion; and he added to those which hailed the coronation, in 1661, the verses entitled " A Panegyric to his Sacred Majesty." These pieces testify, that the author had already made some progress in harmonizing his versification. But they also contain many of those points of wit, and turns of epigram, which he condemned in his more advanced judgment.[1]   The same description applies, in a yet stronger degree, to the verses addressed to Lord Chancellor Hyde (Lord Clarendon) on the New-Year's-Day of 1662, in which Dryden has more closely imitated the metaphysical poetry than in any poem, except the juvenile elegy on Lord Hastings. I cannot but think, that the poet consulted the taste of his patron, rather than his own, in adopting this peculiar style.   Clarendon was educated in the

[1] [In his note (*Dryden*, vol. ix., p. 41) on the lines—

" An horrid stillness first invades the ear,
And in that silence we the tempest fear,"

Sir Walter Scott says " The small wits of the time made themselves very merry with the couplet; because stillness, being a mere absence of sound, could not, it was said, be personified, as an active agent, or invader.   Captain Ratcliffe thus states the objection in his ' News from Hell:'

' Laureat, who was both learn'd and florid,
Was damn'd long since, for *silence horrid* ;
Nor had there been such clatter made,
But that this silence did *invade*.
Invade! and so't might well, 'tis clear ;
But what did it invade?—An ear. '

" In the ' Dialogue in Bedlam,' between Oliver's porter, fiddler, and poet, the first of these persons thus addresses L'Estrange and Dryden, ' the scene being adorned with several of the poet's own flowers :'

' O glory, glory! who are these appear ?
My fellow-servants, poet, fiddler here ?
Old Hodge the constant, Johny the sincere!
Who sent you hither ? and, pray tell me, why ?
A horrid silence does invade my eye,
While not one sound of voice from you I spy. '

But, as Dr Johnson justly remarks, we hesitate not to say, the world is invaded by darkness, which is a privation of light, and why not by silence, which is a privation of sound ?"]

court of Charles I., and Dryden may have thought it necessary, in addressing him, to imitate the " strong verses," which were then admired.

According to the fashion of the times, such copies of occasional verses were rewarded by a gratuity from the person to whom they were addressed; and poets had not yet learned to think this mode of receiving assistance incompatible with the feelings of dignity or delicacy. Indeed, in the common transactions of that age, one sees something resembling the Eastern custom of accompanying with a present, and not always a splendid one, the usual forms of intercourse and civility. Thus we find the wealthy corporation of Hull, backing a polite address to the Duke of Monmouth, their governor, with a present of *six broad pieces;* and his grace deemed it a point of civility to press the acceptance of the same gratuity upon the member of parliament for the city, by whom it was delivered to him.[1] We may therefore believe, that Dryden received

[1] " The Duke of Monmouth returned on Saturday from New-Market. To-day I waited on him, and first presented him with your letter, which he read all over very attentively; and then prayed me to assure you, that he would, upon all occasions, be most ready to give you the marks of his affection, and assist you in any affairs you should recommend to him. I then delivered to him the six broad pieces, telling him, that I was deputed to blush on your behalf for the meanness of the present, &c.; but he took me off, and said he thanked you for it, and accepted it as a token of your kindness. He had, before I came in, as I was told, considered what to do with the gold; and but that I by all means prevented the offer, or I had been endangered of being reimbursed with it."—ANDREW MARVELL's *Works*, vol. i., p. 210. *Letter to the Mayor of Hull.*

some compliment from the king and chancellor ; and I am afraid the same premises authorize us to conclude that it was but trifling. Meantime, our author having no settled means of support, except his small landed property, and having now no assistance to expect from his more wealthy kinsmen, to whom, probably, neither his literary pursuits, nor his commencing them by a panegyric on the Restoration, were very agreeable, and whom he had also offended by a slight change in spelling his name,[1] seems to have been reduced to narrow and uncomfortable circumstances. Without believing, in its full extent, the exaggerated account given by Brown and Shadwell,[2] we may discover from their reproaches, that, at the commencement of his literary career, Dryden was connected, and probably lodged, with Herringman the bookseller, in the New Exchange, for whom he wrote prefaces, and other occasional pieces. But having, as Mr Malone has observed, a patrimony, though a small one, of his

[1] From Driden to Dryden.

[2] Shadwell makes Dryden say, that after some years spent at the university, he came to London. " At first I struggled with a great deal of persecution, took up with a lodging which had a window no bigger than a pocket-looking glass, dined at a three-penny ordinary enough to starve a vacation tailor, kept little company, went clad in homely drugget, and drunk wine as seldom as a rechabite, or the grand seignior's confessor." The old gentleman, who corresponded with the " Gentleman's Magazine," and remembered Dryden before the rise of his fortunes, mentions his suit of plain drugget, being, by the by, the same garb in which he himself has clothed Flecnoe, who " coarsely clad in Norwich drugget came."

own, it seems impossible that our author was ever in that state of mean and abject dependence, which the malice of his enemies afterwards pretended. The same malice misrepresented, or greatly exaggerated, the nature of Dryden's obligations to Sir Robert Howard, with whom he became acquainted probably about the time of the Restoration, whose influence was exerted in his favour, and whose good offices the poet returned by literary assistance.

Sir Robert Howard was a younger son of Thomas Earl of Berkeley, and, like all his family, had distinguished himself as a royalist, particularly at the battle of Cropley Bridge. He had recently suffered a long imprisonment in Windsor Castle during the usurpation. His rank and merits made him, after the Restoration, a patron of some consequence; and upon his publishing a collection of verses very soon after that period, Dryden prefixed an address " to his honoured friend," on "his excellent poems." Sir Robert Howard understood the value of Dryden's attachment, introduced him into his family, and probably aided in procuring his productions that degree of attention from the higher world, for want of which the most valuable efforts of genius have often sunk into unmerited obscurity. Such, in short, were his exertions in favour of Dryden, that, though we cannot believe he was indebted to Howard for those necessaries of life which he had the means to procure for himself, the poet found ground to acknowledge, that his patron had not only been " careful of his fortune, which was the effect of his nobleness, but solicitous of his reputation, which was that of his kindness."

Thus patronised, our author seems to have advanced in reputation as he became more generally known to the learned and ingenious of his time. Yet we have but few traces of the labour, by which he doubtless attained, and secured, his place in society. A short Satire on the Dutch, written to animate the people of England against them, appeared in 1662.[1] It is somewhat in the

[1] [" Be gull'd no longer, for you'll find it true,
They have no more religion, faith! than you.
Interest's the god they worship in their state;
And we, I take it, have not much of that.
Well Monarchies may own religion's name;
But States are atheists in their very frame.
They share a sin; and such proportions fall,
That, like a stink, 'tis nothing to them all.
Think on their rapine, falsehood, cruelty,
And that, what once they were they still would be.
To one well-born the affront is worse and more,
When he's abused and baffled by a boor.
With an ill grace the Dutch their mischiefs do;
They've both ill-nature and ill-manners too.
Well may they boast themselves an ancient nation,
For they were bred ere manners were in fashion;
And their new Commonwealth hath set them free,
Only from honour and civility.
Venetians do not more uncouthly ride,
Than did their lubber State mankind bestride;
Their sway became them with as ill a mien,
As their own paunches swell above their chin."

Works, vol. ix., p. 71.

" The verses are adapted to the comprehension of the vulgar, whom they were intended to inflame. Bold invective, and coarse raillery, supply the place of the wit and argument, with which Dryden, when the time fitted, knew so well how to arm his satire."—*Editor's Note, ib.,* p. 70.]

hard style of invective which Cleveland applied to the Scottish nation; yet Dryden thought it worth while to weave the same verses into the prologue and epilogue of the tragedy of " Amboyna," a piece written in 1673, with the same kind intentions towards the States-General.

Science, as well as poetry, began to revive after the iron dominion of military fanaticism was ended; and Dryden, who through life was attached to experimental philosophy, speedily associated himself with those who took interest in its progress. He was chosen a member of the newly instituted Royal Society, 26th November, 1662; an honour which cemented his connexion with the most learned men of the time, and is an evidence of the respect in which he was already held. Most of these, and the discoveries by which they had distinguished themselves, Dryden took occasion to celebrate in his " Epistle to Dr Walter Charleton," a learned physician, upon his treatise of Stonehenge.[1] Gilbert, Boyle, Harvey, and Ent, are mentioned with enthusiastic applause, as treading in the path

[1] [" Among the assertors of free reason's claim,
  Our nation's not the least in worth or fame.
  The world to Bacon does not only owe
  Its present knowledge, but its future too.
  Gilbert shall live, till loadstones cease to draw,
  Or British fleets the boundless ocean awe.
  And noble Boyle, not less in nature seen,
  Than his great brother, read in states and men.
  The circling streams, once thought but pools of blood,
  (Whether life's fuel, or the body's food,)
  From dark oblivion Harvey's name shall save;
  While Ent keeps all the honour that he gave."
                                  Works, vol. xi., p. 15.]

pointed out by Bacon, who first broke the fetters of Aristotle, and taught the world to derive knowledge from experiment. In these elegant verses, the author divests himself of all the flippant extravagance of point and quibble, in which, complying with his age, he had hitherto indulged, though of late in a limited degree.[1]

While thus united in friendly communion with men of kindred and congenial spirits, Dryden seems to have been sensible of the necessity of applying his literary talents to some line, in which he might derive a steadier and more certain recompense, than by writing occasional verses to the great, or doing literary drudgery for the bookseller. His own genius would probably have directed him to the ambitious labours of an epic poem; but for this the age afforded little encouragement. "Gondibert," the style of which Dryden certainly both admired and copied, became a martyr to the raillery of the critics;[2] and to fill up

---

[1] [" At an age, when Lucian and Tasso had run out their course, and Milton had given the most precious samples of his genius, Dryden had achieved nothing that could raise him much above ordinary men. The first of his poems which possesses any considerable merit, is the epistle to Dr Charleton."—HALLAM, *Edin. Rev.* 1808.]

[2] [" Hobbes, in a letter to the Hon. Edward Howard, says, ' My judgment in poetry hath, you know, been once already censured, by very good wits, for commending GONDIBERT; but yet they have not, I think, disabled my testimony. For what authority is there in wit? A jester may have it; a man in drink may have it, and be fluent over night, and wise and dry in the morning. What is it? or who can tell whether it

the measure of shame, the " Paradise Lost" fell still-born from the press. This last instance of bad taste had not, it is true, yet taken place; but the men who were guilty of it were then living under Dryden's observation, and their manners and habits could not fail to teach him, to anticipate the little encouragement they were likely to afford to the loftier labours of poetry. One only line remained, in which poetical talents might exert themselves, with some chance of procuring their possessor's reward, or at least maintenance, and this was dramatic composition. To this Dryden sedulously applied himself, with various success, for many years. But before proceeding to trace the history of his dramatic career, I proceed to notice such pieces of his poetry, as exhibit marks of his earlier style of composition.

The victory gained by the Duke of York over the Dutch fleet on the 3d of June, 1665, and his Duchess's subsequent journey into the north, furnished Dryden with the subject of a few occasional verses, in which the style of Waller (who came forth with a poem on the same subject) is successfully imitated. In addressing her grace, the poet suppresses all the horrors of the battle, and turns her eyes upon the splendour of a victory, for which the kingdom was indebted to her husband's valour,

---

be better to have it, or to be without it, especially if it be a pointed wit? I will take my liberty to praise what I like, as well as they do to reprehend what they do not like.' "—D'Is-RAELI's *Quarrels of Authors*, vol. ii., p. 242.]

and her " chaste vows."[1] In these verses, not the
least vestige of metaphysical wit can be traced ;
and they were accordingly censured, as wanting
height of fancy, and dignity of words. This criticism Dryden refuted, by alleging, that he had succeeded in what he did attempt, in the softness of
expression and smoothness of the measure, (the
appropriate ornaments of an address to a lady,) and
that he was accused of that only thing which he
could well defend. It seems, however, very possible that these remarks impelled him to undertake
a task, in which vigour of fancy and expression
might, with propriety, be exercised. Accordingly,
his next poem was of greater length and importance. This is an historical account of the events
of the year 1666, under the title of "*Annus Mirabilis*," to which distinction the incidents which had
occurred in that space gave it some title. The
poem being in the elegiac stanza, Dryden relapsed
into an imitation of " Gondibert," from which he

[1] [" The winds were hush'd, the waves in ranks were cast,
As awfully as when God's people past :
These, yet uncertain on whose sails to blow,
These, where the wealth of nations ought to flow.
Then with the duke your Highness ruled the day : ⎫
While all the brave did his command obey,   ⎬
The fair and pious under you did pray.   ⎭
How powerful are chaste vows ! the wind and tide
You bribed to combat on the English side.
Thus to your much-loved lord you did convey
An unknown succour, sent the nearest way.
New vigour to his wearied arms you brought,
(So Moses was upheld while Israel fought,)
While, from afar, we heard the cannon play,
Like distant thunder on a shiny day.
For absent friends we were ashamed to fear,
When we consider'd what you ventured there."
                                Works, vol. ix., p. 77.]

had departed ever since the " Elegy on Cromwell."
From this it appears, that the author's admiration
of Davenant had not decreased. Indeed he, long
afterwards, bore testimony to that author's quick
and piercing imagination ; which at once produced
thoughts remote, new, and surprising, such as could
not easily enter into any other fancy.[1] Dryden
at least equalled Davenant in this quality; and
certainly excelled him in the powers of composition, which are to embody the conceptions of the
imagination ; and in the extent of acquired knowledge, by which they were to be enforced and
illustrated. In his preface, he has vindicated the
choice of his stanza, by a reference to the opinion
of Davenant,[2] which he sanctions by affirming,

[1] [" In the time I writ with him, I had the opportunity to
observe somewhat more nearly of him than I had formerly
done, when I had only a bare acquaintance with him. I
found him then of so quick a fancy, that nothing was proposed
to him, on which he could not suddenly produce a thought
extremely pleasant and surprising ; and those first thoughts
of his, contrary to the old Latin proverb, were not always the
least happy. And as his fancy was quick, so likewise were
the products of it remote and new. He borrowed not of any
other ; and his imaginations were such as could not easily
enter into any other man. His corrections were sober and
judicious; and he corrected his own writings much more
severely than those of another man, bestowing twice the time
and labour in polishing, which he used in invention," &c.—
Dryden's Works, vol. iii., p. 101.]

[2] Davenant alleges the advantages of a respite and pause
between every stanza, which should be so constructed as to
comprehend a period ; and adds, " nor doth alternate rhime,
by any lowliness of cadence, make the sound less heroic, but
rather adapt it to a plain and stately composing of music ;
and the brevity of the stanza renders it less subtle to the com-

that he had always, himself, thought quatrains, or stanzas of verse in alternate rhyme, more noble, and of greater dignity, both for sound and number, than any other verse in use among us.[1] By this attention to sound and rhythm, he improved upon the school of metaphysical poets, which disclaimed attention to either ; but in the thought and ex - pression itself, the style of Davenant more nearly resembled Cowley's than that of Denham and Waller. The same ardour for what Dryden calls " wit-writing," the same unceasing exercise of the memory, in search of wonderful thoughts and allusions, and the same contempt for the subject, except as the medium of displaying the author's learning and ingenuity, marks the style of Dave- nant, though in a less degree than that of the meta- physical poets, and though chequered with many examples of a simpler and chaster character. Some part of this deviation was, perhaps, owing to the nature of the stanza ; for the structure of the quatrain prohibited the bard, who used it, from rambling into those digressive similes, which, in the pindaric strophe, might be pursued through endless ramifications. If the former started an extravagant thought, or a quaint image, he was compelled to bring it to a point within his four-lined stanza. The snake was thus scotched, though not killed ; and conciseness being rendered indis-

---

poser, and more easy to the singer, which, in *stilo recitativo,* when the story is long, is chiefly requisite."—*Preface to Gon-dibert.*

[1] Dryden's Works, vol. ix., p. 95.

pensable, a great step was gained towards concentration of thought, which is necessary to the simple and to the sublime. The manner of Davenant, therefore, though short-lived, and ungraced by public applause, was an advance towards true taste, from the unnatural and frantic indulgence of unrestrained fancy ; and, did it claim no other merit, it possesses that of having been twice sanctioned by the practice of Dryden, upon occasions of uncommon solemnity.

The "*Annus Mirabilis*" evinces a considerable portion of labour and attention ; the lines and versification are highly polished, and the expression was probably carefully corrected. Dryden, as Johnson remarks, already exercised the superiority of his genius, by recommending his own performance, as written upon the plan of Virgil ; and as no unsuccessful effort at producing those well-wrought images and descriptions, which create admiration, the proper object of heroic poetry. The "*Annus Mirabilis*" may indeed be regarded as one of Dryden's most elaborate pieces ; although it is not written in his later, better, and most peculiar style of poetry.[1]

The poem first appeared in octavo, in 1667, and was afterwards frequently reprinted in quarto. It

[1] [In commenting on this opinion as to the "*Annus Mirabilis*," Mr Hallam says " Variety is its chief want, as dignity is its greatest excellence ; but in spite of this defect, and of much bad taste, we doubt whether so continued a strain of poetry could at that time be found in the language. Waller's ' Panegeric,' at least, and Denham's ' Cooper's Hill,' the most celebrated poems of the age, are very inferior to it."—*Ed. Review.*]

was dedicated to the Metropolis of Great Britain, as represented by the lord mayor and magistrates. A letter to Sir Robert Howard was prefixed to the poem, in which the author explains the purpose of the work, and the difficulties which presented themselves in the execution. And in this epistle, as a contrast between the smooth and easy style of writing which was proper in addressing a lady, and the exalted style of heroic, or at least historical poetry, he introduces the verses to the Duchess of York, already mentioned.

The " *Annus Mirabilis*" being the last poetical work of any importance produced by our author, until " Absalom and Achitophel," the reader may here pause, and consider, in the progressive improvement of Dryden, the gradual renovation of public taste. The irregular pindaric ode was now abandoned to Arwaker, Behn, Durfey, and a few inferior authors ; who, either from its tempting facility of execution, or from an affected admiration of old times and fashions, still pestered the public with imitations of Cowley. The rough measure of Donne (if it had any pretension to be called a measure) was no longer tolerated, and it was ex pected, even of those who wrote satires, lampoons, and occasional verses, that their rhymes should be rhymes, both to the ear and eye ; and that they should neither adore their mistresses, nor abuse their neighbours, in lines which differed only from prose in the fashion of printing. Thus the measure used by Rochester, Buckingham, Sheffield, Sedley, and other satirists, if not polished or harmonized, approaches more nearly to modern verse, than that of Hall or Donne. In the " Elegy on Cromwell," and the " *Annus Mirabilis,*" Dryden followed Davenant, who abridged, if he did not explode, the quaintnesses of his predecessors. In " *Astræa Redux,*" and his occasional verses, to Dr Charleton, the Duchess of York, and others, the poet proposed a separate and simpler model, more dignified than that of Suckling or Waller; more harmonious in measure, and chaste in expression, than those of Cowley and Crashaw. Much, there doubtless remained, of ancient subtlety, and ingenious quibbling; but when Dryden declares, that he proposes Virgil, in preference to Ovid, to be his model in the " *Annus Mirabilis,*" it sufficiently implies, that the main defect of the poetry of the last age had been discovered, and was in the way of being amended by gradual, and almost imperceptible, degrees.

In establishing, or refining, the latter style of writing, in couplet verse, our author found great assistance from his dramatic practice; to trace the commencement of which, is the purpose of the next Section.

SECTION II.

Revival of the Drama at the Restoration—Heroic Plays—
Comedies of Intrigue—Commencement of Dryden's Dra-
matic Career—The Wild Gallant—Rival Ladies—
Indian Queen and Emperor—Dryden's Marriage—
Essay on Dramatic Poetry, and subsequent Controversy
with Sir Robert Howard—The Maiden Queen—The
Tempest—Sir Martin Mar-all—The Mock Astrologer
—The Royal Martyr—The Two Parts of the Con-
quest of Granada—Dryden's Situation at this Period.

IT would appear that Dryden, at the period of
the Restoration, renounced all views of making his
way in life except by exertion of the literary talents
with which he was so eminently endowed. His
becoming a writer of plays was a necessary consequence; for the theatres, newly opened after so
long silence, were resorted to with all the ardour
inspired by novelty; and dramatic composition
was the only line which promised something like
an adequate reward to the professors of literature.
In our sketch of the taste of the seventeenth
century previous to the Restoration, this topic
was intentionally postponed.

In the times of James I. and of his successor,
the theatre retained, in some degree, the splendour
with which the excellent writers of the virgin reign

had adorned it. It is true, that authors of the latter period fell far below those gigantic poets, who flourished in the end of the sixteenth and beginning of the seventeenth centuries; but what the stage had lost in dramatic composition, was, in some degree, supplied by the increasing splendour of decoration, and the favour of the court. A private theatre, called the Cockpit, was maintained at Whitehall, in which plays were performed before the court; and the king's company of actors often received command to attend the royal progresses.[1] Masques, a species of representation calculated exclusively for the recreation of the great, in whose halls they were exhibited, were a usual entertainment of Charles and his consort. The machinery and decorations were often superintended by Inigo Jones, and the poetry composed by Ben Jonson the laureat. Even Milton deigned to contribute one of his most fascinating poems to the service of the drama; and, notwithstanding the severity of his puritanic tenets, "Comus" could only have been composed by one who felt the full enchantment of the theatre. But all this splendour vanished at the approach of civil war. The stage and court were almost as closely united in their fate as royalty and episcopacy, had the same enemies, the same defenders, and shared the same overwhelming ruin. "No throne no theatre," seemed as just a dogma as the famous "No king no bishop." The puritans indeed commenced their attack against

---

[1] Malone's "History of the Stage."

royalty in this very quarter; and, while they im-
pugned the political exertions of prerogative, they
assailed the private character of the monarch and
his consort, for the encouragement given to the
profane stage, that rock of offence, and stumbling-
block to the godly. Accordingly, the superiority
of the republicans was no sooner decisive, than
the theatres were closed, and the dramatic poets
silenced. No department of poetry was accounted
lawful; but the drama being altogether unhallowed
and abominable, its professors were persecuted,
while others escaped with censure from the pulpit,
and contempt from the rulers. The miserable shifts
to which the surviving actors were reduced during
the commonwealth, have been often detailed. At
times they were connived at by the caprice or indolence of their persecutors; but, in general, as soon
as they had acquired any slender stock of properties,
they were beaten, imprisoned, and stripped, at the
pleasure of the soldiery.

The Restoration naturally brought with it a
revived taste for those elegant amusements, which,
during the usurpation, had been condemned as
heathenish, or punished as appertaining especially
to the favourers of royalty. To frequent them,
therefore, became a badge of loyalty, and a virtual
disavowal of those puritanic tenets which all now
agree in condemning. The taste of the restored
monarch also was decidedly in favour of the drama.
At the foreign courts, which it had been his lot to
visit, the theatre was the chief entertainment; and
as amusement was always his principal pursuit, it

cannot be doubted that he often sought it there. The interest, therefore, which the monarch took in the restoration of the stage, was direct and personal. Had it not been for this circumstance, it seems probable that the general audience, for a time at least, would have demanded a revival of those pieces which had been most successful before the civil wars ; and that Shakspeare, Massinger, and Fletcher, would have resumed their acknowledged superiority upon the English stage. But as the theatres were re-established and cherished by the immediate influence of the sovereign, and of the court which returned with him from exile, a taste formed during their residence abroad dictated the nature of entertainments which were to be presented to them. It is worthy of remark, that Charles took the models of the two grand departments of the drama from two different countries.

France afforded the pattern of those tragedies which continued in fashion for twenty years after the Restoration, and which were called Rhyming or Heroic Plays. In that country, however, contrary to the general manners of the people, a sort of stately and precise ceremonial early took possession of the theatre. The French dramatist was under the necessity of considering less the situation of the persons of the drama, than that of the performers, who were to represent it before a monarch and his court. It was not, therefore, sufficient for the author to consider how human beings would naturally express themselves in the predicament of the scene ; he had the more embarrassing task of so modifying their expressions of passion and feeling, that they might not exceed the decorum necessary in the august presence of the *Grand Monarque.* A more effectual mode of freezing the dialogue of the drama could hardly have been devised, than by introducing into the theatre the etiquette of the drawingroom. That etiquette also, during the reign of Louis XIV., was of a kind peculiarly forced and unnatural. The romances of Calprenede and Scuderi, those ponderous and unmerciful folios now consigned to utter oblivion, were in that reign not only universally read and admired, but supposed to furnish the most perfect models of gallantry and heroism; although, in the words of an elegant female author, these celebrated writings are justly described as containing only " unnatural representations of the passions, false sentiments, false precepts, false wit, false honour, and false modesty, with a strange heap of improbable, unnatural incidents, mixed up with true history, and fastened upon some of the great names of antiquity."[1] Yet upon the model of such works were framed the court manners of the reign of Louis, and, in imitation of them, the French tragedy, in which every king was by prescriptive right a hero, every female a goddess, every tyrant a fire-breathing chimera, and every soldier an irresistible Amadis; in which,

[1] *Haud inexperta loquitur.* " I have," she continues, "(and yet I am still alive,) drudged through Le Grand Cyrus, in twelve huge volumes; Cleopatra, in eight or ten ; Polexander, Ibraham, Clelie, and some others, whose names, as well as all the rest of them, I have forgotten."—*Letter of Mrs Chapone to Mrs Carter.*

the amusements of the drama would have appeared insipid, unless seasoned with the libertine spirit which governed their lives, and which was encouraged by the example of the monarch. Thus it is acutely argued by Dennis, in reply to Collier, that the depravity of the theatre, when revived, was owing to that very suppression, which had prevented its gradual reformation. And just so a muddy stream, if allowed its free course, will gradually purify itself; but, if dammed up for a season, and let loose at once, its first torrent cannot fail to be impregnated with every impurity. The license of a rude age was thus revived by a corrupted one; and even those plays which were translated from the French and Spanish, were carefully seasoned with as much indelicacy, and double entendre, as was necessary to fit them for the ear of the wittiest and most profligate of monarchs.[1]

Another remarkable feature in the comedies which succeeded the Restoration, is the structure of their plot, which was not, like that of the tragedies, formed upon the Parisian model. The English audience had not patience for the regular

[1] [" The wits of Charles found easier ways to fame,
    Nor wish'd for Jonson's art, or Shakspeare's flame.
    Themselves they studied, as they felt they writ;
    Intrigue was plot, obscenity was wit.
    Vice always found a sympathetic friend,
    They pleas'd their age, and did not aim to mend.
    Yet bards like these aspir'd to lasting praise,
    And proudly hoped to pimp in future days.
    Their cause was gen'ral, their supports were strong,
    Their slaves were willing, and their reign was long;
    Till Shame regain'd the post that Sense betray'd,
    And Virtue call'd Oblivion to her aid."
                                JOHNSON.]

comedy of their neighbours, depending upon delicate turns of expression, and nicer delineation of
character. The Spanish comedy, with its bustle,
machinery, disguise, and complicated intrigue, was
much more agreeable to their taste. This preference did not arise entirely from what the French
term the phlegm of our national character, which
cannot be affected but by powerful stimulants. It
is indeed certain, that an Englishman expects his
eye, as well as his ear, to be diverted by theatrical
exhibition; but the thirst of novelty was another
and separate reason, which affected the style of
the revived drama. The number of new plays
represented every season was incredible; and the
authors were compelled to have recourse to that
mode of composition which was most easily executed. Laboured accuracy of expression, and fine
traits of character, joined to an arrangement of
action, which should be at once pleasing, interesting, and probable, requires sedulous study, deep
reflection, and long and repeated correction and
revision. But these were not to be expected from
a playwright, by whom three dramas were to be
produced in one season; and in their place were
substituted adventures, surprises, rencounters, mistakes, disguises, and escapes, all easily accomplished
by the intervention of sliding panels, closets, veils,
masques, large cloaks, and dark lanterns. If the
dramatist was at a loss for employing these convenient implements, the fifteen hundred plays of
Lope de Vega were at hand for his instruction;
presenting that rapid succession of events, and

those sudden changes in the situation of the personages, which, according to the noble biographer
of the Spanish dramatist, are the charms by which
he interests us so forcibly in his plots.[1]   These
Spanish plays had already been resorted to by the
authors of the earlier part of the century.   But
under the auspices of Charles II., who must often
have witnessed the originals while abroad, and in
some instances by his express command, translations
were executed of the best and most lively Spanish
comedies.[2]

The favourite comedies, therefore, after the
Restoration, were such as depended rather upon
the intricacy, than the probability, of the plot;
rather upon the vivacity and liveliness, than on
the natural expression of the dialogue; and, finally,
rather upon extravagant and grotesque conception
of character, than upon its being pointedly de-
lineated, and accurately supported through the
representation.   These particulars, in which the
comedies of Charles the Second's reign differ from
the example set by Shakspeare, Massinger, and
Beaumont and Fletcher, seem to have been derived
from the Spanish model.   But the taste of the age
was too cultivated to follow the stage of Madrid,

[1] Lord Holland's " Life of Lope de Vega," p. 128.
[2] The " Wild Gallant," which Charles commanded to be
performed before him more than once, was of the class of
Spanish comedies.   The " Maiden Queen," which the witty
monarch honoured with the title of *his play,* is in the same
division.   Sir Samuel Tuke's " Adventures of Five Hours,"
and Crowne's " Sir Courtley Nice," were both translated
from the Spanish by the king's express recommendation.

in introducing, or, to speak more accurately, in reviving, the character of the *gracioso*, or clown, upon that of London.[1] Something of foreign manners may be traced in the license assumed by valets, and domestics, in the English comedy; a freedom which at no time made a part of our national manners, though something like it may still be traced upon the continent. These seem to

[1] The *gracioso*, or buffoon, according to Lord Holland, held an intermediate character between a spectator and a character in the play; interrupting with his remarks, at one time, the performance, of which he forms an essential, but very defective part in another. His part was, I presume, partly written, partly extempore. Something of the kind was certainly known upon our stage. Wilson and Tarleton, in their capacity of clowns, entered freely into a contest of wit with the spectators, which was not at all held inconsistent with their having a share in the performance. Nor was tragedy exempted from their interference. Hall, after telling us of a tragic representation, informs us,

" Now least such frightful showes of fortunes fall,
And bloudy tyrants' rage, should chance appall
The dead-struck audience, 'midst the silent rout
Comes leaping in a selfe-misformed lout,
And laughes, and grins, and frames his mimick face,
And justles straight into the prince's place :
Then doth the theatre echo all aloud
With gladsome noyse of that applauding croud.
A goodly hoch-poch, when vile russetings
Are matcht with monarchs and with mighty kings."

This extemporal comic part seems to have been held essential to dramatic representation, in most countries in Europe, during the infancy of the art. A personification of the same kind is still retained in the lower kinds of popular exhibitions; and the clowns to the shows of tumbling and horsemanship, with my much-respected friend Mr Punch in a puppet-show, bear a pretty close resemblance to the *gracioso* of the Spaniards, the *arlequino* of the Italians, and the clown of the ancient English drama.—See MALONE's *History of the Stage.*

be the leading characteristics of the comedies of Charles the Second's reign; in which the rules of the ancients were totally disregarded. It were to be wished that the authors could have been exculpated from a heavier charge,—that of assisting to corrupt the nation, by nourishing and fomenting their evil passions, as well as by indulging and pandering to their vices.

The theatres, after the Restoration, were limited to two in number; a restriction perhaps necessary, as the exclusive patent expresses it, in regard of the extraordinary licentiousness then used in dramatic representation; but for which no very good reason can be shown, when they are at least harmless, if not laudable places of amusement. One of these privileged theatres was placed under the direction of Sir William Davenant, whose sufferings in the royal cause merited a provision, and whose taste and talents had been directed towards the drama even during its proscription. He is said to have introduced movable scenes upon the English stage; and, without entering into the dispute of how closely this is to be interpreted, we are certain that he added much to its splendour and decoration. His set of performers, which contained the famous Betterton, and others of great merit, was called the Duke's Company. The other licensed theatre was placed under the direction of Thomas Killigrew, much famed by tradition for his colloquial wit, but the merit of whose good things evaporated as soon as he attempted to interweave them with comedy. His performers formed what was entitled the King's Company. With this last theatre

Dryden particularly connected himself, by a contract to be hereafter mentioned.   None of his
earlier plays were acted by the Duke's Company,
unless those in which he had received assistance
from others, whom he might think as well entitled
as himself to prescribe the place of representation.

Such was the state of the English drama when
Dryden became a candidate for theatrical laurels.
So early as the year of the Restoration, he had
meditated a tragedy upon the fate of the Duke of
Guise ; but this, he has informed us, was suppressed
by the advice of some friends, who told him, that
it was an excellent subject, but not so artificially
managed as to render it fit for the stage.   It were
to be wished these scenes had been preserved, since
it may be that the very want of artifice, alleged by
the critics of the day, would have recommended
them to our more simple taste.   We might at
least have learned from them, whether Dryden, in
his first essay, leant to the heroic, or to the ancient
English tragedy.   But the scene of Guise's return
to Paris, is the only part of the original sketch which
Dryden thought fit to interweave with the play, as
acted in 1682 ; and as that scene is rendered literally from Davila, upon the principle that, in so
remarkable an action, the poet was not at liberty to
change the words actually used by the persons
interested, we only learn from it, that the piece
was composed in blank verse, not rhyme.

In the course of the year 1661-2, our author
composed the " Wild Gallant," which was acted

about February 1662–3 without success. The beautiful Countess of Castlemain, afterwards Duchess of Cleveland, extended her protection to the unfortunate performance, and received the incense of the author; who boasts,

> " Posterity will judge by my success,
> I had the Grecian poet's happiness,
> Who, waiving plots, found out a better way,—
> Some god descended and preserved the play."

It was probably by the influence of this royal favourite, that the " Wild Gallant " was more than once performed before Charles by his own command. But the author, his piece, and his poetical compliment, were hardly treated in a Session of the Poets, which appeared about 1670. Nor did Sir Robert Howard, his associate, escape without his share of ridicule :

> " Sir Robert Howard, call'd for over and over,
>   At length sent in Teague with a packet of news,
> Wherein the sad knight, to his grief, did discover
>   How Dryden had lately robb'd him of his Muse.
>
> " Each man in the court was pleased with the theft,
>   Which made the whole family swear and rant,
> Desiring, their Robin in the lurch being left,
>   The thief might be punish'd for his ' Wild Gallant.'
>
> " Dryden, who one would have thought had more wit,
>   The censure of every man did disdain,
> Pleading some pitiful rhymes he had writ
>   In praise of the Countess of Castlemaine."

The play itself contained too many of those prize-fights of wit, as Buckingham called them, in which the plot stood absolutely still, while two of the characters were showing the audience their dexterity at repartee. This error furnishes matter for a lively scene in the " Rehearsal."

The " Rival Ladies," acted in 1663, and published in the year following, was our author's next dramatic essay. It is a tragi-comedy; and the tragic scenes are executed in rhyme,—a style which Dryden anxiously defends, in a Dedication addressed to the Earl of Orrery, who had himself written several heroic plays. He cites against blank verse the universal practice of the most polished and civilized nations, the Spanish, the Italian, and the French; enumerates its advantages in restraining the luxuriance of the poet's imagination, and compelling him to labour long upon his clearest and richest thoughts: but he qualifies his general assertion by affirming, that heroic verse ought only to be applied to heroic situations and personages; and shows to most advantage in the scenes of argumentation, on which the doing or forbearing some considerable action should depend. Accordingly, in the " Rival Ladies," those scenes of the play which approach to comedy (for it contains none properly comic) are written in blank verse. The Dedication contains two remarkable errors: The author mistakes the title of " Ferrex and Porrex," a play written by Sackville Lord Buckhurst, and Norton; and he ascribes to Shakspeare the first introduction of blank verse. The " Rival Ladies" seems to have been well received, and was probably of some advantage to the author.

In 1663-4, we find Dryden assisting Sir Robert

Howard, who must be termed his friend, if not his patron, in the composition of a rhyming play, called the " Indian Queen." The versification of this piece, which is far more harmonious than that generally used by Howard, shows evidently, that our author had assiduously corrected the whole play, though it may be difficult to say how much of it was written by him. Clifford afterwards upbraided Dryden with having copied his Almanzor from the character of Montezuma;[1] and it must be allowed, there is a striking resemblance between these two outrageous heroes, who carry conquest to any side they choose, and are restrained by no human consideration, excepting the tears or commands of their mistress. But whatever share Dryden had in this piece, Sir Robert Howard retained possession of the titlepage without acknowledgment, and Dryden nowhere gives himself the trouble of reclaiming his property, except in a sketch of the connexion between the " Indian Queen," and " Indian Emperor," where he simply states, that he wrote a part of the former. The " Indian Queen" was acted with very great applause, to which, doubtless, the scenery and dresses contributed not a little. Moreover, it presented battles and sacrifices on the stage, aërial demons singing in the air, and the god of dreams ascending through a trap ; the least of which has often saved a worse tragedy. Evelyn, who witnessed this

---

[1] Notes on Mr Dryden's Poems, 1687.

exhibition, has recorded, that the scenes were the
richest ever seen in England, or perhaps elsewhere,
upon a public stage.[1]

The " Indian Queen" having been thus successful, Dryden was encouraged to engraft upon it
another drama, entitled, the " Indian Emperor."
It is seldom that the continuation of a concluded
tale is acceptable to the public.   The present case
was an exception, perhaps because the connexion
between the " Indian Emperor" and its predecessor
was neither close nor necessary. Indeed, the whole
persons of the " Indian Queen" are disposed of by
the bowl and dagger, at the conclusion of that tragedy, excepting Montezuma, who, with a second
set of characters, the sons and daughters of those
deceased in the first part, occupies the stage in the
second play.   The author might, therefore, have
safely left the audience to discover the plot of the
" Indian Emperor," without embarrassing them
with that of the " Indian Queen."   But to prevent
mistakes, and principally, I should think, to explain
the appearance of three ghosts, the only persons
(if they can be termed such) who have any connexion with the former drama, Dryden took the
precaution to print and disperse an argument of
the play, in order, as the " Rehearsal" intimated,
to insinuate into the audience some conception of
his plot.   The " Indian Emperor" was probably
the first of Dryden's performances which drew
upon him, in an eminent degree, the attention of

[1] Evelyn's Memoirs, 5th February, 1664.

the public.   It was dedicated to Anne, Duchess
of Monmouth, whom long afterward our author
styled his first and best patroness.[1]   This lady, in
the bloom of youth and wit, and married to a
nobleman no less the darling of his father than of
the nation, had it in her power effectually to serve
Dryden, and doubtless exerted her influence in
procuring him that rank in public opinion, which
is seldom early attained without the sanction of
those who lead the fashion in literature.   The
Duchess of Monmouth probably liked in the " Indian Emperor," not only the beauty of the numbers,
and the frequently exquisite turn of the description,
but also the introduction of incantations and appa-
ritions, of which romantic style of writing she was
a professed admirer.   The " Indian Emperor" had
the most ample success ; and from the time of its
representation, till the day of his death, our author,
though often rudely assailed, maintained the very
pinnacle of poetical superiority, against all his contemporaries.

The dreadful fire of London, in 1666, put a
temporary stop to theatrical exhibitions, which
were not permitted till the following Christmas.
We may take this opportunity to review the effect
which the rise of Dryden's reputation had upon
his private fortune and habits of life.

While our author was the literary assistant of
Sir Robert Howard, and the hired labourer of
Herringman the bookseller, we may readily pre-

[1] Preface to " King Arthur," Dryden's Works, vol. viii.,
p. 120.

sume, that his pretensions and mode of living were necessarily adapted to that mode of life into which he had descended by the unpopularity of his puritanical connexions. Even for some time after his connexion with the theatre, we learn, from a contemporary, that his dress was plain at least, if not mean, and his pleasures moderate, though not inelegant.[1] But as his reputation advanced, he naturally glided into more expensive habits, and began to avail himself of the license, as well as to partake of the pleasures, of the time. We learn from a poem of his enemy Milbourne, that Dryden's person was advantageous; and that, in the

[1] " I remember," says a correspondent of the Gentleman's Magazine, for 1745, " plain John Dryden, before he paid his court with success to the great, in one uniform clothing of Norwich-drugget. I have eat tarts with him and Madam Reeve at the Mulberry garden, when our author advanced to a sword and a Chadreux wig."—Page 99.—[On this note Mr Hallam (Edin. Rev. 1808) says, " Far less than could be expected is known of Dryden's character and customs of life. The patrons whom he flattered, and the wits who courted his company, have been negligent in preserving any particular memorials of one whose acquaintance did them so much honour. Congreve is an exception, who has drawn his character with elegance, and in the spirit of friendship, but not with sufficient minuteness to satisfy curiosity. It is lamentable that our biographical antiquaries, who are so very learned in epitaphs and extracts from parish registers, are seldom so lucky as to bring any thing to light, by which a man's real character is distinguished. How much has been written upon *Shakespeare* and *Shakespere*,—what long pedigrees of the Halls, Harts, and Hathaways,—while the reader, amidst the profusion of learning, searches in vain for a vestige of the manners and opinions of him, in whom alone he is interested! *Pars minima est ipse poeta sui.*"]

younger part of his life, he was distinguished by the emulous favour of the fair sex.[1] And although it would not be edifying, were it possible, to trace instances of his success in gallantry, we may barely notice his intrigue with Mrs Reeves, a beautiful actress, who performed in many of his plays. This amour was probably terminated before the fair lady's retreat to a cloister, which seems to have taken place before the representation of Otway's " Don Carlos," in 1676.[2] Their connexion is alluded to in the " Rehearsal," which was acted in 1671. Bayes, talking of Amarillis, actually represented by Mrs Reeves, says, " Ay, 'tis a pretty little rogue ; she's my mistress : I knew her face would set off armour extremely ; and to tell you true, I writ that part only for her." There follows an obscure allusion to some gallantry of our author in another quarter. But Dryden's amours were interrupted, if not terminated, in 1665, by his marriage.

Our author's friendship with Sir Robert Howard, and his increasing reputation, had introduced him to the family of the Earl of Berkshire, father to his friend. In the course of this intimacy,

[1] He describes him as,

"Still smooth, as when, adorn'd with youthful pride,
For thy dear sake the blushing virgins died,
When the kind gods of wit and love combined,
And with large gifts thy yielding soul refined."

[2] The epilogue has these lines :—

"But now if by my suit you'll not be won,
You know what your unkindness oft has done,—
I'll e'en forsake the playhouse, and turn nun."

the poet gained the affections of Lady Elizabeth Howard, the earl's eldest daughter, whom he soon afterwards married. The lampoons, by which Dryden's private character was assailed in all points, allege, that this marriage was formed under circumstances dishonourable to the lady. But of this there is no evidence; while the malignity of the reporters is evident and undisguised. We may however believe, that the match was not altogether agreeable to the noble family of Berkshire. Dryden, it is true, might, in point of descent, be admitted to form pretensions to Lady Elizabeth Howard; but his family, though honourable, was in a kind of disgrace, from the part which Sir Gilbert Pickering and Sir John Driden had taken in the civil wars: while the Berkshire family were remarkable for their attachment to the royal cause. Besides, many of the poet's relations were engaged in trade; and the alliance of his brothers-in-law, the tobacconist and stationer, if it was then formed, could not sound dignified in the ears of a Howard. Add to this a very important consideration,—Dryden had no chance of sharing the wealth of his principal relations, which might otherwise have been received as an atonement for the guilty confiscations by which it was procured. He had quarreled with them, or they with him; his present possession was a narrow independence; and his prospects were founded upon literary success, always precarious, and then connected with circumstances of personal abasement, which rendered it almost disreputable. A noble family might be allowed to regret, that one of their members was chiefly to rely for the maintenance of her husband, her family, and herself, upon the fees of dedications, and occasional pieces of poetry, and the uncertain profits of the theatre.

Yet, as Dryden's manners were amiable, his reputation high, and his moral character unexceptionable, the Earl of Berkshire was probably soon reconciled to the match; and Dryden seems to have resided with his father-in-law for some time, since it is from the Earl's seat of Charlton, in Wiltshire, that he dates the Introduction to the "*Annus Mirabilis*," published in the end of 1667.

So honourable a connexion might have been expected to have advanced our author's prospects in a degree beyond what he experienced; but his father-in-law was poor, considering his rank, and had a large family, so that the portion of Lady Elizabeth was inconsiderable. Nor was her want of fortune supplied by patronage, or family influence. Dryden's preferment, as poet laureat, was due to, and probably obtained by, his literary character; nor did he ever receive any boon suitable to his rank, as son-in-law to an earl. But, what was worst of all, the parties did not find mutual happiness in the engagement they had formed. It is difficult for a woman of a violent temper and weak intellects, and such the lady seems to have been, to endure the apparently causeless fluctuation of spirits incident to one doomed to labour incessantly in the feverish exercise of the imagination. Unintentional neglect, and the inevitable relaxa-

tion, or rather sinking of spirit, which follows
violent mental exertion, are easily misconstrued
into capricious rudeness, or intentional offence;
and life is embittered by mutual accusation, not
the less intolerable because reciprocally just. The
wife of one who is to gain his livelihood by poetry,
or by any labour (if any there be) equally exhaust-
ing, must either have taste enough to relish her
husband's performances, or good-nature sufficient
to pardon his infirmities. It was Dryden's misfortune, that Lady Elizabeth had neither the one nor
the other; and I dismiss the disagreeable subject
by observing, that on no one occasion, when a sarcasm against matrimony could be introduced, has
our author failed to season it with such bitterness,
as spoke an inward consciousness of domestic
misery.

During the period when the theatres were closed,
Dryden seems to have written and published the
" *Annus Mirabilis*," of which we spoke at the close
of the last Section. But he was also then labouring upon his " Essay of Dramatic Poesy." It was
a singular trait in the character of our author, that
by whatever motive he was directed in his choice
of a subject, and his manner of treating it, he was,
upon all occasions, alike anxious to persuade the
public, that both the one and the other were the
object of his free choice, founded upon the most
rational grounds of preference. He had, therefore, no sooner seriously bent his thoughts to the
stage, and distinguished himself as a composer of
heroic plays, than he wrote his " Essay of Drama-

tic Poesy," in which he assumes, that the drama was the highest department of poetry; and endeavours to prove, that rhyming, or heroic, tragedies are the most legitimate offspring of the drama.

The subject is agitated in a dialogue between Lord Buckhurst, Sir Charles Sedley, Sir Robert Howard, and the author himself, under the feigned names of Eugenius, Lisideius, Crites, and Neander. This celebrated Essay was first published in the end of 1667, or beginning of 1668. The author revised it with an unusual degree of care, and published it anew in 1684, with a Dedication to Lord Buckhurst.

In the introduction of the dialogue, our author artfully solicits the attention of the public to the improved versification, in which he himself so completely excelled all his contemporaries; and contrasts the rugged lines and barbarous conceits of Cleveland with the more modern style of composition, where the thoughts were moulded into easy and significant words, superfluities of expression retrenched, and the rhyme rendered so properly a part of the verse, that it was led and guided by the sense, which was formerly sacrificed in attaining it. This point being previously settled, a dispute occurs concerning the alleged superiority of the ancient classic models of dramatic composition. This is resolutely denied by all the speakers, excepting Crites; the regulation of the unities is condemned, as often leading to greater absurdities than those they were designed to obviate; and the classic authors are censured for the cold and trite subjects of their comedies, the bloody and horrible topics of many of their tragedies, and their deficiency in painting the passion of love. From all this, it is justly gathered, that the moderns, though with less regularity, possess a greater scope for invention, and have discovered, as it were, a new perfection in writing. This debated point being abandoned by Crites, (or Howard,) the partisan of the ancients, a comparison between the French and English drama is next introduced. Sedley, the celebrated wit and courtier, pleads the cause of the French, an opinion which perhaps was not singular among the favourites of Charles II. But the rest of the speakers unite in condemning the extolled simplicity of the French plots, as actual barrenness, compared to the variety and copiousness of the English stage ; and their authors' limiting the attention of the audience and interest of the piece to a single principal personage, is censured as poverty of imagination, when opposed to the diversification of characters exhibited in the *dramatis personæ* of the English poets. Shakspeare and Jonson are then brought forward and contrasted with the French dramatists, and with each other. The former is extolled, as the man of all modern, and perhaps ancient, poets, who had the largest and most comprehensive soul, and intuitive knowledge of human nature; and the latter, as the most learned and judicious writer which any theatre ever had. But to Shakspeare, Dryden objects, that his comic sometimes degenerates into *clenches*, and his serious into bombast; to Jonson, the sullen and saturnine character of his genius, his borrowing from the ancients, and the insipidity of his latter plays. The examen leads to the discussion of a point, in which Dryden had differed with Sir Robert Howard. This was the use of rhyme in tragedy. Our author had, it will be remembered, maintained the superiority of rhyming plays, in the introduction to the " Rival Ladies." Sir Robert Howard, the catalogue of whose virtues did not include that of forbearance, made a direct answer to the arguments used in the introduction;[1] and while he studiously extolled the plays of Lord Orrery, as affording an exception to his general sentence against rhyming plays, he does not extend the compliment to Dryden, whose defence of rhyme was expressly dedicated to that noble author. Dryden, not much pleased, perhaps, at being left undistinguished in the general censure passed upon rhyming plays by his friend and ally, retaliates in the Essay, by placing in the mouth of Crites the arguments urged by Sir Robert Howard, and replying to them in the person of Neander. To the charge, that rhyme is unnatural, in consequence of the inverted arrangement of the words necessary to produce it, he replies, that, duly ordered, it may be natural in itself, and therefore not unnatural in a play; and that, if the objection be further insisted upon, it is equally conclusive against blank verse, or measure without rhyme. To the objection founded on the formal and uniform recurrence of the measure, he alleges the facility of

---

[1] See Dryden's Works, vol. xv., p. 362, note.

varying it, by throwing the cadence upon different parts of the line, by breaking it into hemistiches, or by running the sense into another line, so as to make art and order appear as loose and free as nature.[1] Dryden even contends, that, for variety's sake, the pindaric measure might be admitted, of which Davenant set an example in the " Siege of Rhodes." But this license, which was probably borrowed from the Spanish stage, has never succeeded elsewhere, except in operas. Finally, it is urged, that rhyme, the most noble verse, is alone fit for tragedies, the most noble species of composition ; that far from injuring a scene, in which quick repartee is necessary, it is the last perfection of wit to put it into numbers ; and that, even where a trivial and common expression is placed, from necessity, in the mouth of an important character, it receives, from the melody of versification, a dignity befitting the person that is to pronounce it. With this keen and animated defence of a mode of composition, in which he felt his own excellence, Dryden concludes the " Essay of Dramatic Poesy."

The publication of this criticism, the first that contained an express attempt to regulate dramatic writing, drew general attention, and gave some offence. Sir Robert Howard felt noways flattered at being made, through the whole dialogue, the champion of unsuccessful opinions: and a partiality

---

[1] Sandford, a most judicious actor, is said, by Cibber, cautiously to have observed this rule, in order to avoid surfeiting the audience by the continual recurrence of rhyme.

to the depreciated blank verse seems to have been hereditary in his family.[1] He therefore hasted to assert his own opinion against that of Dryden, in the preface to one of his plays, called the " Duke of Lerma," published in the middle of the year 1668. It is difficult for two friends to preserve their temper in a dispute of this nature; and there may be reason to believe, that some dislike to the alliance of Dryden, as a brother-in-law, mingled with the poetical jealousy of Sir Robert Howard. The preface to the " Duke of Lerma" is written in the tone of a man of quality and importance, who is conscious of stooping beneath his own dignity, and neglecting his graver avocations, by engaging in a literary dispute. Dryden was not likely, of many men, to brook this tone of affected superiority. He retorted upon Sir Robert Howard very severely, in a tract, entitled, the " Defence of the Essay of Dramatic Poesy," which he prefixed to the second edition of the " Indian Emperor," published in 1668. In this piece, the author mentions his antagonist as master of more than twenty legions of arts and sciences, in ironical allusion to Sir Robert's

---

[1] The honourable Edward Howard, Sir Robert's brother, expresses himself in the preface to the " Usurper," a play published in 1668, " not insensible to the disadvantage it may receive passing into the world upon the naked feet of verse, with other works that have their measures adorned with the trappings of rhyme, which, however they have succeeded in wit or design, is still thought music, as the heroic tone now goes ; but whether so natural to a play, that should most nearly imitate, in some cases, our familiar converse, the judicious may easily determine."

coxcomical affectation of universal knowledge, which had already exposed him to the satire of Shadwell.[1] He is also described, in reference to some foolish appearance in the House of Commons, as having maintained a contradiction *in terminis*, in the face of three hundred persons. Neither does Dryden neglect to hold up to ridicule the slips in Latin and English grammar, which marked the offensive preface to the " Duke of Lerma." And although he concludes, that he honoured his adversary's parts and person as much as any man living, and had so many particular obligations to him, that he should be very ungrateful not to acknowledge them to the world, yet the personal and contemptuous severity of the whole piece must have cut to the heart so proud a man as Sir Robert Howard. This quarrel between the baronet and the poet, who was suspected of having crutched-up many of his lame performances, furnished food for lampoon and amusement to the indolent wits of the day. But the breach between the brothers-in-law, though wide, proved fortunately not irreconcilable; and towards the end of Dryden's literary career, we find him again upon terms of friendship with the person by whom he had been befriended at its

[1] Who drew Sir Robert in the character of Sir Positive Atall in the " Sullen Lovers;" a foolish knight, that pretends to understand every thing in the world, and will suffer no man to understand any thing in his company; so foolishly positive, that he will never be convinced of an error, though never so gross. This character is supported with great humour.

commencement.[1] Edward Howard, who, it appears, had entered as warmly as his brother into the contest with Dryden about rhyming tragedies, also seems to have been reconciled to our poet; at least he pronounced a panegyric on his translation of Virgil before it left the press, in a passage which is also curious, from the author ranking in the same line " the two elaborate poems of Blackmore and Milton."[2] In testimony of total amnesty, the " De-

[1] In a letter from Dryden to Tonson, dated 26th May, 1696, in which he reckons upon Sir Robert Howard's assistance in a pecuniary transaction.

[2] " I am informed Mr Dryden is now translating of Virgil; and although I must own it is a fault to forestall or anticipate the praise of a man in his labours, yet, big with the greatness of the work, and the vast capacity of the author, I cannot here forbear saying, that Mr Dryden, in the translating of Virgil, will of a certain make Maro speak better than ever Maro thought. Besides those already mentioned, there are other ingredients and essential parts of poetry, necessary for the forming of a truly great and happy genius, viz. a free air and spirit, a vigorous and well-governed thought, which are, as it were, the soul which inform and animate the whole mass and body of verse. But these are such divine excellencies as are peculiar only to the brave and the wise. The first chief in verse, who trode in this sweet and delightful path of the Muses, was the renowned Earl of Roscommon, a great worthy, as well as a great wit; and who is, in all respects, resembled by another great Lord of this present age, viz. my Lord Cutts, a person whom all people must allow to be an accomplished gentleman, a great general, and a fine poet.

" The two elaborate poems of Blackmore and Milton, the which, for the dignity of them, may very well be looked upon as the two grand exemplars of poetry, do either of them exceed, and are more to be valued than all the poets, both of

fence of the Essay" was cancelled; and it must be rare indeed to meet with an original edition of it, since Mr Malone had never seen one.[1]

Dryden's fame, as an author, was doubtless exalted by the " Essay of Dramatic Poesy" which showed, that he could not only write plays, but defend them when written. His circumstances rendered it necessary, that he should take the full advantage of his reputation to meet the increasing expense of a wife and family; and it was probably shortly after the Essay appeared, that our author entered into his memorable contract with the King's Company of players. The precise terms of this agreement have been settled by Mr Malone from unquestionable evidence, after being the subject of much doubt and uncertainty. It is now certain, that, confiding in the fertility of his genius, and the readiness of his pen, Dryden undertook to write for the King's house no less than three plays in the course of the year. In consideration of this engagement, he was admitted to hold one share and a quarter in the profits of the theatre, which was stated by the managers to have produced him

the Romans and the Greeks put together. There are two other incomparable pieces of poetry, viz. Mr Dryden's ' Absalom and Achitophel,' and the epistle of a known and celebrated wit (*Mr Charles Montague*) to my Lord of Dorset, the best judge in poetry, as well as the best poet; the tutelar *numen* o' the stage, and on whose breath all the muses have their dependence." — *Proem to an Essay on Pastoral, and Elegy on Queen Mary, by the Honourable Edward Howard,* 21*st January,* 1695.

[1] That now before me is prefixed to the second edition of the " Indian Emperor," 1668.

three or four hundred pounds, *communibus annis.*
Either, however, the players became sensible, that,
by urging their pensioner to continued drudgery,
they in fact lessened the value of his labour, or
Dryden felt himself unequal to perform the task he
had undertaken; for the average number of plays
which he produced was only about half that which
had been contracted for. The company, though
not without grudging, paid the poet the stipulated
share of profit; and the curious document, recovered by Mr Malone, not only establishes the terms
of the bargain, but that the players, although they
complained of the laziness of their indented author,
were jealous of their right to his works, and anxious
to retain possession of him, and of them.[1] It would

---

[1] It seems to have been a memorial addressed to the Lord
Chamberlain for the time, and was long in the possession of
the Killigrew family. It was communicated by the learned
Mr Reed to Mr Malone, and runs as follows :

" Whereas, upon Mr Dryden's binding himself to write
three playes a-yeere, he, the said Mr Dryden, was admitted, and continued as a sharer, in the King's Playhouse for
diverse years, and received for his share and a quarter, three
or four hundred pounds, *communibus annis;* but though he
received the moneys, we received not the playes, not one in a
yeare. After which, the House being burnt, the Company, in
building another, contracted great debts, so that the shares fell
much short of what they were formerly. Thereupon, Mr
Dryden complaining to the Company of his want of proffit,
the Company was so kind to him, that they not only did not
presse him for the playes which he so engaged to write for
them, and for which he was paid beforehand, but they did
also, at his earnest request, give him a third day for his last
new play, called ' All for Love;' and at the receipt of the
money of the said third day, he acknowledged it as a guift,
and a particular kindnesse of the Company. Yet, notwith-

have been well for Dryden's reputation, and perhaps not less productive to the company, had the number of his plays been still farther abridged; for, while we admire the facility that could produce five or six plays in three years, we lament to find it so often exerted to the sacrifice of the more essential qualities of originality and correctness.

Dryden had, however, made his bargain, and was compelled to fulfil it the best he might. As his last tragic piece, the " Indian Emperor," had been eminently successful, he was next to show the public, that his talents were not limited to the buskin;

---

standing this kind proceeding, Mr Dryden has now, jointly with Mr Lee, (who was in pension with us to the last day of our playing, and shall continue,) written a play, called ' Œdipus,' and given it to the Duke's Company, contrary to his said agreement, his promise, and all gratitude, to the great prejudice and almost undoing of the Company, they being the only poets remaining to us. Mr Crowne, being under the like agreement with the Duke's House, writt a play, called the ' Destruction of Jerusalem,' and being forced, by their refusall of it, to bring it to us, the said Company compelled us, after the studying of it, and a vast expense in scenes and cloathes, to buy off their clayme, by paying all the pension he had received from them, amounting to one hundred and twelve pounds paid by the King's Company, besides neere forty pounds he, the said Mr Crowne, paid out of his owne pocket.

" These things considered, if, notwithstanding Mr Dryden's said agreement, promise, and moneys, freely given him for his said last new play, and the many titles we have to his writings, this play be judged away from us, we must submit.

(Signed)   " CHARLES KILLIGREW.
            CHARLES HART.
            RICH. BURT.
            CARDELL GOODMAN.
            MIC. MOHUN."

and accordingly, late in 1667, was represented, the " Maiden Queen," a tragi-comedy, in which, although there is a comic plot separate from the tragic design, our author boasts to have retained all that regularity and symmetry of parts which the dramatic laws require. The tragic scenes of the " Maiden Queen" were deservedly censured, as falling beneath the " Indian Emperor." They have neither the stately march of the heroic dialogue, nor, what we would be more pleased to have found in them, the truth of passion, and natural colouring, which characterised the old English drama. But the credit of the piece was redeemed by the comic part, which is a more light and airy representation of the fashionable and licentious manners of the time than Dryden could afterwards exhibit, excepting in " Marriage a-la-Mode." The king, whose judgment on this subject was unquestionable, graced the " Maiden Queen" with the title of *his play ;* and Dryden insinuates that it would have been dedicated to him, had he had confidence to follow the practice of the French poets in like cases. At least, he avoided the solecism of inscribing the king's own play to a subject ; and, instead of a dedication, we have a preface, in which the sovereign's favourable opinion of the piece is studiously insisted upon. Neither was the praise of Charles conferred without critical consideration ; for he justly censured the concluding scene, in which Celadon and Florimel treat of their marriage in very light terms in presence of the Queen, who stands by, an idle spectator. This insult to Melpomene, and preference of her comic sister, our author acknowledges to be a fault, but seemingly only in deference to the royal opinion; for he instantly adds, that, in his own judgment, the scene was necessary to make the piece go off smartly, and was, in the estimation of good judges, the most diverting of the whole comedy.

Encouraged by the success of the "Maiden Queen," Dryden proceeded to revive the "Wild Gallant;" and, in deference to his reputation, it seems now to have been more favourably received than at its first representation.

The "Maiden Queen" was followed by the "Tempest," an alteration of Shakspeare's play of the same name, in which Dryden assisted Sir William Davenant. It seems probable that Dryden furnished the language, and Davenant the plan of the new characters introduced. They do but little honour to his invention, although Dryden has highly extolled it in his preface. The idea of a counterpart to Shakspeare's plot, by introducing a man who had never seen a woman, as a contrast to a woman who had never seen a man, and by furnishing Caliban with a sister monster, seems hardly worthy of the delight with which Dryden says he filled up the characters so sketched. In mixing his tints, Dryden did not omit that peculiar colouring, in which his age delighted. Miranda's simplicity is converted into indelicacy, and Dorinda talks the language of pro-stitution before she has ever seen a man. But the play seems to have succeeded to the utmost wish of the authors. It was brought out in the Duke's house, of which Davenant was manager, with all the splendour of scenic decoration, of which he was inventor. The opening scene is described as being particularly splendid, and the performance of the spirits, " with mops and mows," excited general applause. Davenant died before the publication of this piece, and his memory is celebrated in the preface.

Our author's next play, if it could be properly called his, was " Sir Martin Mar-all." This was originally a translation of " *L'Etourdi* " of Moliere, executed by the Duke of Newcastle, famous for his loyalty, and his skill in horsemanship. Dryden availed himself of the noble translator's permission to improve and bring " Sir Martin Mar-all" forward for his own benefit. It was attended with the most complete success, being played four times at court, and above thirty times at the theatre in Lincoln's-Inn Fields; a run chiefly attributed to the excellent performance of Nokes, who represented Sir Martin.[1] The " Tempest" and " Sir

[1] Cibber, with his usual vivacity, thus describes the comic powers of Nokes in this admired character; and many of the traits remind us strongly of our own excellent Liston :

" In the ludicrous distresses, which, by the laws of comedy, folly is often involved in, he sunk into such a mixture of piteous pusillanimity, and a consternation so ruefully ludicrous and inconsolable, that when he had shook you to a fatigue of laughter, it became a moot point, whether you ought not to have pity'd him. When he debated any matter by himself, he would shut up his mouth with a dumb studious powt, and roll his full eye into such a vacant amazement, such palpable ignorance of what to think of it, that his silent perplexity

Martin Mar-all" were both acted by the Duke's company, probably because Dryden was in the one assisted by Sir William Davenant, the manager, and because the other was entered in the name of the Duke of Newcastle. Of these two plays, " Sir Martin Mar-all" was printed anonymously in 1668. It did not appear with Dryden's name until 1697. The " Tempest," though acted before " Sir Martin Mar-all," was not printed until 1669-70. They are in the present, as in former editions,[1] arranged according to the date of publication, which gives the precedence to " Sir Martin Mar-all," though last acted.

The "Evening's Love, or the Mock Astrologer,"

(which would sometimes hold him several minutes) gave your imagination as full content, as the most absurd thing he could say upon it.   In the character of Sir Martin Mar-all, who is always committing blunders to the prejudice of his own interest, when he had brought himself to a dilemma in his affairs, by vainly proceeding upon his own head, and was afterwards afraid to look his governing servant and counsellor in the face ; what a copious and distressful harangue have I seen him make with his looks (while the house has been in one continued roar for several minutes) before he could prevail with his courage to speak a word to him! Then might you have, at once, read in his face vexation—that his own measures, which he had piqued himself upon, had failed ; envy of his servant's wit; distress—to retrieve the occasion he had lost; shame—to confess his folly ; and yet a sullen desire to be reconciled, and better advised for the future! What tragedy ever showed us such a tumult of passions rising, at once, in one bosom ! or what buskin hero, standing under the load of them, could have more effectually moved his spectators by the most pathetic speech, than poor miserable Nokes did by this silent eloquence, and piteous plight of his features?"
—CIBBER's *Apology*, p. 86.

[1] Of Dryden's Works.

was Dryden's next composition. It is an imitation of "*Le Feint Astrologus*" of Corneille, which is founded upon Calderon's "*El Astrologo Fingido*." Several of the scenes are closely imitated from Moliere's "*Dépit Amoureux*." Having that lively bustle, intricacy of plot, and surprising situation, which the taste of the time required, and being enlivened by the characters of Wildblood and Jacinta, the "Mock Astrologer" seems to have met a favourable reception in 1668, when it first appeared. It was printed in the same, or in the following year, and inscribed to the Duke of New-castle, to whom Dryden had been indebted for the sketch of "Sir Martin Mar-all." It would appear, that this gallant and chivalrous peer was then a protector of Dryden, though he afterwards seems more especially to have patronised his enemy Shad-well; upon whose *northern* dedications, inscribed to the Duke and his lady, our author is particularly severe. In the preface to the "Evening's Love," Dryden anxiously justifies himself from the charge of encouraging libertinism, by crowning his rake and coquette with success. But after he has ar-rayed all the authority of the ancient and modern poets, and has pleaded that these licentious charac-ters are only made happy after being reclaimed in the last scene, we may be permitted to think, that more proper heroes may be selected than those, who, to merit the reward assigned them, must announce a violent and sudden change from the character they have sustained during five acts; and the attempt to shroud himself under authority of others, is seldom resorted to by Dryden when a cause is otherwise tenable. The excellent Evelyn, who mentions seeing this play under the inaccurate title of the "Evening's Love," adds, "A foolish plot, and very profane; it affected me to see how much the stage was degenerated and polluted by the licentious times."[1] In this preface also he justified himself from the charge of plagiarism, by showing that the mere story is the least part either of the labour of the poet, or of the graces of the poem; quoting against his critics the expression of the king, who had said, he wished those, who charged Dryden with theft, would always steal him plays like Dryden's.

The "Royal Martyr" was acted in 1668-9, and printed in 1670. It is, in every respect, a proper heroic tragedy, and had a large share of the applause with which those pieces were then received. It abounds in bombast, but is not deficient in specimens of the sublime and of the tender. The preface is distinguished by that tone of superiority, which Dryden often assumed over the critics of the time. Their general observations he cuts short, by observing, that those who make them produce nothing of their own, or only what is more ridiculous than any thing they reprehend. Special objections are refuted, by an appeal to classical authority. Thus the couplet,

"And he who servilely creeps after sense,
Is safe, but ne'er will reach an excellence,"

is justified from the "*serpit humi tutus*" of Ho-

[1] Evelyn's Memoirs, 19th June, 1668.

race ; and, by a still more forced derivation, the line,

> " And follow fate, which does too fast pursue,"

is said to be borrowed from Virgil,

> " *Eludit gyro interior sequiturque sequentem.*"

And he concludes by exulting, that, though he might have written nonsense, none of his critics had been so happy as to discover it. These indications of superiority, being thought to savour of vanity, had their share in exciting the storm of malevolent criticism, of which Dryden afterwards so heavily complained. " Tyrannic Love " is dedicated to the Duke of Monmouth ; but it would seem the compliment was principally designed to his duchess. The duke, whom Dryden was afterwards to celebrate in very different strains, is however compared to an Achilles, or Rinaldo, who wanted only a Homer, or Tasso, to give him the fame due to him.

It was in this period of prosperity, of general reputation, of confidence in his genius, and perhaps of presumption, (if that word can be applied to Dryden,) that he produced those two very singular plays, the First and Second Parts of the " Conquest of Granada." In these models of the pure heroic drama, the ruling sentiments of love and honour are carried to the most passionate extravagance.[1] And, to maintain the legitimacy

---

1 [Sir Walter Scott says elsewhere, (Dryden's Works, vol. iv., p. 7, 8,) " In the conduct of the story there is much brilliancy

of this style of composition, our author, ever ready
to vindicate with his pen to be right, that which
his timid critics murmured at as wrong, threw the
gauntlet down before the admirers of the ancient
English school, in the epilogue to the " Second
Part of the Conquest of Granada," and in the
defence of that epilogue.   That these plays might
be introduced to the public with a solemnity corresponding in all respects to models of the rhyming
tragedy, they were inscribed to the Duke of York,
and prefaced by an " Essay upon Heroic Plays."
They were performed in 1669–70, and received
with unbounded applause.   Before we consider
the effect which they, and similar productions, produced on the public, together with the progress
and decay of the taste for heroic dramas, we may
first notice the effect which the ascendency of our
author's reputation had produced upon his situation
and fortunes.

of event.   The reader, or spectator, is never allowed to repose
on the scene before him; and although the changes of fortune
are too rapid to be either probable, or altogether pleasing, yet
they arrest the attention by their splendour and importance,
and interest us in spite of our more sober judgment."......
" If the reader can abstract his mind from the qualities now
deemed essential to a play, and consider the Conquest of
Granada as a piece of romantic poetry, there are few compositions in the English language, which convey a more lively
and favourable display of the magnificence of fable, of
language, and of action, proper to that style of composition.
Amid the splendid ornaments of the structure, we lose sight
of occasional disproportion and incongruity; and, at an early
age particularly, there are few poems which make a more
deep impression upon the imagination, than the Conquest of
Granada."]

Whether we judge of the rank which Dryden held in society by the splendour of his titled and powerful friends, or by his connexions among men of genius, we must consider him as occupying, at this time, as high a station, in the very foremost circle, as literary reputation could gain for its owner. Independent of the notice with which he was honoured by Charles himself, the poet numbered among his friends most of the distinguished nobility. The great Duke of Ormond had already begun that connexion, which subsisted between Dryden and three generations of the house of Butler ; Thomas Lord Clifford, one of the Cabal ministry, was uniform in patronising the poet, and appears to have been active in introducing him to the king's favour ; the Duke of Newcastle, as we have seen, loved him sufficiently to present him with a play for the stage ; the witty Earl of Dorset, then Lord Buckhurst, and Sir Charles Sedley, admired in that loose age for the peculiar elegance of his loose poetry, were his intimate associates, as is evident from the turn of the " Essay of Dramatic Poesy," where they are speakers ; Wilmot Earl of Rochester (soon to act a very different part) was then anxious to vindicate Dryden's writings, to mediate for him with those who distributed the royal favour, and was thus careful, not only of his reputation, but his fortune.[1] In short, the first

[1] [" It is to your Lordship's favour we generally owe our protection and patronage ; and to the nobleness of your nature, which will not suffer the least shadow of your wit to be contemned in other men. You have been often pleased, not only

author of what was then held the first style of
poetry, was sought for by all among the great and
gay who wished to maintain some character for
literary taste ; a description which included all of
the court of Charles whom nature had not positively incapacitated from such pretension. It was
then Dryden enjoyed those genial nights described
in the dedication of the " Assignation," when " discourse was neither too serious nor too light, but
always pleasant, and for the most part instructive ;
the raillery neither too sharp upon the present, nor
too censorious upon the absent ; and the cups such
only as raised the conversation of the night, without disturbing the business of the morrow." [1] He
had not yet experienced the disadvantages atten-
dant on such society, or learned how soon literary
eminence becomes the object of detraction, of envy,
of injury, even from those who can best feel its
merit, if they are discouraged by dissipated habits

---

to excuse my imperfections, but to vindicate what was tolerable
in my writings from their censures, and, what I never can
forget, *you have not only been careful of my reputation, but of
my fortune.* You have been solicitous to supply my neglect
of myself, and to overcome the fatal modesty of poets, which
submits them to perpetual wants, rather than to become impor-
tunate with those people who have the liberality of kings in
their disposing, and who, dishonouring the bounty of their
master, suffer such to be in necessity who endeavour at least
to please him ; and for whose entertainment he has generously
provided, if the fruits of his royal favour were not often
stopped in other hands."—*Epistle dedicatory to Marriage a-la-
Mode, Dryden's Works*, vol. iv., p. 238.]

[1] Ibid. vol. iv., p. 351.

from emulating its flight, or hardened by perverted feeling against loving its possessors.

But, besides the society of these men of wit and pleasure, Dryden enjoyed the affection and esteem of the ingenious Cowley, who wasted his brilliant talents in the unprofitable paths of metaphysical poetry; of Waller and of Denham, who had done so much for English versification; of Davenant, as subtle as Cowley, and more harmonious than Denham, who, with a happier model, would probably have excelled both. Dryden was also known to Milton, though it may be doubted whether they justly appreciated the talents of each other. Of all the men of genius at this period, whose claims to immortality our age has admitted, Butler alone seems to have been the adversary of our author's reputation.

While Dryden was thus generally known and admired, the advancement of his fortune bore no equal progress to the splendour of his literary fame. Something was, however, done to assist it. The office of royal historiographer had become vacant in 1666 by the decease of James Howell, and in 1668 the death of Davenant opened the situation of poet laureat. These two offices, with a salary of L.200 paid quarterly, and the celebrated annual butt of canary, were conferred upon Dryden 18th August, 1670. The grant bore a retrospect to the term after Davenant's demise, and is declared to be to " John Dryden, master of arts, in considera‧ tion of his many acceptable services theretofore done to his present Majesty, and from an observation of his learning and eminent abilities, and his great skill and elegant style, both in verse and prose." [1] Thus was our author placed at the head of the literary class of his countrymen, so far as that high station could be conferred by the favour of the monarch.

If we compute Dryden's share in the theatre at L.300 annually, which is lower than it was rated by the actors in their petition; [2] if we make, at the same time, some allowance for those presents which authors of that time received upon presenting dedications, or occasional pieces of poetry ; if we recollect, that Dryden had a small landed property, and that his wife, Lady Elizabeth, had probably some fortune, or allowance, however trifling, from her family,—I think we will fall considerably under the mark in computing the poet's income, during this period of prosperity, at L.600 or L.700 annually ; [3] a sum more adequate to procure all the

[1] Pat. 22 Car. ii., p. 6, n. 6.   Malone, i., p. 88.

[2] Their account was probably exaggerated. Upon a similar occasion, the master of the revels stated the value of his winter and summer benefit plays at L.50 each ; although, in reality, they did not, upon an average, produce him L.9.—See MALONE's *Historical Account of the Stage.*

[3] [This point has been investigated by Malone with a minuteness which, in this instance, we certainly think well-employed (Malone's Life, p. 144). From his data, it seems that Mr Scott has rated Dryden's income rather too high ; but if we suppose him to have possessed but L.500 a-year, equal at least to L.1500 at present, this is placing the circumstances of a poet, who has been a proverb, even among his own tribe, for penury, in a very new light. Yet he has never been accused of extravagance, or over-stating his own distresses.

comforts, and many of the luxuries, of life, than thrice the amount at present. We must, at the same time, recollect, that, though Dryden is nowhere censured for extravagance, poets are seldom capable of minute economy, and that Lady Elizabeth was by education, and perhaps by nature, unfitted for supplying her husband's deficiencies. These halcyon days, too, were but of short duration. The burning of the theatre, in 1670, greatly injured the poet's income from that quarter; his pension, like other appointments of the household establishment of Charles II., was very irregularly paid; and thus, if his income was competent in amount, the payment was precarious and uncertain.

Leaving Dryden for the present in the situation which we have described, and which he occupied during the most fortunate period of his life, the next Section may open with an account of the public taste at this time, and of the revolution in it which shortly took place.

We must suppose, therefore, that his income was irregular, and his salary not regularly forthcoming from the scanty exchequer of Charles.—HALLAM, 1808.]

SECTION III.

*Heroic Plays—The Rehearsal—Marriage a-la-Mode—
The Assignation—Controversy with Clifford—with Leigh
—with Ravenscroft—Massacre of Amboyna—State of
Innocence.*

THE rage for imitating the French stage, joined
to the successful efforts of our author, had now
carried the heroic or rhyming tragedy to its highest
pitch of popularity.[1] The principal requisites of

[1] [" It is justly observed by Mr Scott, that the French
theatre, which was now thought to be in perfection, guided
the criticism of Charles the Second's court, and afforded the pattern of those tragedies, which continued in fashion for twenty
years after the Restoration, and which were called rhyming
or heroic plays. He finds the origin of that unnatural and
pedantic dialogue which prevailed through these performances,
in the romances of Calprenede and Scuderi; and in the necessity of modifying every expression of passion and feeling,
so as not to exceed the decorum prescribed by the presence of
a royal spectator. It may be doubtful, however, whether the
inflexible nature of French verse, and its want of a proper
poetical dialect, will not principally account for these defects.
They were, too, established and rendered legitimate by the
authority of Corneille, whose genius, in many respects, resembled that of Dryden. It would be ridiculous (although
we think Dryden, upon the whole, by far the superior) to
balance his heroic plays against Cinna and Polyeucte; but
the merits and defects of the two writers are much of the same
class. Voltaire somewhere confesses of his countrymen, that
he has written no line that ever drew a tear; an avowal, by

such a drama are summed up by Dryden in the two first lines of the " *Orlando Furioso*,"

> " *Le Donne, i cavalieri, l' arme, gli amori*
> *Le cortesie, l' audaci imprese.*"

The story thus partaking of the nature of a romance of chivalry, the whole interest of the play necessarily turned upon love and honour, those supreme idols of the days of knight-errantry. The love introduced was not of that ordinary sort, which exists between persons of common mould; it was the love of Amadis and Oriana, of Oroondates and Statira; that love which required a sacrifice of every wish, hope, and feeling, unconnected with itself, and which was expressed in the language of prayer and of adoration. It was that love which was neither to be chilled by absence, nor wasted by time, nor quenched by infidelity. No caprice in the object beloved entitled her slave to emancipate himself from her fetters; no command, however unreasonable, was to be disobeyed; if required by the fair mistress of his affections, the hero was not only to sacrifice his interest, but his friend, his honour, his word, his country, even the gratification of his love itself, to maintain the character of a submissive and faithful adorer.

---

the way, which ought to have silenced him, when he affected to set the name of Corneille above that of Shakspeare. Of Dryden, the same may perhaps be said, with very little exception; but each had great knowledge of men; great power of reasoning in forcible and compressed language; and a command of the versification of his own tongue. The following account of these heroic tragedies is lively and just."— HALLAM.]

Much of this mystery is summed up in the following speech of Almahide to Almanzor, and his answer ; from which it appears, that a lover of the true heroic vein never thought himself so happy, as when he had an opportunity of thus showing the purity and disinterestedness of his passion. Almanzor is commanded by his mistress to stay to assist his rival, the king, her husband. The lover very naturally asks,

> " *Almanz.* What recompense attends me, if I stay ?
> *Almah.* You know I am from recompense debarr'd,
> But I will grant your merit a reward ;
> Your flame's too noble to deserve a cheat,
> And I too plain to practise a deceit.
> I no return of love can ever make,
> But what I ask is for my husband's sake ;
> He, I confess, has been ungrateful too,
> But he and I are ruin'd if you go :
> Your virtue to the hardest proof I bring ;—
> Unbribed, preserve a mistress and a king.
> *Almanz.* I'll stop at nothing that appears so brave :
> I'll do't, and now I no reward will have.
> You've given my honour such an ample field,
> That I may die, but that shall never yield."

The king, however, not perhaps understanding this nice point of honour, grows jealous, and wishes to dismiss the disinterested ally, whom his spouse's beauty had enlisted in his service. But this did not depend upon him ; for Almanzor exclaims,

> " *Almanz.* I wonnot go ; I'll not be forced away :
> I came not for thy sake ; nor do I stay.
> It was the queen who for my aid did send ;
> And 'tis I only can the queen defend :
> I, for her sake, thy sceptre will maintain ;
> And thou, by me, in spite of thee, shalt reign."

partakes more of the Spanish than of the French tragedy, although it does not demand that the parody shall be so very strict, as to re-echo noun for noun, or verb for verb, which Lord Holland gives us as a law of the age of Lope de Vega.[1] The English heroic poet did enough if he displayed sufficient point in the dialogue, and alertness in adopting and retorting the image presented by the preceding speech; though, if he could twist the speaker's own words into an answer to his argument, it seems to have been held the more ingenious mode of confutation.

While the hero of a rhyming tragedy was thus unboundedly submissive in love, and dexterous in applying the metaphysical logic of amorous jurisprudence, it was essential to his character that he should possess all the irresistible courage and fortune of a *preux chevalier*. Numbers, however unequal, were to be as chaff before the whirlwind of his valour; and nothing was to be so impossible, that, at the command of his mistress, he could not with ease achieve. When, in the various changes of fortune which such tragedies demand, he quarreled with those whom he had before assisted to conquer,

> " Then to the vanquish'd part his fate he led,
> The vanquish'd triumph'd, and the victor fled."

The language of such a personage, unless when engaged in argumentative dialogue with his mistress, was, in all respects, as magnificent and inflated

---

[1] Life of Lope de Vega, p. 208.

as might beseem his irresistible prowess.   Witness
the famous speech of Almanzor :

> " *Almanz.* To live !
> If from thy hands alone my death can be,
> I am immortal, and a god to thee.
> If I would kill thee now, thy fate's so low,
> That I must stoop ere I can give the blow :
> But mine is fix'd so far above thy crown,
> That all thy men,
> Piled on thy back, can never pull it down :
> But, at my ease, thy destiny I send,
> By ceasing from this hour to be thy friend.
> Like heaven, I need but only to stand still,
> And, not concurring to thy life, I kill.
> Thou canst no title to my duty bring ;
> I'm not thy subject, and my soul's thy king.
> Farewell.   When I am gone,
> There's not a star of thine dare stay with thee :
> I'll whistle thy tame fortune after me ;
> And whirl fate with me wheresoe'er I fly,
> As winds drive storms before them in the sky."

It was expected by the audience, that the pomp
of scenery, and bustle of action, in which such
tremendous heroes were engaged, should in some
degree correspond with their lofty sentiments and
superhuman valour.   Hence solemn feasts, processions, and battles by sea and land, filled the
theatre.   Hence, also, the sudden and violent
changes of fortune, by which the hero and his
antagonists are agitated through the whole piece.
Fortune has been often compared to the sea ; but
in a heroic play, her course resembled an absolute
Bay of Biscay, or Race of Portland, disturbed by
an hundred contending currents and eddies, and
never continuing a moment in one steady flow.

That no engine of romantic surprise might be wanting, Dryden contends, that the dramatist, as he is not confined to the probable in character, so he is not limited by the bounds of nature in the action, but may let himself loose to visionary objects, and to the representation of such things as, not depending upon sense, leave free exercise for the imagination. Indeed, if ghosts, magicians, and demons, might with propriety claim a place anywhere, it must be in plays which throughout disclaim the common rules of nature, both in the incidents narrated, and the agents interested.[1]

Lastly, the action of the heroic drama was to be laid, not merely in the higher, but in the very highest walk of life. No one could with decorum aspire to share the sublimities which it annexed to character, except those made of the " porcelain clay of the earth," dukes, princes, kings, and kaisars. The matters agitated must be of moment, proportioned to their characters and elevated station, the fate of cities and the fall of kingdoms.

That the language, as well as actions and character of the *dramatis personæ*, might be raised

[1] Dryden was severely censured by the critics for his supernatural persons, and ironically described as the " man, nature seemed to make choice of to enlarge the poet's empire, and to complete those discoveries others had begun to shadow. That Shakspeare and Fletcher (as some think) erected the pillars of poetry, is a grosse errour ; this Zany of Columbus has discovered a poeticall world of greater extent than the naturall, peopled with Atlantick colonies of notionali creatures, astrall spirits, ghosts, and idols, more various than ever the Indians worshipt, and heroes more lawless than their savages."—*Censure of the Rota.*

above the vulgar, their sentiments were delivered in rhyme, the richest and most ornate kind of verse, and the farthest removed from ordinary colloquial diction. Dryden has himself assigned the following reasons:—" The plot, the characters, the wit, the passions, the descriptions, are all exalted above the level of common converse, as high as the imagination of the poet can carry them, with proportion to verisimility. Tragedy, we know, is wont to image to us the minds and fortunes of noble persons, and to portray these exactly; heroic rhyme is nearest nature, as being the noblest kind of modern verse.

> *Indignatur enim privatis, et prope socco*
> *Dignis carminibus, narrari cœna Thyestæ—*

says Horace: and in another place,

> *Effutire leves indigna tragœdia versus.—*

Blank verse is acknowledged to be too low for a poem, nay more, for a paper of verses; but if too low for an ordinary sonnet, how much more for tragedy, which is by Aristotle, in the dispute betwixt the epic poesy and the dramatic, for many reasons he there alleges, ranked above it."

When we consider these various essentials of a rhyming play, we may perhaps, without impropriety, define it to be *a metrical romance of chivalry in form of a drama.* The hero is a perfect knight-errant, invincible in battle, and devoted to his dulcinea by a love, subtle, metaphysical, and abstracted from all the usual qualities of the instinctive passion; his adventures diversified by splendid descriptions of bull-feasts, battles, and tournaments ; his fortune undergoing the strangest, most causeless, and most unexpected varieties ; his history chequered by the marvellous interference of ghosts, spectres, and hell itself ; his actions effecting the change of empires, and his co-agents being all lords, and dukes, and noble princes, in order that their rank might, in some slight degree, correspond to the native exaltation of the champion's character.

The reader may smile at this description, and feel some surprise how compositions, involving such gross absurdities, were tolerated by an audience, having pretence to taste and civilisation. But something may be said for the heroic drama.

Although the manners were preposterous, and the changes of fortune rapid and improbable, yet the former often attained a sublime, though forced elevation of sentiment ; and the latter, by rapidity of transition and of contrast, served in no slight degree to interest as well as to surprise the audience. If the spectators were occasionally stunned with bombast, or hurried and confused by the accumulation of action and intrigue, they escaped the languor of a creeping dialogue, and the tedium of a barren plot, of which the termination is descried full three acts before it can be attained. Besides, if these dramas were sometimes extravagant, beautiful passages often occurred to atone for these sallies of fury. In others, ingenuity makes some amends for the absence of natural feeling, and the reader's fancy is pleased at the expense of his taste. In representation, the beauty of the verse,

assisted by the enunciation of such actors as Betterton and Mohun, gilded over the defects of the
sense, and afforded a separate gratification. The
splendour of scenery also, in which these plays
claimed a peculiar excellence, afforded a different
but certain road to popular favour; and thus this
drama, with all its faults, was very far from wanting the usual requisites for success. But another
reason for its general popularity may be sought in
a certain correspondence with the manners of the
time.

Although in Charles the Second's reign the age
of chivalry was totally at an end, yet the sentiments, which had ceased to be motives of action,
were not so obsolete as to sound totally strange to
the public ear. The French romances of the lower
class, such as " Cassandra," " Cleopatra," &c., were
the favourite pastime of the ladies, and retained all
the extravagances of chivalrous sentiment, with a
double portion of tedious form and metaphysical
subtlety. There were occasionally individuals
romantic enough to manage their correspondence
and amours on this exploded system. The admired
Mrs Philips carried on an extensive correspondence with ingenious persons of both sexes, in which
she called herself *Orinda*, and her husband, Mr
Wogan, by the title of *Antenor*. Shadwell, an
acute observer of nature, in one of his comedies,
describes a formal coxcomb of this class, who
courts his mistress out of the " Grand Cyrus," and
rejoices in an opportunity of showing that his

passion could subsist in despite of her scorn.[1]   It
is probable he had met with such an original in
the course of his observation.   The *Précieuses* of
Moliere, who affected a strange mixture of the
romantic heroine and modern fine lady, belong to
the same class of oddities, and had their prototypes
under the observation of the satirist.   But even
those who were above such foppery had been early
taught to read and admire the conceits of Donne,
and the metaphysical love-poems of Cowley.   They
could not object to the quaint and argumentative
dialogues which we have described; for the course
of their studies had formed their taste upon a
model equally artificial and fantastic : and thus,
what between real excellence, and false brilliancy,
the age had been accustomed, not only to admit,
but to admire heroic plays.

Perhaps even these favourable circumstances, of
taste and opportunity, would hardly have elevated
the rhyming drama so high in the public opinion,
had it been supported by less powers than those of
Dryden, or even by equal talents less happily
adapted to that style of composition.   His versification flowed so easily, as to lessen the bad effects

---

[1] His mistress having fallen in love with a disguised barber,
a less polished rival exclaims,—

" *Sir Hum.* Nay, for my part, madam, if you must love a
cudgeled barber, and take him for a valiant count, make much
of him ; I shall desist : there are more ladies, heaven be
thanked.

Trim. Yes, sir, there are more ladies ; but if any man affirms
that my fair Dorinda has an equal, I thus fling down my glove,
and do demand the combat for her honour.—This is a nice
point of honour I have hit."—*Bury fair.*

of rhyme in dialogue; and, at the same time, abounded with such splendid and sonorous passages, as, in the mouth of a Betterton, awed into silence even those critics, who could distinguish that the tumid and unnatural was sometimes substituted for the heroic and sublime. The felicity of his language, the richness of his illustrations, and the depth of his reflections, often supplied what the scene wanted in natural passion; and, while enjoying the beauty of his declamation, it was only on cool reflection, that the hearer discovered it had passed upon him for the expression of genuine feeling. Even then the pleasure which he actually received from the representation, was accepted as an apology for the more legitimate delight which the rules of criticism entitled him to have expected. To these considerations, the high rank and consequent influence, which Dryden already held in the fashionable and literary circles of the time, must unquestionably be added. Nor did he fail to avail himself of his access to the great, whose applause was often cheaply secured by a perusal of the piece, previous to its being presented to the public; and thus it afterwards came forth with all the support of a party eminent for rank and literature, already prepossessed in its favour.[1]

[1] The author of the " Friendly Vindication of Mr Dryden from the Censure of the Rota," (Cambridge, 1673,) mentions, " his humble and supplicant addresses to men and ladies of honour, to whom he presented the most of his plays to be read, and so passing through their families, to comply with

For all these reasons, the heroic drama appears to have gradually risen in reputation, from the return of Charles till about the year 1670–1, when Dryden's " Conquest of Granada " was received with such enthusiastic applause. The reputation of the poet himself kept pace with that of his favourite style of composition ; and though posterity has judged more correctly, it may be questioned, whether " Tyrannic Love " and the " Conquest of Granada " did not place Dryden higher in public esteem, in 1670, than his " Virgil " and " Fables " in 1700. He was, however, now to experience the inconveniences of elevation, and to sustain an attack upon the style of writing which he had vindicated and practised, as well as to repel the efforts of rivals, who boasted of outstripping him in the very road to distinction, which he had himself pointed out. The Duke of Buckingham attacked the system of rhyming plays from the foundation ; Leigh, Clifford, and other scribblers, wrote criticisms upon those of our author in particular ; and Elkanah Settle was able to form a faction heretical enough to maintain, that he could write such compositions better than Dryden.

The witty farce of the " Rehearsal " is said to have been meditated by its authors, (for it was the work of several hands,) so early as a year or two

---

their censures before-hand ; confessing ingenuously, that had he ventured his wits upon the tenter-hooks of Fortune, (like other poets who depended more upon the merits of their pens,) he had been more severely entangled in his own lines long ago."—Page 7.

after the Restoration, when Sir William Davenant's operas and tragedies were the favourite
exhibitions. The ostensible author was the witty
George Villiers, Duke of Buckingham, whose
dissipation was marked with shades of the darkest
profligacy. He lived an unprincipled statesman,
a fickle projector, a wavering friend, a steady
enemy ; and died a bankrupt, an outcast, and a proverb. The Duke was unequal to that masculine
satire, which depends for edge and vigour upon
the conception and expression of the author.[1] But
he appears to have possessed considerable powers
of discerning what was ludicrous ; and enough of
subordinate humour to achieve an imitation of colloquial peculiarities, or a parody upon remarkable
passages of poetry,—talents differing as widely from
real wit, as mimicry does from true comic action.
Besides, Buckingham, as a man of fashion and a
courtier, was master of the *persiflage*, or jargon of
the day, so essentially useful as the medium of
conveying light humour. He early distinguished
himself as an opponent of the rhyming plays. Those
of the Howards, of Davenant, and others, the first
which appeared after the "Reformation," experienced his opposition. At the representation of the
" United Kingdoms," by the Honourable Edward
Howard, a brother of Sir Robert, the Duke's active
share in damning the piece was so far resented by
the author and his friends, that he narrowly escaped

---

[1] Of this want of talent the reader may find sufficient proof
in the extracts from his Grace's reflections upon " Absalom
and Achitophel."—See *Dryden's Works*, vol. ix., p. 273.

longer a well-known or worthy object of ridicule. Perhaps also there was a difficulty in bringing the piece forward, while, of the persons against whom its satire was chiefly directed, Davenant was manager of the one theatre, and Dryden a sharer in the other. The death of Davenant probably removed this difficulty: and the success of Dryden in the heroic drama; the boldness with which he stood forth, not only as a practiser, but as the champion of that peculiar style; a certain provoking tone of superiority in his critical essays, which, even when flowing from conscious merit, is not easily tolerated by contemporaries; and perhaps his situation as poet laureat, a post which has been always considered as a fair butt for the shafts of ridicule,—induced Buckingham to resume the plan of his satire, and to place Dryden in the situation designed originally for Davenant or Howard. That the public might be at no loss to assign the character of Bayes to the laureat, his peculiarities of language were strictly copied. Lacy the actor was instructed by Buckingham himself how to mimic his voice and manner; and, in performing the part, he wore a dress exactly resembling Dryden's usual habit. With these ill-natured precautions, the "Rehearsal" was, in 1671, brought forward for the first time by the King's Company. As, besides the reputation of Dryden, that of many inferior poets, but greater men, was assailed by the Duke's satire, it would appear that the play met a stormy reception on the first night of representation. The friends of the Earl of Orrery, of Sir Robert Howard and his brothers, and other men of rank, who had produced heroic plays, were loud and furious in their opposition. But, as usually happens, the party who laughed got the advantage over that which was angry, and finally drew the audience to their side. When once received, the success of the " Rehearsal" was unbounded. The very popularity of the plays ridiculed aided the effect of the satire, since every body had in their recollection the originals of the passages parodied. Besides the attraction of personal severity upon living and distinguished literary characters, and the broad humour of the burlesque, the part of Bayes had a claim to superior praise, as drawn with admirable attention to the foibles of the poetic tribe. His greedy appetite for applause; his testy repulse of censure or criticism; his inordinate and overwhelming vanity, not unmixed with a vein of flattery to those who he hopes will gratify him by returning it in kind; finally, that extreme, anxious, and fidgeting attention to the minute parts of what even in whole is scarce worthy of any,—are, I fear, but too appropriate qualities of the " *genus vatum.*"

Almost all Dryden's plays, including those on which he set the highest value, and which he had produced, with confidence, as models of their kind, were parodied in the " Rehearsal." He alone contributed more to the farce than all the other poets together. His favourite style of comic dialogue, which he had declared to consist rather in a quick sharpness of dialogue than in delineations of humour,[1] is paraphrased in the scene between Tom Thimble and Prince Prettyman; the lyrics of his astral spirits are cruelly burlesqued in the song of the two lawful Kings of Brentford, as they descend to repossess their throne; above all, Almanzor, his favourite hero, is parodied in the magnanimous Drawcansir; and, to conclude, the whole scope of heroic plays, with their combats, feasts, processions, sudden changes of fortune, embarrassments of chivalrous love and honour, splendid verse and unnatural rants, are so held up to ridicule, as usually to fix the resemblance upon some one of his own dramas. The " Wild Gallant," the " Maiden Queen," and " Tyrannic Love," all furnish parodies, as do both parts of the " Conquest of Granada," which had been frequently acted before the representation of the " Rehearsal," though not printed till after. What seems more strange, the play of " Marriage a-la-Mode" is also alluded to, although it was neither acted nor printed till 1673, a year after the appearance of the " Rehearsal." But there being no parody of any particular passage, although the plot and conduct of the piece are certainly ridiculed, it seems probable, that, as Dryden often showed his plays in manuscript to those whom he accounted his patrons, the plan of " Marriage a-la-Mode" may have transpired in the

[1] Preface to " An Evening's Love."—*Dryden's Works*, vol. iii., p. 225.

circles which Buckingham frequented, who may thus have made it the subject of satire by anticipation.[1]

It is easy to conceive what Dryden must have felt, at beholding his labours, and even his person, held up to public derision, on the theatre where he had so often triumphed. But he was too prudent to show outward signs of resentment; and in conversation allowed, that the farce had a great many good things in it, though so severe against himself. " Yet I cannot help saying," he added, in a well-judged tone of contempt, " that Smith and Johnson are two of the coolest and most insignificant fellows I ever met with upon the stage."[2] Many years afterwards he assigned nearly the same reason to the public for not replying to the satire.[3] But

---

[1] Mr Malone inclines to think, there is no allusion to " Marriage a-la-Mode" in the " Rehearsal." But surely the whimsical distress of Prince Prettyman, " sometimes a fisher's son, sometimes a prince," is precisely that of Leonidas, who is first introduced as the son of a shepherd; secondly, discovered to be the son of an unlawful king called Polydamus; thirdly, proved anew to be the son of the shepherd; and, finally, proved to be the son of neither of them, but of the lawful king, Theogenes. Besides, the author of the " Key to the Rehearsal" points out a parallel between the revolution of state in the farce, and that by which Leonidas, after being carried off to execution, on a sudden snatches a sword from one of the guards, proclaims himself rightful king, and, without more ceremony, deposes the powerful and jealous usurper, who had sentenced him to death.

[2] Spence's " Anecdotes," quoted by Mr Malone, vol. i., p. 106.

[3] " I answered not the ' Rehearsal,' because I knew the author sat to himself when he drew the picture, and was the very Bayes of his own farce; because also I knew, that my

though he veiled his resentment under this mask of indifference at the time, he afterwards avowed, that the exquisite character of Zimri in " Absalom and Achitophel," was laboured with so much felicitous skill, as a requital in kind to the author of the " Rehearsal." [1]

The ridicule cast upon heroic plays by the " Rehearsal," did not prevent their being still exhibited. They contained many passages of splendid poetry, which continued to delight the audience after they had laughed at Buckingham's parody. But the charm began to dissolve ; and from the time of that representation, they seem gradually, but perceptibly, to have declined in favour. Accordingly, Dryden did not trust to his powers of numbers in

---

betters were more concerned than I was in that satire ; and, lastly, because Mr Smith and Mr Johnson, the main pillars of it, were two such languishing gentlemen in their conversation, that I could liken them to nothing but to their own relations, those noble characters of men of wit and pleasure about the town."—*Dedication to Juvenal, Dryden's Works*, vol. xiii. p. 10.

[1] The pains which Dryden bestowed on the character of Zimri, and the esteem in which he held it, is evident from his quoting it as the master-piece of his own satire. " The character of Zimri in my ' Absalom,' is, in my opinion, worth the whole poem : it is not bloody, but it is ridiculous enough ; and he, for whom it was intended, was too witty to resent it as an injury. If I had railed, I might have suffered for it justly ; but I managed my own work more happily, perhaps more dexterously. I avoided the mention of great crimes, and applied myself to the representing of blind sides, and little extravagances ; to which, the wittier a man is, he is generally the more obnoxious. It succeeded as I wished ; the jest went round, and he was laughed at in his turn who began the frolic."

his next play, but produced the " Marriage a-la-
Mode," a tragi-comedy, or rather a tragedy and
comedy, the plots and scenes of which are inter-
mingled, for they have no natural connexion with
each other. The state-intrigue bears evident
marks of hurry and inattention ; and it is at least
possible, that Dryden originally intended it for the
subject of a proper heroic play, but, startled at the
effect of Buckingham's satire, hastily added to it
some comic scenes, either lying by him, or composed on purpose. The higher or tragic plot is not
only grossly inartificial and improbable, but its incidents are so perplexed and obscure, that it would
have required much more action to detail them
intelligibly. Even the language has an abridged
appearance, and favours the idea, that the tragic
intrigue was to have been extended into a proper
heroic play, instead of occupying a spare corner in a
comedy. But to make amends, the comic scenes
are executed with spirit, and in a style resembling
those in the " Maiden Queen."[1] They contained
much witty and fashionable raillery ; and the character of Melantha is pronounced by Cibber to
exhibit the most complete system of female foppery
that could possibly be crowded into the tortured
form of a fine lady. It was admirably acted by
Mrs Monfort, afterwards Mrs Verbruggen. The
piece thus supported was eminently successful ; a
fortunate circumstance for the King's Company,

[1] In one of Cibber's moods of alteration, he combined the
comic scenes of these two plays into a comedy entitled, " The
Comical Lovers."

who were then in distressful circumstances. Their
house in Drury-Lane had been destroyed by fire,
after which disaster they were compelled to occupy
the old theatre in Lincoln's-Inn Fields, lately deserted by the rival company for a splendid one in
Dorset Gardens.   From a prologue which our
author furnished, to be spoken at the opening of
this house of refuge, it would seem, that even
the scenes and properties of the actors had been
furnished by the contributions of the nobility. [1]
Perhaps their present reduced situation was an
additional reason with Dryden for turning his
attention to comedy, which required less splendour
of exhibition and decoration than the heroic plays.

   " Marriage a-la-mode" was inscribed to Wilmot, Earl of Rochester, in strains of adulation not
very honourable to the dedicator.   But as he
expresses his gratitude for Rochester's care, not
only of his reputation, but of his fortune ; for his
solicitude to overcome the fatal modesty of poets,
which leads them to prefer want to importunity ;
and, finally, for the good effects of his mediation in
all his concerns at court ; it may be supposed some
recent benefit, perhaps an active share in procuring
the appointment of poet laureat, had warmed the
heart of the author towards the patron.   The
dedication was well received, and the compliment
handsomely acknowledged, as we learn by a letter

---

   [1] " You are changed too, and your pretence to see
       Is but a nobler name for charity.
       Your own provisions furnish out our feasts,
       While you, the founders, make yourselves the guests."
                            Dryden's Works, vol. x., p. 319.

from Dryden to Rochester, where he says that the shame of being so much overpaid for an ill dedication, made him almost repent of his address.   But he had shortly afterwards rather more substantial reasons for regretting his choice of a patron.

The same cause for abstaining from tragic composition still remaining in force, Dryden, in 1672, brought forward a comedy, called " The Assignation, or Love in a Nunnery."   The plot was after the Spanish model.   The author seems to have apprehended, and experienced, some opposition on account of this second name; and although he deprecates, in the epilogue, the idea of its being a party play, or written to gratify the puritans with satire at the expense of the catholics;[1] yet he complains, in the dedication, of the number of its enemies, who came prepared to damn it on account of the title.   The Duke of York having just made public profession of the Roman faith, any reflections upon it were doubtless watched with a jealous eye.   But, though guiltless in this respect, the " Assignation" had worse faults.   The Plot is but indifferently conducted, and was neither enlivened

[1] " Some have expected, from our bills to-day,
     To find a satire in our poet's play.
     The zealous rout from Coleman-street did run,
     To see the story of the Friar and Nun ;
     Or tales, yet more ridiculous to hear,
     Vouch'd by their vicar of ten pounds a-year,—
     Of Nuns, who did against temptation pray,
     And discipline laid on the pleasant way :
     Or that, to please the malice of the town,
     Our poet should in some close cell have shown
     Some sister, playing at content alone :
     This they did hope; the other side did fear ;
     And both, you see, alike are cozen'd here."

with gay dialogue, nor with striking character : the play, accordingly, proved unsuccessful in the representation. Yet, although upon reading the "Assignation," we cannot greatly wonder at this failure, still, considering the plays which succeeded about the same time, we may be disposed to admit, that the weight of a party was thrown into the scale against its reception. Buckingham, who shortly afterwards published a revised edition of the "Rehearsal," failed not to ridicule the absurd and coarse trick, by which the enamoured prince prevents his father from discovering the domino of his mistress, which had been left in his apartment.[1] And Dryden's rivals and enemies, now a numerous body, hailed, with malicious glee, an event which seemed to foretell the decay of his popularity.

The "Assignation" was published in 1673, and inscribed, by Dryden, to his much honoured friend Sir Charles Sedley. There are some acrimonious

[1] " *Bayes.* I remember once, in a play of mine, I set off a scene, i'gad, beyond expectation, only with a petticoat and the belly-ach.

Smith. Pray, how was that, sir?

Bayes. Why, sir, I contrived a petticoat to be brought in upon a chair, (nobody knew how,) into a prince's chamber, whose father was not to see it, that came in by chance.

Johns. God's-my-life, that was a notable contrivance indeed!

Smith. Ay, but, Mr Bayes, how could you contrive the belly-ach?

Bayes. The easiest i'the world, i'gad : I'll tell you how; I made the prince sit down upon the petticoat, no more than so, and pretended to his father that he had just then got the belly-ach; whereupon his father went to call a physician, and his man ran away with the petticoat."—*Rehearsal.*

passages in this dedication, referring to the controversies in which the author had been engaged; and, obscure as these have become, it is the biographer's duty to detail and illustrate them.

It cannot be supposed, that the authors of the time saw with indifference Dryden's rapid success, and the measures which he had taken, by his critical essays, to guide the public attention, and to fix it upon himself and the heroic plays, in which he felt his full superiority. But no writer of the time could hope to be listened to by the public, if he entered a claim of personal competition against a poet so celebrated. The defence of the ancient poets afforded a less presumptuous and more favourable pretext for taking the field, and for assailing Dryden's writings, and avenging the slight notice he had accorded to his contemporaries, under the colour of defending the ancients against his criticism. The " Essay of Dramatic Poesy " afforded a pretence for commencing this sort of warfare. In that piece, Dryden had pointed out the faults of Shakspeare, Jonson, and Fletcher, with less ceremony than the height of their established reputation appeared to demand from a young author. But the precedence which he undauntedly claimed for the heroic drama, and, more generally, the superiority of the plays of Dryden's own age, whether tragic or comic, over those of the earlier part of the seventeenth century, was asserted, not only distinctly, but irreverently, in the Epilogue to the " Conquest of Granada : "

" They, who have best succeeded on the stage,
Have still conform'd their genius to their age.
Thus Jonson did mechanic humour show,
When men were dull, and conversation low.
Then comedy was faultless, but 'twas coarse :
Cob's tankard was a jest, and Otter's horse.
And, as their comedy, their love was mean,
Except, by chance, in some one labour'd scene,
Which must atone for an ill-written play,
They rose, but at their height could seldom stay.
Fame then was cheap, and the first comer sped ;
And they have kept it since, by being dead.
But, were they now to write, when critics weigh
Each line, and every word, throughout a play,
None of them, no not Jonson in his height,
Could pass, without allowing grains for weight.
Think it not envy, that these truths are told ;
Our poet's not malicious, though he's bold.
'Tis not to brand them, that their faults are shown,
But, by their errors, to excuse his own.
If love and honour now are higher raised,
'Tis not the poet, but the age is praised.
Wit's now arrived to a more high degree ;
Our native language more refined and free.
Our ladies and our men now speak more wit
In conversation, than those poets writ.
Then, one of these is, consequently, true ;
That what this poet writes comes short of you,
And imitates you ill (which most he fears),
Or else his writing is not worse than theirs.
Yet, though you judge (as sure the critics will),
That some before him writ with greater skill,
In this one praise he has their fame surpast,
To please an age more gallant than the last."

The daring doctrine laid down in these obnoxious lines, our author ventured to maintain, in what
he has termed a " Defence of the Epilogue, or an
Essay on the Dramatic Poetry of the last age."
It is subjoined to the " Conquest of Granada ;"

and, as that play was not printed till after the
" Rehearsal," it serves to show how little Dryden's
opinions were altered, or his tone lowered, by the
success of that witty satire. It was necessary, he
says, either not to print the bold epilogue, which
we have quoted, or to show that he could defend
it. He censures decidedly the antiquated language,
irregular plots, and anachronisms of Shakspeare
and Fletcher; but his main strength seems directed
against Jonson. From his works he selects several
instances of harsh, inelegant, and even inaccurate
diction. In describing manners, he claims for the
modern writers a decided superiority over the poets
of the earlier age, when there was less gallantry,
and when the authors were not admitted to the
best society. The manners of their low, or Dutch
school of comedy, in which Jonson led the way,
by his " Bartholomew Fair," and similar pieces,
are noticed, and censured, as unfit for a polished
audience. The characters in what may be termed
genteel comedy are reviewed, and restricted to the
Truewit of Jonson's " Silent Woman," the Mercutio of Shakspeare, and Fletcher's Don John in
the " Chances." Even this last celebrated character, he observes, is better carried on in the modern
alteration of the play, than in Fletcher's original;
a singular instance of Dryden's liberality of criticism, since the alteration of the " Chances " was
made by that very Duke of Buckingham, from
whom he had just received a bitter and personal
offence. Dryden proceeds to contend, that the
living poets, from the example of a gallant king

and sprightly court, have learned, in their comedies, a tone of light discourse and raillery, in which the solidity of English sense is blended with the air and gaiety of their French neighbours; in short, that those who call Jonson's the golden age of poetry, have only this reason, that the audience were then content with acorns, because they knew not the use of bread. In all this criticism there was much undeniable truth; but sufficient weight was not given to the excellences of the old school, while their faults were ostentatiously and invidiously enumerated. It would seem that Dryden, perhaps from the rigour of a puritanical education, had not studied the ancient dramatic models in his youth, and had only begun to read them with attention when it was his object rather to depreciate than to emulate them. But the time came when he did due homage to their genius.

Meanwhile, this avowed preference of his own period excited the resentment of the older critics, who had looked up to the era of Shakspeare as the golden age of poetry; and no less that of the playwrights of his own standing, who pretended to discover, that Dryden designed to establish less the reputation of his age, than of himself individually, upon the ruined fame of the ancient poets. They complained, that, as the wild bull in the Vivarambla of Granada,

—— " monarch-like he ranged the listed field,
And some he trampled down, and some he kill'd."

Many, therefore, advancing under pretence of vindicating the fame of the ancients, gratified their

spleen by attacking that of Dryden, and strove less
to combat his criticisms, than to criticise his productions. We shall have too frequent occasion to
observe, that there was, during the reign of Charles
II., a semi-barbarous virulence of controversy, even
upon abstract points of literature, which would be
now thought injudicious and unfair, even by the
newspaper advocates of contending factions. A
critic of that time never deemed he had so effectually refuted the reasoning of his adversary, as
when he had said something disrespectful of his
talents, person, or moral character. Thus, literary
contest was embittered by personal hatred, and
truth was so far from being the object of the com-
batants, that even victory was tasteless unless
obtained by the disgrace and degradation of the
antagonist. This reflection may serve to introduce
a short detail of the abusive controversies in which
it was Dryden's lot to be engaged.

One of those, who most fiercely attacked our
author's system and opinions, was Matthew Clifford,
already mentioned as engaged in the " Rehearsal."
At what precise time he began his Notes upon
Dryden's Poems, in Four Letters, or how they
were originally published, is uncertain. The last
of the letters is dated from the Charter-House,
1st July, 1672, and is signed with his name : probably the others were written shortly before. The
only edition now known was printed along with
some " Reflections on the Hind and Panther, by
another Hand," (Tom Brown,) in 1687. If these
letters were not actually printed in 1672, they were

Friendly Vindication of Mr Dryden from the Author of the Censure of the Rota," was printed at Cambridge. All these appeared previous to the publication of the " Assignation." The first, as Wood informs us, was written by Richard Leigh, educated at Queen's College, Oxford, where he entered in 1665, and was probably resident when this piece was there published. He was afterwards a player in the Duke's Company, but must be carefully distinguished from the celebrated comedian of the same name. It seems likely that he wrote also the second tract, which is a continuation of the first. Both are in a frothy, flippant style of raillery, of which the reader will find a specimen in the note.[1] The Cambridge Vindication seems

[1] " Amongst several other late exercises of the Athenian virtuosi in the Coffee-academy, instituted by Apollo for the advancement of Gazette Philosophy, Mercury's Diurnalli, &c. this day was wholly taken up in the examination of the ' Conquest of Granada.' A gentleman on the reading of the First Part, and there in the description of the bull-baiting, said, that Almanzor's playing at the bull was according to the standard of the Greek heroes, who, as Mr Dryden had learnedly observed (Essay of Dramatic Poesy), were great beef-eaters. And why might not Almanzor as well as Ajax, or Don Quixote, worry mutton, or take a bull by the throat, since the author had elsewhere explained himself, by telling us the heroes were more noble beasts of prey, in his Epistle to his ' Conquest of Granada,' distinguishing them into wild and tame; and in his play we have Almanzor shaking his chains, and frighting his keeper, broke loose, and tearing those that would reclaim his rage. To this he added, that his bulls excelled other heroes, as far as his own heroes surpassed his gods; that the champion bull was divested of flesh and blood, and made immortal by the poet, and bellowed after death; that the fantastic bull seemed fiercer than the true, and the

to have been written by a different hand, though
in the same taste.   It is singular in bringing a
charge against our author, which has been urged
by no other antagonist ; for he is there upbraided
with exhibiting in his comedies the persons and
follies of living characters.[1]

The friends and admirers of Dryden did not see
with indifference these attacks upon his reputation;
for he congratulates[2] himself upon having found
defenders even among strangers, alluding probably
to a tract by Mr Charles Blount, entitled, " Mr
Dryden Vindicated, in answer to the Friendly
Vindication of Mr Dryden, with Reflections on
the Rota."   This piece is written with all the
honest enthusiasm of youth in defence of that

---

dead bellowings in verse were louder than the living; concluding with a wish, that Mr Dryden had the good luck to
have varied that old verse quoted in his Dramatic Essay:

      ' *Atque Ursum, et Pugiles media inter carmina poscunt*
      Tauros, et Pugiles prima inter carmina posco ; '

and prefixed it to the front of his play, instead of

      ———— ' *Major rerum mihi nascitur ordo,*
    Majus opus moveo.' "

—*Censure of the Rota*, p. 1.

[1] " But, however, if he were taken for no good comic
poet, or satirist, he had found a way of much easier license,
(though more remarkable in the sense of some,) which was,
not only to libel men's persons, but to represent them on the
stage too :   That to this purpose he made his observations of
men, their words and actions, with so little disguise, that
many beheld themselves acted for their half-crown ; yet, after
all, was unwilling to believe, that this was not both good
comedy, and no less good manners."—*Friendly Vindication of
Mr Dryden*, p. 8.

[2] Dedication to the " Assignation."

croft's play, which is a bald translation from the "*Bourgeois Gentilhomme*" of Moliere, was successful, chiefly owing to the burlesque procession of Turks employed to dub the citizen a *Mamamouchi*, or Paladin. Dryden, with more indignation than the occasion warranted, retorted, in the prologue to the "Assignation," by the following attack on Ravenscroft's jargon and buffoonery:

> "You must have Mamamouchi, such a fop
> As would appear a monster in a shop;
> He'll fill your pit and boxes to the brim,
> Where, ramm'd in crowds, you see yourselves in him.
> Sure there's some spell, our poet never knew,
> In *Hullibabilah de*, and *Chu, chu, chu;*
> But *Marababah sahem* most did touch you;
> That is, Oh how we love the Mamamouchi!
> Grimace and habit sent you pleased away;
> You damn'd the poet, and cried up the play."

About this time, too, the actresses in the King's theatre, to vary the amusements of the house, represented "Marriage a-la-Mode" in men's dresses. The Prologue and Epilogue were furnished by Dryden; and in the latter, mentioning the projected union of the theatres,—

> —— "all the women most devoutly swear,
> Each would be rather a poor actress here,
> Than to be made a Mamamouchi there."

Ravenscroft, thus satirized, did not fail to exult in the bad success of the "Assignation," and celebrated his triumph in some lines of a Prologue to the "Careless Lovers," which was acted in the

———

Addle is a similar character, in a play called "Sir Solomon, or The Courteous Coxcomb," attributed to one John Caryll.]

vacation succeeding the ill fate of Dryden's play.
They are thrown into the note, that the reader may
judge how very unworthy this scribbler was of the
slightest notice from the pen of Dryden.[1]   And
with this *Te Deum*, on the part of Ravenscroft,
ended a petty controversy, which gives him his only
title to be named in the life of an English classic.

From what has been detailed of these disputes
we may learn, that, even at this period, the laureat's
wreath was not unmingled with thorns; and that if
Dryden still maintained his due ascendency over
the common band of authors, it was not without
being occasionally under the necessity of descend-
ing into the *arena* against very inferior antagonists.

In the course of these controversies, Dryden
was not idle, though he cannot be said to have
been worthily or fortunately employed; his muse
being lent to the court, who were at this time
anxious to awake the popular indignation against
the Dutch.   It is a characteristic of the English
nation, that their habitual dislike against their
neighbours is soon and easily blown into animosity.

[1] " An author did, to please you, let his wit run,
Of late much on a serving man and cittern;
And yet, you would not like the serenade,—
Nay, and you damn'd his nuns in masquerade;
You did his Spanish sing-song too abhor;
Ah! que locura con tanto rigor!
In fine, the whole by you so much was blamed,
To act their parts, the players were ashamed.
Ah, how severe your malice was that day!
To damn, at once, the poet and his play:
But why was your rage just at that time shown,
When what the author writ was all his own?
Till then, he borrow'd from romance, and did translate;
And those plays found a more indulgent fate."

But, although Dryden chose for his theme the horrid massacre of Amboyna, and fell to the task with such zeal, that he accomplished it in a month, his play was probably of little service to the cause in which it was written. The story is too disgusting to produce the legitimate feelings of pity and terror, which tragedy should excite: the black hole of Calcutta would be as pleasing a subject. The character of the Hollanders, as there represented, is too grossly vicious and detestable to give the least pleasure. They are neither men, nor even devils; but a sort of lubbar fiends, compounded of cruelty, avarice, and brutal debauchery, like Dutch swabbers possessed by demons. But of this play the author has himself admitted, that the subject is barren, the persons low, and the writing not heightened by any laboured scenes: and, without attempting to contradict this modest description, we may dismiss the tragedy of "Amboyna." It was dedicated to Lord Clifford of Chudleigh, an active member of the Cabal administration of Charles II.; but who, as a catholic, on the test act being passed, resigned his post of lord high treasurer, and died shortly afterwards. There is great reason to think, that this nobleman had essentially favoured Dryden's views in life. On a former occasion, he had termed Lord Clifford a better Mæcenas than the friend of Horace;[1] and,

---

[1] " For my own part, I, who am the least among the poets, have yet the fortune to be honoured with the *best patron*, and the best friend; for (to omit some great persons of our court, to whom I am many ways obliged, and have taken care of me

in the present dedication, he mentions the numerous favours received through so many years, as forming one continued act of his patron's generosity and goodness; so that the excess of his gratitude had led the poet to receive those benefits, as the Jews received their law, with mute wonder, rather than with outward and ceremonious acclamation. These sentiments of obligation he continued, long after Lord Clifford's death, to express in terms equally glowing;[1] so that we may safely do this statesman's memory the justice to record him as an active and discerning patron of Dryden's genius.

In the course of 1673, our author's pen was engaged in a task, which may be safely condemned as presumptuous, though that pen was Dryden's. It was no other than that of new-modelling the " Paradise Lost " of Milton into a dramatic poem, called the " State of Innocence, or the Fall of Man." The coldness with which Milton's mighty epic was received upon the first publication is almost proverbial. The character of the author,

---

during the exigencies of a war) I have found a better Mæcenas in the person of my Lord Treasurer Clifford, and a more elegant Tibullus in that of Sir Charles Sedley."—*Dedication to the Assignation, Dryden's Works,* vol. iv., p. 350.

[1] In his Dedication of the Pastorals of Virgil to Hugh Lord Clifford, he says, " I have no reason to complain of fortune, since, in the midst of that abundance, I could not have chosen better than the worthy son of so illustrious a father.   He was the patron of my manhood, when I flourished in the opinion of the world, though with small advantage to my fortune, till he awakened the remembrance of my royal master.   He was that Pollio, or that Varus, *who introduced me to Augustus.*"
—*Ibid.* vol. xiii., p. 338.

obnoxious for his share in the usurped government;
the turn of the language, so different from that of
the age; the seriousness of a subject, so discordant
with its lively frivolities—gave to the author's
renown the slowness of growth with the perma-
nency of the oak.   Milton's merit, however, had
not escaped the eye of Dryden.[1]   He was acquainted with the author, perhaps even before the
Restoration; and who can doubt Dryden's power
of feeling the sublimity of the " Paradise Lost,"
even had he himself not assured us, in the prefatory essay to his own piece, that he accounts it
" undoubtedly, one of the greatest, most noble,
and most sublime poems, which either this age or
nation has produced ?"   We are, therefore, to
seek for the motive which could have induced him,
holding this opinion, " to gild pure gold, and set a
perfume on the violet."   Dennis has left a curious
record upon this subject :—" Dryden," he observes,
" in his Preface before the ' State of Innocence,'
appears to have been the first, those gentlemen
excepted whose verses are before Milton's poem,
who discovered in so public a manner an extraordinary opinion of Milton's extraordinary merit.

[1] The elder Richardson has told a story, that Lord Buckhurst, afterwards Earl of Dorset, was the first who introduced
the " Paradise Lost," then lying like waste paper in the bookseller's hands, to the notice of Dryden.   But this tradition
has been justly exploded by Mr Malone.—*Life of Dryden*, vol.
i., p. 114.   Indeed, it is by no means likely, that Dryden
could be a stranger to the very existence of a large poem,
written by a man of such political as well as literary eminence, even if he had not happened, as was the case, to be
personally known to the author.

And yet Mr Dryden at that time knew not half the extent of his excellence, as more than twenty years afterwards he confessed to me, and is pretty plain from his writing the ' State of Innocence.' " Had he known the full extent of Milton's excellence, Dennis thought he would not have ventured on this undertaking, unless he designed to be a foil to him : " but they," he adds, " who knew Mr Dryden, knew very well, that he was not of a temper to design to be a foil to any one." [1]   We are therefore to conclude, that it was only the hope of excelling his original, admirable as he allowed it to be, which impelled Dryden upon this unprofitable and abortive labour ; and we are to examine the improvements which Dryden seemed to meditate, or, in other words, the differences between his taste and that of Milton.

And first we may observe, that the difference in their situations affected their habits of thinking upon poetical subjects.   Milton had retired into solitude, if not into obscurity, relieved from every thing like external agency either influencing his choice of a subject, or his mode of treating it ; and, in consequence, instead of looking abroad to consult the opinion of his age, he appealed only to the judge which Heaven had implanted within him, when he was endowed with severity of judgment, and profusion of genius.   But the taste of Dryden was not so independent.   Placed by his very office at the head of what was fashionable in literature,

[1] Dennis's Letters, quoted by Malone.

as he terms Sir George Mackenzie, the issue of which, in his apprehension, pointed out farther room for improving upon the epic of Milton. This was an enquiry into the " turn of words and thoughts" requisite in heroic poetry. These " turns," according to the definition and examples which Dryden has given us, differ from the points of wit, and quirks of epigram, common in the metaphysical poets, and consist in a happy, and at the same time a natural recurrence of the same form of expression, melodiously varied. Having failed in his search after these beauties in Cowley, the darling of his youth, " I consulted," says Dryden, " a greater genius, (without offence to the manes of that noble author,) I mean—Milton ; but as he endeavours everywhere to express Homer, whose age had not arrived to that fineness, I found in him a true sublimity, lofty thoughts, which were clothed with admirable Grecisms, and ancient words, which he had been digging from the mines of Chaucer and Spenser, and which, with all their rusticity, had somewhat of venerable in them. But I found not there neither that for which I looked." This judgment Addison has proved to be erroneous, by quoting from Milton the most beautiful example of a turn of words which can be found in English poetry.[1] But Dryden, holding it for just, conceived,

[1] " ' With thee conversing, I forget all time,
All seasons, and their change ; all please alike :
Sweet is the breath of morn, her rising sweet,
With charm of earliest birds : pleasant the sun,
When first on this delightful land he spreads
His orient beams, on herb, tree, fruit, and flower,
Glist'ring with dew : fragrant the fertile earth

doubtless, that, in his " State of Innocence," he might exert his skill successfully, by supplying the supposed deficiency, and for relieving those " flats of thought " which he complains of, where Milton, for a hundred lines together, runs on in a " track of Scripture ;" but which Dennis more justly ascribes to the humble nature of his subject in those passages. The graces, also, which Dryden ventured to interweave with the lofty theme of Milton, were rather those of Ovid than of Virgil, rather turns of verbal expression than of thought. Such is that conceit which met with censure at the time:

> " Seraph and cherub, careless of their charge,
> And wanton, in full ease now live at large;
> Unguarded leave the passes of the sky,
> And all dissolved in hallelujahs lie."

" I have heard," said a petulant critic, " of anchovies dissolved in sauce ; but never of an angel

---

> After soft show'rs, and sweet the coming on
> Of grateful evening mild : then silent night,
> With this her solemn bird, and this fair moon,
> And these the gems of heaven, her starry train :
> But neither breath of morn, when she ascends
> With charm of earliest birds; nor rising sun
> On this delightful land; nor herb, fruit, flower,
> Glist'ring with dew; nor fragrance after show'rs;
> Nor grateful evening mild ; nor silent night,
> With this her solemn bird ; nor walk by moon ;
> Or glist'ring star-light, without thee is sweet.'

" The variety of images in this passage is infinitely pleasing, and the recapitulation of each particular image, with a little varying of the expression, makes one of the finest turns of words that I have ever seen ; which I rather mention, because Mr Dryden has said, in his Preface to Juvenal, that he could meet with no turn of words in Milton."—*Tatler*, Nos. 114, 115.

dissolved in hallelujahs." But this raillery Dryden, rebuffs with a quotation from Virgil:

" Invadunt urbem, somno vinoque sepultam."

It might have been replied, that Virgil's analogy was familiar and simple, and that of Dryden was far-fetched, and startling by its novelty.

The majesty of Milton's verse is strangely degraded in the following speeches, which precede the rising of Pandæmonium. Some of the couplets are utterly flat and bald, and, in others, the balance of point and antithesis is substituted for the simple sublimity of the original:

" *Moloch.* Changed as we are, we're yet from homage free;
We have, by hell, at least gain'd liberty:
That's worth our fall; thus low though we are driven,
Better to rule in hell, than serve in heaven.
   Lucifer. There spoke the better half of Lucifer!
   Asmoday. 'Tis fit in frequent senate we confer,
And then determine how to steer our course;
To wage new war by fraud, or open force.
The doom's now past, submission were in vain.
   Mol. And were it not, such baseness I disdain;
I would not stoop, to purchase all above,
And should contemn a power, whom prayer could move,
As one unworthy to have conquer'd me.
   Beelzebub. Moloch, in that all are resolved, like thee.
The means are unproposed; but 'tis not fit
Our dark divan in public view should sit;
Or what we plot against the Thunderer,
The ignoble crowd of vulgar devils hear.
   Lucif. A golden palace let be raised on high;
To imitate? No, to outshine the sky!
All mines are ours, and gold above the rest:
Let this be done; and quick as 'twas exprest."

I fancy the reader is now nearly satisfied with

Dryden's improvements on Milton. Yet some of his alterations have such peculiar reference to the taste and manners of his age, that I cannot avoid pointing them out. Eve is somewhat of a coquette, even in the state of innocence. She exclaims,

> ———— " from each tree
> The feather'd kind press down to look on me ;
> The beasts, with up-cast eyes, forsake their shade,
> And gaze, as if I were to be obey'd.
> Sure, I am somewhat which they wish to be,
> And cannot,—I myself am proud of me."

Upon receiving Adam's addresses, she expresses, rather unreasonably in the circumstances, some apprehensions of his infidelity ; and, upon the whole, she is considerably too knowing for the primitive state. The same may be said of Adam, whose knowledge in school divinity, and use of syllogistic argument, Dryden, though he found it in the original, was under no necessity to have retained.

The " State of Innocence," as it could not be designed for the stage, seems to have been originally intended as a mere poetical prolusion ; for Dryden, who was above affecting such a circumstance, tells us, that it was only made public, because, in consequence of several hundred copies, every one gathering new faults, having been dispersed without his knowledge, it became at length a libel on the author, who was forced to print a correct edition in his own defence. As the incidents and language were ready composed by Milton, we are not surprised when informed, that the composition and revision were completed in

a single month. The critics having assailed the
poem even before publication, the author has prefixed an " Essay upon Heroic Poetry and Poetic
Licence ;" in which he treats chiefly of the use of
metaphors, and of the legitimacy of machinery.

The Dedication of the " State of Innocence,"
addressed to Mary of Este, Duchess of York, is a
singular specimen of what has been since termed
the *celestial* style of inscription.   It is a strain of
flattery in the language of adoration ; and the elevated station of the princess is declared so suited to
her excellence, that Providence has only done justice to its own works in placing the most perfect
work of heaven where it may be admired by all
beholders.   Even this flight is surpassed by the
following ;—

" 'Tis true, you are above all mortal wishes ; no man desires impossibilities, because they are beyond the reach of
nature.   To hope to be a god, is folly exalted into madness ;
but, by the laws of our creation, we are obliged to adore him,
and are permitted to love him too at human distance.   'Tis
the nature of perfection to be attractive : but the excellency
of the object refines the nature of the love.   It strikes an impression of awful reverence ; 'tis indeed that love which is
more properly a zeal than passion.   'Tis the rapture which
anchorites find in prayer, when a beam of the divinity shines
upon them ; that which makes them despise all worldly objects ; and yet 'tis all but contemplation.   They are seldom
visited from above ; but a single vision so transports them,
that it makes up the happiness of their lives.   Mortality
cannot bear it often : it finds them in the eagerness and height
of their devotion ; they are speechless for the time that it continues, and prostrate and dead when it departs."

Such eulogy was the taste of the days of Charles,
when ladies were deified in dedications, and painted

as Venus or Diana upon canvass. In our time, the elegance of the language would be scarcely held to counterbalance the absurdity of the compliments.

Lee, the dramatic writer, an excellent poet, though unfortunate in his health and circumstances, evinced his friendship for Dryden, rather than his judgment, by prefixing to the " State of Innocence " a copy of verses, in which he compliments the author with having refined the ore of Milton. Dryden repaid this favour by an epistle, in which he beautifully apologizes for the extravagances of his friend's poetry, and consoles him for the censure of those cold judges, whose blame became praise when they accused the warmth which they were incapable of feeling.[1]

Having thus brought the account of our author's productions down to 1674, from which period we date a perceptible change in his taste and mode of composition, I have only to add, that his private situation was probably altered to the worse, by the burning of the King's theatre, and the debts contracted in rebuilding it. The value of his share in that company must consequently have fallen far short of what it was originally. In other respects, he was probably nearly in the same condition as in 1672. The critics, who assailed his literary reputation, had hitherto spared his private character ; and, excepting Rochester, whose malignity towards Dryden now began to display itself, he probably

1 See this Epistle, Dryden's Works, vol. xi., p. 22. It was prefixed to " Alexander the Great ; " a play, the merits and faults of which are both in extreme.

had not lost one person whom he had thought worthy to be called a friend. Lee, who seems first to have distinguished himself about 1672, was probably then added to the number of his intimates. Milton died shortly before the publication of the " State of Innocence ;" and we may wish in vain to know his opinion of that piece ; but if tradition can be trusted, he said, perhaps on that undertaking, that Dryden was a good rhymer, but no poet. Blount, who had signalized himself in Dryden's defence, was now added to the number of his friends. This gentleman dedicated his " *Religio Laici* " to Dryden in 1683, as his " much-honoured friend ;" and the poet speaks of him with kindness and respect in 1696, three years after his unfortunate and violent catastrophe.

Dryden was, however, soon to experience the mutability of the friendship of wits and courtiers. A period was speedily approaching, when the violence of political faction was to effect a breach between our author and many of those with whom he was now intimately connected ; indeed, he was already entangled in the quarrels of the great, and sustained a severe personal outrage, in consequence of a quarrel with which he had little individual concern.

SECTION IV.

" The State of Innocence" was published in 1674, and " Aureng-Zebe," Dryden's next tragedy, appeared in 1675. In the interval, he informs us, his ardour for rhyming plays had considerably abated. The course of study which he imposed on himself, doubtless led him to this conclusion. But it is also possible, that he found the peculiar facilities of that drama had excited the emulation of very inferior poets, who, by dint of show, rant, and clamorous hexameters, were likely to divide with him the public favour. Before proceeding, therefore, to state the gradual alteration in Dryden's own taste, we must perform the task of detailing the literary quarrels in which he was at this period engaged. The chief of his rivals was Elkanah Settle, a person afterwards utterly contemptible ; but who, first by the strength of a party at court, and afterwards by a faction in the state, was, for a time, buoyed up in opposition to

Dryden. It is impossible to detail the progress of the contest for public favour between these two ill-matched rivals, without noticing at the same time Dryden's quarrel with Rochester, who appears to have played off Settle in opposition to him, as absolutely, and nearly as successfully, as Settle ever played off the literal puppets, for which, in the ebb of his fortune, he wrote dramas.

In the year 1673, Dryden and Rochester were on such friendly terms, that our poet inscribed to his lordship his favourite play of " Marriage a-la-Mode;" not without acknowledgment of the deepest gratitude for favours done to his fortune and reputation. The dedication, we have seen, was so favourably accepted by Rochester, that the reception called forth a second tribute of thanks from the poet to the patron. But at this point, the interchange of kindness and of civility received a sudden and irrecoverable check. This was partly owing to Rochester's fickle and jealous temper, which induced him alternately to raise and depress the men of parts whom he loved to patronise; so that no one should ever become independent of his favour, or so rooted in the public opinion, as to be beyond the reach of his satire; but it may also in part be attributed to Dryden's attachment to Sheffield, Earl of Mulgrave, afterwards Duke of Buckingham, then Rochester's rival in wit and court-favour, and from whom he had sustained a deadly affront, on an occasion, which, as the remote cause of a curious incident in Dryden's life, I have else-

where detailed in the words of Sheffield himself. [1]
Rochester, who was branded as a coward in con-

[1] [" No one could know the cowardice of Lord Rochester so
well as Mulgrave, who, in his Memoirs, records the following
infamous instance of it.	He had heard it reported, that Lord
Rochester had said something of him very malicious: ' I
therefore sent Colonel Aston, a very mettled friend of mine,
to call him to account for it.	He denied the words; and,
indeed, I was soon convinced he had never said them; but
the mere report, though I found it to be false, obliged me (as
I then foolishly thought) to go on with the quarrel; and the
next day was appointed for us to fight on horseback, a way in
England a little unusual, but it was his part to choose. Accordingly, I and my second lay the night before at Knightsbridge,
privately, to avoid the being secured at London upon any
suspicion; which yet we found ourselves more in danger of
there, because we had all the appearance of highwaymen, that
had a mind to lie skulking in an odd inn for one night; but
this, I suppose, the people of that house were used to, and so
took no notice of us, but liked us the better. In the morning
we met the Lord Rochester at the place appointed, who,
instead of James Porter, whom, he assured Aston, he would
make his second, brought an errant lifeguard-man, whom
nobody knew.	To this Mr Aston took exception, upon the
account of his being no suitable adversary; especially considering how extremely well he was mounted, whereas we had
only a couple of pads. Upon which, we all agreed to fight on
foot.	But, as my Lord Rochester and I were riding into the
next field, in order to it, he told me, that he had at first
chosen to fight on horseback, because he was so weak with a
distemper that he found himself unfit to fight at all in any way,
much less a-foot.	I was extremely surprised, because, at that
time, no man had a better reputation for courage; and (my
anger against him being quite over, because I was satisfied that
he never spoke those words I resented) I took the liberty of
representing, what a ridiculous story it would make if we
returned without fighting; and therefore advised him, for
both our sakes, especially for his own, to consider better of it;
since I must be obliged, in my own defence, to lay the fault on
him, by telling the truth of the matter.	His answer was, that

This playwright, whom the jealous spleen of a favourite courtier, and the misjudging taste of a promiscuous audience, placed for some time in so high a station, came into notice in 1671, on the representation of his first play, " Cambyses, King of Persia," which was played six nights successively. This run of public favour gave Rochester some pretence to bring Settle to the notice of the King; and, through the efforts of this mischievous wit, joined to the natural disposition of the people to be carried by show, rant, and tumult, Settle's second play, the " Empress of Morocco," was acted with unanimous and overpowering applause for a month together. To add to Dryden's mortification, Rochester had interest enough to have this tragedy of one whom he had elevated into the rank of his rival, first acted at Whitehall by the lords and

----

and the first that ever was printed with cuts. The booksellers at that time of day had not discovered so much of the weakness of their gentle readers as they have done since, nor so plainly discovered that fools, like children, are to be drawn in by gewgaws. Well, but what was the event of this great success? Mr Settle began to grow insolent, as any one may see, who reads the epistle dedicatory to ' The Empress of Morocco.' Mr Dryden, Mr Shadwell, and Mr Crowne, began to grow jealous; and they three in confederacy wrote ' Remarks on the Empress of Morocco.' Mr Settle answered them; and, according to the opinion which the town then had of the matter, (for I have utterly forgot the controversy,) had by much the better of them all. In short, Mr Settle was then a formidable rival to Mr Dryden; and I remember very well, that not only the town, but the university of Cambridge, was very much divided in their opinions about the preference that ought to be given to them; and in both places the younger fry inclined to Elkanah."

ladies of the court; an honour which had never been paid to any of Dryden's compositions, however more justly entitled to it, both from intrinsic merit, and by the author's situation as poet laureat. Rochester contributed a prologue upon this brilliant occasion, to add still more grace to Settle's triumph; but what seems yet more extraordinary, and has, I think, been unnoticed in all accounts of the controversy, Mulgrave,[1] Rochester's rival, and the friend of Dryden, did the same homage to the " Empress of Morocco." From the King's private theatre, the " Empress of Morocco" was transferred, in all its honours, to the public stage in Dorset Garden, and received with applause corresponding to the expectation excited by its favour at Whitehall. While the court and city were thus worshipping the idol which Rochester had set up, it could hardly be expected of poor Settle, that he should be first to discern his own want of desert. On the contrary, he grew presumptuous on success; and when he printed his performance, the dedication to the Earl of Norwich was directly levelled against the poet laureat, who termed it the " most arrogant, calumniatory, ill-mannered, and senseless preface he ever saw."[2] And, to add gall

[1] Lord Mulgrave wrote the prologue when Settle's play was first acted at court; Lord Rochester's was written for the second occasion; both were spoken by the beautiful Lady Elizabeth Howard.

[2] See this offensive dedication in the account of Settle's controversy with Dryden, in Dryden's Works, vol. xv., p. 398. [A spectacle, founded on Lalla Rookh, having been performed at the Court of Berlin in 1821, Lord Byron thus writes to

to bitterness, the bookseller thought the "Empress of Morocco" worthy of being decorated with engravings, and sold at the advanced price of two shillings; being the first drama advanced to such honourable distinction.[1] Moreover, the play is ostentatiously stated in the title to be written by Elkanah Settle, *Servant to his Majesty*;[2] an addition which the laureat had assumed with greater propriety.

If we are asked the merit of a performance which made such an impression at the time, we may borrow an expression applied to a certain orator,[3] and say, that the "Empress of Morocco" must have acted *to the tune* of a good heroic play. It had all the outward and visible requisites of splendid scenery, prisons, palaces, fleets, combats

---

Mr Moore:—" Your Berlin drama is an honour, unknown since the days of Elkanah Settle, whose ' Empress of Morocco' was represented by the Court ladies, which was, as Johnson says, 'the last blast of inflammation' to poor Dryden, who could not bear it, and fell foul of Settle without mercy or moderation on account of that and a frontispiece, which he dared to put before his play."—BYRON, vol. v., p. 213.]

[1] A copy of this rare edition (the gift of my learned friend, the Rev. Henry White of Lichfield) is now before me. The engravings are sufficiently paltry; and had the play been published even in the present day, it would have been accounted dear at two shillings. The name of the publisher is William Cademan, the date 1673. This play I had afterwards the pleasure to give to my friend, Mr John Kemble, who had not met that copy, even in his extensive research after dramatic rarities.

[2] This title is omitted in subsequent editions.

[3] Of whom it was said, that he spoke, " to the tune of a good speech."

of desperate duration and uncertain issue,[1] assassinations, a dancing tree, a rainbow, a shower of hail, a criminal executed,[2] and hell itself opening upon the stage. The rhyming dialogue too, in which the play was written, had an imperative and tyrannical sound ; and to a foreigner, ignorant of the language, might have appeared as magnificent as that of Dryden. But it must raise our admiration that the witty court of Charles could patiently listen to a " tale told by an idiot, full of sound and fury, signifying nothing," and give it a preference over the poetry of Dryden. The following description of a hail-storm in Africa, will vindicate our wonder :—

> " This morning, as our eyes we upward cast,
> The desert regions of the air lay waste.
> But straight, as if it had some penance bore,
> A mourning garb of thick black clouds it wore.
> But on the sudden,
> Some aëry demon changed its form, and now
> That which look'd black above, look'd white below ;

[1] As for example, this stage-direction: " Here a company of villains, in ambush, from behind the scenes discharge their guns at Muly-Hamet; at which Muly-Hamet starting and turning, Hametalhaz from under his priest's habit draws a sword, and passes at Muly-Hamet, which pass is intercepted by Abdelcader. They engage in a very fierce fight with the villains, who also draw and assist Hametalhaz, and go off several ways fighting; after the discharge of other guns heard from within, and the clashing of swords, enter again Muly-Hamet, driving in some of the former villains, which he kills."

[2] In the fifth act the scene draws and discovers Crimalhaz cast down on the *guanches*, i. e. hung on a wall set with spikes, scythe-blades, and hooks of iron ; which scene (to judge from the engraving) exhibited the mangled limbs and wasted bones of former sufferers, suspended in agreeable confusion. With this pleasing display the piece concluded.

The clouds dishevell'd, from their crusted locks,
Something like gems coin'd out of crystal rocks.
The ground was with this strange bright issue spread,
As if heaven in affront to nature had
Design'd some new-found tillage of its own,
And on the earth these unknown seeds had sown.
Of these I reach'd a grain, which to my sense
Appear'd as cool as virgin-innocence ;
And like that too, (which chiefly I admired,)
Its ravish'd whiteness with a touch expired.
At the approach of heat, this candied rain
Dissolved to its first element again.

    Muley H. Though showers of hail Morocco never see,
Dull priest, what does all this portend to me?
    Ham. It does portend—
    Muley. What?
    Ham. That the fates design—
    Muley. To tire me with impertinence like thine."

Such were the strains once preferred to the
magnificent verses of Dryden; whose very worst
bombast is sublimity compared to them. To prove
which, the reader need only peruse the Indian's
account of the Spanish fleet in the " Indian Emperor," to which the above lines are a parallel;[1]
each being the description of an object familiar to

[1] [" *Montezuma.* I sent thee to the frontiers; quickly tell
The cause of thy return; are all things well?
    Guyomar. I went, in order, sir, to your command,
To view the utmost limits of the land:
To that sea-shore where no more world is found,
But foaming billows breaking on the ground;
Where, for a while, my eyes no object met,
But distant skies, that in the ocean set;
And low-hung clouds, that dipt themselves in rain,
To shake their fleeces on the earth again.
At last, as far as I could cast my eyes
Upon the sea, somewhat, methought, did rise,
Like blueish mists, which, still appearing more,
Took dreadful shapes, and moved towards the shore.
    Mont. What forms did these new wonders represent?
    Guy. More strange than what your wonder can invent.

the audience, but new to the describer. The poet felt the disgraceful preference more deeply than was altogether becoming; but he had levelled his powers, says Johnson, when he levelled his desires to those of Settle, and placed his happiness in the claps of multitudes. The moral may be carried yet farther; for had not Dryden stooped to call to the aid of his poetry the auxiliaries of scenery, gilded truncheons, and verse of more noise than meaning, it is impossible his plays could have been drawn into comparison with those of Settle. But the meretricious ornaments which he himself had introduced were within the reach of the meanest capacity; and, having been among the first to debauch the taste of the public, it was retributive justice that he should experience their inconstancy. Indeed Dryden seems himself to admit, that the

----

    The object, I could first distinctly view,
Was tall straight trees, which on the waters flew;
Wings on their sides, instead of leaves, did grow,
Which gathered all the breath the winds could blow;
And at their roots grew floating palaces,
Whose outblowed bellies cut the yielding seas.
    Mont. What divine monsters, O ye Gods, were these,
That float in air, and fly upon the seas?—
Came they alive or dead upon the shore?
    Guy. Alas, they lived too sure; I heard them roar.
All turn'd their sides, and to each other spoke;
I saw their words break out in fire and smoke.
Sure 'tis their voice that thunders from on high,
Or these the younger brothers of the sky.
Deaf with the noise, I took my hasty flight;
No mortal courage can support the fright.
    High Priest. Old prophecies foretel our fall at hand;
When bearded men in floating castles land.
I fear it is of dire portent.
    Mont. Go see
What it foreshows, and what the Gods decree."

principal difference between his heroic plays and
" The Empress of Morocco," was, that the former
were good sense, that looked like nonsense, and
the latter nonsense, which yet looked very like
sense.   A nice distinction, and which argued some
regret at having opened the way to such a rival.

The feelings of contempt ought to have suppressed those of anger; but Dryden, who pro-
fessedly lived to please his own age, had not
temper to wait till time should do him justice.
Angry he was; and unfortunately he determined
to show the world that he did well in being so.
With this view, in conjunction with Shadwell and
Crowne, two brother-dramatists, equally jealous
of Settle's success, he composed a pamphlet, entitled, " Remarks upon the Empress of Morocco."
This piece is written in the same tone of boisterous
and vulgar raillery with which Clifford and Leigh
had assailed Dryden himself; and little resembles
our poet's general style of controversy. He seems
to have exchanged his satirical scourge for the
clumsy flail of Shadwell, when he stooped to use
such raillery as the following description of Settle:
" In short, he is an animal of a most deplored
understanding, without reading and conversation;
his being is in a twilight of sense, and some glimmering of thought, which he can never fashion
either into wit or English. His style is boisterous and rough-hewn; his rhyme incorrigibly
lewd, and his numbers perpetually harsh and ill-
sounding."

Settle, nothing dismayed with this vehement

attack, manfully retorted the abuse which had been thrown upon him, and answered the insulting clamour of his three antagonists with clamorous insult.[1] It was obvious, that the weaker poet must be the winner by this contest in abuse; and Dryden gained no more by his dispute with Settle. than a well-dressed man who should condescend to wrestle with a chimney-sweeper. The feud between them was carried no farther, until, after the publication of " Absalom and Achitophel," party animosity added spurs to literary rivalry.

We must now return to Rochester; who, observing Settle's rise to this unmerited elevation in the public opinion, became as anxious to lower his presumption as he had formerly been to diminish the reputation of Dryden. With this view, that tyrannical person of honour availed himself of his credit to recommend Crowne to write the masque of " Calisto," which was acted by the lords and ladies of the court of Charles in 1675. Nothing could be more galling towards Dryden, a part of whose duty as poet laureat was to compose the pieces designed for such occasions. Crowne, though he was a tolerable comic writer,[2] had no turn whatever for tragedy, or indeed for poetry of

[1] Settle's pamphlet was contumaciously entitled, " Notes and Observations on the Empress of Morocco revised, with some few erratas; to be printed instead of the Postscript with the next edition of the Conquest of Granada, 1674." See some quotations from this piece, Dryden's Works, vol. xv., p. 399.

[2] His comedy of " Sir Courtly Nice " exhibits marks of comic power. [" There is a forgotten rhyming tragedy in two parts, called the Destruction of Jerusalem. It was written by

any kind. But the splendour of the scenery and dresses, the quality of the performers, selected from the first nobility, and the favour of the sovereign, gave "Calisto" a run of nearly thirty nights. Dryden, though mortified, tendered his services in the shape of an epilogue, to be spoken by Lady Henrietta Maria Wentworth.[1] But the influence of his enemy, Rochester, was still predominant, and the epilogue of the laureat was rejected.

The author of "Calisto" also lost his credit with Rochester, as soon as he became generally popular; and shortly after the representation of that piece, its fickle patron seems to have recommended to the royal protection, a rival more formidable to Dryden than either Settle or "starch Johnny Crowne."[2] This was no other than Otway, whose "Don Carlos" appeared in 1676, and was hailed as one of the best heroic plays which had been

---

Crowne, (the ridiculous rival of Dryden,) and is said to have been acted with applause about the year 1677. It does not appear that it ever fell into Mr Milman's hands; nor, indeed, if it had, could he have turned it to any advantage. Both parts are taken, in some measure, from the narrative of Josephus, but absurdly mixed up in the fashion of the day with Court intrigue and party politics. They are, however, among the best of Crowne's dramas, and the first part is not without merit."—*Quarterly Review* (of Milman's ' Fall of Jerusalem·') *May* 1820.

John Crown, an American, was the son of an Independent minister in Nova Scotia, and author of about fifteen dramatic pieces. He died about the beginning of the 18th century.]

[1] See Dryden's Works, vol. x., p. 336.

[2] So called, according to the communicative old correspondent of the Gentleman's Magazine in 1745, from the unalterable stiffness of his long cravat.

written. The author avows in his preface the obligations he owed to Rochester, who had recommended him to the King and the Duke, to whose favour he owed his good success, and on whose indulgence he reckoned as ensuring that of his next attempt.[1] These effusions of gratitude did not, as Mr Malone observes, withhold Rochester, shortly after, from lampooning Otway, with circumstances of gross insult, in the " Session of the Poets."[2] In the same preface, Otway, in very intelligible language, bade defiance to Dryden, whom he charges with having spoken slightly of his play.[3]

[1] " I am well satisfied I had the greatest party of men of wit and sense on my side : amongst which I can never enough acknowledge the unspeakable obligations I received from the Earl of R., who, far above what I am ever able to deserve from him, seemed almost to make it his business to establish it in the good opinion of the king and his royal highness; from both of which I have since received confirmations of their good-liking of it, and encouragement to proceed. And it is to him, I must, in all gratitude, confess, I owe the greatest part of my good success in this, and on whose indulgency I extremely build my hopes of a next." Accordingly, next year, Otway's play of " Titus and Berenice " is inscribed to Rochester, " his good and generous patron."

[2] " Tom Otway came next, Tom Shadwell's dear zany,
And swears for heroics he writes best of any ;
' Don Carlos ' his pockets so amply had fill'd,
That his mange was quite cured, and his lice were all kill'd.
But Apollo had seen his face on the stage,
And prudently did not think fit to engage
The scum of a playhouse for the prop of an age."

[3] " Though a certain writer, that shall be nameless, (but you may guess at him by what follows,) being ask'd his opinion of this play, very gravely cock't, and cry'd, *I'gad* he knew not a line in it he would be authour of. But he is a fine

In the preface to " All for Love," published in 1678, he gives a severe rebuke to those men of rank, who, having acquired the credit of wit, either by virtue of their quality, or by common fame, and finding themselves possessed of some smattering of Latin, become ambitious to distinguish themselves by their poetry from the herd of gentlemen.

" And is not this," he exclaims, " a wretched affectation, not to be contented with what fortune has done for them, and sit down quietly with their estates, but they must call their wits in question, and needlessly expose their nakedness to public view ?   Not considering that they are not to expect the same approbation from sober men, which they have found from their flatterers after the third bottle.   If a little glittering in discourse has passed them on us for witty men, where was the necessity of undeceiving the world ?   Would a man who has an ill title to an estate, but yet is in possession of it; would he bring it of his own accord to be tried at Westminster ? We who write, if we want the talent, yet have the excuse, that we do it for a poor subsistence : but what can be urged in their defence, who, not having the vocation of poverty to scribble, out of mere wantonness take pains to make themselves ridiculous ?   Horace was certainly in the right, where he said, ' That no man is satisfied with his own condition.' A poet is not pleased, because he is not rich ; and the rich are discontented, because the poets will not admit them of their number. Thus the case is hard with writers; if they succeed not, they must starve ; and if they do, some malicious satire is prepared to level them, for daring to please without their leave.   But while they are so eager to destroy the fame of others, their ambition is manifest in their concernment ; some poem of their own is to be produced, and the slaves are to be laid flat with their faces on the ground, that the monarch may appear in the greater majesty."

This general censure of the persons of wit and honour about town, is fixed on Rochester in particular, not only by the marked allusion in the last sentence, to the despotic tyranny which he claimed over the authors of his time, but also by a direct attack upon such imitators of Horace, who make doggrel of his Latin, misapply his censures, and often contradict their own. It is remarkable, however, that he ascribes this imitation rather to some zany of the great, than to one of their number; and seems to have thought Rochester rather the patron than the author.

At the expense of anticipating the order of events, and that we may bring Dryden's dispute with Rochester to a conclusion, we must recall to the reader's recollection our author's friendship with Mulgrave. This appears to have been so intimate, that, in 1675, that nobleman intrusted him with the task of revising his " Essay upon Satire:" a poem which contained dishonourable mention of many courtiers of the time, and was particularly severe on Sir Car Scrope and Rochester. The last of these is taxed with cowardice, and a thousand odious and mean vices; upbraided with the grossness and scurrility of his writings, and with the infamous profligacy of his life.[1] The

[1] " Rochester I despise for's mere want of wit,
Though thought to have a tail and cloven feet;
For while he mischief means to all mankind,
Himself alone the ill effects does find;
And so, like witches, justly suffers shame,
Whose harmless malice is so much the same.
False are his words, affected is his wit,
So often does he aim, so seldom hit.
To every face he cringes, while he speaks,
But when the back is turn'd the head he breaks.
Mean in each action, lewd in every limb,
Manners themselves are mischievous in him;

versification of the poem is as flat and inharmonious as the plan is careless and ill-arranged ; and though the imputation was to cost Dryden dear, I cannot think that any part of the " Essay on Satire" received additions from his pen. Probably he might contribute a few hints for revision ; but the author of " Absalom and Achitophel" could never completely disguise the powers which were shortly to produce that brilliant satire. Dryden's verses must have shone among Mulgrave's as gold beside copper. The whole Essay is a mere stagnant level, no one part of it so far rising above the rest as to bespeak the work of a superior hand. The

A proof that chance alone makes every creature,—
A very Killigrew, without good-nature.
For what a Bessus has he always lived,
And his own kickings notably contrived ;
For (there's the folly that's still mixed with fear)
Cowards more blows than any hero bear.
Of fighting sparks Fame may her pleasure say,
But 'tis a bolder thing to run away.
The world may well forgive him all his ill,
For every fault does prove his penance still.
Falsely he falls into some dangerous noose,
And then as meanly labours to get loose.
A life so infamous is better quitting ;
Spent in base injury and low submitting.—
I'd like to have left out his poetry,
Forgot by all almost as well as me.
Sometimes he has some humour, never wit,
And if it rarely, very rarely hit,
'Tis under such a nasty rubbish laid,
To find it out's the cinder-woman's trade ;
Who for the wretched remnants of a fire,
Must toil all day in ashes and in mire.
So lewdly dull his idle works appear,
The wretched text deserves no comments here ;
Where one poor thought sometimes left all alone,
For a whole page of dulness to atone :
'Mongst forty bad, one tolerable line,
Without expression, fancy, or design."

thoughts, even when conceived with some spirit, are clumsily and unhappily brought out; a fault never to be traced in the beautiful language of Dryden, whose powers of expression were at least equal to his force of conception. Besides, as Mr Malone has observed, he had now brought to the highest excellence his system of versification; and is it possible he could neglect it so far as to write the rugged lines in the note, where all manner of elliptical barbarisms are resorted to, for squeezing the words into a measure " lame and o'erburdened, and screaming its wretchedness ?" The " Essay on Satire" was finally subjected by the noble author to the criticism of Pope, who, less scrupulous than Dryden, appears to have made large improvements; but after having undergone the revision of two of the first names in English poetry, it continues to be a very indifferent performance.

In another point of view, it seems inconsistent with Dryden's situation to suppose he had any active share in the " Essay on Satire." The character of Charles is treated with great severity, as well as those of the Duchesses of Portsmouth and Cleveland, the royal mistresses. This was quite consistent with Mulgrave's disposition, who was at this time discontented with the ministry; but certainly would not have beseemed Dryden, who held an office at court. Sedley also, with whom Dryden always seems to have lived on friendly terms, is harshly treated in the " Essay on Satire." It may be owned, however, that these reasons were not held powerful at the time, since they must, in that case, have saved Dryden from the inconvenient suspicion, which, we will presently see, attached to him. The public were accustomed to see the friendship of wits end in mutual satire; and the good-natured Charles was so generally the subject of the ridicule which he loved, that no one seems to have thought there was improbability in a libel being composed on him by his own laureat.

The "Essay on Satire," though written, as appears from the titlepage of the last edition, in 1675, was not made public until 1679, when several copies were handed about in manuscript. Rochester sends one of these to his friend, Henry Saville, on the 21st of November, 1679, with this observation:— " I have sent you herewith a libel, in which my own share is not the least. The king having perused it, is no way dissatisfied with his. The author is apparently Mr Dr[yden], his patron, Lord M[ulgrave,] having a panegyric in the midst." From hence it is evident, that Dryden obtained the reputation of being the author; in consequence of which, Rochester meditated the base and cowardly revenge which he afterwards executed; and he thus coolly expressed his intention in another of his letters:—" You write me word, that I'm out of favour with a certain poet, whom I have admired for the disproportion of him and his attributes. He is a rarity which I cannot but be fond of, as one would be of a hog that could fiddle, or a singing owl. If he falls on me at the blunt, which is his very good

weapon in wit, I will forgive him if you please;
and *leave the repartee to black Will with a cud-
gel.*"

In pursuance of this infamous resolution, Dryden, upon the night of the 18th December, 1679,
was waylaid by hired ruffians, and severely beaten,
as he passed through Rose-street, Covent-Garden,
returning from Will's Coffee-house to his own
house in Gerard-street. A reward of L.50 was in
vain offered, in the London Gazette, and other
newspapers, for the discovery of the perpetrators
of this outrage.[1] The town was, however, at no
loss to pitch upon Rochester as the employer of the
bravoes, with whom the public suspicion joined the
Duchess of Portsmouth, equally concerned in the
supposed affront thus avenged. In our time, were
a nobleman to have recourse to hired bravoes to
avenge his personal quarrel against any one, more
especially a person holding the rank of a gentleman,
he might lay his account with being hunted out of
society. But in the age of Charles, the ancient

---

[1] " Whereas John Dryden, Esq. was on Monday the 18th
instant, at night, barbarously assaulted, and wounded, in
Rose-street, in Covent-Garden, by divers men unknown; if
any person shall make discovery of the said offenders to the
said Mr Dryden, or to any justice of the peace, he shall not
only receive fifty pounds, which is deposited in the hands of
Mr Blanchard, goldsmith, next door to Temple-bar, for the
said purpose; but if he be a principal, or an accessory, in the
said fact, his Majesty is graciously pleased to promise him his
pardon for the same."—*London Gazette*, from December 18th
to December 22d, 1679. Mr Malone mentions the same advertisement in a newspaper, entitled, " Domestic Intelligence,
or News from City and Country."

high and chivalrous sense of honour was esteemed Quixotic, and the civil war had left traces of ferocity in the manners and sentiments of the people. Rencounters, where the assailants took all advantages of number and weapons, were as frequent, and held as honourable, as regular duels. Some of these approached closely to assassination; as in the famous case of Sir John Coventry, who was waylaid, and had his nose slit by some young men of high rank, for a reflection upon the king's theatrical amours. This occasioned the famous statute against maiming and wounding, called the Coventry Act; an act highly necessary, since so far did our ancestors' ideas of manly forbearance differ from ours, that Killigrew introduces the hero of one of his comedies, a cavalier, and the fine gentleman of the piece, lying in wait for, and slashing the face of a poor courtezan, who had cheated him.[1]

It will certainly be admitted, that a man, surprised in the dark and beaten by ruffians, loses no honour by such a misfortune. But, if Dryden had received the same discipline from Rochester's own hand without resenting it, his drubbing could not have been more frequently made a matter of reproach to him;—a sign surely of the penury of subjects for satire in his life and character, since an

---

[1] I might also mention the sentiment of Count Conigsmarck, who allowed, that the barbarous assassination of Mr Thynne by his bravoes was a stain on his blood, but such a one as a good action in the wars, or a lodging on a counterscarp, would easily wash out. See his Trial, " State Trials," vol. iv. But Conigsmarck was a foreigner

accident, which might have happened to the greatest
hero who ever lived, was resorted to as an imputation on his honour. The Rose-alley ambuscade
became almost proverbial;[1] and even Mulgrave,
the real author of the satire, and upon whose shoulders the blows ought in justice to have descended,
mentions the circumstances in his " Art of Poetry,"
with a cold and self-sufficient complacent sneer :

> " Though prais'd and punish'd for another's rhymes,
> His own deserve as great applause *sometimes*."

To which is added in a note, " A libel for which he
was both applauded and wounded, though entirely
ignorant of the whole matter." This flat and con-
ceited couplet, and note, the noble author judged it
proper to omit in the corrected edition of his poem.
Otway alone, no longer the friend of Rochester,

---

[1] For example, a rare broadside in ridicule of Benjamin
Harris the Whig publisher, entitled, " The Saint turned
Courtezan, or a new plot discovered by a precious Zealot of
an Assault and Battery designed upon the Body of a sanctified
Sister,

> " Who, in her husband's absence, with a brother
> Did often use to comfort one another,
> Till wide-mouth'd Crop, who is an old Italian,
> Took his mare nappy, and surprised her stallion,
> Who stead of entertainment from his mistress,
> Did meet a cudgelling not match'd in histories.
>   ' Who's there ?' quoth watchful Argus.
>   ' 'Tis I, in longing passion ;
>   Give me a kiss.'
> Quoth Ben, ' Take this,
>   *A Dryden salutation.*'
>   Help Care, Vile, Smith, and Curtes,
>   Each zealous covenanter !
>   What wonder the atheist
>   L'Estrange should turn papist,
>   When a zealot turns a ranter."

and perhaps no longer the enemy of **Dryden**, has spoken of the author of this dastardly **outrage** with the contempt his cowardly malice deserved :

> " Poets in honour of the truth should write,
> With the same spirit brave men for it fight ;
> And though against him causeless hatreds rise,
> And daily where he goes, of late, he spies
> The scowls of sullen and revengeful eyes ;
> 'Tis what he knows with much contempt to bear,
> And serves a cause too good to let him fear :
> He fears no poison from incensed Drabb,
> No ruffian's five-foot sword, nor rascal's stab ;
> Nor any other snares of mischief laid,
> *Not a Rose-alley cudgel ambuscade ;*
> From any private cause where malice reigns,
> Or general pique all blockheads have to brains. "

It does not appear that Dryden ever thought it worth his while to take revenge on Rochester ; and the only allusion to him in his writings may be found in the Essay prefixed to the translation of Juvenal, where he is mentioned as a man of quality, whose ashes our author was unwilling to disturb, and who had paid Dorset, to whom that piece is inscribed, " the highest compliment which his self-sufficiency could afford to any man."[1] Perhaps Dryden remembered Rochester among others, when, in the same piece, he takes credit for resisting opportunities and temptation to take revenge, even upon those by whom he had been notoriously and wantonly provoked.[2]

[1] [Viz. the famous couplet—
" For pointed satire I would Buckhurst chuse ;
The best good man, with the worst natured muse."]

[2] [" More libels have been written against me, than almost any man now living ; and I had reason on my side to have

The detail of these quarrels has interrupted our account of Dryden's writings, which we are now to resume.

"Aureng-Zebe" was his first performance after the failure of the "Assignation." It was acted in 1675, with general applause. "Aureng-Zebe" is a heroic, or rhyming, play, but not cast in a mould quite so romantic as the "Conquest of Granada." There is a grave and moral turn in many of the speeches, which brings it nearer the style of a French tragedy. It is true, the character of Morat borders upon extravagance; but a certain license has been always given to theatrical tyrants, and we excuse bombast in him more readily than in Almanzor. There is perhaps some reason for this indulgence. The possession of unlimited power, vested in active and mercurial characters, naturally drives them to an extravagant indulgence of passion, bordering upon insanity; and it follows, that their language must outstrip the modesty of nature. Propriety of diction in the drama is relative, and

---

defended my own innocence. I speak not of my poetry, which I have wholly given up to the critics; let them use it as they please; posterity, perhaps, may be more favourable to me; for interest and passion will be buried in another age, and partiality and prejudice be forgotten. I speak of my morals, which have been sufficiently aspersed; that only sort of reputation ought to be dear to every honest man, and is to me. But let the world witness for me, that I have often been wanting to myself in that particular. I have seldom answered any scurrilous lampoon, when it was in my power to have exposed my enemies; and, being naturally vindictive, have suffered in silence, and possessed my soul in quiet."—*Dryden's Works*, vol. xiii., p. 80.]

to be referred more to individual character than to
general rules : to make a tyrant sober-minded, is
to make a madman rational.   But this discretion
must be used with great caution by the writer, lest
he should confound the terrible with the burlesque.
Two great actors, Kynaston and Booth, differed
in their style of playing Morat.   The former, who
was the original performer, and doubtless had his
instructions from the author, gave full force to the
sentiments of avowed and barbarous vainglory,
which mark the character.   When he is determined
to spare Aureng-Zebe, and Nourmahal pleads,

" 'Twill not be safe to let him live an hour,"

Kynaston gave all the stern and haughty insolence
of despotism to his answer,

" I'll do't to show my arbitrary power." [1]

But Booth, with modest caution, avoided marking
and pressing upon the audience a sentiment hover-
ing between the comic and terrible, however consonant to the character by whom it was delivered.
The principal incident in "Aureng-Zebe" was suggested by King Charles himself.   The tragedy is
dedicated to Mulgrave, whose patronage had been
so effectual, as to introduce Dryden and his poetical schemes to the peculiar notice of the king and
duke.   The dedication and the prologue of this
piece throw considerable light upon these plans, as
well as upon the revolution which had gradually
taken place in Dryden's dramatic taste.

[1] Cibber's Apology, 4to., p. 74.

During the space which occurred between writing the "Conquest of Granada" and "Aureng-Zebe," our author's researches into the nature and causes of harmony of versification had been unremitted, and he had probably already collected the materials of his intended English *Prosodia*. Besides this labour, he had been engaged in a closer and more critical examination of the ancient English poets, than he had before bestowed upon them. These studies seem to have led Dryden to two conclusions; first, that the drama ought to be emancipated from the fetters of rhyme; and secondly, that he ought to employ the system of versification, which he had now perfected, to the more legitimate purpose of epic poetry. Each of these opinions merits consideration.

However hardly Dryden stood forward in defence of the heroic plays, he confessed, even in the heat of argument, that Rhyme, though he was brave and generous, and his dominion pleasing, had still somewhat of the usurper in him. A more minute enquiry seems to have still farther demonstrated the weakness of this usurped dominion; and our author's good taste and practice speedily pointed out deficiencies and difficulties, which Sir Robert Howard, against whom he defended the use of rhyme, could not show, because he never aimed at the excellences which they impeded. The perusal of Shakspeare, on whom Dryden had now turned his attention, led him to feel, that something farther might be attained in tragedy than the expression of exaggerated sentiment in

smooth verse, and that the scene ought to represent, not a fanciful set of agents exerting their
superhuman faculties in a fairy-land of the poet's
own creation, but human characters, acting from
the direct and energetic influence of human passions, with whose emotions the audience might
sympathize, because akin to the feelings of their
own hearts.   When Dryden had once discovered
that fear and pity were more likely to be excited
by other causes than the logic of metaphysical love,
or the dictates of fantastic honour, he must have
found, that rhyme sounded as unnatural in the
dialogue of characters drawn upon the usual scale
of humanity, as the plate and mail of chivalry would
have appeared on the persons of the actors.   The
following lines of the prologue to " Aureng-Zebe,"
although prefixed to a rhyming play, the last which
he ever wrote, expresses Dryden's change of sentiment on these points.

" Our author, by experience, finds it true,
'Tis much more hard to please himself than you :
And, out of no feign'd modesty, this day
Damns his laborious trifle of a play :
Not that it's worse than what before he writ,
But he has now another taste of wit ;
And, to confess a truth, though out of time,
Grows weary of his long-loved mistress, Rhyme.
Passion's too fierce to be in fetters bound,
And nature flies him like enchanted ground.
What verse can do, he has perform'd in this,
Which he presumes the most correct of his ;
But spite of all his pride, a secret shame
Invades his breast at Shakspeare's sacred name :
Awed when he hears his godlike Romans rage,
He, in a just despair, would quit the stage ;

And to an age less polish'd, more unskill'd,
Does, with disdain, the foremost honours yield."

It is remarkable, as a trait of character, that
though our author admitted his change of opinion
on this long disputed point, he would not consent
that it should be imputed to any arguments which
his opponents had the wit to bring against him.
On this subject he enters a protest in the Preface
to his revised edition of the " Essay of Dramatic
Poesy" in 1684.

" I confess, I find many things in this discourse which I do
not now approve; my judgment being not a little altered since
the writing of it; but whether for the better or the worse, I
know not: neither indeed is it much material, in an essay,
where all I have said is problematical. For the way of writing plays in verse, which I have seemed to favour, I have,
since that time, laid the practice of it aside, till I have more
leisure, because I find it troublesome and slow: but I am no
way altered from my opinion of it, *at least with any reasons
which have opposed it;* for your lordship may easily observe,
that none are very violent against it, but those who either
have not attempted it, or who have succeeded ill in their
attempt."

Thus cautious was Dryden in not admitting a
victory, even in a cause which he had surrendered.

But, although the poet had admitted, that, with
powers of versification superior to those possessed
by any earlier English author, and a taste corrected
by the laborious study both of the language and
those who had used it, he found rhyme unfit for
the use of the drama, he at the same time discovered a province where it might be employed in
all its splendour. We have the mortification to

learn, from the dedication of " Aureng-Zebe," that
Dryden only wanted encouragement to enter upon
the composition of an epic poem, and to abandon
the thriftless task of writing for the promiscuous
audience of the theatre,—a task which, rivalled as
he had lately been by Crowne and Settle, he most
justly compares to the labour of Sisyphus.   His
plot, he elsewhere explains, was to be founded
either upon the story of Arthur, or of Edward the
Black Prince ; and he mentions it to Mulgrave in
the following remarkable passage, which argues
great dissatisfaction with dramatic labour, arising
perhaps from a combined feeling of the bad taste of
rhyming plays, the degrading dispute with Settle,
and the failure of the " Assignation," his last theatrical attempt :—

" If I must be condemned to rhyme, I should find some
ease in my change of punishment.   I desire to be no longer
the Sisyphus of the stage ; to roll up a stone with endless labour, which, to follow the proverb, *gathers no moss*, and which
is perpetually falling down again.   I never thought myself
very fit for an employment, where many of my predecessors
have excelled me in all kinds ; and some of my contemporaries,
even in my own partial judgment, have outdone me in comedy.
Some little hopes I have yet remaining, (and those too, considering my abilities, may be vain,) that I may make the world
some part of amends for many ill plays, by an heroic poem.
Your lordship has been long acquainted with my design ; the
subject of which you know is great, the story English, and
neither too far distant from the present age, nor too near approaching it.   Such it is in my opinion, that I could not have
wished a nobler occasion to do honour by it to my king, my
country, and my friends ; most of our ancient nobility being
concerned in the action.   And your lordship has one particular
reason to promote this undertaking, because you were the first
who gave me the opportunity of discoursing it to his majesty,

and his royal highness; they were then pleased both to com-
mend the design, and to encourage it by their commands;
but the unsettledness of my condition has hitherto put a stop
to my thoughts concerning it. As I am no successor to Homer
in his wit, so neither do I desire to be in his poverty. I can
make no rhapsodies, nor go a begging at the Grecian doors,
while I sing the praises of their ancestors. The times of
Virgil please me better, because he had an Augustus for his
patron; and, to draw the allegory nearer you, I am sure I
shall not want a Mæcenas with him. It is for your lordship
to stir up that remembrance in his majesty, which his many
avocations of business have caused him, I fear, to lay aside;
and, as himself and his royal brother are the heroes of the
poem, to represent to them the images of their warlike predecessors; as Achilles is said to be roused to glory with the
sight of the combat before the ships. For my own part, I am
satisfied to have offered the design; and it may be to the advantage of my reputation to have it refused me." [1]

Dr Johnson and Mr Malone remark, that Dryden observes a mystery concerning the subject of
his intended epic, to prevent the risk of being anticipated, as he finally was by Sir Richard Blackmore on the topic of Arthur. This, as well as
other passages in Dryden's life, allows us the
pleasing indulgence of praising the decency of our
own time. Were an author of distinguished merit
to announce his having made choice of a subject
for a large poem, the writer would have more
than common confidence who should venture to
forestall his labours. But, in the seventeenth
century, such an intimation would, it seems, have
been an instant signal for the herd of scribblers to
souse upon it, like the harpies on the feast of the

---

[1] Dryden's Works, vol. v., pp. 183, 184.

Trojans, and leave its mangled relics too polluted
for the use of genius ;—

> " *Turba sonans prædam pedibus circumvolat uncis ;*
> *Polluit ore dapes.* ———— ————
>
> *Semesam prædam et vestigia fœda relinquunt.*"

"Aureng-Zebe" was followed, in 1678, by "All
for Love," the only play Dryden ever wrote for
himself; the rest, he says, were given to the people.
The habitual study of Shakspeare, which seems
lately to have occasioned, at least greatly aided,
the revolution in his taste, induced him, among a
crowd of emulous shooters, to try his strength in
this bow of Ulysses. I have, in some preliminary
remarks to the play, endeavoured to point out the
difference between the manner of these great
artists in treating the misfortunes of Antony and
Cleopatra.[1] If these are just, we must allow Dryden the praise of greater regularity of plot, and a
happier combination of scene ; but in sketching
the character of Antony, he loses the majestic and
heroic tone which Shakspeare has assigned him.
There is too much of the love-lorn knight-errant,
and too little of the Roman warrior, in Dryden's
hero. The passion of Antony, however overpowering and destructive in its effects, ought not
to have resembled the love of a sighing swain of
Arcadia. This error in the original conception
of the character must doubtless be ascribed to
Dryden's habit of romantic composition. Monte-

---

[1] Dryden's Works, vol. v., p. 287.

zuma and Almanzor were, like the prophet's image,
formed of a mixture of iron and clay ; of stern and
rigid demeanour to all the universe, but unbounded
devotion to the ladies of their affections.   In Antony, the first class of attributes are discarded ; he
has none of that tumid and outrageous dignity
which characterised the heroes of the rhyming
plays, and in its stead is gifted with even more
than a usual share of devoted attachment to his
mistress.[1]   In the preface, Dryden piques himself
upon venturing to introduce the quarrelling scene
between Octavia and Cleopatra, which a French
writer would have rejected, as contrary to the
decorum of the theatre.   But our author's idea of
female character was at all times low ; and the
coarse, indecent violence, which he has thrown into
the expressions of a queen and a Roman matron,
is misplaced and disgusting, and contradicts the
general and well-founded observation on the address and self-command, with which even women
of ordinary dispositions can veil mutual dislike
and hatred, and the extreme keenness with which
they can arm their satire, while preserving all the
external forms of civil demeanour.   But Dryden
more than redeemed this error in the scene between
Antony and Ventidius, which he himself preferred

---

[1] This distinction our author himself points out in the
Prologue.   The poet there says,

> " His hero, whom you wits his bully call,
> Bates of his mettle, and scarce rants at all ;
> He's somewhat lewd, but a well-meaning mind,
> Keeps much, fights little, but is wondrous kind."
> *Dryden's Works*, vol. v., p. 321.

to any that he ever wrote, and perhaps with justice, if we except that between Dorax and Sebastian : both are avowedly written in imitation of
the quarrel between Brutus and Cassius. "All for
Love" was received by the public with universal
applause. Its success, with that of "Aureng-Zebe,"
gave fresh lustre to the author's reputation, which
had been somewhat tarnished by the failure of the
" Assignation," and the rise of so many rival dramatists. We learn from the Players' petition to
the Lord Chamberlain, that " All for Love" was
of service to the author's fortune as well as to his
fame, as he was permitted the benefit of a third
night, in addition to his profits as a sharer with
the company. The play was dedicated to the
Earl of Danby, then a minister in high power, but
who, in the course of a few months, was disgraced
and imprisoned at the suit of the Commons. As
Danby was a great advocate for prerogative, Dryden fails not to approach him with an encomium
on monarchical government, as regulated and cir-
cumscribed by law. In reprobating the schemes
of those innovators, who, surfeiting on happiness,
endeavoured to persuade their fellow-subjects to
risk a change, he has a pointed allusion to the
Earl of Shaftesbury, who, having left the royal
councils in disgrace, was now at the head of the
popular faction.

In 1678 Dryden's next play, a comedy, entitled
" Limberham," was acted at Dorset-garden theatre,
but was endured for three nights only. It was
designed, the author informs us, as a satire on

" the crying sin of keeping;" and the crime for
which it suffered was, that " it expressed too much
of the vice which it decried." Grossly indelicate
as this play still is, it would seem, from the dedication to Lord Vaughan, that much which offended
on the stage was altered, or omitted in the press; [1]
yet more than enough remains to justify the sentence pronounced against it by the public. Mr
Malone seems to suppose Shaftesbury's party had
some share in its fate, supposing that the character
of Limberham had reference to their leader. Yet
surely, although Shaftesbury was ridiculous for
aiming at gallantry, from which his age and personal infirmity should have deterred him, Dryden
would never have drawn the witty, artful politician,
as a silly, hen-pecked cully. Besides, Dryden was
about this time supposed even himself to have
some leaning to the popular cause; a supposition
irreconcilable with his caricaturing the foibles of
Shaftesbury.

The tragedy of " Œdipus " was written by
Dryden in conjunction with Lee; the entire first
and third acts were the work of our author, who
also arranged the general plan, and corrected the
whole piece. Having offered some observations [2]
elsewhere upon this play, and the mode in which
its celebrated theme has been treated by the dra-

[1] Mr Malone has seen a MS. copy of " Limberham " in its
original state, found by Bolingbroke in the sweepings of
Pope's study. It contained several exceptionable passages,
afterwards erased or altered.

[2] Dryden's Works, vol. vi., p. 117.

matists of different nations, I need not here resume
the subject.   The time of the first representation
is fixed to the beginning of the playing season, in
winter 1678–9, although it was not printed until
1679.[1]   Both "Limberham" and " Œdipus" were
acted at the Duke's theatre; so that it would seem
that our author was relieved from his contract with
the King's house, probably because the shares were
so much diminished in value, that his appointment
was now no adequate compensation for his labour.
The managers of the King's company complained
to the lord chamberlain, and endeavoured, as we
have seen, by pleading upon the contract, to assert
their right to the play of " Œdipus."[2]   But their
claim to reclaim the poet and the play appears to
have been set aside, and Dryden continued to give
his performances to the Duke's theatre until the
union of the two companies.

Dryden was now to do a new homage to Shakspeare, by refitting for the stage the play of " Troilus and Cressida," which the author left in a state
of strange imperfection, resembling more a chro-
nicle, or legend, than a dramatic piece.   Yet it
may be disputed whether Dryden has greatly improved it even in the particulars which he censures
in his original.   His plot, though more artificial, is
at the same time more trite than that of Shakspeare.
The device by which Troilus is led to doubt the
constancy of Cressida is much less natural than
that she should have been actually inconstant; her

[1] By allusion to the act for burying in woollen.
[2] See their Petition, *ante*, p. 86.

vindication by suicide is a clumsy, as well as a hackneyed expedient; and there is too much drum and trumpet in the grand *finale*, where " Troilus and Diomede fight, and both parties engage at the same time. The Trojans make the Greeks retire, and Troilus makes Diomede give ground, and hurts him. Trumpets sound. Achilles enters with his Myrmidons, on the backs of the Trojans, who fight in a ring, encompassed round. Troilus, singling Diomede, gets him down and kills him; and Achilles kills Troilus upon him. All the Trojans die upon the place, Troilus last." Such a *bellum internecinum* can never be waged to advantage upon the stage. One extravagant passage in this play serves strongly to evince Dryden's rooted dislike to the clergy.[1] Troilus exclaims,—

That I should trust the daughter of a priest!
Priesthood, that makes a merchandise of heaven!
Priesthood, that sells even to their prayers and blessings,
And forces us to pay for our own cozenage!
 Thersites. Nay, cheats heaven too with entrails and with
   offals;
Gives it the garbage of a sacrifice,
And keeps the best for private luxury.

[1] ["Malevolence to the clergy is seldom at a great distance from irreverence of religion, and Dryden affords no exception to this observation. His writings exhibit many passages, which, with all the allowance that can be made for characters and occasions, are such as piety would not have admitted, and such as may vitiate light and unprincipled minds. But there is no reason for supposing that he disbelieved the religion which he disobeyed. He forgot his duty rather than disowned it. His tendency to profaneness is the effect of levity, negligence, and loose conversation, with a desire of accommodating himself to the corruption of the times, by venturing to be wicked as far as he durst. When he professed himself a convert to Popery, he did not pretend to have received any new conviction of the fundamental doctrines of Christianity."—JOHNSON.]

Troilus. Thou hast deserved thy life for cursing priests.
Let me embrace thee; thou art beautiful:
That back, that nose, those eyes are beautiful:
Live; thou art honest, for thou hat'st a priest."

Dryden prefixed to " Troilus and Cressida" his excellent remarks on the Grounds of Criticism in Tragedy, giving up, with dignified indifference, the faults even of his own pieces, when they contradict the rules his later judgment had adopted. How much his taste had altered since his " Essay of Dramatic Poesy," or at least since his " Remarks on Heroic Plays," will appear from the following abridgement of his new maxims. The Plot, according to these remarks, ought to be simply and naturally detailed from its commencement to its conclusion,—a rule which excluded the crowded incidents of the Spanish Drama; and the personages ought to be dignified and virtuous, that their misfortunes might at once excite pity and terror. The plots of Shakspeare and Fletcher are meted by this rule, and pronounced inferior in mechanic regularity to those of Ben Jonson. The Characters of the agents, or persons, are next to be considered; and it is required that their Manners shall be at once marked, dramatic, consistent, and natural. And here the supereminent powers of Shakspeare, in displaying the manners, bent, and inclination of his characters, is pointed out to the reader's admiration. The copiousness of his invention, and his judgment in sustaining the ideas which he started, are illustrated by referring to Caliban, a creature of the fancy, begot by an incubus upon a witch, and furnished with a person, language, and character, befitting his pedigree on both sides. The Passions are then considered as included in the Manners; and Dryden, at once and peremptorily, condemns both the extravagance of language, which substitutes noise for feeling, and those points and turns of wit, which misbecome one actuated by real and deep emotion. He candidly gives an example of the last error from his own Montezuma, who, pursued by his enemies, and excluded from the fort, describes his situation in a long simile, taken besides from the sea, which he had only heard of for the first time in the first act. As a description of natural passion, the famous procession of King Richard in the train of the fortunate usurper is quoted, in justice to the divine author. From these just and liberal rules of criticism, it is easy to discover that Dryden had already adopted a better taste, and was disgusted with comedies, where the entertainment arose from bustling incident, and tragedies, where sounding verse was substituted for the delineation of manners and expression of feeling. These opinions he pointedly delivers in the Prologue to " Troilus and Cressida," which was spoken by Betterton, representing the ghost of Shakspeare:

" See, my loved Britons, see your Shakspeare rise,
An awful ghost confess'd to human eyes!
Unnamed, methinks, distinguish'd I had been,
From other shades, by this eternal green,
About whose wreaths the vulgar poets strive,
And, with a touch, their wither'd bays revive.

Untaught, unpractised, in a barbarous age,
I found not, but created first the stage.
And, if I drain'd no Greek or Latin store,
'Twas, that my own abundance gave me more.
On foreign trade I needed not rely,
Like fruitful Britain, rich without supply.
In this, my rough-drawn play, you shall behold
Some master-strokes, so manly and so bold,
That he who meant to alter, found 'em such,
He shook, and thought it sacrilege to touch.
Now, where are the successors to my name?
What bring they to fill out a poet's fame?
Weak, short-lived issues of a feeble age;
Scarce living to be christen'd on the stage!
For humour *farce,* for love they *rhyme* dispense,
That tolls the knell for their departed sense."

It is impossible to read these lines, remembering
Dryden's earlier opinions, without acknowledging
the truth of the ancient proverb, *Magna est veritas,*
et prevalebit.

The " Spanish Friar," our author's most successful comedy, succeeded " Troilus and Cressida."
Without repeating the remarks which are prefixed
to the play in the present edition,[1] we may briefly

[1] [See Scott's edition of Dryden, vol. vi., p. 367. The Editor there says, " The Spanish Friar, or the Double Discovery,
is one of the best and most popular of our poet's dramatic
efforts. The plot is, as Johnson remarks, particularly happy,
for the coincidence and coalition of the tragic and comic plots.
The grounds for this eminent critic's encomium will be found
to lie more deep than appears at first sight. It was, indeed,
a sufficiently obvious connexion, to make the gay Lorenzo an
officer of the conquering army, and attached to the person of
Torrismond. This expedient could hardly have escaped the
invention of the most vulgar playwright that ever dovetailed
tragedy and comedy together. The felicity of Dryden's plot,
therefore, does not consist in the ingenuity of his original
conception, but in the minutely artificial strokes, by which

notice, that in the tragic scenes our author has attained that better strain of dramatic poetry, which he afterwards evinced in " Sebastian." In the comic part, the well-known character of Father Dominic, though the conception only embodies the abstract idea which the ignorant and prejudiced fanatics of the day formed to themselves of a Romish priest, is brought out and illustrated with peculiar spirit. The gluttony, avarice, debauchery, and meanness of Dominic, are qualified with the talent and wit necessary to save him from being utterly detestable; and, from the beginning to the end of the piece, these qualities are so happily tinged with insolence, hypocrisy, and irritability, that they cannot be mistaken for the avarice, debauchery, gluttony, and meanness of any other profession than that of a bad churchman. In the tragic plot, we principally admire the general management of the opening, and chiefly censure the cold-blooded barbarity and perfidy of the young

---

the reader is perpetually reminded of the dependence of the one part of the play on the other. These are so frequent, and appear so very natural, that the comic plot, instead of diverting our attention from the tragic business, recalls it to our mind by constant and unaffected allusion. No great event happens in the higher region of the camp or court, that has not some indirect influence upon the intrigues of Lorenzo and Elvira; and the part which the gallant is called upon to act in the revolution that winds up the tragic interest, while it is highly in character, serves to bring the catastrophe of both parts of the play under the eye of the spectator, at one and the same time. Thus much seemed necessary to explain the felicity of combination, upon which Dryden justly valued himself, and which Johnson sanctioned by his high commendation," &c.]

queen, in instigating the murder of the deposed sovereign, and then attempting to turn the guilt on her accomplice. I fear Dryden here forgot his own general rule, that the tragic hero and heroine should have so much virtue as to entitle their distress to the tribute of compassion. Altogether, however, the " Spanish Friar," in both its parts, is an interesting, and almost a fascinating play; although the tendency, even of the tragic scenes, is not laudable, and the comedy, though more decent in language, is not less immoral in tendency than was usual in that loose age.

Dryden attached considerable importance to the art with which the comic and tragic scenes of the " Spanish Friar " are combined; and in doing so, he has received the sanction of Dr Johnson. Indeed, as the ardour of his mind ever led him to prize that task most highly, on which he had most lately employed his energy, he has affirmed in the dedication to the " Spanish Friar," that there was an absolute necessity for combining two actions in tragedy, for the sake of variety. " The truth is," he adds, " the audience are grown weary of continued melancholy scenes; and I dare venture to prophesy, that few tragedies, except those in verse, shall succeed in this age, if they are not lightened with a course of mirth; for the feast is too dull and solemn without the fiddles." The necessity of the relief alluded to may be admitted, without allowing that we must substitute either the misplaced charms of versification, or a secondary comic plot, to relieve the solemn weight and monotony of tragedy. It is no doubt true, that a highly-buskined tragedy, in which all the personages maintain the funeral pomp usually required from the victims of Melpomene, is apt to be intolerably tiresome, after all the pains which a skilful and elegant poet can bestow upon finishing it. But it is chiefly tiresome, because it is unnatural; and, in respect of propriety, ought no more to be relieved by the introduction of a set of comic scenes, independent of those of a mournful complexion, than the *sombre* air of a funeral should be enlivened by a concert of fiddles. There appear to be two legitimate modes of inter-weaving tragedy with something like comedy. The first and most easy, which has often been resorted to, is to make the lower or less marked characters of the drama, like the porter in " Mac-beth," or the fool in " King Lear," speak the language appropriated to their station, even in the midst of the distresses of the piece; nay, they may be permitted to have some slight under-intrigue of their own. This, however, requires the exertion of much taste and discrimination; for if we are once seriously and deeply interested in the distress of the play, the intervention of any thing like buffoonery may unloose the hold which the author has gained on the feelings of the audience. If such subordinate comic characters are of a rank to inter-mix in the tragic dialogue, their mirth ought to be chastened, till their language bears a relation to that of the higher persons. For example, nothing can be more absurd than in " Don Sebastian," and some of Southerne's tragedies, to hear the comic character answer in prose, and with a would-be witticism, to the solemn, unrelaxed blank verse of his tragic companion.[1] Mercutio is, I think, one of the best instances of such a comic person as may be reasonably and with propriety admitted into tragedy: From which, however, I do not exclude those lower characters, whose conversation appears absurd if much elevated above their rank. There is, however, another mode, yet more difficult to be used with address, but much more fortunate in effect when it has been successfully employed. This is, when the principal personages themselves do not always remain in the buckram of tragedy, but reserve, as in common life, lofty expressions for great occasions, and at other times evince themselves capable of feeling the lighter, as well as the more violent or more deep, affections of the mind. The shades of comic humour in Hamlet, in Hotspur, and in Falconbridge, are so far from injuring, that they greatly aid the effect of the tragic scenes, in which these same persons take a deep and tragical share. We grieve with them, when grieved, still more, because we have rejoiced with them when they rejoiced ; and, on the whole, we acknowledge a deeper *frater feeling*, as Burns has termed it, in men who are actuated by the usual changes of human temperament, than in those who, contrary to the nature of humanity, are eternally actuated by an unvaried strain of tragic feeling. But whether the poet diversifies his melancholy

[1] This is ridiculed in " Chrononhotonthologos."

scenes by the passing gaiety of subordinate characters ; or whether he qualifies the tragic state of his
heroes by occasionally assigning lighter tasks to
them ; or whether he chooses to employ both modes
of relieving the weight of misery through five long
acts ; it is obviously unnecessary that he should
distract the attention of his audience, and destroy
the regularity of his play, by introducing a comic
plot with personages and interest altogether distinct, and intrigue but slightly connected with that
of the tragedy. Dryden himself afterwards acknowledged, that, though he was fond of the " Spanish
Friar," he could not defend it from the imputation
of Gothic and unnatural irregularity ; " for mirth
and gravity destroy each other, and are no more to
be allowed for decent, than a gay widow laughing
in a mourning habit." [1]

The " Spanish Friar" was brought out in 1681–2,
when the nation was in a ferment against the Catholics, on account of the supposed plot.   It is dedicated to John, Lord Haughton, as a *protestant
play* inscribed to a *protestant patron*.   It was also
the last dramatic work, excepting the political
play of the " Duke of Guise," and the masque of
" Albion and Albanius," brought out by our author
before the Revolution.   And in political tendency,
the " Spanish Friar" has so different colouring
from these last pieces, that it is worth while to
pause to examine the private relations of the author
when he composed it.

[1] Parallel of Poetry and Painting, Dryden's Works, vol
xvii., p. 325.

Previous to 1678, Lord Mulgrave, our author's constant and probably effectual patron, had given him an opportunity of discoursing over his plan of an epic poem to the King and Duke of York; and in the preface to " Aureng-Zebe " in that year, the poet intimates an indirect complaint, that the royal brothers had neglected his plan.[1]   About two years afterwards, Mulgrave seems himself to have fallen into disgrace, and was considered as in opposition to the court.[2]   Dryden was deprived of his intercession, and appears in some degree to have shared his disgrace.   The " Essay on Satire " became public in November, 1679, and being generally imputed to Dryden, it is said distinctly by one libeller, that his pension was for a time interrupted.[3]   This does not seem likely; it is more probable, that Dryden shared the general fate of

[1] See ante, p. 184.

[2] He is said to have cast the eyes of ambitious affection on the Lady Anne, (afterwards queen,) daughter of the Duke of York; at which presumption Charles was so much offended, that when Mulgrave went to relieve Tangier in 1680, he is said to have been appointed to a leaky and frail vessel, in hopes that he might perish; an injury which he resented so highly, as not to permit the king's health to be drunk at his table till the voyage was over.   On his return from Tangier he was refused the regiment of the Earl of Plymouth; and, considering his services as neglected, for a time joined those who were discontented with the government.   He was probably reclaimed by receiving the government of Hull and lieutenancy of Yorkshire.—See Dryden's Works, vol. ix., pp. 504, 505.

[3] In a poem called " The Laureat," the satirist is so ill informed, as still to make Dryden the author of the " Essay on Satire."   Surely it is unlikely to suppose, that he should have submitted to the loss of a pension, which he so much needed,

the household of Charles II., whose appointments were but irregularly paid ; but perhaps his supposed delinquency made it more difficult for him than others to obtain redress.   At this period broke out the pretended discovery of the Popish Plot, in which Dryden, even in "Absalom and Achitophel," evinces a partial belief.[1]   Not encouraged, if not actually discountenanced, at court; sharing in some degree the discontent of his patron Mulgrave ; above all, obliged by his situation to please the age in which he lived, Dryden did not probably hold the reverence of the Duke of York so sacred, as to prevent his making the ridicule of the Catholic religion the means of recommending his play to the passions of the audience.   Neither was his situation at court in any danger from his closing on this occasion with the popular tide.   Charles, during the heat of the Popish Plot, was so far

---

rather than justify himself, where justification was so easy. Yet his resentment is said to have been

> " For pension lost, and justly, without doubt:
> When servants snarl we ought to kick them out.
> — — — — — —
> That lost, the visor changed, you turn about,
> And strait a true-blue Protestant crept out.
> The *Friar* now was wrote ; and some will say,
> They smell a malecontent through all the play."

See the whole passage, *Dryden's Works*, vol. vi., p. 369.

[1] See, for this point also, the volume and page last quoted :

> [" From hence began that plot, the nation's curse,
> Bad in itself, but represented worse ;
> Raised in extremes, and in extremes decried,
> With oaths affirm'd, with dying vows denied ;
> Nor weigh'd nor winnow'd by the multitude,
> But swallow'd in the mass unchew'd and crude.
> *Some truth there was, but dash'd and bruis'd with lies,*
> To please the fools, and puzzle all the wise."]

from being in a situation to incur odium by dismissing a laureat for having written a *Protestant play*, that he was obliged for a time to throw the reins of government into the hands of those very persons, to whom the Papists were most obnoxious. The inference drawn from Dryden's performance was, that he had deserted the court; and the Duke of York was so much displeased with the tenor of the play, that it was the only one, of which, on acceding to the crown, he prohibited the representation. The " Spanish Friar " was often objected to the author by his opponents, after he had embraced the religion there satirized. Nor was the idea of his apostasy from the court an invention of his enemies after his conversion, for it prevailed at the commencement of the party disputes ; and the name of Dryden is, by a partisan of royalty, ranked with that of his bitter foe Shadwell, as followers of Shaftesbury in 1680.[1] But whatever cause of coolness or disgust our author had received from Charles or his brother, was removed, as usual, as soon as his services became necessary; and thus the supposed author of a libel on the king became the ablest defender of the cause of monarchy, and the author of the " Spanish Friar," the advocate and convert of the Catholic religion.

In his private circumstances Dryden must have been even worse situated than at the close of the

<hr>

[1] In " A Modest Vindication of Antony, Earl of Shaftesbury, in a Letter to a Friend concerning his having been elected King of Poland," Dryden is named poet laureat to the supposed king-elect, and Shadwell his deputy.—See *Dryden's Works*, vol. ix., p. 453.

last Section. His contract with the King's Company was now ended, and long before seems to have produced him little profit. If Southerne's biographer can be trusted, Dryden never made by a single play more than one hundred pounds ; so that, with all his fertility, he could not, at his utmost exertion, make more than two hundred a-year by his theatrical labours.[1] At the same time, they so totally engrossed his leisure, that he produced no other work of consequence after the " *Annus Mirabilis.*" [2] If, therefore, the payment of his pension was withheld, whether from the resentment of the court, or the poverty of the exchequer, he might well complain of the " unsettled state," which doomed him to continue these irksome and ill-paid labours.

[1] " Dryden being very desirous of knowing how much Southerne had made by the profits of one of his plays, the other, conscious of the little success Dryden had met with in theatrical compositions, declined the question, and answered, he was really ashamed to acquaint him. Dryden continuing to be solicitous to be informed, Southerne owned he had cleared by his last play L.700 ; which appeared astonishing to Dryden, who was perhaps ashamed to confess, that he had never been able to acquire, by any of his most successful pieces, more than L.100."—*Life of Southerne* prefixed to his Plays. [For a curious account of the prices obtained for poems and plays in those times, see D'ISRAELI's *Quarrels of Authors,* Appendix to vol. i.]

[2] There was published 1679, a translation of Appian, printed for John Amery at the Peacock, against St Dunstan's Church, Fleet-street. It is inscribed by the translator, J. D., to the Earl of Ossory ; and seems to have been undertaken by his command. This work is usually termed, in catalogues, Dryden's Appian. I presume it may be the work of that Jonathan Dryden, who is mentioned, *ante,* p. 24.

SECTION V.

Dryden engages in Politics—Absalom and Achitophel, Part First—The Medal—Mac-Flecknoe—Absalom and Achitophel, Part Second—The Duke of Guise.

THE controversies in which Dryden had hitherto been engaged, were of a private complexion, arising out of literary disputes and rivalry. But the country was now deeply agitated by political faction; and so powerful an auxiliary was not permitted by his party to remain in a state of inactivity. The religion of the Duke of York rendered him obnoxious to a large proportion of the people, still agitated by the terrors of the Popish Plot. The Duke of Monmouth, handsome, young, brave, and courteous, had all the external requisites for a popular idol; and what he wanted in mental qualities was amply supplied by the Machiavel subtlety of Shaftesbury. The life of Charles was the only isthmus between these contending tides, " which, mounting, viewed each other from afar, and strove in vain to meet." It was already obvious, that the king's death was to be the signal of civil war. His situation was doubly embarrassing, because, in all probability, Monmouth, whose claims were both unjust in themselves, and highly derogatory to the authority of the crown, was personally amiable, and more beloved by Charles than was his inflexible and bigoted brother. But to consent to the bill for excluding the lawful heir from the crown, would have been at the same time putting himself in a state of pupilage for the rest of his reign, and evincing to his subjects, that they had nothing to expect from attachment to his person, or defence of his interest. This was a sacrifice not to be thought of so long as the dreadful recollection of the wars in the preceding reign determined a large party to support the monarch, while he continued willing to accept of their assistance. Charles accordingly adopted a determined course; and, to the rage rather than confusion of his partisans, Monmouth was banished to Holland, from whence he boldly returned without the king's license, and openly assumed the character of the leader of a party. Estranged from court, he made various progresses through the country, and employed every art which the genius of Shaftesbury could suggest, to stimulate the courage, and to increase the number, of his partisans. The press, that awful power, so often and so rashly misused, was not left idle. Numbers of the booksellers were distinguished as Protestant or fanatical publishers; and their shops teemed with the furious declamations of Ferguson, the inflammatory sermons of Hickeringill, the political disquisitions of Hunt, and the party plays and libellous poems of Settle and Shadwell. A host of rhymers, inferior even to those last named, attacked the king, the Duke of York, and the ministry, in songs and libels, which, however paltry, were read, sung, rehearsed, and applauded. It was time that some champion should appear in behalf of the crown, before the public should have been irrecoverably alienated by the incessant and slanderous clamour of its opponents. Dryden's place, talents, and mode of thinking, qualified him for this task. He was the poet laureat and household servant of the king, thus tumultuously assailed. His vein of satire was keen, terse, and powerful, beyond any that has since been displayed. From the time of the Restoration, he had been a favourer of monarchy, perhaps more so, because the opinion divided him from his own family. If he had been for a time neglected, the smiles of a sovereign soon made his coldness forgotten; and if his narrow fortune was not increased, or even rendered stable, he had promises of provision, which inclined him to look to the future with hope, and endure the present with patience. If he had shared in the discontent which for a time severed Mulgrave from the royal party, that cause ceased to operate when his patron was reconciled to the court, and received a share of the spoils of the disgraced Monmouth.[1] If there wanted further impulse to induce Dryden, conscious of his strength, to mingle in an affray where it might be displayed to advantage, he had the stimulus of personal attachment and personal en-

[1] Mulgrave was created lieutenant of Yorkshire and governor of Hull, when Monmouth was deprived of these and other honours.

mity, to sharpen his political animosity. Ormond, Halifax, and Hyde, Earl of Rochester, among the nobles, were his patrons; Lee and Southerne, among the poets, were his friends. These were partisans of royalty. The Duke of York, whom the "Spanish Friar" probably had offended, was conciliated by a prologue on his visiting the theatre at his return from Scotland,[1] and, it is said, by the omission of certain peculiarly offensive passages, as soon as the play was reprinted.[2] The opposite ranks contained Buckingham, author of the "Rehearsal;" Shadwell, with whom our poet now urged open war; and Settle, the insolence of whose rivalry was neither forgotten, nor duly avenged. The respect due to Monmouth was probably the only consideration to be overcome: but his character was to be handled with peculiar lenity; and his duchess, who, rather than himself, had patronised Dryden, was so dissatisfied with his politics, as well as the other irregularities of her husband, that there was no danger of her taking a gentle correction of his ambition as any affront to herself. Thus stimulated by every mo-

---

[1] See Dryden's Works, vol. x., p. 366.

[2] This is objected to Dryden by one of his antagonists: "Nor could ever Shimei be thought to have cursed David more bitterly, than he permits his friend to blaspheme the Roman priesthood in his epilogue to the 'Spanish Friar.' In which play he has himself acted his own part like a true younger son of Noah, as may be easily seen in the first edition of that comedy, which would not pass muster a second time without emendations and corrections."—*The Revolter*, 1687, p. 29.

tive, and withheld by none, Dryden composed, and, on the 17th November, 1681, published, the satire of "Absalom and Achitophel."

The plan of the satire was not new to the public. A catholic poet had, in 1679, paraphrased the scriptural story of Naboth's vineyard, and applied it to the condemnation of Lord Stafford, on account of the Popish Plot.[1] This poem is written in the style of a scriptural allusion; the names and situations of personages in the holy text being applied to those contemporaries, to whom the author assigned a place in his piece. Neither was the obvious application of the story of Absalom and Achitophel to the persons of Monmouth and Shaftesbury first made by our poet. A prose paraphrase, published in 1680, had already been composed upon this allusion.[2] But the vigour of the satire, the happy adaptation, not only of the incidents, but of the very names to the individuals characterised, gave Dryden's poem the full effect of novelty. It appeared a very short time after Shaftesbury had been committed to the Tower, and only a few days before the grand jury were to take under consideration the bill preferred against him for high treason. Its sale was rapid beyond example; and even those who were most severely characterised, were compelled to acknowledge the beauty, if not the justice, of the satire.

---

[1] See Dryden's Works, vol. ix., p. 198.

[2] See Dryden's Works, vol. ix., p. 199. This piece, entitled "Absalom's Conspiracy, or the Tragedy of Treason," is printed on p. 205 of the same volume.

The character of Monmouth, an easy and gentle temper, inflamed beyond its usual pitch by ambition, and seduced by the arts of a wily and interested associate, is touched with exquisite delicacy. The poet is as careful of the offending Absalom's fame, as the father in Scripture of the life of his rebel son.   The fairer side of his character is industriously presented, and a veil drawn over all that was worthy of blame.   But Shaftesbury pays the lenity with which Monmouth is dismissed. The traits of praise, and the tribute paid to that statesman's talents, are so qualified and artfully blended with censure, that they seem to render his faults even more conspicuous, and more hateful. In this skilful mixture of applause and blame lies the nicest art of satire.   There must be an appearance of candour on the part of the poet, and just so much merit allowed, even to the object of his censure, as to make his picture natural.   It is a child alone who fears the aggravated terrors of a Saracen's head ; the painter, who would move the awe of an enlightened spectator, must delineate his tyrant with human features.   It seems likely, that Dryden considered the portrait of Shaftesbury, in the first edition of "Absalom and Achitophel," as somewhat deficient in this respect ; at least the second edition contains twelve additional lines, the principal tendency of which is to praise the ability and integrity with which Shaftesbury had discharged the office of Lord High Chancellor.[1]   It

[1] [" In drawing the character of Achitophel," says Sir Walter, (in *Note*, Dryden's Works, vol. ix., p. 201,) " such a de-

has been reported, that this mitigation was intended to repay a singular exertion of generosity on
Shaftesbury's part, who, while smarting under the
lash of Dryden's satire, and in the short interval
between the first and second edition of the poem,
had the liberality to procure admission for the poet's
son upon the foundation of the Charter-house, of
which he was then governor. But Mr Malone has
fully confuted this tale, and shown, from the records
of the seminary, that Dryden's son Erasmus was

---

gree of justice is rendered to his acute talents, and to his merits
as a judge, that we are gained by the poet's apparent candour
to give him credit for the truth of the portrait in its harsher
features. It is remarkable, that the only considerable additions made to the poem, after the first edition, have a tendency rather to mollify than to sharpen the satire. The following additional passage, in the character of Achitophel,
stands in this predicament:

> " A name to all succeeding ages curst,
>
>   *   *   *   *   *
>
> In friendship false, implacable in hate;
> Resolved to ruin, or to rule the state.
> To compass this the triple bond he broke;
> The pillars of the public safety shook;
> And fitted Israel for a foreign yoke;
> Then, seiz'd with fear, yet still affecting fame,
> Usurp'd a patriot's all-atoning name.
> *So easy still it proves in factious times,*
> *With public zeal to cancel private crimes.*
> *How safe is treason, and how sacred ill,*
> *Where none can sin against the people's will?*
> *Where crowds can wink, and no offence be known,*
> *Since in another's guilt they find their own?*
> *Yet fame deserved no enemy can grudge;*
> *The statesman we abhor, but praie the judge.*
> *In Israel's courts ne'er sat an Abethdin,*
> *With more discerning eyes, or hands more clean,*
> *Unbribed, unsought, the wretched to redress;*
> *Swift of despatch, and easy of access.*"]

admitted upon the recommendation of the king himself.[1] The insertion, therefore, of the lines in commemoration of Shaftesbury's judicial character, was a voluntary effusion on the part of Dryden, and a tribute which he seems to have judged it proper to pay to the merit even of an enemy. Others of the party of Monmouth, or rather of the opposition party, (for it consisted, as is commonly the case, of a variety of factions, agreeing in the single principle of opposition to the government,) were stigmatized with severity, only inferior to that applied to Achitophel.   Among these we distinguish the famous Duke of Buckingham, with whom, under the character of Zimri, our author balanced accounts for his share in the " Rehearsal;"[2]

[1] See Dryden's Works, vol. ix., p. 201.

[" Some of their chiefs were princes of the land :
In the first rank of these did Zimri stand ;
A man so various, that he seem'd to be
Not one, but all mankind's epitome ;
Stiff in opinions, always in the wrong,
Was every thing by starts, and nothing long ;
But, in the course of one revolving moon,
Was chemist, fiddler, statesman, and buffoon ;
Then all for women painting, rhyming, drinking,
Besides ten thousand freaks that died in thinking.
Blest madman, who could every hour employ,
With something new to wish, or to enjoy !
Railing and praising were his usual themes ;
And both, to show his judgment, in extremes ;
So over violent, or over civil,
That every man with him was God or devil.
In squandering wealth was his peculiar art ;
Nothing went unrewarded but desert.
Beggar'd by fools, whom still he found too late ;
He had his jest, and they had his estate.
He laugh'd himself from Court ; then sought relief
By forming parties, but could ne'er be chief ;

Bethel, the Whig sheriff, whose scandalous avarice was only equalled by his factious turbulence; and Titus Oates, the pretended discoverer of the Popish Plot. The account of the Tory chiefs, who retained, in the language of the poem, their friendship for David at the expense of the popular hatred, included, of course, most of Dryden's personal protectors. The aged Duke of Ormond is panegyrized with a beautiful apostrophe to the memory of his son, the gallant Earl of Ossory. The Bishops of London and Rochester; Mulgrave, our author's constant patron, now reconciled with Charles and his government; the plausible and trimming Halifax; and Hyde, Earl of Rochester, second son to the great Clarendon, appear in this list. The poet having thus arrayed and mustered the forces on each side, some account of the combat is naturally expected; and Johnson complains, that, after all the interest excited, the story is but lamely winded up by a speech from the throne, which produces the instantaneous and even marvellous effect, of reconciling all parties, and subduing the whole phalanx of opposition. Even thus, says the critic, the walls, towers, and battlements of an enchanted castle disappear, when the destined knight winds his horn before it. Spence records in his Anecdotes, that Charles himself imposed on Dryden the task of paraphrasing the speech to his Oxford

For, spite of him, the weight of business fell
On Absalom and wise Achitophel;
Thus, wicked but in will, of means bereft,
He left not faction, but of that was left."]

parliament, at least the most striking passages, as a conclusion to his poem of " Absalom and Achitophel."

But let us consider whether the nature of the poem admitted of a different management in the close.   Incident was not to be attempted ; for the poet had described living characters and existing factions, the issue of whose contention was yet in the womb of fate, and could not safely be anticipated in the satire. Besides, the dissolution of the Oxford parliament with that memorable speech, was a remarkable era in the contention of the factions, after which the Whigs gradually declined, both in spirit, in power, and in popularity.   Their boldest leaders were for a time appalled ;[1] and when they resumed their measures, they gradually approached rather revolution than reform, and thus alienated the more temperate of their own party, till at length their schemes terminated in the Rye-house conspiracy.   The speech having such an effect, was therefore not improperly adopted as a termination to the poem of " Absalom and Achitophel."

[1] Lord Grey says in his narrative, " After the dissolution of the Oxford parliament, we were all very peaceably inclined, and nothing passed amongst us that summer of importance, which I can call to mind : I think my Lord Shaftesbury was sent to the Tower just before the long vacation ; and the Duke of Monmouth, Mr Montague, Sir Thomas Armstrong, and myself, went to Tunbridge immediately after his lordship's imprisonment, where we laid aside the thoughts of disturbing the peace of the government for those of diverting ourselves."

The success of this wonderful satire was so great, that the court had again recourse to the assistance of its author. Shaftesbury was now liberated from the Tower; for the grand jury, partly influenced by deficiency of proof, and partly by the principles of the Whig party, out of which the sheriffs had carefully selected them, refused to find the bill of high treason against him. This was a subject of unbounded triumph to his adherents, who celebrated his acquittal by the most public marks of rejoicing. Amongst others, a medal was struck, bearing the head and name of Shaftesbury, and on the reverse, a sun, obscured with a cloud, rising over the Tower and city of London, with the date of the refusal of the bill, (24th November, 1681,) and the motto LÆTAMUR. These medals, which his partisans wore ostentatiously at their bosoms, excited the general indignation of the Tories; and the king himself is said to have suggested it as a theme for the satirical muse of Dryden, and to have rewarded his performance with a hundred broad pieces. To a poet of less fertility, the royal command, to write again upon a character, which, in a former satire, he had drawn with so much precision and felicity, might have been as embarrassing at least as honourable. But Dryden was inexhaustible; and easily discovered, that, though he had given the outline of Shaftesbury in " Absalom and Achitophel," the finished colouring might merit another canvass. About the 16th of March, 1681, he published, anonymously, " The

Medal, a Satire against Sedition," with the apt motto,

> " *Per Graium populos, mediæque per Elidis urbem*
> *Ibat ovans ; Divumque sibi poscebat honores.*" [1]

In this satire, Shaftesbury's history ; his frequent political apostasies ; his licentious course of life, so contrary to the stern rigour of the fanatics, with whom he had associated ; his arts in instigating the fury of the anti-monarchists ; in fine, all the political and moral bearings of his character,—are sounded and exposed to contempt and reprobation, the beauty of the poetry adding grace to the severity of the satire. What impression these vigorous and well-aimed darts made upon Shaftesbury, who was so capable of estimating their sharpness and force, we have no means to ascertain; but long afterwards, his grandson, the author of the "Characteristics," speaks of Dryden and his works with a bitter affectation of contempt, offensive to every reader of judgment, and obviously formed

---

[1] [" It was Charles II. who gave Mr Dryden the hint for writing his poem called the Medal. One day as the king was walking in the Mall, and talking with Dryden, he said, ' If I was a poet, (and I think I am poor enough to be one,) I would write a poem on such a subject in the following manner,' and then gave him the plan for it. Dryden took the hint, carried the poem as soon as it was written to the King, and had a present of a hundred broad pieces for it. (This was said by a priest that I often met with at Mr Pope's, who seemed to confirm it, and added, that King Charles obliged Dryden to put his Oxford speech into verse, and to insert it towards the close of his Absalom and Achitophel.)"—POPE, *Spence's Anecdotes,* (*Malone,*) p. 112.]

on prejudice against the man, rather than dislike
to the poetry.[1] It is said, that he felt more resentment on account of the character of imbecility adjudged to his father in "Absalom and Achitophel,"
than for all the pungent satire, there and in the
"Medal," bestowed upon his grandfather; an ad-

[1] He usually distinguishes Dryden by his "Rehearsal" title
of Bayes; and, among many other oblique expressions of
malevolence, he has this note:—" To see the incorrigibleness
of our poets in their pedantic manner, their vanity, defiance
of criticism, their rhodomontade, and poetical bravado, we
need only turn to our famous poet laureat, (the very Mr
Bayes himself,) in one of his latest and most valued pieces,
writ many years after the ingenious author of the ' Rehearsal' had drawn his picture. ' I have been listening, (says
our poet, in his Preface to ' Don Sebastian,') what objections
had been made against the conduct of the play, but found
them all so trivial, that if I should name them, a true critic
would imagine that I played booty. Some are pleased to say
the writing is dull; but *ætatem habet, de se loquatur.* Others,
that the double poison is unnatural; let the common received
opinion, and Ausonius's famous epigram, answer that. Lastly,
a more ignorant sort of creatures than either of the former
maintain, that the character of Dorax is not only unnatural,
but inconsistent with itself; let them read the play, and think
again. A longer reply is what those cavillers deserve not.
But I will give them and their fellows to understand, that
the Earl of ———— was pleased to read the tragedy twice
over before it was acted, and did me the favour to send me
word, that I had written beyond any of my former plays,
and that he was displeased any thing should be cut away. If
I have not reason to prefer his single judgment to a whole
faction, let the world be judge; for the opposition is the same
with that of Lucan's hero against an army, *concurrere bellum
atque virum.* I think I may modestly conclude,' &c. Thus
he goes on, to the very end, in the self-same strain. Who, after
this, can ever say of the ' Rehearsal' author, that his picture
of our poet was overcharged, or the national humour wrong
described?"

ditional proof, how much more easy it is to bear
those reflections which render ourselves or our
friends hateful, than those by which they are only
made ridiculous and contemptible.[1]

The Whig poets, for many assumed that title,
did not behold these attacks upon their leader and
party with patience or forbearance; but they rushed
to the combat with more zeal, or rather fury, than
talent or policy. Their efforts are numbered and
described elsewhere;[2] so that we need here only
slightly notice those which Dryden thought worthy
of his own animadversion. Most of them adopted
the clumsy and obvious expedient of writing their
answers in the style of the successful satire which
had provoked them. Thus, in reply to "Absalom
and Achitophel," Pordage and Settle imitated the
plan of bestowing scriptural names on their poem
and characters; the former entitling his piece,
"Azaria and Hushai," the latter, "Absalom Senior,
or Absalom and Achitophel transprosed." But
these attempts to hurl back the satire at him, by
whom it was first launched, succeeded but indifferently, and might have convinced the authors,
that the charm of "Absalom and Achitophel" lay

[1] [" Great wits are sure to madness near allied,
And thin partitions do their bounds divide;
Else, why should he, with wealth and honour blest,
Refuse his age the needful hours of rest;
Punish a body which he could not please;
Bankrupt of life, yet prodigal of ease?
And all to leave what with his toil he won
To that unfeather'd two-legg'd thing, a son;
Got, while his soul did huddled notions try;
And born a shapeless lump, like anarchy."]

[2] See Dryden's Works, vol. ix., pp. 372 *et seq.;* also p. 415.

not in the plan, but in the power of execution. It
was easy to give Jewish titles to their heroes, but
the difficulty lay in drawing their characters with
the force and precision of their prototype. Buckingham himself was rash enough to engage in this
conflict; but, whether his anger blunted his wit,
or that his share in the " Rehearsal " was less even
than what is generally supposed, he loses, by his
" Reflections on Absalom and Achitophel," the
credit we are disposed to allow him for talent on
the score of that lively piece.[1] A non-conformist
clergyman published two pieces, which I have
never seen, one entitled, " A Whip for the Fool's
Back, who styles honourable Marriage a cursed
confinement, in his profane Poem of Absalom and
Achitophel;" the other, " A Key, with the Whip,
to open the Mystery and Iniquity of the Poem
called Absalom and Achitophel." Little was to
be hoped or feared from poems bearing such absurd titles: I throw, however, into the note, the
specimen which Mr Malone has given of their contents.[2] The reverend gentleman having announced,

[1] See some extracts from these " Reflections," in Dryden's
Works, vol. ix., p. 272.

[2]   " How well this Hebrew name with sense doth sound,
    A fool's my brother,[3] though in wit profound!
    Most wicked wits are the devil's chiefest tools,
    Which, ever in the issue, God befools.
    Can thy compare, vile varlet, once hold true,
    Of the loyal lord, and this disloyal Jew?
    Was e'er our English earl under disgrace,
    And, as unconscionable, put out of place?

[3] *Achi*, my brother, and *tophel*, a fool.—*Orig. Note.*

that Achitophel, in Hebrew, means " the brother of a fool," Dryden retorted with infinite coolness, that in that case the author of the discovery might pass with his readers for next a-kin, and that it was probably the relation which made the kindness.

" The Medal" was answered by the same authors who replied to " Absalom and Achitophel," as if the Whigs had taken in sober earnest the advice which Dryden bestowed on them in the preface to that satire.   And moreover (as he there expressly recommends) they railed at him abundantly, without a glimmering of wit to enliven their scurrility. Hickeringill, a crazy fanatic, began the attack with a sort of mad poem, called the " The Mushroom." It was written and sent to press the very day on which " The Medal" appeared; a circumstance on which the author valued himself so highly, as to ascribe it to divine inspiration.[1]   With more labour, and equal issue, Samuel Pordage, a minor poet of the day, produced " The Medal Reversed ;" for which, and his former aggression, Dryden brands

----

> Hath he laid lurking in his country-house
> To plot rebellions, as one factious?
> Thy bog-trot bloodhounds hunted have this stag,
> Yet cannot fasten their foul fangs,—they flag.
> Why didst not *thou* bring in thy evidence
> With them, to rectify the brave jury's sense,
> And so prevent the *ignoramus?*—nay,
> Thou wast cock-sure he would be damn'd for aye,
> Without thy presence,—thou wast then employ'd
> To brand him 'gainst he came to be destroy'd:
> 'Forehand preparing for the hangman's axe,
> Had not the witnesses been found so lax."

[1] Dryden's Works, vol. ix., p. 452.

him, in a single line of the Second Part of " Absalom and Achitophel," as

" Lame Mephibosheth, the wizard's [1] son."

There also appeared " The Loyal Medal Vindicated," and a piece entitled " Dryden's Satire to
his Muse," imputed to Lord Somers, but which, in
conversation with Pope, he positively disavowed.
All these, and many other pieces, the fruits of
incensed and almost frantic party-fury, are marked
by the most coarse and virulent abuse. The events
in our author's life were few, and his morals, gene-

---

[1] He was the son of Dr John Pordage, minister of Bradfield,
expelled his charge for insufficiency in the year 1646. Among
other charges against him were the following, which, extraordinary as they are, he does not seem to have denied :

" That he hath very frequent and familiar converse with
angels.

" That a great dragon came into his chamber with a tail of
eight yards long, four great teeth, and did spit fire at him ;
and that he contended with the dragon.

" That his own angel came and stood by him while he was
expostulating with the dragon ; and the angel came in his
own shape and fashion, the same clothes, bands, and cuffs, the
same bandstrings ; and that his angel stood by him and upheld him.

" That Mrs Pordage and Mrs Flavel had their angels
standing by them also, Mrs Pordage singing sweetly, and
keeping time upon her breast ; and that his children saw the
spirits coming into the house, and said, Look there, father ;
and that the spirits did after come into the chamber, and
drew the curtains when they were in bed.

" That the said Mr Pordage confessed, that a strong enchantment was upon him, and that the devil did appear to
him in the shape of Everard, and in the shape of a fiery dragon ; and the whole roof of the house was full of spirits."—
State Trials.

rally speaking, irreproachable; so that the topics
for the malevolence of his antagonists were both
scanty and strained. But they ceased not, with
the true pertinacity of angry dulness, to repeat, in
prose and verse, in couplet, ballad, and madrigal,
the same unvaried accusations, amounting in sub-
stance to the following :—That Dryden had been
bred a puritan and republican; that he had written
a Eulogy on Cromwell (which one wily adversary
actually reprinted); that he had been in poverty at
the Restoration; that Lady Elizabeth Dryden's
character was tarnished by the circumstances attending their nuptials; that Dryden had written
the " Essay on Satire," in which the king was
libelled; that he had been beaten by three men
in Rose-alley; finally, that he was a Tory and
a tool of arbitrary power. This cuckoo song,
garnished with the burden of *Bayes* and *Poet
Squab,*[1] was rung in the ear of the public again
and again, and with an obstinacy which may convince us how little there was to be said, when that
little was so often repeated. Feeble as these
attacks were, their number, like that of the gnats
described by Spenser,[2] seems to have irritated

[1] How little Dryden valued these nicknames appears from
a passage in the " Vindication of the Duke of Guise: "—
" Much less am I concerned at the noble name of Bayes; that
is a brat so like his own father, that he cannot be mistaken
for any body else. They might as reasonably have called
Tom Sternhold Virgil, and the resemblance would have held
as well."—Dryden's Works, vol. vii., p. 165.

[2] " As when a swarm of gnats at even tide
   Out of the fennes of Allan doe arise,

Dryden to exert the power of his satire, and like the blast of the northern wind, to sweep away at once these clamorous and busy, though ineffectual assailants. Two, in particular, claimed distinction from the nameless crowd; Settle, Dryden's ancient foe, and Shadwell, who had been originally a dubious friend.

Of Dryden's controversy with Settle we have already spoken fully; but we may here add, that, in addition to former offences of a public and private nature, Elkanah, in the prologue to the " Empress of Morocco," acted in March, 1681-2, had treated Dryden with great irreverence.[1] Shadwell had been for some time in good habits with Dryden; yet an early difference of taste and practice in comedy, not only existed between them, but was the subject of reciprocal debate, and something approaching to rivalry. Dryden, as we have seen, had avowed his preference of lively dialogue in

Their murmuring small trompetts sownde winde,
Whiles in the aire their clustring army flies,
That as a cloud doth seeme to dim the skies;
No man nor beast may rest or take repast
For their sharpe wounds and noyous injuries,
Till the fierce northern wind with blustring blast
Doth blow them quite away, and in the ocean cast."

[1] " How finely would the sparks be caught to-day,
Should a Whig poet write a Tory play,
And you, possessed with rage before, should send
Your random shot abroad and maul a friend !
For you, we find, too often hiss and clap,
Just as you live, speak, think, and fight—by hap.
And poets, we all know, can change, like you,
And are alone to their own interest true ;
Can write against all sense, nay even their own :
The vehicle called *pension* makes it down.
No fear of cudgels, where there's hope of bread ;
A well-filled paunch forgets a *broken head*."

comedy to delineation of character ; or, in other
words, of wit and repartee to what was then called
humour.   On this subject Shadwell early differed
from the laureat. Conscious of considerable powers
in observing nature, while he was deficient in that
liveliness of fancy which is necessary to produce
vivacity of dialogue, Shadwell affected, or perhaps
entertained, a profound veneration for the memory
of Ben Jonson, and proposed him as his model in
the representation of such characters as were to
be marked by *humour*, or an affectation of singu-
larity of manners, speech, and behaviour. Dryden,
on the other hand, was no great admirer either of
Jonson's plays in general, or of the low and coarse
characters of vice and folly, in describing which
lay his chief excellency ; and this opinion he had
publicly intimated in the " Essay of Dramatic
Poesy."   In the preface to the very first of Shadwell's plays, printed in 1668, he takes occasion
bitterly, and with a direct application to Dryden,
to assail the grounds of this criticism, and the
comedies of the author who had made it.[1]   If this

[1] I quote the passage at length, as evincing the difference
between Dryden's taste in comedy and that of Shadwell :
" I have endeavoured to represent variety of humours (most
of the persons of the play differing in their characters from
one another), which was the practice of Ben Jonson, whom I
think all dramatick poets ought to imitate, though none are
like to come near ; he being the onely person that appears to me
to have made perfect representation of human life : most other
authors that I ever read, either have wild romantick tales,
wherein they strain love and honour to that ridiculous height,
that it becomes burlesque ; or in their lower comedies content
themselves with one or two humours at most, and those not

petulance produced any animosity, it was not lasting ; for, in the course of their controversy, Dryden
appeals to Shadwell, whether he had not rather

---

near so perfect characters as the admirable Jonson always
made, who never wrote comedy without seven or eight considerable humours.   I never saw one, except that of Falstaffe,
that was, in my judgment, comparable to any of Jonson's considerable humours.   You will pardon this digression when I
tell you, he is the man, of all the world, I most passionately
admire for his excellency in dramatick poetry.

" Though I have known *some of late so insolent to say*, that
Ben Jonson wrote his best playes without wit, imagining, that
all the wit playes consisted in bringing two persons upon the
stage to break jest, and to bob one another, which they call
repartie, not considering, that there is more wit and invention
required in the finding out good humour and matter proper
for it, then in all their smart reparties : for, in the writing
of a humour, a man is confined not to swerve from the character, and obliged to say nothing but what is proper to it ;
but in the playes which have been wrote of late, there is no
such thing as perfect character, but the two chief persons are
most commonly a swearing, drinking, whoring ruffian for a
lover, and impudent, ill-bred tomrig for a mistress, and these
are the fine people of the play ; and there is that latitude in
this, that almost any thing is proper for them to say ; but
their chief subject is bawdy, and profaneness, which they call
brisk writing, when the most dissolute of men, that rellish
those things well enough in private, are choked at 'em in pub-
lick ; and, methinks, if there were nothing but the ill manners
of it, it should make poets avoid that indecent way of writing."—*Preface to the Sullen Lovers.*

Lest this provocation should be insufficient, the Prologue of
the same piece has a fling at heroic plays.   The poet says he
has

> " No kind romantic lover in his play
> To sigh and whine out passion, as they may
> Charm waiting-women with heroic chime,
> And still resolve to live and die in rhyme ;
> Such as your ears with love and honour feast,
> And play at crambo for three hours at least ;

countenanced than impeded his first rise in public
favour; and, in 1674, they made common cause
with Crowne to write those remarks, which were
to demolish Settle's " Empress of Morocco." Even
in 1676, while Shadwell expresses the same dissent
from Dryden's opinion concerning the merit of
Jonson's comedy, it is in very respectful terms, and
with great deference to his respected and admired
friend, of whom, though he will not say his is the
best way of writing, he maintains his manner of
writing it is most excellent.[1] But the irreconcilable difference in their taste soon after broke
out in less seemly terms; for Shadwell permitted
himself to use some very irreverent expressions
towards Dryden's play of " Aureng-Zebe," in the
prologue and epilogue to his comedy of the " Vir-
tuoso;" and in the preface to the same piece he
plainly intimated, that he wanted nothing but a
pension to enable him to write as well as the poet
laureat.[2] This attack was the more intolerable,
as Dryden, in the Preface to that very play of
" Aureng-Zebe," probably meant to include Shadwell among those contemporaries who, even in his
own judgment, excelled him in comedy. In 1678,
Dryden accommodated with a prologue Shadwell's

That fight and woo in verse in the same breath,
And make similitude and love in death."

Whatever symptoms of reconciliation afterwards took place
between the poets, I greatly doubt if this first offence was
ever cordially forgiven.

[1] Dryden's Works, vol. vii., p. 141.
[2] See these offensive passages, Dryden's Works, vol. x., p.
427.

play of the " True Widow ;" but to write these occasional pieces was part of his profession, and the circumstance does not prove that the breach between these rivals for public applause was ever thoroughly healed; on the contrary, it seems likely, that, in the case of Shadwell, as in that of Settle, political hatred only gangrened a wound inflicted by literary rivalry. After their quarrel became desperate, Dryden resumed his prologue, and adapted it to a play by Afra Behn, called the " Widow Ranter, or Bacon in Virginia." [1] Whatever was the progress of the dispute, it is certain that Shadwell, as zealously attached to the Whig faction as Dryden to the Tories, buckled on his armour among their other poetasters to encounter the champion of royalty. His answer to " The Medal " is entitled " The Medal of John Bayes:" it appeared in autumn 1681, and is distinguished by scurrility, even among the scurrilous lampoons of Settle, Care, and Pordage. " Those," he coolly says, " who know Dryden, know there is not an untrue word spoke of him in the poem ;" although he is there charged with the most gross and infamous crimes. Shadwell also seems to have had a share in a lampoon, entitled " The Tory Poets," in which both Dryden and Otway were grossly reviled. [2]   On both occasions, his satire was as

[1] Dryden's Works, vol. x., p. 343.

[2] " The laurel makes a wit ; a brave, the sword;
And all are wise men at a Council-board :
Settle's a coward, 'cause fool Otway fought him,
And Mulgrave is a wit, because I taught him."
The Tory Poets, 4to, 1682.

clumsy as his overgrown person, and as brutally coarse as his conversation : for Shadwell resembled Ben Jonson in his vulgar and intemperate pleasures, as well as in his style of comedy and corpulence of body.[1] Dryden seems to have thought, that such reiterated attacks, from a contemporary of some eminence, whom he had once called friend, merited a more severe castigation than could be administered in a general satire. He therefore

[1] Jonson is described as wearing a loose coachman's coat, frequenting the Mermaid tavern, where he drunk seas of Canary, then reeling home to bed, and, after a profuse perspiration, arising to his dramatic studies. Shadwell appears, from the slight traits which remain concerning him, to have followed, as closely as possible, the same course of pleasure and of study. He was brutal in his conversation, and much addicted to the use of opium, to which, indeed, he is said finally to have fallen a victim.

I observe, the ingenious editor of the late excellent edition of Jonson's Works, expresses some indignation at the charge brought against that eminent author in this note, and denies the authority of the letter-writer, who characterises Jonson as indulging in vulgar excess. Few men have more sincere admiration for Jonson's talents than the present writer. But surely that coarseness of taste, which tainted his powerful mind, is proved from his writings. Many authors of that age are indecent, but Jonson is filthy and gross in his pleasantry, and indulges himself in using the language of scavengers and night-men. His Bartholomew-fair furnishes many examples of this unhappy predilection, and his " Famous Voyage" seems to have disgusted even the zeal of his editor. But, in marking these faults, I was far from meaning to assail the well-earned reputation of " Rare Ben Jonson," who could well afford to be guilty of these sins against decorum, while his writings afford so strong and masculine a support to the cause of virtue and religion. [Sir Walter Scott argues this question with Mr Gifford more at length in his Essay on Hawthornden, in the " Provincial Antiquities."]

composed " Mac-Flecknoe, or a Satire on the True Blue Protestant Poet, T. S., by the author of Absalom and Achitophel," which was published 4th October, 1682. Richard Flecknoe, from whom the piece takes its title, was so distinguished as a wretched poet, that his name had become almost proverbial. Shadwell is represented as the adopted son of this venerable monarch, who so long

> " In prose and verse was own'd without dispute,
> Through all the realms of Nonsense absolute."

The solemn inauguration of Shadwell as his successor in this drowsy kingdom, forms the plan of the poem ; being the same which Pope afterwards adopted on a broader canvass for his " Dunciad." The vices and follies of Shadwell are not concealed, while the awkwardness of his pretensions to poetical fame are held up to the keenest ridicule. In an evil hour, leaving the composition of low comedy, in which he held an honourable station, he adventured upon the composition of operas and pastorals. On these the satirist falls without mercy ; and ridicules, at the same time, his pretensions to copy Ben Jonson :—

> " Nor let false friends seduce thy mind to fame,
> By arrogating Jonson's hostile name ;
> Let father Flecknoe fire thy mind with praise,
> And uncle Ogleby thy envy raise.
> Thou art my blood, where Jonson has no part :
> What share have we in nature or in art ?
> Where did his wit on learning fix a brand,
> And rail at arts he did not understand ?
> Where made he love in ' Prince Nicander's ' vein,
> Or swept the dust in ' Psyche's ' humble strain ? "

This unmerciful satire was sold off in a very short time ; and it seems uncertain whether it was again published until 1684, when it appeared with the author's name in Tonson's first Miscellany. It would seem that Dryden did not at first avow it, though, as the titlepage assigned it to the author of " Absalom and Achitophel," we cannot believe Shadwell's assertion, that he had denied it with oaths and imprecations. Dryden, however, omits this satire in the printed list of his plays and poems, along with the Eulogy on Cromwell. But he was so far from disowning it, that in his " Essay on Satire," he quotes " Mac-Flecknoe " as an instance given by himself of the Varronian satire. Poor Shadwell was extremely disturbed by this attack upon him ; the more so, as he seems hardly to have understood its tendency.   He seriously complains, that he is represented by Dryden as an Irishman, " when he knows that I never saw Ireland till I was three-and-twenty years old, and was there but for four months." He had understood Dryden's parable literally ; so true it is, that " a knavish speech sleeps in a foolish ear."

" Mac-Flecknoe," though so cruelly severe, was not the only notice which Shadwell received of Dryden's displeasure at his person and politics. " Absalom and Achitophel," and " The Medal," having been so successful, a second part to the first poem was resolved on, for the purpose of sketching the minor characters of the contending factions. Dryden probably conceiving that he had already done his part, only revised this additional book, and contributed about two hundred lines. The body of the poem was written by Nahum Tate, one of those second-rate bards, who, by dint of pleonasm and expletive, can find smooth lines if any one will supply them with ideas. The Second Part of " Absalom and Achitophel" is, however, much beyond his usual pitch, and exhibits considerable marks of a careful revision by Dryden, especially in the satirical passages; for the eulogy on the Tory chiefs is in the flat and feeble strain of Tate himself, as is obvious when it is compared with the description of the Green-Dragon Club, the character of Corah, and other passages exhibiting marks of Dryden's hand.

But if the Second Part of " Absalom and Achitophel" fell below the First in its general tone, the celebrated passage inserted by Dryden possessed even a double portion of the original spirit.   The victims whom he selected out of the partisans of Monmouth and Shaftesbury for his own particular severity, were Robert Ferguson, afterwards well known by the name of the Plotter; Forbes; Johnson, author of the parallel between James, Duke of York, and Julian the Apostate; but, above all, Settle and Shadwell,[1] whom, under the names of Doeg and Og, he has depicted in the liveliest colours his poignant satire could afford.

[1] [" Three of the characters in Tate's second part of Absalom and Achitophel are of Dryden's writing, and are all excellently well writ; that of Julian Johnson, under the name of Ben; Tochannan Shadwell, under the name of Og; and Settle, under that of Doeg."—LOCKIER—*Spence's Anecdotes,* (*Malone,*) p. 111.]

They who have patience to look into the lampoons which these worthies had published against Dryden, will, in reading his retort, be reminded of the combats between the giants and knights of romance. His antagonists came on with infinite zeal and fury, discharged their ill-aimed blows on every side, and exhausted their strength in violent and ineffectual rage. But the keen and trenchant blade of Dryden never makes a thrust in vain, and never strikes but at a vulnerable point. This we have elsewhere remarked is a peculiar attribute of his satire ;[1] and it is difficult for one assailed on a single ludicrous foible, to make good his respectability, though possessed of a thousand valuable qualities ; as it

[1] [" It is no inconsiderable part of the merit of ' Mac-Flecknoe,' that it led the way to the ' Dunciad ;' yet, while we acknowledge the more copious and variegated flow of Pope's satire, we must not forget, that, independent of the merit of originality, always inestimable, Dryden's poem claims that of a close, and more compact fable, of a single and undisturbed aim. Pope's ridicule and sarcasm is scattered so wide, and among such a number of authors, that it resembles small shot discharged at random among a crowd ; while that of Dryden, like a single well-directed bullet, prostrates the individual object against whom it was directed. Besides, the reader is apt to sympathize with the degree of the satirist's provocation, which in Dryden's case cannot be disputed ; whereas Pope sometimes confounds those, from whom he had received gross incivility, with others who had given him no offence, and with some whose characters were above his accusation. To posterity, the ' Mac-Flecknoe' possesses a decided superiority over the ' Dunciad,' for a very few facts make us master of the argument ; while that of the latter poem, excepting the Sixth Book, where the satire is more general, requires a note at every tenth line to render it even intelligible."—*Notes, Dryden's Works,* vol. x., p. 430.]

patron Shaftesbury was gradually becoming weaker,
fairly abandoned him to his fate, and read a solemn
recantation of his political errors in a narrative
published in 1683.   The truth seems to be, that
honest Doeg was poet laureat to the city, and
earned some emolument by composing verses for
pageants and other occasions of civic festivity; so
that when the Tory interest resumed its ascendency
among the magistrates, he had probably no alterna-
tive but to relinquish his principles or his post, and
Elkanah, like many greater men, held the former
the easier sacrifice.   Like all converts, he became
outrageous in his new faith, wrote a libel on Lord
Russell a few days after his execution; indited a
panegyric on Judge Jefferies; and, being *tam
Marte quam Mercurio*, actually joined as a trooper
the army which King James encamped upon
Hounslow Heath.   After the Revolution, he is
enumerated, with our author and Tate, among
those poets whose strains had been stifled by that
great event.[1]   He continued, however, to be the

termed to-day by the same persons, a Cowley, a man of
honour, an hero, and a zealous upholder of the Protestant
cause and interest."

[1] In the " Deliverance," an address to the Prince of Orange,
published about 9th February, 1689:

" Alas! the famous Settle, Durfey, Tate,
That early propp'd the deep intrigues of state,
Dull Whiggish lines the world could ne'er applaud,
While your swift genius did appear abroad:
And thou, great Bayes, whose yet unconquer'd pen
Wrote with strange force as well of beasts as men,
Whose noble genius grieved from afar,
Because new worlds for Bayes did not appear,
Now to contend with the ambitious elf,
Begins a civil war against himself," &c.

city-laureat;[1] but, in despite of that provision, was reduced by want to write plays, like Ben Jonson's Littlewit, for the profane *motions*, or puppet-shows, of Smithfield and Bartholomew fairs. Nay, having proceeded thus far in exhibiting the truth of Dryden's prediction, he actually mounted the stage in person among these wooden performers, and combated St George for England in a green dragon of his own proper device. Settle was admitted into the Charter-House in his old age, and died there in 1723. The lines of Pope on poor Elkanah's fate are familiar to every poetical reader :

" In Lud's old walls though long I ruled, renown'd
Far as loud Bow's stupendous bells resound ;
Though my own aldermen conferr'd the bays,
To me committing their eternal praise,
Their full-fed heroes, their pacific mayors,
Their annual trophies, and their monthly wars ;
Though long my party built on me their hopes,
For writing pamphlets, and for roasting popes ;
Yet lo ! in me what authors have to brag on !
Reduced at last to hiss in my own dragon.
Avert it, heaven ! that thou, or Cibber, e'er
Should wag a serpent-tail in Smithfield fair !
Like the vile straw that's blown about the streets,
The needy poet sticks to all he meets ;
Coach'd, carted, trod upon, now loose, now fast,
And carried off in some dog's tail at last." [2]

[1] In 1702, probably in the capacity of civic-laureat, he wrote " *Carmen Irenicum,*" upon the union of the two East India companies ; and long afterward, in 1717, he is mentioned by Dennis as still the city poet.

[2] [The curious reader is referred, for various particulars about Settle, to Nichol's Literary Anecdotes of the 18th Century, vol. i., p. 41, &c. He was entered of Trinity College, Oxon, in 1665, but left the University without a degree ; and having, according to Gildon, profligately squandered a fair fortune, betook himself to poetry, as

As Dryden was probably more apprehensive of
Shadwell, who, though a worse poet than Settle,

---

the means of gaining bread. We owe to Mr D'Israeli, the detection
of Pope as the writer, when only in his 14th year, of a satire upon
Settle, included in the first edition of Lintot's Miscellaneous Poems.
It is entitled " To the author of the Successio," and begins,

> " Begone, ye critics, and restrain your spite,
> *Codrus* writes on, and will for ever write :
> The heaviest muse the swiftest course has gone,
> As clocks run fastest when the lead is on," &c.

Mr D'Israeli says : " The juvenile composition bears the marks of
Pope's future excellences ; it has the tune of his verse, and the
images of his wit. Thirty years afterwards, when occupied by the
DUNCIAD, he transplanted and pruned again some of the original
images.

" The hero of this satire is ELKANAH SETTLE. The subject is one of
those Whig Poems, designed to celebrate the happiness of an uninterrupted ' Succession ' in the Crown, at the time the Act of Settle-
ment passed, which transferred it to the Hanoverian line. The rhimer
and his theme, were equally contemptible to the juvenile Jacobite
poet.

" The hoarse and voluminous Codrus of Juvenal aptly designates
this eternal verse-maker,—one who has written with such constant
copiousness, that no bibliographer has presumed to form a complete
list of his works.

" When Settle had outlived his temporary rivalship with Dryden,
and was reduced to mere Settle, he published party-poems, in folio,
composed in Latin, accompanied by his own translations. These folio
poems, uniformly bound, except that the arms of his patrons, or rather
his purchasers, richly gilt, emblazon the black morocco, may still be
found. These presentation copies were sent round to the chiefs of
the party, with a mendicant's petition, of which some still exist. To
have a clear conception of the *present views* of some politicians, it is
necessary to read their history backwards. In 1702, when Settle published " Successio," he must have been a Whig. In 1685 he was a
Tory, commemorating, by an heroic poem, the coronation of James II.,
and writing periodically against the Whigs. In 1680, he had left the
Tories for the Whigs, and conducted the whole management of burning the Pope, then a very solemn national ceremony.

" Settle, in his latter state of wretchedness, had one standard *elegy*
and *epithalamium* printed off with blanks. By the ingenious contrivance of inserting the name of any considerable person who died, or
was married, no one who had gone out of the world, or was entering
into it, but was equally welcome, to this dinnerless liveryman of the
draggle-tailed Muses. I have elsewhere noticed his last exit from
this state of poetry and of pauperism ; when, leaping into a green dra-

has excelled even Dryden in the lower walks of comedy, he has treated him with sterner severity. His person, his morals, his manners, and his politics, all that had escaped or been but slightly touched upon in " Mac-Flecknoe," are bitterly reviewed in the character of Og ; and there probably never existed another poet, who, at the distance of a month, which intervened between the publication of the two poems, could resume an exhausted theme with an energy which gave it all the charms of novelty.   Shadwell did not remain silent beneath the lash ; but his clamorous exclamations only tended to make his castigation more ludicrous.[1]

The Second Part of " Absalom and Achitophel " was followed by the " *Religio Laici*," a poem which Dryden published in the same month of November 1682.   Its tendency, although of a political nature, is so different from that of the satires, that it will be most properly considered when we can place it in contrast to the " Hind and Panther." It was addressed to Henry Dickinson, a young gentleman, who had just published a translation of Simon's " Critical History of the New Testament."

As the publication of the two Parts of " Absalom and Achitophel," " The Medal," and " Mac-

gon, which his own creative genius had invented, in a theatrica. booth, Codrus, in hissing flames, and terrifying morocco folds, disco-vered the fate of talents misapplied."—*Quarrels of Authors*, vol. i. , p. 298.]

[1] He published a translation of the tenth satire of Juvenal, in the preface to which he rails plentifully against Dryden.

Flecknoe," all of a similar tone, and rapidly succeeding each other, gave to Dryden, hitherto chiefly
known as a dramatist, the formidable character of
an inimitable satirist, we may here pause to consider
their effect upon English poetry. The witty Bishop
Hall had first introduced into our literature that
species of poetry; which, though its legitimate use
be to check vice and expose folly, is so often applied
by spleen or by faction to destroy domestic happiness, by assailing private character. Hall possessed
a good ear for harmony; and, living in the reign of
Elizabeth, might have studied it in Spenser, Fairfax, and other models. But from system, rather
than ignorance or inability, he chose to be " hard
of conceit, and harsh of style," in order that his
poetry might correspond with the sharp, sour, and
crabbed nature of his theme.[1] Donne, his successor,
was still more rugged in his versification, as well
as more obscure in his conceptions and allusions.
The satires of Cleveland (as we have indeed formerly noticed) are, if possible, still harsher and
more strained in expression than those of Donne.
Butler can hardly be quoted as an example of the
sort of satire we are treating of. " Hudibras " is
a burlesque tale, in which the measure is inten-

---

[1] I infer, that the want of harmony was intentional, from
these expressions: " It is not for every one to relish a true
and natural satire; being of itself, besides the nature and in-
bred bitterness and tartness of particulars, both hard of conceit and harsh of style, and therefore cannot but be unpleasing
both to the unskilful and over-musical ear; the one being
affected with only a shallow and easy, the other with a smooth
and current, disposition."—*Postscript to* HALL's *Satires.*

tionally and studiously rendered as ludicrous as the characters and incidents. Oldham, who flourished in Dryden's time, and enjoyed his friendship, wrote his satires in the crabbed tone of Cleveland and Donne. Dryden, in the copy of verses dedicated to his memory, alludes to this deficiency, and seems to admit the subject as an apology :—

> " O early ripe ! to thy abundant store
> What could advancing age have added more!
> It might (what nature never gives the young)
> Have taught the numbers of thy native tongue.
> But satire needs not those, and wit will shine
> Through the harsh cadence of a rugged line."

Yet the apology which he admitted for Oldham, Dryden disdained to make use of himself. He did not, as has been said of Horace, wilfully untune his harp when he commenced satirist. Aware that a wound may be given more deeply with a burnished than with a rusty blade, he bestowed upon the versification of his satires the same pains which he had given to his rhyming plays and serious poems. He did not, indeed, for that would have been pains misapplied, attempt to smooth his verses into the harmony of those in which he occasionally celebrates female beauty; but he gave them varied tone, correct rhyme, and masculine energy, all which had hitherto been strangers to the English satire. Thus, while Dryden's style resembled that of Juvenal rather than Horace, he may claim a superiority, for uniform and undeviating dignity, over the Roman satirist. The age, whose appetite

the prologues and epilogues, which then served as a sort of moral to the plays, the veil, thin as it was, was completely raised, and the political analogies pointed out to such of the audience as might otherwise have been too dull to apprehend them. In this sharp though petty war, Dryden bore a considerable share. His necessities obliged him, among other modes of increasing his income, to accept of a small pecuniary tribute for furnishing prologues on remarkable occasions, or for new plays; and his principles determined their tendency.[1] But this was not all the support which his party expected, and which he afforded them on the theatre, even while labouring in their service in a different department.

When Dryden had but just finished his "*Religio Laici*," Lee, who had assisted in the play of " Œdipus," claimed Dryden's promise to requite the obligation. It has been already noticed, that Dryden had, in the year succeeding the Restoration, designed a play on the subject of the Duke of Guise; and he has informed us he had preserved one or two of the scenes. These, therefore, were revised, and inserted in the new play, of which Dryden wrote the first scene, the whole fourth act, and great part of the fifth. Lee composed the rest of the " Duke of Guise." The general

express command, imitated from the Spanish, the furious Tory is ridiculed in the character of Hothead, as well as the fanatical Whig under that of Testimony.

[1] See the Prologues and Epilogues in Dryden's Works, vol. x.; particularly those on pages 352, 358, 366, 368, 370.

parallel between the League in France and the Covenant in England, was too obvious to escape early notice; but the return of Monmouth to England, against the king's express command, in order to head the opposition, perhaps the insurrection, of London, presented a still closer analogy to the entry of the Duke of Guise into Paris, under similar circumstances, on the famous day of the barricades. Of this remarkable incident, the united authors of the " Duke of Guise" naturally availed themselves; though with such precaution, that almost the very expressions of the scene are taken from the prose of Davilla. Yet the plot, though capable of an application so favourable for the royal party, contained circumstances of offence to it. If the parallel between Guise and Monmouth was on the one hand felicitous, as pointing out the nature of the duke's designs, the moral was revolting, as seeming to recommend the assassination of Charles's favourite son. The king also loved Monmouth to the very last; and was slow and reluctant in permitting his character to be placed in a criminal or odious point of view.[1] The play, therefore, though ready for exhibition before midsummer, 1682, remained in the hands of Arlington, the lord chamberlain, for two months, without being licensed for representation. But during that time

[1] The concealed partiality of Charles towards Monmouth survived even the discovery of the Rye-House plot. He could not dissemble his satisfaction upon seeing him after his surrender, and pressed his hand affectionately.—See Monmouth's Diary in *Wellwood's Memorials*, p. 322.

the scene darkened. The king had so far suppressed his tenderness for Monmouth, as to authorize
his arrest at Stafford; and the influence of the
Duke of York at court became daily more predominant. Among other evident tokens that no
measures were henceforward to be kept between
the king and Monmouth, the representation of the
" Duke of Guise" was at length authorized.

The two companies of players, after a long and
expensive warfare, had now united their forces;
on which occasion Dryden furnished them with
a prologue, full of violent Tory principles. By
this united company " The Duke of Guise " was
performed on the 30th December, 1682. It was
printed, with a dedication to Hyde, Earl of Rochester, subscribed by both authors, but evidently the
work of Dryden. It is written in a tone of defiance
to the Whig authors, who had assailed the dedica-
tors, it alleges, " like footpads in the dark," though
their blows had done little harm, and the objects of
their malice yet lived to vindicate their loyalty in
open day. The play itself has as determined a
political character as the dedication. Besides the
general parallel between the leaguers and the fanatical sectaries, and the more delicate, though not
less striking connexion between the story of Guise
and of Monmouth, there are other collateral allusions in the piece to the history of that unfortunate
nobleman, and to the state of parties. The whole
character of Marmoutiere, high-spirited, loyal, and
exerting all her influence to deter Guise from the
prosecution of his dangerous schemes, corresponds

to that of Anne, Duchess of Monmouth.[1] The
love too which the king professes to Marmoutiere,
and which excites the jealousy of Guise, may bear
a remote and delicate allusion to that partiality
which the Duke of York is said to have entertained
for the wife of his nephew.[2] The amiable colours
in which Marmoutiere is painted, were due to the

---

[1] Carte, in his "Life of the Duke of Ormond," says, that
Monmouth's resolutions varied from submission to resistance
against the king, according to his residence with the Duchess
at Moor-park, who schooled him to the former course, or with
his associates and partisans in the city, who instigated him to
more desperate resolutions.

[2] This Dryden might learn from Mulgrave, who mentions
in his Memoirs, as a means of Monmouth's advancement, the
" great friendship which the Duke of York had openly professed to his wife, a lady of wit and reputation, who had both
the ambition of making her husband considerable, and the
address of succeeding in it, by using her interest in so friendly
an uncle, whose design I believe was only to convert her.
Whether this familiarity of theirs was contrived or only connived at by the Duke of Monmouth himself, is hard to determine. But I remember, that after these two princes had become declared enemies, the Duke of York one day told me,
with some emotion, as conceiving it a new mark of his nephew's insolence, that he had forbidden his wife to receive
any more visits from him; at which I could not help frankly
replying, that I, who was not used to excuse him, yet could
not hold from doing it in that case, wishing his highness
might have no juster cause to complain of him. Upon which
the Duke, surprised to find me excuse his and my own
enemy, changed the discourse immediately."—*Memoirs*, p. 13.

I have perused letters from Sir Gideon Scott of Highchester
to the Duchess of Monmouth, recommending a prudent and
proper attention to the Duke of York: and this advice she
probably followed; for, after her husband's execution, James
restored to her all her family estates. Sir Gideon's son had
been married to the Duchess's eldest sister.

Duchess of Monmouth, Dryden's especial patroness. Another more obvious and more offensive parallel existed between the popular party in the city, with the Whig sheriffs at their head, and that of the *Echevins,* or sheriffs of Paris, violent demagogues and adherents to the League, and who, in the play, are treated with great contumely by Grillon and the royal guards.   The tumults which had taken place at the election of these magistrates were warm in the recollection of the city ; and the com- mitment of the ex-sheriffs, Shute and Pilkington, to the Tower, under pretext of a riot, was consi- dered as the butt of the poet's satire.   Under these impressions the Whigs made a violent opposition to the representation of the piece, even when the king gave it his personal countenance. And although in despite of them, " The Duke of Guise " so far succeeded, as " to be frequently acted, and never without a considerable attendance," we may con- clude from these qualified expressions of the author himself, that the play was never eminently popular. He who writes for a party, can only please at most one half of his audience.

It was not to be expected that, at a time so very critical, a public representation, including such bold allusions, or rather parallels, should pass without critical censure.   " The Duke of Guise" was at- tacked by Dryden's old foe Shadwell, in some verses, entitled, " A Lenten Prologue refused by the Players ;"[1] and more formally, in " Reflections

---

[1] Bought by Mr Luttrell, 11th April, 1683. See it, Dryden's Works, vol. x., p. 131. It is expressly levelled against the

on the pretended Parallel in the Play called the Duke of Guise." In this pamphlet Shadwell seems to have been assisted by a gentleman of the Temple, so zealous for the popular cause, that Dryden says he was detected disguised in a livery-gown, proffering his vote at the Common-hall. Thomas Hunt, a barrister,[1] likewise stepped forth on this occasion; and in his " Defence of the Charter of London," then challenged by the famous process of *Quo Warranto*, he accuses Dryden of having prepared the way for that arbitrary step, by the degrading representation of their magistrates executed in effigy upon the stage. Dryden thought these pamphlets of consequence enough to deserve an answer, and published, soon after, " The Vindication of the Duke of Guise." In perusing the controversy, we may admire two circumstances, eminently characteristic of the candour with which such controversies are usually maintained: First, the anxiety with which the critics labour to fix upon Dryden a disrespectful parallel between Charles II. and Henry II. of France, which certainly our author did not propose to carry farther than their common point of situation; and secondly, the labour with which he disavows what he unquestionably did intend,—a parallel between the rebellious conduct of Monmouth and of Guise. The Vindication

---

" Duke of Guise," and generally against Dryden as a court poet. I may, however, be wrong in ascribing it to Shadwell.

[1] I observe Anthony Wood, as well as Mr Malone, suppose Hunt and the Templar associated in the Reflections to be the same person. But in the " Vindication of the Duke of Guise," Shadwell and they are spoke of as three distinct persons.

is written in a tone of sovereign contempt for the adversaries, particularly for Shadwell. Speaking of Thomas Hunt, Dryden says,—

" Even this their celebrated writer knows no more of style and English than the Northern dictator; as if dulness and clumsiness were fatal to the name of *Tom*. It is true, he is a fool in three languages more than the poet; for, they say, ' he understands Latin, Greek, and Hebrew,' from all which, to my certain knowledge, I acquit the other. Og may write against the king, if he pleases, so long as he drinks for him, and his writings will never do the government so much harm, as his drinking does it good; for true subjects will not be much perverted by his libels; but the wine-duties rise considerably by his claret. He has often called me an atheist in print; I would believe more charitably of him, and that he only goes the broad way, because the other is too narrow for him. He may see, by this, I do not delight to meddle with his course of life, and his immoralities, though I have a long bead-roll of them. I have hitherto contented myself with the ridiculous part of him, which is enough, in all conscience, to employ one man; even without the story of his late fall at the Old Devil, where he broke no ribs, because the hardness of the stairs could reach no bones; and, for my part, I do not wonder how he came to fall, for I have always known him heavy: the miracle is, how he got up again. I have heard of a sea captain as fat as he, who, to escape arrests, would lay himself flat upon the ground, and let the bailiffs carry him to prison, if they could. If a messenger or two, nay, we may put in three or four, should come, he has friendly advertisment how to escape them. But to leave him, who is not worth any further consideration, now I have done laughing at him,— would every man knew his own talent, and that they, who are only born for drinking, would let both poetry and prose alone! "

This was the last distinct and prolonged animadversion which our author bestowed upon his corpulent antagonist.

Soon after this time, Dryden wrote a biographical preface to Plutarch's Lives, of which a new translation, by several hands, was in the press. The dedication is addressed to the Duke of Ormond, the Barzillai of " Absalom and Achitophel," whom Charles, after a long train of cold and determined neglect, had in emergency recalled to his favour and his councils. The first volume of Plutarch's Lives, with Dryden's Life of the author, appeared in 1683.

About the same time, the king's express command engaged Dryden in a work, which may be considered as a sort of illustration of the doctrines laid down in the " Vindication of the Duke of Guise." It was the translation of Maimbourg's " History of the League," expressly composed to draw a parallel between the Huguenots of France and the Leaguers, as both equal enemies of the monarchy. This comparison was easily transferred to the sectaries of England, and the association proposed by Shaftesbury. The work was published with unusual solemnity of titlepage and frontispiece ; the former declaring, that the translation was made by his majesty's command ; the latter representing Charles on his throne, surrounded by emblems expressive of hereditary and indefeasible right.[1] The dedication to the king contains sentiments which savour strongly of party violence, and even ferocity. The forgiving disposition of the king is, according to the dedicator, the encouragement of the conspirators. Like

---

[1] See Dryden's Works, vol. xvii., p. 80.

Antæus, they rise refreshed from a simple over-throw. " These sons of earth are never to be trusted in their mother element; they must be hoisted into the air, and strangled." Thus exasperated were the most gentle tempers in those times of doubt and peril. The rigorous tone adopted, confirms the opinion of those historians who observe, that, after the discovery of the Rye-house Plot, Charles was fretted out of his usual debonair ease, and became more morose and severe than had been hitherto thought consistent with his disposition.

This translation was to be the last service which Dryden was to render his good-humoured, selfish, and thoughtless patron. While the laureat was preparing for the stage the opera of " Albion and Albanius," intended to solemnize the triumph of Charles over the Whigs, or, as the author expressed it, the double restoration of his sacred majesty, the king died of an apoplexy upon the 6th February, 1684-5. His death opened to many, and to Dryden among others, new hopes, and new prospects, which were, in his instance, doomed to terminate in disappointment and disgrace. We may therefore pause, and review the private life of the poet during the period which has occupied our last sections.

The vigour and rapidity with which Dryden poured forth his animated satire, plainly intimates, that his mind was pleased with the exercise of that formidable power. It was more easy for him, he has himself told us, to write with severity, than with forbearance; and indeed, where is the expert swordsman who does not delight in the flourish of his weapon? Neither could this self-complacent feeling be much allayed, by the vague and abusive ribaldry with which his satire was repaid. This was natural to the controversy, was no more than he expected, and was easily retorted with treble interest. " As for knave," says he, " and sycophant, and rascal, and impudent, and devil, and old serpent, and a thousand such good-morrows, I take them to be only names of parties; and could return murderer, and cheat, and whignapper, and sodomite; and, in short, the goodly number of the seven deadly sins, with all their kindred and relations, which are names of parties too; but saints will be saints, in spite of villany." With such feelings, we may believe Dryden's rest was little disturbed by the litter of libels against him:

" Sons of a day just buoyant on the flood,
Then number'd with the puppies in the mud."

But he who keenly engages in political controversy, must not only encounter the vulgar abuse, which he may justly contemn, but the altered eye of friends, whose regard is chilled, or alienated. That Dryden sustained such misfortune we cannot doubt, when he informs us, that, out of the large party in opposition, comprehending, doubtless, many men of talent and eminence, who were formerly familiar with him, he had, during the course of a whole year, only spoken to four, and to those but casually and cursorily, and only to express a wish, that the times might come when the names of Whig and Tory might be abolished, and men live together as they had done before they were introduced.

Neither did the protecting zeal of his party-friends compensate for the loss of those whom Dryden had alienated in their service. True it is, that a host of Tory rhymers came forward with complimentary verses to the author of "Absalom and Achitophel," and of "The Medal." But of all payment, that in kind is least gratifying to a poverty-struck bard, and the courtly patrons of Dryden were in no haste to make him more substantial requital. A gratuity of a hundred broad pieces is said to have been paid him by Charles for one of his satires; but no permanent provision was made for him. He was coolly left to increase his pittance by writing occasional pieces; and it was probably with this view that he arranged for publication a miscellaneous collection of poetry, which he afterwards continued. It was published for Tonson, in 1683-4, and contained several versions of Epistles from Ovid, and translations of detached pieces of Virgil, Horace, and Theocritus, with some smaller pieces by Dryden himself, and a variety of poems by other hands. The epistles had appeared in 1680, in a version of the original by several hands, to which Dryden also contributed an introductory discourse on translation. Contrary to our author's custom, the miscellany appeared without either preface or dedication.

The miscellany, among other minor poems of

Dryden, contained many of his occasional prologues and epilogues, the composition of which his
necessity had rendered so important a branch of
income, that, in the midst of his splendour of satirical reputation, the poet was obliged to chaffer
about the scanty recompense which he drew from
such petty sources. Such a circumstance attended
the commencement of his friendship with Southerne.
That poet then opening his dramatic career with
the play of the " Loyal Brother," came, as was
usual, to request a prologue from Dryden, and to
offer him the usual compliment of five guineas.
But the laureat demurred, and insisted upon double
the sum; " not out of disrespect," he added, " to
you, young man; but the players have had my
goods too cheap." Hence Southerne, who was
peculiarly fortunate in his dramatic revenue, is designed by Pope as

> —— " Tom sent down to raise
> The price of prologues and of plays."

It may seem surprising, that Dryden should be
left to make an object of such petty gains, when,
labouring for the service of government, he had in
little more than twelve months produced both Parts
of " Absalom and Achitophel," " The Medal,"
" Mac-Flecknoe," " *Religio Laici*," and " The
Duke of Guise." But this was not the worst; for,
although his pension as poet laureat was apparently
all the encouragement which he received from the
crown, so ill-regulated were the finances of Charles,
so expensive his pleasures, and so greedy his fa-

vourites, that our author, shortly after finishing these immortal poems, was compelled to sue for more regular payment of that very pension, and for a more permanent provision, in the following affecting Memorial, addressed to Hyde, Earl of Rochester :—

" I would plead," says he, " a little merit, and some hazards of my life from the common enemies; my refusing advantages offered by them, and neglecting my beneficial studies, for the king's service; but I only think I merit not to starve. I never applied myself to any interest contrary to your lordship's; and, on some occasions, perhaps not known to you, have not been unserviceable to the memory and reputation of my lord, your father. [1] After this, my lord, my conscience assures me, I may write boldly, though I cannot speak to you. I have three sons, growing to man's estate. I breed them all up to learning, beyond my fortune; but they are too hopeful to be neglected, though I want. Be pleased to look on me with an eye of compassion : some small employment would render my condition easy. The King is not unsatisfied of me; the Duke has often promised me his assistance; and your lordship is the conduit through which their favours pass. Either in the customs, or the appeals of the excise, or some other way, means cannot be wanting, if you please to have the will. *'Tis enough for one age to have neglected Mr Cowley, and starved Mr Butler;* but neither of them had the happiness to live till your lordship's ministry. In the mean time be pleased to give me a gracious and a speedy answer to my present request of half a year's pension for my necessities. I am going to write somewhat by his Majesty's command, [2] and cannot stir into the country for my health and studies till I secure my family from want."

We know that this affecting remonstrance was in part successful; for long afterwards, he says, in

[1] Probably alluding to the author having defended Clarendon in public company; for nothing of the kind occurs in Dryden's publications.

[2] Probably the translation of " *Religio Laici.*"

allusion to this period, " Even from a bare trea-
sury, my success has been contrary to that of Mr
Cowley; and Gideon's fleece has there been mois-
tened, when all the ground was dry."   But in the
admission of this claim to the more regular payment of his pension, was comprehended all Rochester's title to Dryden's gratitude.   The poet could
not obtain the small employment which he so
earnestly solicited; and such was the recompense
of the merry monarch and his counsellors, to one
whose productions had strengthened the pillars of
his throne, as well as renovated the literary taste
of the nation.

SECTION VI.

Threnodia Augustalis—Albion and Albanius—Dryden becomes a Catholic—The Controversy of Dryden with Stillingfleet—The Hind and Panther—Life of St Francis Xavier—Consequences of the Revolution to Dryden—Don Sebastian—King Arthur—Cleomenes—Love Triumphant.

THE accession of James II. to the British throne excited new hopes in all orders of men. On the accession of a new prince, the loyal looked to rewards, the rebellious to amnesty. The catholics exulted in beholding one of their persuasion attain the crown after an interval of two centuries ; the Church of England expected the fruits of her unlimited devotion to the royal line ; even the sectaries might hope indulgence from a prince, whose religion deviated from that established by law as widely as their own. All, therefore, hastened, in sugared addresses, to lament the sun which had set, and hail the beams of that which had arisen. Dryden, among other expectants, chose the more honourable of these themes ; and in the " *Threnodia Augustalis,*" at once paid a tribute to the memory of the deceased monarch, and decently solicited the attention of his successor. But although he had enjoyed personal marks of the favour of

Charles, they were of a nature too unsubstantial to demand a deep tone of sorrow. " Little was the muses' hire, and light their gain ;" and " the pension of a prince's praise " is stated to have been all their encouragement. Dryden, therefore, by no means sorrowed as if he had no hope ; but, having said all that was decently mournful over the bier of Charles, tuned his lyrics to a sounding close in praise of James.

About the same time, Dryden resumed, with new courage, the opera of " Albion and Albanius," which had been nearly finished before the death of Charles. This was originally designed as a masque, or emblematical prelude to the play of " King Arthur;" for Dryden, wearied with the inefficient patronage of Charles, from whom he only "received fair words," had renounced in despair the task of an epic poem, and had converted one of his themes, that of the tale of Arthur, into the subject of a romantic drama. As the epic was to have been adapted to the honour and praise of Charles and his brother, the opera had originally the same political tendency. " Albion and Albanius" was a sort of introductory masque, in which, under a very thin veil of allegory, first, the restoration of the Stuarts to the throne, and, secondly, their escape from the Rye-house plot, and the recent conquest over their Whig opponents, were successively represented. The death of Charles made little alteration in this piece : it cost but the addition of an apotheosis ; and the opera concluded with the succession of James to the throne, from which he had been so nearly excluded. These topics were however temporary; and, probably from the necessity of producing it while the allusions were fresh and obvious, " Albion and Albanius" was detached from " King Arthur," which was not in such a state of forwardness. Great expense was bestowed in bringing forward this piece, and the scenery seems to have been unusually perfect; particularly, the representation of a celestial phenomenon, actually seen by Captain Gunman of the navy, whose evidence is quoted in the printed copies of the play.[1]   The music of " Albion and Albanius"

1 It formed the machine on which Iris appeared—Dryden's Works, vol. vii., p. 241. I have been favoured by Sir Egerton Brydges, with the following " Extract from the Journal of Captain Christopher Gunman, commander of his Royal Highness's yacht the Mary, lying in Calais pier, Tuesday, 18th March:

   " 1683-4,

   " March 18th. It was variable cloudy weather: this morning about seven o'clock saw in the firmament three suns, with two demi-rainbows; and all within one whole rainbow, in form and shape as here pourtrayed:

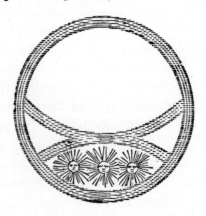

was arranged by Grabut, a Frenchman, whose name does not stand high as a composer. Yet Dryden pays him some compliments in the preface of the piece, which were considered as derogatory to Purcel and the English school, and gave great offence to a class of persons at least as irritable as their brethren the poets. This, among other causes, seems to have injured the success of the piece. But its death-blow was the news of the Duke of Monmouth's invasion, which reached London on Saturday, 13th June, 1685, while " Albion and Albanius" was performing for the sixth time : the audience broke up in consternation, and the piece was never again repeated. [1] This opera was prejudicial

---

" The sun towards the left hand bore east, and that on the right hand bore south-east of me. I did sit and draw it as well as the time and place would permit me; for it was seen in its full form about the space of half an hour ; but part of the rainbow did see above two hours. It appeared first at three quarters past six, and was over-clouded at a quarter past seven. The wind north-by-west."

Mr Gunman, the descendant of the captain, has lately had a picture on the subject painted by Serres, the marine painter ; which makes an interesting history-piece. It represents the phenomenon in the heavens—the harbour of Calais—and the yacht lying off it, &c. &c.

[1] This tradition is thus critically examined and proved by Mr Malone :

" From a letter written by King James to the Prince of Orange, June 15, 1685, it appears, that though the Duke of Monmouth landed at Lyme, in Dorsetshire, on Thursday evening, June 11th, an account of his landing did not reach the King at Whitehall till *Saturday* morning the 13th. The House of Commons, having met on that day at the usual hour, between nine and ten o'clock, the news was soon afterwards communicated to them by a Message from the King, delivered

to the company, who were involved by the expense
in a considerable debt, and never recovered half
the money laid out.   Neither was it of service to
our poet's reputation, who had, on this occasion, to
undergo the gibes of angry musicians, as well as the
reproaches of disappointed actors and hostile poets.
One went so far as to suggest, with some humour,
that probably the laureat and Grabut had mistaken
their trade ; the former writing the music, and the
latter the verse.

We have now reached a remarkable incident
in our author's life, namely, his conversion to the
Catholic faith, which took place shortly after the
accession of James II. to the British throne.
The biographer of Dryden must feel considerable
difficulty in discussing the probable causes of his
change.   Although this essay be intended to con-

---

by the Earl of Middleton to (whom Etheredge afterwards
wrote two poetical Epistles from Ratisbon).—Having voted
and drawn up an Address to his Majesty, desiring him to take
care of his royal person, they adjourned to *four o'clock;*
in which interval they went to Whitehall, presented their
Address, and then met again.—*Com. Jour.* vol. ix., p. 735.
About this time, therefore, it may be presumed, the news
transpired, and in an hour afterwards probably reached the
Theatre, where an audience was assembled at the representation of the opera of ' Albion and Albanius ;' for plays at that
time began at four o'clock.   It seems from Mr Luttrell's MS.
note, that the first representation of this opera was on Saturday the 6th of June ; and Downes (*Rosc. Ang.* p. 40) says,
that in consequence of Monmouth's invasion, it was only performed *six* times ; so that the sixth representation was, without doubt, on Saturday, the 13th of June.   An examination
of dates is generally fatal to tales of this kind : here, however,
they certainly support the tradition mentioned in the text."—
Life of Dryden, p. 188.

tain the life, not the apology of the poet, it is the duty of the writer to place such circumstances in view, as may qualify the strong prepossession at first excited by a change of faith against the individual who makes it. This prepossession, powerful in every case, becomes doubly so, if the step be taken at a time when the religion adopted seems more readily to pave the way for the temporal prosperity of the proselyte. Even where the grounds of conviction are ample and undeniable, we have a respect for those who suffer, rather than renounce a mistaken faith, when it is discountenanced or persecuted. A brave man will least of all withdraw himself from his ancient standard when the tide of battle beats against it. On the other hand, those who at such a period admit conviction to the better and predominant doctrine, are viewed with hatred by the members of the deserted creed, and with doubt by their new brethren in faith. Many who adopted Christianity in the reign of Constantine were doubtless sincere proselytes, but we do not find that any of them have been canonized. These feelings must be allowed powerfully to affect the mind, when we reflect, that Dryden, a servant of the court, and zealously attached to the person of James, to whom he looked for the reward of long and faithful service, did not receive any mark of royal favour until he professed himself a member of the religion for which that king was all but an actual martyr. There are other considerations, however, greatly qualifying the conclusions which might be drawn from these suspicious circumstances, and tending to show, that Dryden's conversion was at least in a great measure effected by sincere conviction. The principal clue to the progress of his religious principles is to be found in the poet's own lines in " The Hind and the Panther ;" and may, by a very simple commentary, be applied to the state of his religious opinions at different periods of his life:

> " My thoughtless youth was wing'd with vain desires;
> My manhood, long misled by wandering fires,
> Follow'd false lights; and, when their glimpse was gone,
> My pride struck out new sparkles of her own.
> Such was I, such by nature still I am;
> Be thine the glory, and be mine the shame ! "

The " vain desires " of Dryden's " thoughtless youth " require no explanation; they obviously mean, that inattention to religious duties which the amusements of youth too frequently occasion. The " false lights " which bewildered the poet's manhood, were, I doubt not, the puritanical tenets, which, coming into the world under the auspices of his fanatical relations, Sir Gilbert Pickering and Sir John Driden, he must have at least professed, but probably seriously entertained. It must be remembered, that the poet was thirty years of age at the Restoration; so that a considerable space of his full-grown manhood had passed while the rigid doctrines of the fanatics were still the order of the day. But the third state of his opinions, those " sparkles which his pride struck out," after the delusions of puritanism had vanished; in other words, those sentiments which he

imbibed after the Restoration, and which immediately preceded his adoption of the Catholic faith,
cannot be ascertained without more minute investigation. We may at the outset be easily permitted
to assume, that the adoption of a fixed creed of
religious principles was not the first business of
our author, when that merry period set him free
from the rigorous fetters of fanaticism. Unless he
differed more than we can readily believe from
the public feeling at that time, Dryden was satisfied to give to Cæsar the things that were Cæsar's,
without being in a hurry to fulfil the counterpart
of the precept. Foremost in the race of pleasure,
engaged in labours alien from serious reflection, the
favourite of the most lively and dissolute nobility
whom England ever saw, religious thoughts were
not, at this period, likely to intrude frequently
upon his mind, or to be encouraged when they did
so. The time, therefore, when Dryden began
seriously to compare the doctrines of the contending sects of Christianity, was probably several
years after the Restoration, when reiterated disappointment, and satiety of pleasure, prompted his
mind to retire within itself, and think upon hereafter. The " *Religio Laici*," published in 1682,
evinces, that, previous to composing that poem, the
author had bestowed serious consideration upon
the important subjects of which it treats ; and I
have postponed the analysis of it to this place, in
order that the reader may be able to form his own
conjecture from what faith Dryden changed when
he became a Catholic.

The "*Religio Laici*" has indeed a political tendency, being written to defend the church of England against the sectaries: it is not, therefore, so much from the conclusions of the piece, as from the mode of the author's deducing these conclusions, that Dryden's real opinions may be gathered;— as we learn nothing of the bowl's bias from its having reached its mark, though something may be conjectured by observing the course which it described in attaining it. From many minute particulars, I think it almost decisive, that Dryden, when he wrote the "*Religio Laici,*" was sceptical concerning revealed religion. I do not mean, that his doubts were of that fixed and permanent nature, which have at different times induced men, of whom better might have been hoped, to pronounce themselves freethinkers on principle. On the contrary, Dryden seems to have doubted with such a strong wish to believe, as, accompanied with circumstances of extrinsic influence, led him finally into the opposite extreme of credulity. His view of the doctrines of Christianity, and of its evidence, were such as could not legitimately found him in the conclusions he draws in favour of the Church of England; and accordingly, in adopting them, he evidently stretches his complaisance towards the national religion, while perhaps in his heart he was even then disposed to think there was no middle course between natural religion and the Church of Rome. The first creed which he examines is that of Deism; which he rejects because the worship of one sole deity was not known to the philosophers of antiquity, and is therefore obviously to be ascribed to revelation. Revelation thus proved, the puzzling doubt occurs, whether the Scripture, as contended by Calvinists, was to be the sole rule of faith, or whether the rules and traditions of the church are to be admitted in explanation of the holy text. Here Dryden does not hesitate to point out the inconveniences ensuing from making the sacred page the subject of the dubious and contradictory commentary of the laity at large: when

> " The common rule was made the common prey,
> And at the mercy of the rabble lay;
> The tender page with horny fists was gall'd,
> And he was gifted most that loudest bawl'd;
> The spirit gave the doctoral degree,
> And every member of a company
> Was of his trade and of the Bible free."

This was the rule of the sectaries,—of those whose innovations seemed, in the eyes of the Tories, to be again bursting in upon monarchy and episcopacy with the strength of a land-flood. Dryden, therefore, at once, and heartily, reprobates it. But the opposite extreme of admitting the authority of the church as omnipotent in deciding all matters of faith, he does not give up with the same readiness. The extreme convenience, nay, almost necessity, for such authority, is admitted in these remarkable lines:

> " Such an omniscient church we *wish* indeed;
> *'Twere worth both Testaments, cast in the Creed.*"

A wish, so forcibly expressed, shows a strong desire on the part of the poet to be convinced of the existence of that authority to which he so ardently desired to submit himself. And the argument which Dryden considers as conclusive against the existence of such an omniscient church, is precisely that which a subtle Catholic would find little trouble in repelling. If there be such a church, says Dryden, why does it not point out the corruption of the canon, and restore it where lost? The answer is obvious, providing that the infallibility of the church be previously assumed; for where can be the necessity of restoring or explaining scripture, if God has given, to Pope and Council, the inspiration necessary to settle all doubts in matters of faith? Dryden must have perceived where this argument led him, and he rather compounds with the difficulty than faces it. The scripture, he admits, must be the rule on the one hand; but, on the other, it was to be qualified by the traditions of the earlier ages, and the exposition of learned men. And he concludes boldly enough:

> " Shall I speak plain, and, in a nation free,
> Assume an honest layman's liberty?
> I think, according to my little skill,
> To my own mother-church submitting still,
> That many have been saved, and many may,
> Who never heard this question brought in play.
> The unletter'd Christian, who believes in gross,
> Plods on to heaven, and ne'er is at a loss;
> For the strait gate would be made straiter yet,
> Were none admitted there but men of wit."

This seems to be a plain admission, that the author was involved in a question from which he saw no very decided mode of extricating himself;

and that the best way was to think as little as possible upon the subject. But this was a sorry conclusion for affording firm foundation in religious faith.

Another doubt appears to have puzzled Dryden so much, as to lead him finally to the Catholic faith for its solution. This was the future fate of those who never heard the gospel preached, supposing belief in it essential to salvation:

> " Because a general law is that alone,
> Which must to all, and every where, be known."

Dryden, it is true, founds upon the mercy of the Deity a hope, that the benefit of the propitiatory sacrifice of our Mediator may be extended to those who knew not of its power. But the creed of St Athanasius stands in the poet's road; and though he disposes of it with less reverence to the patriarch than is quite seemly, there is an indecision, if not in his conclusion, at least in his mode of deducing it, that shows an apt inclination to cut the knot, and solve the objection of the Deist, by alleging, that belief in the Christian religion is an essential requisite to salvation.

If I am right in these remarks, it will follow, that Dryden never could be a firm or steady believer in the Church of England's doctrines. The arguments, by which he proved them, carried him too far; and when he commenced a teacher of faith, or when, as he expresses it, " his pride struck out new sparkles of its own," at that very time, while in words he maintained the doctrines of his mother-church, his conviction really hovered between natu-

ral religion and the faith of Rome.   It is remarkable, that his friends do not seem to have considered
the " *Religio Laici* " as expressive of his decided
sentiments;   for Charles Blount, a noted free-
thinker, in consequence of that very work, wrote a
deistical treatise in prose, bearing the same title,
and ascribed it with great testimony of respect
to " his much-honoured friend, John Dryden,
Esquire."[1]   Mr Blount, living in close habits with
Dryden, must have known perfectly well how to
understand his polemical poem ; and, had he supposed it was written under a deep belief of the truth
of the English creed, can it be thought he would
have inscribed to the author a tract against all revelation ?[2]   The inference is, therefore, sufficiently
plain, that the dedicator knew that Dryden was
sceptical on the subject, on which he had, out of
compliment to church and state, affected a convic-

[1] The expressions in the dedication are such as to preclude
all idea but of profound respect : " Sir, The value I have ever
had for your writings, makes me impatient to peruse all treatises that are crowned with your name ; whereof, the last that
fell into my hands was your ' *Religio Laici;* ' which expresses
as well your great judgment in, as value for, religion : a thing
too rarely found in this age among gentlemen of your parts ;
and, I am confident, (with the blessing of God upon your
endeavours,) not unlikely to prove of great advantage to the
public ; since, as Mr Herbert well observes,

> ' A verse may find him who a sermon flies,
> And turn delight into a sacrifice.' "

[2] Blount preserves, indeed, that affectation of respect for the
doctrines of the Established Church which decency imposes ;
but the tendency of his work is to decry all revelation.   It is
founded on the noted work of Lord Herbert of Cherbury,
" *De Veritate.*"

tion ; and that his " *Religio Laici* " no more inferred a belief in the doctrines of Christianity, than
the sacrifice of a cock to Esculapius proved the
heathen philosopher's faith in the existence of that
divine leech.   Thus far Dryden had certainly proceeded.   His disposition to believe in Christianity
was obvious, but he was bewildered in the maze of
doubt in which he was involved ; and it was already
plain, that the church, whose promises to illuminate
him were most confident, was likely to have the
honour of this distinguished proselyte.   Dryden
did not, therefore, except in outward profession,
abandon the Church of England for that of Rome,
but was converted to the Catholic faith from a state
of infidelity, or rather of Pyrrhonism.   This is made
more clear by his own words, from which it appears,
that, having once admitted the mysterious doctrines
of the Trinity and of Redemption, so incomprehen-
sible to human reason, Dryden felt no right to make
any further appeal to that fallible guide :

> " Good life be now my task ; my doubts are done ;
> What more could fright my faith than three in one ?
> Can I believe Eternal God could lie
> Disguised in mortal mould, and infancy ?
> That the great Maker of the world could die ?
> And after that trust my imperfect sense,
> Which calls in question his omnipotence ? "

From these lines it may be safely inferred, that
Dryden's sincere acquiescence in the more abstruse
points of Christianity, did not long precede his
adoption of the Roman faith.   In some preceding
verses, it appears how eagerly he received the
conviction of the church's infallibility, as affording

that guide, the want of whom he had in some degree lamented in the " *Religio Laici :*"

> " What weight of ancient witness can prevail,
> If private reason hold the public scale ?
> But, gracious God, how well dost thou provide
> For erring judgments an unerring guide !
> Thy throne is darkness in the abyss of light,
> A blaze of glory that forbids the sight.
> O teach me to believe thee, thus conceal'd,
> And search no farther than thyself reveal'd ;
> But her alone for my director take,
> Whom thou hast promised never to forsake !"

We find, therefore, that Dryden's conversion was not of that sordid kind which is the consequence of a strong temporal interest ; for he had expressed intelligibly the imagined *desiderata* which the church of Rome alone pretends to supply, long before that temporal interest had an existence. Neither have we to reproach him, that, grounded and rooted in a pure Protestant creed, he was foolish enough to abandon it for the more corrupted doctrines of Rome. He did not unloose from the secure haven to moor in the perilous road ; but, being tossed on the billows of uncertainty, he dropped his anchor in the first moorings to which the winds, waves, and perhaps an artful pilot, chanced to convey his bark. We may indeed regret, that, having to choose between two religions, he should have adopted that which our education, reason, and even prepossessions, combine to point out as foully corrupted from the primitive simplicity of the Christian church. But neither the Protestant Christian, nor the sceptic philosopher, can claim a right to despise the sophistry which bewildered the judgment of Chillingworth, or the toils which enveloped the active and suspicious minds of Bayle and of Gibbon. The latter, in his account of his own conversion to the Catholic faith, fixes upon the very arguments pleaded by Dryden, as those which appeared to him irresistible. The early traditions of the church, the express words of the text, are referred to by both as the grounds of their conversion; and the works of Bossuet, so frequently referred to by the poet, were the means of influencing the determination of the philosopher.[1] The victorious argument

---

[1] " I was unable to resist the weight of historical evidence, that within the same period most of the leading doctrines of Popery were already introduced in theory and practice; nor was my conclusion absurd, that miracles are the test of truth, and that the church must be orthodox and pure, which was so often approved by the visible interposition of the Deity. The marvellous tales which are so boldly attested by the Basils and Chrysostoms, the Austins and Jeroms, compelled me to embrace the superior merits of celibacy, the institution of the monastic life, the use of the sign of the Cross, of holy oil, and even of images, the invocation of saints, the worship of relics, the rudiments of purgatory in prayers for the dead, and the tremendous mystery of the sacrifice of the body and blood of Christ, which insensibly swelled into the prodigy of transubstantiation. In these dispositions, and already more than half a convert, I formed an unlucky intimacy with a young gentleman of our college, whose name I shall spare. With a character less resolute, Mr ***** had imbibed the same religious opinions; and some Popish books, I know not through what channel, were conveyed into his possession. I read, I applauded, I believed; the English translations of two famous works of Bossuet, Bishop of Meaux, the ' Exposition of the Catholic Doctrine,' and the ' History of the Protestant Variations,' achieved my conversion; and I surely fell by a noble hand. I have since examined the originals with a more dis-

to which Chillingworth himself yielded was, " that there must be somewhere an infallible judge, and the church of Rome is the only Christian society which either does or can pretend to that character."

It is also to be observed, that, towards the end of Charles the Second's reign, the High-Church-men and the Catholics regarded themselves as on the same side in political questions, and not greatly divided in their temporal interests. Both were sufferers in the Plot, both were enemies of the sectaries, both were adherents of the Stuarts. Alternate conversion had been common between

---

cerning eye, and shall not hesitate to pronounce, that Bossuet is indeed a master of all the weapons of controversy. In the ' Exposition,' a specious apology, the orator assumes, with consummate art, the tone of candour and simplicity ; and the ten-horned monster is transformed, at his magic touch, into the milk-white Hind, who must be loved as soon as she is seen.   In the ' History,' a bold and well-aimed attack, he displays, with a happy mixture of narrative and argument, the faults and follies, the changes and contradictions of our first reformers ; whose variations (as he dexterously contends) are the mark of historical error, while the perpetual unity of the Catholic church is the sign and test of infallible truth. To my present feelings, it seems incredible, that I should ever believe that I believed in transubstantiation.   But my conqueror oppressed me with the sacramental words, ' *Hoc est corpus meum,*' and dashed against each other the figurative half-meanings of the Protestant sects ; every objection was resolved into omnipotence ; and, after repeating at St Mary's the Athanasian creed, I humbly acquiesced in the mystery of the real presence.

" ' To take up half on trust, and half to try,
Name it not faith, but bungling bigotry.
Both knave and fool, the merchant we may call,
To pay great sums, and to compound the small ;
For who would break with heaven, and would not break for all ? ' "
GIBBON'S *Memoirs of his own Life.*

them, so early as since Milton made a reproach to
the English universities of the converts to the
Roman faith daily made within their colleges ; of
those sheep,

> _____" Whom the grim wolf with privy paw
> Daily devours apace and nothing said."

In approaching Dryden, therefore, a Catholic priest
had to combat few of those personal prejudices,
which, in other cases, have been impediments to
their making converts.   The poet had, besides,
before him the example of many persons, both of
rank and talent, who had adopted the Catholic
religion.

Such being the disposition of Dryden's mind,
and such the peculiar facilities of the Roman
churchmen in making proselytes, it is by no means
to be denied, that circumstances in the poet's
family and situation strongly forwarded his taking
such a step.   His wife, Lady Elizabeth, had for
some time been a Catholic ; and though she may
be acquitted of any share in influencing his determination, yet her new faith necessarily brought
into his family persons both able and disposed to
do so.   His eldest and best beloved son, Charles,
is also said, though upon uncertain authority, to
have been a Catholic before his father, and to have
contributed to his change.[1]   Above all, James,
his master, to whose fortunes he had so closely

_____

[1] In a libel in the " State Poems," vol. iii., Dryden is made
to say,

> " One son turn'd me, I turn'd the other two,
> But had not an indulgence, sir, like you."
>
> Page 244.

attached himself, had now become as parsimonious of his favour as his church is of salvation, and restricted it to those of his own sect. It is more than probable, though only a conjecture, that Dryden might be made the subject of those private exhortations, which in that reign were called *closeting ;* and, predisposed as he was, he could hardly be supposed capable of resisting the royal eloquence. For, while pointing out circumstances of proof, that Dryden's conversion was not made by manner of bargain and sale, but proceeded upon a sincere though erroneous conviction, it cannot be denied, that his situation as poet laureat, and his expectations from the king, must have conduced to his taking his final resolution. All I mean to infer from the above statement is, that his interest and internal conviction led him to the same conclusion.

If we are to judge of Dryden's sincerity in his new faith, by the determined firmness with which he retained it through good report and bad report, we must allow him to have been a martyr, or at least a confessor, in the Catholic cause. If, after the Revolution, like many greater men, he had changed his principles with the times, he was not a person of such mark as to be selected from all the nation, and punished for former tenets. Supported by the friendship of Rochester, and most of the Tory nobles who were active in the Revolution, of Leicester, and many Whigs, and especially of the Lord-Chamberlain Dorset, there would probably have been little difficulty in permitting so eminent an author to remain poet laureat, if he had

recanted the errors of popery. But the Catholic
religion, and the consequent disqualifications, were
an insurmountable obstacle to his holding that or
any other office under government; and Dryden's
adherence to it, with all the poverty, reproach, and
even persecution which followed the profession,
argued a deep and substantial conviction of the
truth of the doctrines it inculcated. So late as
1699, when a union, in opposition to King William,
had led the Tories and Whigs to look on each
other with some kindness, Dryden thus expresses
himself in a letter to his cousin, Mrs Steward:

" The court rather speaks kindly of me, than does any
thing for me, though they promise largely; and perhaps they
think I will advance as they go backward, in which they
will be much deceived: for I can never go an inch beyond my
conscience and my honour. If they will consider me as a man
who has done my best to improve the language, and especially
the poetry, and will be content with my acquiescence under
the present government, and forbearing satire on it, that I can
promise, because I can perform it: but I can neither take the
oaths, nor forsake my religion; because I know not what
church to go to, if I leave the Catholic; they are all so divided
amongst themselves in matters of faith, necessary to salvation,
and yet all assuming the name of Protestants. May God be
pleased to open your eyes, as he has opened mine! Truth is
but one, and they who have once heard of it can plead no
excuse if they do not embrace it. But these are things too
serious for a trifling letter." [1]

If, therefore, adherence to the communion of a
falling sect, loaded too at the time with heavy
disqualifications, and liable to yet more dangerous
suspicions, can be allowed as a proof of sincerity,
we can hardly question that Dryden was, from the

[1] Dryden's Works, vol. xviii., p. 162.

date of his conviction, a serious and sincere Roman Catholic.

The conversion of Dryden did not long remain unrewarded, nor was his pen suffered to be idle in the cause which he had adopted. On the 4th of March, 1685-6, an hundred pounds a-year, payable quarterly, was added to his pension;[1] and probably he found himself more at ease under the regular and economical government of James, than when his support depended on the exhausted exchequer of Charles. Soon after the granting of this boon, he was employed to defend the reasons of conversion to the Catholic faith, alleged by Anne Hyde, Duchess of York, which, together with two papers on a similar subject, said to have been found in Charles the Second's strong box, James had with great rashness given to the public. Stillingfleet, now at the head of the champions of the Protestant faith, published some sharp remarks on these papers. Another hand, probably that of a Jesuit, was employed to vindicate against him the royal grounds of conversion; while to Dryden was committed the charge of defending those alleged by the Duchess. The tone of Dryden's apology was, to say the least, highly injudicious, and adapted to irritate the feelings of the clergy of the Established

[1] The grant bears this honourable consideration, which I extract from Mr Malone's work: " Pat. 2. Jac. p. 4., n. 1. Know ye, that we, for and in consideration of the many good and acceptable services done by John Dryden, Master of Arts, to our late dearest brother King Charles the Second, as also to us done and performed, and taking notice of the learning and eminent abilities of the said J. D.," &c.

Church, already sufficiently exasperated to see the sacrifices which they had made to the royal cause utterly forgotten, the moment that they paused in the extremity of their devotion towards the monarch. The name of " Legion," which the apologist bestows on his adversaries, intimates the committee of the clergy by whom the Protestant cause was then defended; and the tone of his arguments is harsh, contemptuous, and insulting. A raker up of the ashes of princes, an hypocrite, a juggler, a latitudinarian, are the best terms which he affords the advocate of the Church of England, in defence of which he had so lately been himself a distinguished champion. Stillingfleet returned to the charge; and when he came to the part of the Defence written by Dryden, he did not spare the personal invective, to which the acrimonious style of the poet laureat had indeed given an opening. " Zeal," says Stillingfleet, " in a new convert, is a terrible thing, for it not only burns, but rages like the eruptions of Mount Ætna; it fills the air with noise and smoke, and throws out such a torrent of living fire, that there is no standing before it." In another passage, Stillingfleet talks of the " temptation of changing religion for bread;" in another, our author's words, that

" Priests of all religions are the same," [1]

are quoted to infer, that he who has no religion may declare for any. Dryden took his revenge both on Stillingfleet the author, and on Burnet,

[1] " Absalom and Achitophel," Part I., Dryden's Works, vol. ix., p. 220.

whom he seems to have regarded as the reviser of this answer, in his polemical poem of " The Hind and the Panther."

If we can believe an ancient tradition, this poem was chiefly composed in a country retirement at Rushton, near his birth-place in Huntingdon. There was an embowered walk at this place, which, from the pleasure which the poet took in it, retained the name of Dryden's Walk; and here was erected, about the middle of last century, an urn, with the following inscription : " In memory of Dryden, who frequented these shades, and is here said to have composed his poem of ' The Hind and the Panther.' " [1]

" The Hind and the Panther " was written with a view to obviate the objections of the English clergy and people to the power of dispensing with the test laws, usurped by James II. A change of political measures, which took place while the poem was composing, has greatly injured its unity and consistence. In the earlier part of his reign, James endeavoured to gain the Church of England, by fair means and flattery, to submit to the remission which he claimed the liberty of granting to the Catholics. The first part of Dryden's poem is written upon this soothing plan ; the Panther, or Church of England, is

> —— " sure the noblest next the Hind,
> And fairest offspring of the spotted kind.
> Oh, could her in-born stains be wash'd away,
> She were too good to be a beast of prey ! "

[1] I am indebted for this anecdote to Mr Octavius Gilchrist, the editor of the poems of the witty Bishop Corbett.

The sects, on the other hand, are characterised, wolves, bears, boars, foxes,—all that is odious and horrible in the brute creation. But ere the poem was published, the king had assumed a different tone with the Established Church. Relying upon the popularity which the suspension of the penal laws was calculated to procure among the Dissenters, he endeavoured to strengthen his party by making common cause between them and the Catholics, and bidding open defiance to the Church of England. For a short time, and with the most ignorant of the sectaries, this plan seemed to succeed; the pleasure of a triumph over their ancient enemies rendering them blind to the danger of the common Protestant cause. During this interval the poem was concluded; and the last book seems to consider the cause of the Hind and Panther as gone to a final issue, and incapable of any amicable adjustment. The Panther is fairly resigned to her fate.

——— " Her hour of grace was pass'd,"

and the downfall of the English hierarchy is foretold in that of the Doves, who, in a subaltern allegory, represent the clergy of the Established Church:

" 'Tis said, the Doves repented, though too late,
Become the smiths of their own foolish fate:
Nor did their owner hasten their ill hour,
But, sunk in credit, they decreased in power;
Like snows in warmth that mildly pass away,
Dissolving in the silence of decay."

In the preface, as well as in the course of the

poem, Dryden frequently alludes to his dispute
with Stillingfleet; and perhaps none of his poems
contain finer lines than those in which he takes
credit for the painful exertion of Christian forbearance, when called by injured feeling to resent
personal accusation :

> " If joys hereafter must be purchased here
> With loss of all that mortals hold so dear,
> Then welcome infamy and public shame,
> And last, a long farewell to worldly fame!
> 'Tis said with ease; but, oh, how hardly tried
> By haughty souls to human honour tied!
> O sharp convulsive pangs of agonizing pride!
> Down then, thou rebel, never more to rise!
> And what thou didst, and dost, so dearly prize,
> That fame, that darling fame, make that thy sacrifice.
> 'Tis nothing thou hast given; then add thy tears
> For a long race of unrepenting years:
> 'Tis nothing yet, yet all thou hast to give;
> Then add those may-be years thou hast to live:
> Yet nothing still : then poor and naked come,
> Thy father will receive his unthrift home,
> And thy blest Saviour's blood discharge the mighty sum."

Stillingfleet is, however, left personally undistinguished; but Burnet, afterwards Bishop of
Salisbury, receives chastisement in his stead. The
character of this prelate, however unjustly exaggerated, preserves many striking and curious traits
of resemblance to the original; and, as was natural,
gave deep offence to the party for whom it was
drawn. For not only did Burnet at the time
express himself with great asperity of Dryden,
but long afterwards, when writing his history, he
pronounced a severe censure on the immorality

of his plays, so inaccurately expressed as to be applicable, by common construction, to the author's private character.[1] From this coarse and inexplicit accusation, the memory of Dryden was indignantly vindicated by his friend Lord Lansdowne.[2]

[1] [" When Burnet adds that ' Dryden, the great master of dramatic poesy, was a monster of immodesty and impurity of all sorts,' the Bishop betrays his own vitiated taste and his political animosity, for Dryden's plays, bad as they are, are not worse than those of his contemporaries, and his life was at least decorous. This was the case also with Shadwell his rival; for such is the blindness of faction, that Shadwell was extolled by the Whigs as a rival to Dryden." — *Quarterly Review, April,* 1823.]

[2] [On this subject Mr D'Israeli somewhat strongly and wildly expresses himself: " The spirit of party has touched with its plague-spot the character of Burnet; it has mildewed the page of a powerful mind, and tainted by its suspicions, its rumours, and its censures, his probity as a man. Can we forbear listening to all the vociferations which faction has thrown out? and do we not fear to trust ourselves amidst the multiplicity of his facts? And when we are familiarized with the variety of his historical portraits, are we not startled when it is suggested that ' they are tinged with his own passions and his own weaknesses?' Burnet has indeed made ' his humble appeal to the great God of Truth,' that he has given it as fully as he could find it; and he has expressed his abhorrence of ' a lie in history,' so much a greater sin than a lie in common discourse, by its lasting and universal nature. Yet these hallowing protestations have not saved him! A cloud of witnesses, from different motives, have rose up to attaint his veracity and his candour, while all the Tory wits have ridiculed his style, impatiently inaccurate, and uncouthly negligent, and would sink his vigour and ardour, while they expose the meanness and poverty of his genius. Thus the literary and the moral character of no ordinary author have fallen a victim to party feeling.

" But this victim to political criticism on literature was himself criminal, and has wreaked his own party feelings on

It is also worth remarking, that in the allegory of the swallows, introduced in the Third Part of " The Hind and the Panther," the author seems to have had in his eye the proposal made at a grand consult of the Catholics, that they should retire from the general and increasing hatred of all ranks, and either remain quiet at home, or settle abroad. This plan, which originated in their despair of James's being able to do any thing effectual in their favour, was set aside by the fiery opposition of Father Petre, the martin of the fable told by the Panther to the Hind.[1]

The appearance of " The Hind and the Panther" excited a clamour against the author far more general than the publication of " Absalom and Achitophel." Upon that occasion, the offence was given only to a party; but this open and

the *Papist* Dryden, and the *Tory* Prior; Dryden, he calls, in the most unguarded language, ' a monster of immodesty and impurity of all sorts,' yet no man's life was purer in its decent habits, and less free from dissipation. There had been a literary quarrel between Dryden and Burnet respecting a translation of Varillas's History of Heresies; Burnet had ruined the credit of the papistical author, while Dryden was busied on the translation; and as Burnet says, ' he has wreaked his malice on me for spoiling his three months' labour,' and in return, he kindly informs Dryden, alluding to his poem of The Hind and the Panther, ' that he is the author of the *worst* poem the age has produced;' and as for ' his morals, it is scarce possible to grow a worse man than he was '—a style not to be permitted in any controversy, but to have brought this passion on the hallowed ground of history, was not to have ' cast away his shoe' in the presence of the Divinity of Truth," &c.—*Quarrels of Authors*, vol. ii., p. 282, *et seq.*]

[1] See a long note upon this subject, in Dryden's Works, vol. x., p. 254.

avowed defence of James's strides towards arbitrary power, with the unpopular circumstance of
its coming from a new convert to the royal faith,
involved our poet in the general suspicion with
which the nation at large now viewed the slightest
motions of their infatuated monarch. The most
noted amongst those who appeared to oppose the
triumphant advocate of the Hind, were Montague
and Prior, young men now rising into eminence.
They joined to produce a parody, entitled the
" Town and Country Mouse ;" with part of which
Mr Bayes is supposed to gratify his old friends,
Smith and Johnson, by repeating to them. The
piece is, therefore, founded upon the twice-told jest
of the " Rehearsal." Of the parody itself, we have
given ample specimen in its proper place.[1] There is
nothing new or original in the idea, which chiefly
turns upon the ridiculing the poem of Dryden,
where religious controversy is made the subject
of dispute and adjustment between a Hind and a
Panther, who vary between their typical character
of animals, and their real character as the Catholic
and English church. In this piece, Prior, though
the younger man, seems to have had by far the
larger share. Lord Peterborough, on being asked
whether the satire was not written by Montague,
in conjunction with Prior, answered, " Yes ; as if
I, seated in Mr Cheselden's chaise drawn by his
fine horse, should say, *Lord !* how finely we draw
this chaise ! " Indeed, although the parody was

[1] [See Notes to " The Hind and Panther," Dryden's
Works, vol. x.]

trite and obvious, the satirists had the public upon their side; and it now seems astonishing with what acclamations this attack upon the most able champion of James's faith was hailed by his discontented subjects. Dryden was considered as totally overcome by his assailants; they deemed themselves, and were deemed by others, as worthy of very distinguished and weighty recompense;[1] and what was yet a more decisive proof that their bolt had attained its mark, the aged poet is said to have lamented, even with tears, the usage he had received from two young men, to whom he had been always civil. This last circumstance is probably exaggerated. Montague and Prior had doubtless been frequenters of Will's Coffee-house, where Dryden held the supreme rule in criticism, and had thus, among other rising wits, been distinguished by him. That he should have felt their satire, is natural; for the arrow flew with the wind, and popularity amply supplied its deficiency in real vigour: but the reader may probably conclude, with Johnson, that Dryden was too much

[1] That Prior was discontented with his share of preferment, appears from the verses entitled " Earl Robert's Mice," and an angry expostulation elsewhere:

" My friend Charles Montague's preferr'd;
Nor would I have it long observed,
That one mouse eats while t'other's starved."

There is a popular tradition, but no farther to be relied on than as showing the importance attached to the " Town and Country Mouse," which says, that Dorset, in presenting Montague to King William, said, " I have brought a *Mouse* to wait on your majesty." " I will make a man of him," said the king; and settled a pension of L.500 upon the fortunate satirist.

hackneyed in political warfare to suffer so deeply
from the parody, as Dr Lockier's anecdote would
lead us to believe.[1] " If we can suppose him
vexed," says that accurate judge of human nature,
" we can hardly deny him sense to conceal his
uneasiness."

Although Prior and Montague were first in place
and popularity, there wanted not the usual crowd
of inferior satirists and poetasters to follow them
to the charge. " The Hind and the Panther " was
assailed by a variety of pamphlets, by Tom Brown
and others, of which an account, with specimens,
perhaps more than sufficient, is annexed to the
notes on the poem in this edition.[2] It is worth
mentioning, that on this, as on a former occasion,
an adversary of Dryden chose to select one of his
own poems as a contrast to his latter opinions.
The " *Religio Laici* " was reprinted, and carefully
opponed to the various passages of " The Hind
and the Panther," which appeared most contradictory to its tenets. But while the Grub-street
editor exulted in successfully pointing out the
inconsistency between Dryden's earlier and later
religious opinions, he was incapable of observing,

[1] [" Dryden was most touched with the Hind and the Panther transverst.   I have heard him say, ' For two young fellows that I have always been so civil to, to use an old man
in so cruel a manner.'   And he wept as he said it."—LOCKIER
—*Spence's Anecdotes* (Malone), p. 111.]

[2] [" Nothing can surpass the admirable version of the Hind
and the Panther, yet Dryden has *denaturalised* the character
of the apologue and of the animals which appear in it ; and
his talents have not protected him against the criticisms
which he deserves."—*Quarterly Review,* April, 1819.]

that the change was adopted in consequence of the same unbroken train of reasoning, and that Dryden, when he wrote the "*Religio Laici*," was under the impulse of the same conviction, which, further prosecuted, led him to acquiesce in the faith of Rome.

The king appears to have been hardly less anxious to promote the dispersion of the "Hind and the Panther," than the Protestant party to ridicule the piece and its author. It was printed about the same time at London and in Edinburgh, where a printing-press was maintained in Holyrood-House, for the dispersion of tracts favouring the Catholic religion. The poem went rapidly through two or three editions; a circumstance rather to be imputed to the celebrity of the author, and to the anxiety which foes, as well as friends, entertained to learn his sentiments, than to any disposition to acquiesce in his arguments.

But Dryden's efforts in favour of the Catholic cause, were not limited to this controversial poem. He is said to have been at first employed by the court, in translating Varillas's "History of Heresies," a work held in considerable estimation by the Catholic divines. Accordingly, an entry to that purpose was made by Tonson in the Stationers' books, of such a translation made by Dryden at his majesty's command. This circumstance is also mentioned by Burnet, who adds, in very coarse and abusive terms, that the success of his own remarks having destroyed the character of Varillas as a historian, the disappointed translator

revenged himself by the severe character of the
Buzzard, under which the future Bishop of Sarum
is depicted in " The Hind and the Panther."[1]
The credulity of Burnet, especially where his

[1] The passage, as quoted at length by Mr Malone, removes
an obscurity which puzzled former biographers, at least as far
as any thing can be made clear, which must ultimately depend
upon such clumsy diction as the following. " It (the answer
of Burnet) will perhaps be a little longer a digesting to Mons.
Varillas, than it was a preparing to me. One proof will
quickly appear, whether the world is so satisfied with his
Answer, as upon that to return to any thoughts of his history; for I have been informed from England, that a gentleman, who is known both for poetry and other things, had
spent three months in translating M. Varillas's History; but
that, as soon as my Reflections appeared, he discontinued his
labour, finding the credit of his author was gone.   Now, if
he thinks it is recovered by his answer, he will perhaps go on
with his translation; and this may be, for aught I know, as
good an entertainment for him as the conversation that he had
set on between the Hinds and Panthers, and all the rest of the
animals, for whom M. Varillas may serve well enough for an
author : and this history and that poem are such extraordinary things of their kind, that it will be but suitable to see the
author of the worst poem, become likewise the translator of the
worst history, that the age has produced. If his grace and his
wit improve both proportionably, he will hardly find that he
has gained much by the change he has made, from having no
religion to choose one of the worst.   It is true, he had something to sink from, in matter of wit; but as for his morals, it
is scarce possible for him to grow a worse man than he was.
He has lately wreaked his malice on me for spoiling his three
months' labour; but in it he has done me all the honour that
any man can receive from him, which is to be railed at by
him. If I had ill-nature enough to prompt me to wish a very
bad wish for him, it should be, that he would go on and finish
his translation.   By that it will appear, whether the English
nation, which is the most competent judge in this matter,
has, upon the seeing our debate, pronounced in M. Varillas's
favour, or in mine.   It is true, Mr D. will suffer a little by

vanity was concerned, was unbounded; and there seems room to trace Dryden's attack upon him, rather to some real or supposed concern in the controversy about the Duchess of York's papers, so often alluded to in the poem, than to the commentary on Varillas, which is not once mentioned. Yet it seems certain that Dryden entertained thoughts of translating "The History of Heresies;" and, for whatever reason, laid the task aside. He soon after was engaged in a task, of a kind as unpromising as remote from his poetical studies, and connected, in the same close degree, with the religious views of the unfortunate James II. This was no other than the translation of "The Life of St Francis Xavier," one of the last adopted saints of the Catholic church, at least whose merits and supposed miracles were those of a missionary. Xavier is perhaps among the latest also, whose renown for sanctity, and the powers attending it, appears to have been extensive, even while he was yet alive.[1] Above all, he was of the order of Jesuits, and the very saint to whom Mary of Este had addressed her vows, in hopes to secure a Catholic successor to the throne of England.[2] It was,

---

it; but at least it will serve to keep him in from other extravagances; and if he gains little honour by this work, yet he cannot lose so much by it, as he has done by his last employment."

[1] In the "Staple of News," act iii., scene 2, Jonson talks of the miracles done by the Jesuits in Japan and China, as current articles of intelligence.

[2] In the Dedication to the Queen, this is stated with a gravity suitable to the occasion. "The reverend author of

therefore, natural enough, that Dryden should have
employed himself in translating the life of a saint,
whose virtues must at that time have appeared so
peculiarly meritorious ; whose praises were so acceptable to his patroness ; and whose miracles were
wrought for the credit of the Catholic church,
within so late a period. Besides, the work had been
composed by Bartoli, in Portuguese ; and by Bou-
hours, in French. With the merits of the latter
we are well acquainted; of the former, Dryden
speaks highly in the dedication. It may perhaps
be more surprising, that the present editor should
have retained this translation, than that Dryden
should have undertaken it. But surely the only
work of this very particular and enthusiastic nature,
which the modern English language has to exhibit,
was worthy of preservation, were it but as a curiosity. The creed and the character of Catholic faith,

this Life, in his dedication to his most Christian Majesty,
affirms, that France was owing for him to the intercession of
St Francis Xavier. That Anne of Austria, his mother, after
twenty years of barrenness, had recourse to heaven, by her
fervent prayers, to draw down that blessing, and addressed
her devotions, in a particular manner, to this holy apostle of
the Indies. I know not, madam, whether I may presume to
tell the world, that your majesty has chosen this great saint
for one of your celestial patrons, though I am sure you will
never be ashamed of owning so glorious an intercessor ; not
even in a country where the doctrine of the holy church is
questioned, and those religious addresses ridiculed. Your
majesty, I doubt not, has the inward satisfaction of knowing,
that such pious prayers have not been unprofitable to you ;
and the nation may one day come to understand, how happy
it will be for them to have a son of prayers ruling over
them."

are now so much forgotten among us, (popularly speaking,) that, in reading the " Life of Xavier," the Protestant finds himself in a new and enchanted land. The motives, and the incidents, and the doctrines, are alike new to him, and, indeed, occasionally form a strange contrast among themselves. There are few who can read, without a sentiment of admiration, the heroic devotion with which, from the highest principle of duty, Xavier exposes himself to hardship, to danger, to death itself, that he may win souls to the Christian faith. The most rigid Protestant, and the most indifferent philosopher, cannot deny to him the courage and patience of a martyr, with the good sense, resolution, ready wit, and address, of the best negotiator that ever went upon a temporal embassy. It is well that our admiration is qualified by narrations so monstrous, as his actually restoring the dead to life;[1] so profane, as the inference concerning the sweating crucifix;[2] so trivial and absurd, as a crab's fishing up Xavier's cross, which had fallen into the sea;[3] and, to conclude, so shocking to humanity, as the account of the saint passing by the house of his ancestors, the abode of his aged mother, on his road to leave Europe for ever, and conceiving he did God good service in denying himself the melancholy consolation of a last farewell.[4] Altogether it forms a curious picture of the human mind, strung to a pitch of enthusiasm, which we can only learn from such narratives: and those to whom this

[1] See Dryden's Works, vol. xvi., pp. 155, 423.
[2] Ibid. p. 456.   [3] Ibid. p. 162.   [4] Ibid. p. 46.

affords no amusement, may glean some curious particulars from the " Life of Xavier," concerning the state of India and Japan, at the time of his mission, as well as of the internal regulations and singular policy adopted by the society, of which the saint was a member. Besides the " Life of Xavier," Dryden is said to have translated Bossuet's " Exposition of the Catholic doctrine ;" but for this we have but slight authority.[1]

Dryden's political and polemic discussions naturally interfered at this period with his more general poetical studies. About the period of James's accession, Tonson had indeed published a second Volume of Miscellanies, to which our poet contributed a critical preface, with various translations from Virgil, Lucretius, and Theocritus, and four Odes of Horace ; of which the third of the First Book is happily applied to Lord Roscommon, and the twenty-ninth to Lawrence Hyde, Earl of Rochester. Upon these and his other translations Garth has the following striking and forcible observations, though expressed in language somewhat

---

[1] " In the Bodleian Catalogue another work is attributed to our author, on very slight grounds : ' An Exposition of the Doctrine of the Catholic Church,' translated from Bossuet, Bishop of Meaux, and published at London in 1685. The only authority for attributing this translation to Dryden, should seem to have been the following note in Bishop Barlow's handwriting, at the bottom of the titlepage of the copy belonging to the Bodleian Library : ' By Mr Dryden, then only a poet, now a papist too: may be, he was a papist before, but not known till of late.' This book had belonged to Bishop Barlow, who died in 1691."—MALONE.

quaint. " I cannot pass by that admirable English poet, without endeavouring to make his country sensible of the obligations they have to his muse. Whether they consider the flowing grace of his versification, the vigorous sallies of his fancy, or the peculiar delicacy of his periods, they all discover excellences never to be enough admired. If they trace him from the first productions of his youth to the last performances of his age, they will find, that as the tyranny of rhyme never imposed on the perspicuity of sense, so a languid sense never wanted to be set off by the harmony of rhyme. And, as his earlier works wanted no maturity, so his latter wanted no force or spirit. The falling off of his hair had no other consequence than to make his laurels be seen the more.

" As a translator, he was just; as an inventor, he was rich. His versions of some parts of Lucretius, Horace, Homer, and Virgil, throughout, gave him a just pretence to that compliment which was made to Monsieur d'Ablancourt, a celebrated French translator. *It is uncertain who have the greatest obligation to him, the dead or the living.*

" With all these wondrous talents he was libelled, in his lifetime, by the very men who had no other excellences but as they were his imitators. Where he was allowed to have sentiments superior to all others, they charged him with theft. But how did he steal? no otherwise than like those who steal beggars' children, only to clothe them the better."

In this reign Dryden wrote the first Ode to St

Cecilia, for her festival, in 1687. This and the
Ode to the Memory of Mrs Anne Killigrew, a
performance much in the manner of Cowley, and
which has been admired perhaps fully as much as
it merits, were the only pieces of general poetry
which he produced between the accession of James
and the Revolution. It was, however, about this
time, that the poet became acquainted with the
simple and beautiful hymns of the Catholic ritual,
the only pieces of uninspired sacred poetry which
are worthy of the purpose to which they are dedicated. It is impossible to hear the " *Dies Iræ*,"
or the " *Stabat Mater dolorosa*," without feeling,
that the stately simplicity of the language, differing
almost as widely from classical poetry as from that
of modern nations, awes the congregation, like the
architecture of the Gothic cathedrals in which they
are chanted. The ornaments which are wanting
to these striking effusions of devotion, are precisely
such as would diminish their grand and solemn
effect; and nothing but the cogent and irresistible
propriety of addressing the Divinity in a language
understood by the whole worshipping assembly,
could have justified the discarding these magnificent hymns from the reformed worship.[1] We

---

[1] [In a letter to Mr Crabbe, on the subject of Church
Psalmody, written in 1813, Sir Walter Scott thus expresses
himself : " I think those hymns which do not immediately
recall the warm and exalted language of the Bible, are apt to be,
however elegant, rather cold and flat for the purposes of devotion. You will readily believe that I do not approve of the vague
and indiscriminate scripture language which the fanatics of
old and the modern Methodists have adopted; but merely

must suppose that Dryden, as a poet, was interested in the poetical part of the religion which he·had chosen; and his translation of " *Veni, Creator Spiritus,*" which was probably recommended to him as being the favourite hymn of St Francis Xavier,[1] shows he was so.   But it is less generally known, that the English Catholics have preserved two other translations ascribed to Dryden; one of the " *Te Deum,*" the other of the Hymn for St John's Eve; which are inserted in the poet's works.

A characteristic of James's administration was rigid economy, not only in ordinary matters, but towards his own partisans;—a wretched quality in a prince, who was attempting a great and unpopular revolution both in religion and politics, and ought, by his liberality, and even profusion, to have attached the hearts and excited the hopes of those fiery and unsettled spirits, who are ever foremost in times of national tumult.   Dryden, one of his

---

that solemnity and peculiarity of diction which at once puts the reader and hearer on his guard as to the purpose of the poetry.   To my Gothic ear, indeed, the *Stabat Mater*, the *Dies Iræ*, and some of the other hymns of the Catholic church, are more solemn and affecting than the fine classical poetry of Buchanan : the one has the gloomy dignity of a Gothic church, and reminds us instantly of the worship to which it is dedicated; the other is more like a Pagan temple, recalling to our memory the classical and fabulous deities," &c.—*Life of the Rev. Geo. Crabbe*, p. 209.]

[1] " Before the beginning of every canonical hour, he always said the hymn of ' *Veni, Creator Spiritus ;*' and it was observed, that while he said it, his countenance was enlightened, as if the Holy Ghost, whom he invoked, was visibly descended on him."—*Dryden's Works*, vol. xvi., p. 473.

most efficient and zealous supporters, and who had taken the step which of all others was calculated to please James, received only, as we have seen, after the interval of nearly a year from that prince's accession, an addition of L.100 to his yearly pension. There may, however, on occasion of " The Hind and the Panther," the Controversy with Stillingfleet, and other works undertaken with an express view to the royal interest, have been private communications of James's favour. But Dryden, always ready to supply with hope the deficiency of present possession, went on his literary course rejoicing. A lively epistle to his friend Etherege, then envoy for James at Ratisbon, shows the lightness and buoyancy of his spirits at this supposed auspicious period.

An event, deemed of the utmost and most bene-ficial importance to the family of Stuart, but which, according to their usual ill fortune, helped to precipitate their ruin, next called forth the public gratulation of the poet laureat. This was the birth of that " son of prayers" prophesied in the dedication to Xavier, whom the English, with obstinate incredulity, long chose to consider as an impostor, grafted upon the royal line to the prejudice of the Protestant succession. Dryden's " Britannia Rediviva" hailed, with the enthusiasm of a Catholic and a poet, the very event, which, removing all hope of succession in the course of nature, precipitated the measures of the Prince of Orange, exhausted the patience of the exasperated people, and led them violently to extirpate a hated dynasty, which seemed likely to be protracted by a new reign. The merits of the poem have been considered in the introductory remarks prefixed in this edition.[1]

Whatever hopes Dryden may have conceived in consequence of " The Hind and the Panther," " Britannia Rediviva," and other works favourable to the cause of James and of his religion, they were suddenly and for ever blighted by the REVOLUTION. It cannot be supposed that the poet viewed without anxiety the crisis while yet at a distance; and perhaps his own tale of the Swallows may have begun to bear, even to the author, the air of a prophecy. He is said, in an obscure libel, to have been among those courtiers who encouraged, by frequent visits, the camp on Hounslow Heath,[2] upon which the king had grounded his hopes of subduing the contumacy

---

[1] Dryden's Works, vol. x., p. 285.

" Here daily swarm prodigious wights,
And strange variety of sights,
As ladies lewd, and foppish knights,
Priests, poets, pimps, and parasites;
Which now we'll spare, and only mention
The hungry bard that writes for pension:
Old Squab, (who's sometimes here, I'm told,)
That oft has with his prince made bold,
Call'd the late king a saunt'ring cully,
To magnify the Gallic bully;
Who lately put a senseless banter
Upon the world, with Hind and Panther;
Making the beasts and birds o'the wood
Debate, what he ne'er understood,
Deep secrets in philosophy,
And mysteries in theology,
All sung in wretched poetry;
Which rambling piece is as much farce all,
As his true mirror, the ' Rehearsal;'
For which he has been soundly bang'd,
But ha'n't his just reward till hang'd.",
                    Poem on the Camp at Hounslow.

of his subjects, and repelling the invasion of the Prince of Orange. If so, he must there have learned how unwilling the troops were to second their monarch in his unpopular and unconstitutional attempts; and must have sadly anticipated the event of a struggle between a king and his whole people. When this memorable catastrophe had taken place, our author found himself at once exposed to all the insult, calumny, and sarcasm, with which a successful party in politics never fail to overwhelm their discomfited adversaries. But, what he must have felt yet more severely, the unpopularity of his religion and principles rendered it not merely unsafe, but absolutely impossible, for him to make retaliation. His powers of satire, at such a period, were of no more use to Dryden, than a sword to a man who cannot draw it; only serving to render the pleasure of insulting him more poignant to his enemies, and the necessity of passive submission more bitter to himself. Of the numerous satires, libels, songs, parodies, and pasquinades, which solemnized the downfall of Popery and of James, Dryden had not only some exclusively dedicated to his case, but engaged a portion, more or less, of almost every one which appeared. Scarce Father Petre, or the Papal envoy Dada, themselves, were more distinguished, by these lampoons, than the poet laureat; the unsparing exertion of whose satirical powers, as well as his unrivalled literary preeminence, had excited a strong party against him among the inferior wits, whose political antipathy was aggravated by ancient resentment and literary envy. An extract from one of each kind may serve to show, how very little wit was judged necessary by Dryden's contemporaries to a successful attack upon him.[1]

[1] Extracts from " The Address of John Dryden, Laureat, to his Highness the Prince of Orange :"

> " In all the hosannas our whole world's applause,
> Illustrious champion of our church and laws !
> Accept, great Nassau ! from unworthy me,
> Amongst the adoring crowd, a bended knee ;
> Nor scruple, sir, to hear my echoing lyre,
> Strung, tuned, and join'd to the universal choir ;
> From my suspected mouth thy glories told,
> A known out-lyer from the English fold."

After renewing the old reproach about Cromwell :

> " If thus all this I could unblushing write,
> Fear not that pen that shall thy praise indite,
> When high-born blood my adoration draws,
> Exalted glory and unblemish'd cause ;
> A theme so all divine my muse shall wing,
> What is't for thee, great prince, I will not sing ?
> No bounds shall stop my Pegasian flight,
> I'll spot my Hind, and make my Panther white
>
> — — — — — — —
>
> But if, great prince, my feeble strength shall fail,
> Thy theme I'll to my successors entail ;
> My heirs the unfinish'd subject shall complete :
> I have a son, and he, by all that's great,
> That very son (and trust my oaths, I swore
> As much to my great master James before)
> Shall, by his sire's example, Rome renounce,
> For he, young stripling, yet has turn'd but once ;
> That Oxford nursling, that sweet hopeful boy,
> His father's and that once Ignatian joy,
> Designed for a new Bellarmin Goliah,
> Under the great Gamaliel, Obadiah ;
> This youth, great sir, shall your fame's trumpets blow,
> And soar when my dull wings shall flag below.
>
> — — — — — — —
>
> Why should I blush to turn, when my defence
> And plea's so plain ?—for if Omnipotence
> Be the highest attribute that heaven can boast,
> That's the truest church that heaven resembles most.

Nor was the "pelting of this pitiless storm" of abusive raillery the worst evil to which our author

> The tables then are turn'd: and 'tis confest,
> The strongest and the mightiest is the best:
> In all my changes I'm on the right side,
> And by the same great reason justified.
> When the bold Crescent late attack'd the Cross,
> Resolved the empire of the world to engross,
> Had tottering Vienna's walls but fail'd
> And Turkey over Christendom prevail'd,
> Long ere this I had cross'd the Dardanello,
> And reign'd the mighty Mahomet's hail fellow;
> Quitting my duller hopes, the poor renown
> Of Eaton College, or a Dublin gown,
> And commenced graduate in the grand divan,
> Had reign'd a more immortal Mussulman."

The lines which follow are taken from "The Deliverance," a poem to the Prince of Orange, by a Person of Quality. 9th February, 1688-9.

> "Alas! how cruel is a poet's fate!
> Or who indeed would be a laureat,
> That must or fall or turn with every change of state?
> Poor bard! if thy hot zeal for loyal Wem [1]
> Forbids thy tacking, sing his requiem;
> Sing something, prithee, to enure thy thumb;
> Nothing but conscience strikes a poet dumb.
> Conscience, that dull chimera of the schools,
> A learned imposition upon fools,
> Thou, Dryden, are not silenced with such stuff,
> Egad thy conscience has been large enough.
> But here are loyal subjects still, and foes,
> Many to mourn, for many to oppose.
> Shall thy great master, thy almighty Jove,
> Whom thou to place above the gods hast strove,
> Shall he from David's throne so early fall,
> And laureat Dryden not one tear let fall;
> Nor sings the bard his exit in one poor pastoral?
> Thee fear confines, thee, Dryden, fear confines,
> And grief, nor shame, stops thy recanting lines.
> Our Damon is as generous as great,
> And well could pardon tears that love create,
> Shouldst thou, in justice to thy vexed soul,
> Not sing to him, but thy lost lord condole.
> But silence is a damning error, John;
> I'd or my master or myself bemoan."

[1] *Lord Jefferies, Baron of Wem.*

was subjected. The religion which he professed, rendered him incapable of holding any office under the new government, even if he could have bended his political principles to take the oaths to William and Mary. We may easily believe, that Dryden's old friend Dorset, now lord high-chamberlain, felt repugnance to render vacant the places of poet laureat and royal historiographer, by removing the man in England most capable of filling them; but the sacrifice was inevitable. Dryden's own feelings, on losing the situation of poet laureat, must have been greatly aggravated by the selection of his despised opponent Shadwell as his successor; a scribbler whom, in " Mac-Flecknoe," he had himself placed preeminent in the regions of dulness, but who now, so far as royal mandate can arrange such precedence, was raised in his stead as chief among English poets. This very remarkable coincidence has led several of Dryden's biographers, and Dr Johnson among others, to suppose that the satire was actually written to ridicule Shadwell's elevation to the honours of the laurel; though nothing is more certain than that it was published while Dryden was himself laureat, and could be hardly supposed to anticipate the object of his satire becoming his successor. Shadwell, however, possessed merits with King William, which were probably deemed by that prince of more importance than all the genius of Shakspeare, Milton, and Dryden, if it could have been combined in one individual. He was a stanch Whig, and had suffered under the former government, being "silenced as a non-conforming poet;" the doors of the theatre closed against his plays; and, if he may himself be believed, even his life was endangered, not only by the slow process of starving, but some more active proceeding of his powerful enemies.[1] Shadwell, moreover, had not failed to hail the dawn of the Revolution by a congratulatory poem to the Prince of Orange, and to Queen Mary on her arrival. In every point of view, his principles, fidelity, and alacrity, claimed William's countenance; he was presented to him by Dorset, not as the best poet, but as the most honest man, politically speaking, among the competitors;[2] and accordingly succeeded to Dryden's situation as poet laureat and royal historiographer, with the appointment of L.300 a-year. Shadwell, as might have been expected, triumphed in his success over his great antagonist; but his triumph was expressed in strains which showed he was totally unworthy of it.[3]

[1] In the dedication of " Bury-Fair " to his patron the Earl of Dorset, he claims the merit due to his political constancy and sufferings: " I never could recant in the worst of times, when my ruin was designed, and my life was sought, and for near ten years I was kept from the exercise of that profession which had afforded me a competent subsistence; and surely I shall not now do it, when there is a liberty of speaking common sense, which, though not long since forbidden, is now grown current."

[2] See Cibber or Shiels's Life of Shadwell.

[3] " These wretched poëtitos, who got praise
For writing most confounded loyal plays,
With viler, coarser jests than at Bear-garden,
And silly Grub-street songs worse than Tom-farthing.
If any noble patriot did excel,
His own and country's rights defending well,

Dryden, deprived by the Revolution of present possession and future hope, was now reduced to the same, or a worse situation, than he had occupied in the year of the Restoration, his income resting almost entirely upon his literary exertions, his expenses increased by the necessity of providing for and educating his family, and the advantage of his high reputation perhaps more than counterbalanced by the popular prejudice against his religion and party. So situated, he patiently and prudently bent to the storm which he could not resist; and though he might privately circulate a few light pieces in favour of the exiled family, as the " Lady's Song,"[1] and the translation of Pitcairn's beautiful Epitaph[2] on the Viscount of Dundee, it seems certain, that he made no formal attack on the government, either in verse or prose. Those who imputed to him the satires on the Revolution,

These yelping curs were straight loo'd on to bark,
On the deserving man to set a mark.
These abject, fawning parasites and knaves,
Since they were such, would have all others slaves.
'Twas precious loyalty that was thought fit
To atone for want of honesty and wit.
No wonder common-sense was all cried down,
And noise and nonsense swagger'd through the town.
Our author, then opprest, would have you know it,
Was silenced for a non-conformist poet;
In those hard times he bore the utmost test,
And now he swears he's loyal as the best.
Now, sirs, since common-sense has won the day,
Be kind to this, as to his last year's play.
His friends stood firmly to him when distress'd;
He hopes the number is not now decreased.
He found esteem from those he valued most,
Proud of his friends, he of his foes could boast."

Prologue to Bury-Fair.

[1] Dryden's Works, vol. xi., p. 175.   [2] Ibid. p. 113.

called " *Suum Cuique*," and " Tarquin and Tullia,"
did injustice both to his prudence and his poetry.
The last, and probably both satires, were written
by Mainwaring, who lived to change his opinions,
and become very sorry for what he had done.

The theatre again became Dryden's immediate
resource.   Indeed, the very first play Queen Mary
attended was one of our poet's, which had been
prohibited during the reign of James II.   But
the revival of the " Spanish Friar " could afford
but little gratification to the author, whose newly-
adopted religion is so severely satirized in the person of father Dominic.   Nor was this ill-fated
representation doomed to afford more pleasure to
the personage by whom it was appointed.   For the
audience applied the numerous passages, concerning the deposing the old king and planting a female
usurper on the throne, to the memorable change
which had just taken place ; and all eyes were fixed
upon Queen Mary, with an expression which threw
her into extreme confusion. [1]

Dryden, after the Revolution, began to lay the
foundation for a new structure of fame and popularity in the tragedy of " Don Sebastian."   This
tragedy, which has been justly regarded as the
chef-d'œuvre of his plays, was not, he has informed
us, " huddled up in haste."   The author knew the
circumstances in which he stood, while, as he expresses it, his ungenerous enemies were taking
advantage of the times to ruin his reputation ; and

[1] Introduction to " Spanish Friar," Dryden's Works, vol.
vi., p. 371.

was conscious, that the full exertion of his genius was necessary to secure a favourable reception from an audience prepossessed against him and his tenets. Nor did he neglect to smooth the way, by inscribing the piece to the Earl of Leicester, brother of Algernon Sidney, who had borne arms against Charles in the civil war; and yet, Whig or republican as he was, had taste and feeling enough to patronise the degraded laureat and proscribed Catholic. The dedication turns upon the philosophical and moderate use of political victory, the liberality of considering the friend rather than the cause, the dignity of forgiving and relieving the fallen adversary; themes, upon which the eloquence of the suffering party is usually unbounded, although sometimes forgotten when they come again into power. With all this deprecatory reasoning, Dryden does not recede, or hint at receding, one inch from his principles, but concludes his preface with a resolution to adopt the counsel of the classic :—

" *Tu ne cede malis, sed contra audentior ito.*" ¹

The merits of this beautiful tragedy I have

¹ [" Soon after the accession of James the Second, Dryden, as is well known, threw additional suspicion upon his character, by embracing, not only the politics, but the religion of the court. The grounds of this charge are investigated by Mr Scott with much candour and ingenuity; and we concur with him in thinking, that a good deal of sincerity was mingled with a readiness to make use of the lucky opportunity. This opinion is founded upon the ' *Religio Laici,*' published in 1682, three years before his conversion; a poem indicating a very vigorous, but a very sceptical mind; unable to solve the problems in religion which it raised to itself, and already willing

attempted to analyze in another place,[1] and at considerable length. It was brought forward in 1690 with great theatrical pomp.[2] But with all these advantages, the first reception of " Don Sebastian " was but cool; nor was it until several retrenchments and alterations had been made, that it rose to the high pitch in public favour which it maintained for many years, and deserved to maintain for ever.

In the same year, " Amphitryon," in which Dryden displays his comic powers to more advantage than anywhere, excepting in the " Spanish Friar," was acted with great applause, calling

to cut the knot, by resorting to an infallible director. There is much reason, therefore, to believe, that Dryden felt sincerely the conviction that he was right in his change of faith; though it would probably never have taken place in other times, and under another master. But we cannot coincide in laying any stress upon his continuing a Catholic after the Revolution. Every man must keep some measures with public opinion; and so gross an avowal of want of principle, would have forfeited the esteem of his friends, and certainly not rendered his enemies less bitter. We do not know what law forbids a Catholic to be poetlaureat, nor why Dryden's expulsion from that place, which Mr Malone is absurd enough to call conscientiously relinquishing it, should be ascribed merely to his religion. But he had gone all lengths, both of adulation and virulence, in support of a party now fallen; it was just, therefore, that he should share their fate, and though befriended by many Whigs, he must naturally have been obnoxious to the greater number."—HALLAM.]

[1] Dryden's Works, vol. vii., p. 273.

[2] " A play well dressed, you know, is half in half, as a great writer says. The Morocco dresses, when new, formerly for ' Sebastian,' they say, enlivened the play as much as the ' pudding and dumpling ' song did Merlin."—*The Female Wits*, a comedy by Mountfort.

forth the gratulations even of Milbourne, who afterwards made so violent an attack upon the translation of Virgil.　The comedy was inscribed to Sir William Leveson Gower, whose name, well known in the history of the Revolution, may be supposed to have been invoked as a talisman against misconstructions, to which Dryden's situation so peculiarly exposed him, and to which he plainly alludes in the prologue.[1]　Our author's choice of this patron was probably dictated by Sir William Gower's connexion with the Earl of Rochester, whose grand-daughter he had married.

Encouraged by the revival of his popularity, Dryden now ventured to bring forward the opera of " King Arthur," originally designed as an entertainment to Charles II.; " Albion and Albanius" being written as a sort of introductory masque upon the occasion.[2]　When we consider the strong and even violent political tendency of that prefatory piece, we may readily suppose, that the opera was originally written in a strain very different from the present; and that much must have been

[1] " The labouring bee, when his sharp sting is gone,
　Forgets his golden work, and turns a drone ;
　Such is a satire, when you take away
　That rage, in which his noble vigour lay.
　What gain you by not suffering him to tease ye ?
　He neither can offend you now, nor please ye.
　The honey-bag and venom lay so near,
　That both together you resolved to tear,
　And lost your pleasure to secure your fear.
　How can he show his manhood, if you bind him
　To box, like boys, with one hand tied behind him ?
　This is plain levelling of wit; in which
　The poor has all the advantage, not the rich
　The blockhead stands excused for wanting sense;
　And wits turn blockheads in their own defence."

[2] See *ante*, p. 257.

softened, altered, and erased, ere a play, designed
to gratulate the discovery of the Rye-house plot,
could, without hazard, be acted after the Revolution. The odious, though necessary, task of defa-
cing his own labours, was sufficiently disgusting to
the poet, who complains, that " not to offend the
present times, nor a government which has hitherto
protected me, I have been obliged so much to alter
the first design, and take away so many beauties
from the writing, that it is now no more what it
was formerly, than the present ship of the Royal
Sovereign, after so often taking down and altering, is the vessel it was at the first building." Persevering in the prudent system of seeking patrons
among those whose patronage was rendered effectual by their influence with the prevailing party,
Dryden prefixed to " King Arthur" a beautiful
dedication to the Marquis of Halifax, to whose
cautious and nice policy he ascribes the nation's
escape from the horrors of civil war, which seemed
impending in the latter years of Charles II.; and
he has not failed, at the same time, to pay a passing
tribute to the merits of his original and good-
humoured master. The music of " King Arthur"
being composed by Purcel, gave Dryden occasion
to make that eminent musician some well-deserved
compliments, which were probably designed as a
peace-offering for the injudicious preference given
to Grabut in the introduction to " Albion and Albanius."[1] The dances were composed by Priest;

[1] See *ante*, p. 259.

and the whole piece was eminently successful. Its good fortune, however, was imputed, by the envious, to a lively song in the last act, which had little or nothing to do with the business of the piece. In this opera ended all the hopes which the world might entertain of an epic poem from Dryden on the subject of King Arthur.

Our author was by no means so fortunate in " Cleomenes," his next dramatic effort. The times were something changed since the Revolution. The Tories, who had originally contributed greatly to that event, had repented them of abandoning the Stuart family, and, one after another, were returning to their attachment to James. It is probable that this gave new courage to Dryden, who, although upon the accession of King William, he saw himself a member of an odious and proscribed sect, now belonged to a broad political faction, which a variety of events was daily increasing. Hence his former caution was diminished, and the suspicion of his enemies increased in proportion. The choice of the subject, the history of a Spartan prince exiled from his kingdom, and waiting the assistance of a foreign monarch to regain it, corresponded too nearly with that of the unfortunate James. The scene of a popular insurrection, where the minds of a whole people were inflamed, was liable to misinterpretation. In short, the whole story of the Spartan Cleomenes was capable of being wrested to political and jacobitic purposes; and there wanted not many to aver, that to such purposes it had been actually applied by Dryden. Neither was the state of our author such at the time, as to permit his pleading his own cause. The completion of the piece having been interrupted by indisposition, was devolved upon his friend Southerne, who revised and concluded the last act. The whispers of the author's enemies in the meantime procured a prohibition, at least a suspension, of the representation of " Cleomenes" from the Lord Chamberlain. The exertions of Hyde, Earl of Rochester, who, although a Tory, was possessed necessarily of some influence as maternal-uncle to the Queen, procured a recall of this award against a play which was in every respect truly inoffensive. But there was still a more insuperable obstacle to its success. The plot is flat and unsatisfactory, involving no great event, and in truth being only the question, whether Cleomenes should or should not depart upon an expedition, which appears far more hazardous than remaining where he was. The grave and stoical character of the hero is more suitable to the French than the English stage; nor had the general conduct of the play that interest, or perhaps bustle, which is necessary to fix the attention of the promiscuous audience of London. In a theatre, where every man may, if he will, express his dissatisfaction, in defiance of *beaux-esprits*, *nobles*, or *movsquetaires*, that which is dull will seldom be long fashionable : " Cleomenes" was accordingly coldly received. Dryden published it with a dedication to Lord Rochester, and the Life of Cleomenes prefixed, as translated from Plutarch by Creech, that it might appear how false those reports were, which imputed to him the composing a Jacobite play.

Omitting, for the present, Dryden's intermediate employments, I hasten to close his dramatic career, by mentioning, that " Love Triumphant," his last play, was acted in 1692, with very bad success. Those who look over this piece, which is in truth one of the worst our author ever wrote, can be at no loss to discover sufficient reason for its condemnation. The comic part approaches to farce, and the tragic unites the wild and unnatural changes and counterchanges of the Spanish tragedy, with the involutions of unnatural and incestuous passion, which the British audience has been always averse to admit as a legitimate subject of dramatic pity or terror. But it cannot be supposed that Dryden received the failure with any thing like an admission of its justice. He was a veteran foiled in the last of his theatrical trials of skill, and retreated for ever from the stage, with expressions which transferred the blame from himself to his judges ; for, in the dedication to James, the fourth Earl of Salisbury, a relation of Lady Elizabeth, and connected with the poet by a similarity of religious and political opinions, he declares, that the characters of the persons in the drama are truly drawn, the fable not injudiciously contrived, the changes of fortune not unartfully managed, and the catastrophe happily introduced : thus leaving, were the author's opinion to be admitted as decisive, no foundation upon which the critics could ground their opposition. The enemies of Dryden, as usual, triumphed greatly in the fall of this piece;[1] and thus the dramatic career of Dryden began and closed with bad success.

This section cannot be more properly concluded than with the list which Mr Malone has drawn out of Dryden's plays, with the respective dates of their being acted and published; which is a correction and enlargement of that subjoined by the author himself to the opera of " Prince Arthur." Henceforward we are to consider Dryden as unconnected with the stage.

[1] For example, in a Session of the Poets, under the fictitious name of Matthew Coppinger, Dryden is thus irreverently introduced :

> " A reverend grisly elder first appear'd,
> With solemn pace through the divided herd ;
> Apollo, laughing at his clumsy mien,
> Pronounced him straight the poets' alderman.
> His labouring muse did many years excel
> In ill inventing, and translating well,
> Till ' Love Triumphant ' did the cheat reveal.
>
> So when appears, midst sprightly births, a sot,
> Whatever was the other offspring's lot,
> This we are sure was lawfully begot."

PLAYS.	Acted by	Entered at Stationers Hall.	Published in
1. The Wild Gallant. C.	The King's Servants.	Aug. 7, 1667.	1669.
2. The Rival Ladies. T. C.	K. S.	June 27, 1664.	1664.
3. The Indian Emperor. T.	K. S.	May 26, 1665.	1667.
4. Secret Love, or The Maiden Queen. C.	K. S.	Aug. 7, 1667.	1668.
5. Sir Martin Marall. C.	The Duke of York's Servants.	June 24, 1668.	1668.
6. The Tempest. C.	D. S.	Jan. 8, 1669-70.	1670.
7. An Evening's Love, or The Mock Astrologer. C.	K. S.	Nov. 20, 1668.	1671. Q. also 1668.
8. Tyrannic Love, or The Royal Martyr. T.	K. S.	July 14, 1669.	1670.
9. & 10. The Conquest of Granada, Two Parts. T.	K. S.	Feb. 20, 1670-1.	1672.
11. Marriage a-la-Mode. C.	K. S.	March 18, 1672-3.	1673.
12. The Assignation, or Love in a Nunnery. C.	K. S.	March 18, 1672-3.	1673.
13. Amboyna. T.	K. S.	June 26, 1673.	1673.
14. The State of Innocence. O.			1674.
15. Aureng-Zebe. T.	K. S.	April 17, 1674.	1676.
16. All for Love. T.	K. S.	Nov. 29, 1675.	1678.
17. The Kind Keeper, or Mr Limberham. C.	D. S.	Jan. 31, 1677-8.	1678.
18. Œdipus. T.	D. S.		1679.
19. Troilus and Cressida. T.	D. S.		1679.
20. The Spanish Friar. T. C.	D. S.	April 14, 1679.	1681.
21. The Duke of Guise. T.	The United Companies.		1683.
22. Albion and Albanius. O.	U. C.		1685.
23. Don Sebastian. T.	U. C.		1690.
24. Amphitryon. C.	U. C.		1690.
25. King Arthur. O.	U. C.		1691.
26. Cleomenes. T.	U. C.		1692.
27. Love Triumphant. T. C.	U. C.		1694.

SECTION VII.

State of Dryden's Connexions in Society after the Revolu-
tion—Juvenal and Persius—Smaller Pieces—Eleonora
— Third Miscellany—Virgil— Ode to St Cecilia—Dis-
pute with Milbourne— With Blackmore—Fables— The
Author's Death and Funeral—His private Character—
Notices of his Family.

THE evil consequences of the Revolution upon
Dryden's character and fortunes, began to abate
sensibly within a year or two after that event.   It
is well known, that King William's popularity
was as short-lived as it had been universal.   All
parties gradually drew off from the king, under
their ancient standards.   The clergy returned to
their maxims of hereditary right, the Tories to
their attachment to the house of Stuart, the Whigs
to their jealousy of the royal authority.   Dryden,
we have already observed, so lately left in a small
and detested party, was now associated among
multitudes, who, from whatever contradictory motives, were joined in opposition to the government.
A reconciliation took place betwixt him and some
of his kinsmen ; particularly with John Driden of
Chesterton, his first cousin ; with whom, from
about this period till his death, he lived upon terms

of uninterrupted friendship. The influence of Clarendon and Rochester, the queen's uncles, were, we have seen, often exerted in the poet's favour; and through them he became connected with the powerful families with which they were allied. Dorset, by whom he had been deprived of his office, seems to have softened this harsh, though indispensable exertion of authority, by a liberal present; and to his bounty Dryden had frequently recourse in cases of emergency.[1] Indeed, upon one occasion it is said to have been administered in a mode savouring more of ostentation than delicacy; for there is a tradition, that Dryden and Tom Brown, being invited to dine with the lord-chamberlain, found under their covers, the one a

[1] Such, I understand, is the general purport of some letters of Dryden's, in possession of the Dorset family, which contain certain particulars rendering them unfit for publication. Our author himself commemorates Dorset's generosity in the Essay on Satire, in the following affecting passage : " Though I must ever acknowledge to the honour of your lordship, and the eternal memory of your charity, that since this Revolution, wherein I have patiently suffered the ruin of my small fortune, and the loss of that poor subsistence which I had from two kings, whom I had served more faithfully than profitable to myself—then your lordship was pleased, out of no other motive but your own nobleness, without any desert of mine, or the least solicitation from me, to make me a most bountiful present, which at that time, when I was most in want of it, came most seasonably and unexpectedly to my relief. That favour, my lord, is of itself sufficient to bind any grateful man to a perpetual acknowledgment, and to all the future service which one of my mean condition can be ever able to perform. May the Almighty God return it for me, both in blessing you here, and rewarding you hereafter ! "— Essay on Satire, vol. xii., p. 31.

bank-note for L.100, the other for L.50. I have already noticed, that these pecuniary benefactions were not held so degrading in that age as at present; and, probably, many of Dryden's opulent and noble friends took, like Dorset, occasional opportunities of supplying wants, which neither royal munificence, nor the favour of the public, now enabled the poet fully to provide for.

If Dryden's critical empire over literature was at any time interrupted by the mischances of his political party, it was in abeyance for a very short period; since, soon after the Revolution, he appears to have regained, and maintained till his death, that sort of authority in Will's Coffee-house, to which we have frequently had occasion to allude. His supremacy, indeed, seems to have been so effectually established, that a "pinch out of Dryden's snuff-box"[1] was equal to taking a degree in that academy of wit. Among those by whom it was frequented, Southerne and Congreve were principally distinguished by Dryden's friendship.[2] His intimacy with the former, though oddly commenced, seems soon to have ripened into such sincere friendship, that the aged poet selected

---

[1] So says Ward, in the London Spy.

[2] [" It was Dryden who made Will's Coffee-house the great resort for the wits of his time. After his death, Addison transferred it to Button's, (in Russell Street, Covent Garden, on the south side,) who had been a servant of his. . . . . Addison passed each day alike, and much in the same manner as Dryden did. Dryden employed his mornings in writing, dined *en famille*, and then went to Will's, only he came home earlier at nights."—POPE—*Spence's Anecdotes*, (Malone,) p. 114.]

Dryden's unusual economy of adulation ; at least he disappointed some expectations which the poet and bookseller seem to have entertained of his liberality.[1] This dedication indicates, that a quarrel was commenced between our author and the critic Rymer. It appears from a passage in a letter to Tonson, that Rymer had spoken lightly of him in his last critique, (probably in the short view of tragedy,) and that the poet took this opportunity, as he himself expresses it, to snarl again. He therefore acquaints us roundly, that the corruption of a poet was the generation of a critic ; exults a little over the memory of Rymer's " Edgar," a tragedy just reeking from damnation ; and hints at the difference which the public is likely to experience between the present royal historiographer and him whose room he occupied. In his epistle to Congreve, alluding to the same circumstance of Rymer's succeeding to the office of historiographer, as Tate did to the laurel, on the death of Thomas Shadwell, in 1692, Dryden has these humorous lines :

> " O that your brows my laurel had sustain'd !
> Well had I been deposed, if you had reign'd ;
> The father had descended for the son ;
> For only you are lineal to the throne.
> Thus, when the state one Edward did depose,
> A greater Edward in his room arose :

[1] 30th August, 1693, Dryden writes to Tonson, " I am sure you thought my Lord Ratcliffe would have done something ; I guessed more truly, that he could not."—*Dryden's Works*, vol. xviii., p. 109. The expression, perhaps, applies rather to his lordship's want of ability than inclination ; and Dryden says indeed, in the dedication, that it is in his nature to be an encourager of good poets, though fortune has not yet put into his hands the power of expressing it. In a letter to Mrs Steward, Dryden speaks of Ratcliffe as a poet, " and none of the best."—*Ibid.*, p. 177.

But now not I, but poetry, is cursed;
For Tom the second reigns like Tom the first.
But let them not mistake my patron's part,
Nor call his charity their own desert."

From the letter to Tonson above referred to,
it would seem that the dedication of the Third
Miscellany gave offence to Queen Mary, being
understood to reflect upon her government, and
that she had commanded Rymer to return to the
charge, by a criticism on Dryden's plays. But the
breach does not appear to have become wider; and
Dryden has elsewhere mentioned Rymer with
civility.

The Third Miscellany contained, of Dryden's
poetry, a few Songs, the First Book, with part of
the Ninth and Sixteenth Books of the Metamorphoses, and the parting of Hector and Andro-
mache, from the Iliad. It was also to have had
the poem of Hero and Leander, from the Greek;
but none such appeared, nor is it clear whether
Dryden ever executed the version, or only had it
in contemplation.[1] The contribution, although
ample, was not satisfactory to old Jacob Tonson,
who wrote on the subject a most mercantile expos-
tulatory letter to Dryden, which is fortunately still
preserved, as a curious specimen of the minutiæ
of a literary bargain in the seventeenth century.
Tonson, with reference to Dryden having offered
a strange bookseller six hundred lines for twenty
guineas, enters into a question in the rule of three,
by which he discovers, and proves, that for fifty

[1] Dryden's Works, vol. xviii., p. 107.

guineas he has only 1446 lines, which he seems
to take more unkindly, as he had not *counted* the
lines until he had paid the money; from all which
Jacob infers, that Dryden ought, out of generosity,
at least to throw him in something to the bargain,
especially as he had used him more kindly in Juvenal, which, saith the said Jacob, is not reckoned
so easy to translate as Ovid. What weight was
given to this supplication does not appear; probably very little, for the translations were not
extended; and as to getting back any part of the
copy-money, it is not probable Tonson's most
sanguine expectations ever reached that point.
Perhaps the songs were thrown in as a make-
weight. There was a Fourth Miscellany published
in 1694; but to this Dryden only gave a version
of the Third Georgic, and his Epistle to Sir Godfrey Kneller, the requital of a copy of the portrait
of Shakspeare.[1]

In 1693, Dryden addressed the beautiful lines
to Congreve, on the cold reception of his " Double
Dealer." He was himself under a similar cloud,
from the failure of " Love Triumphant," and therefore in a fit mood to administer consolation to his
friend. The epistle contains, among other striking
passages, the affecting charge of the care of his
posthumous fame, which Congreve did not forget
when Dryden was no more.[2]

---

[1] Copied from the Chandos picture. Kneller's copy is now
at Wentworth-House, the seat of Earl Fitzwilliam.

[2] [See Congreve's Preface to Dryden's Plays, in Works,
vol. ii., p. 7. The lines of Dryden alluded to, are

" Already I am worn with cares and age,
And just abandoning the ungrateful stage;

But, independently of occasional exertions, our author, now retired from the stage, had bent his thoughts upon one great literary task, the translation of Virgil.   This weighty and important undertaking was probably suggested by the experience of Tonson, the success of whose " Miscellanies " had taught him the value placed by the public on Dryden's translations from the classics.   From hints thrown out by contemporary authors, there is reason to think that this scheme was meditated even before 1694 ; but in that year the poet, in a letter to Dennis, speaks of it as under his immediate contemplation.   The names of Virgil and of Dryden were talismans powerful to arrest all the literature of England, and fix universal attention upon the progress of the work.   Mr Malone has recorded the following particulars concerning it, with pious enthusiasm :—

" Dr Johnson has justly remarked, that the nation seemed to consider its honour interested in the event.   Mr Gilbert Dolben gave him the various editions of his author : Dr Knightly Chetwood furnished him with the Life of Virgil, and the Preface to the Pastorals ; and Addison supplied the arguments of the several books, and an Essay on the Georgics. The first lines of this great poet which he translated, he wrote with a diamond on a pane of glass in one of the windows of Chesterton-house, in Huntingdonshire, the residence of his

Unprofitably kept at heaven's expense,
I live a rent-charge on his providence :
But you, whom every muse and grace adorn,
Whom I forsee to better fortune born,
Be kind to my remains ; and O defend,
Against your judgment, your departed friend !
Let not the insulting foe my fame pursue,
But shade those laurels which descend to you ;
And take for tribute what these lines express ;
You merit more, nor could my love do less."

Epistle to Congreve, Dryden's Works, vol. xi., p. 62.]

kinsman and namesake, John Driden, Esq. [1] The version of the first Georgic, and a great part of the last Æneid, was made at Denham-Court, in Buckinghamshire, the seat of Sir William Bowyer, Baronet ; and the seventh Æneid was translated at Burleigh, the noble mansion of the Earl of Exeter. These circumstances, which must be acknowledged to be of no great importance, I yet have thought it proper to record, because they will for ever endear those places to the votaries of the Muses, and add to them a kind of celebrity, which neither the beauties of nature, nor the exertions of art, can bestow."

Neither was the liberality of the nation entirely disproportioned to the general importance attached to the translation of Virgil, by so eminent a poet. The researches of Mr Malone have ascertained, in some degree, the terms. There were two classes of subscribers, the first set of whom paid five guineas a-piece to adorn the work with engravings ; beneath each of which, in due and grateful remembrance, was blazoned the arms of a subscriber : this class amounted to one hundred and one persons,[2] and presents an assemblage of noble names, few of whom are distinguished more to their credit than by the place they there occupy. The second subscribers were two hundred and fifty in number, at two guineas each. But from these sums was to be deduced the expense of the engravings, though these were only the plates used for Ogilby's Virgil,[3] a little retouched. Besides the subscriptions,

[1] The antiquary may now search in vain for this frail memorial ; for the house of Chesterton was, 1807, pulled down for the sake of the materials.

[2] [See a list of their names in Dryden's Works, vol. xiii., p. 283, et seq.]

[3] [This Virgil was one of the first books that had any thing of a subscription (and even that was a good deal on account

it would seem, that Dryden received from Tonson fifty pounds for each Book of the " Georgics" and " Æneid," and probably the same for the " Pastorals" collectively. On the other hand, it is probable, that Jacob charged a price for the copies delivered to the subscribers, which, with the expense of the plates, reduced Dryden's profit to about twelve or thirteen hundred pounds ;—a trifling sum when compared to what Pope received for the " Iliad," which was certainly between L.5000 and L.6000 ; yet great in proportion to what the age of Dryden had ever afforded, as an encouragement to literature. It must indeed be confessed, that the Revolution had given a new impulse and superior importance to literary pursuits. The semi-barbarous age, which succeeded the great civil war, had been civilized but by slow degrees. It is true, the king and courtiers, among their disorderly and dissolute pleasures, enumerated songs and plays, and, in the course of their political intrigues, held satires in request ; but they had neither money nor time to spare for the encouragement or study of any of the higher and more elaborate departments of poetry. Meanwhile, the bulk of the nation neglected verse, as what they could not understand, or, with puri-

---

of the prints, which were Ogilby's plates touched up) ; as the Tatlers were the first great subscription . . . . Dryden cleared every way about L.1200 by his Virgil, and had sixpence each line for his Fables. For some time he wrote a play (at least) every year; but in those days ten broad pieces was the usual highest price for a play; and if they got L.50 more in the acting, it was reckoned very well."—Pope, 1742.— *Spence's Anecdotes* (Malone), p. 113.]

Classics, witness those on "Juvenal" and "Persius," he neither indulged in critical dissertations on particular beauties and defects, nor in general remarks upon the kind of poetry before him; but contented himself with rendering into English the antiquarian dissertations of Dacier and other foreign commentators, with now and then an explanatory paraphrase of an obscure passage. The parodies of Martin Scriblerus had not yet consigned to ridicule the verbal criticism, and solemn trifling, with which the ancient schoolmen pretended to illustrate the classics. But besides the dispute about the notes in particular, and the various selfish advantages which Dryden suspected Tonson of attempting to secure in the course of the transaction, he seems to have been particularly affronted at a presumptuous plan of that publisher, (a keen Whig, and secretary of the Kit-cat club,) to drive him into inscribing the translation of Virgil to King William. With this view, Tonson had an especial care to make the engraver aggravate the nose of Æneas in the plates into a sufficient resemblance of the hooked promontory of the Deliverer's countenance;[1] and, foreseeing Dryden's repugnance to his favourite plan, he had recourse, it would seem,

[1] This gave rise to a good epigram:

"Old Jacob, by deep judgment sway'd,
 To please the wise beholders,
Has placed old Nassau's hook-nosed head
 On poor old Æneas' shoulders.

"To make the parallel hold tack,
 Methinks there's little lacking;
One took his father pick-a-pack,
 And 'tother sent his packing."

to more unjustifiable means to further it; for the poet expresses himself, as convinced, that, through Tonson's means, his correspondence with his sons, then at Rome, was intercepted.[1] I suppose Jacob, having fairly laid siege to his author's conscience, had no scruple to intercept all foreign supplies, which might have confirmed him in his pertinacity. But Dryden, although thus closely beleaguered, held fast his integrity; and no prospect of personal advantage, or importunity on the part of Tonson, could induce him to take a step inconsistent with his religious and political sentiments. It was probably during the course of these bickerings with his publisher, that Dryden, incensed at some refusal of accommodation on the part of Tonson, sent him three well-known coarse and forcible satirical lines, descriptive of his personal appearance :

"With leering looks, bull-faced, and freckled fair,
With two left legs, and Judas-colour'd hair,
And frowzy pores, that taint the ambient air."

"Tell the dog," said the poet to the messenger,

[1] "I am of your opinion," says the poet to his son Charles, "that, by Tonson's means, almost all our letters have miscarried for this last year. But, however, he has missed of his design in the dedication, though he had prepared the book for it; for, in every figure of Æneas, he has caused him to be drawn, like King William, with a hooked nose."—Dryden hints to Tonson himself his suspicion of this unworthy device, desiring him to forward a letter to his son Charles, but not by post. "Being satisfied, that Ferrand will do by this as he did by two letters which I sent my sons, about my dedicating to the king, of which they received neither."—Dryden's Works, vol. xviii., pp. 132, 140.

" that he who wrote these can write more." But Tonson, perfectly satisfied with this single triplet, hastened to comply with the author's request, without requiring any further specimen of his poetical powers.[1] It would seem, on the other

[1] [" These descriptive lines," says Mr Nichols, " which had the desired effect, by some means got abroad in manuscript ; and not long after Dryden's death, were inserted in 'Faction Displayed,' a satirical poem, said to have been written by Shippen, and extremely popular among the Tories. Tonson being secretary to the *Kit-Cat* Club, which was composed of the most distinguished Whigs, could not escape the notice of a Tory satirist, who gave vent to his spleen against him in lines, by which he has preserved a description that Dryden probably never intended to be transmitted to posterity." After quoting eleven couplets, Mr Nichols adds, " Jacob Tonson, however plain in his appearance, was certainly a worthy man, and was not only respected as an honest and opulent trader, but after Dryden's death lived in familiar intimacy with some of the most considerable persons of the early part of the last century. John Dunton says of him, ' He was a very good judge of persons and authors ; and as there is nobody more competently qualified to give their opinion of another, so there is none who does it with more severe exactness or with less partiality ; for to do Mr Tonson justice, he speaks his mind upon all occasions, and will flatter nobody.' He used to say, that ' Dryden was jealous of rivals.'"—*Literary Anecdotes*, vol. i., p. 293.

On the other hand, we find the poet thus addressing his publisher. " You know," says Dryden, (in a letter to Tonson, Works, vol. xviii., p. 119,) " money is now very scrupulously received. In the last which you did me the favour to change for my wife, besides the *clipped money*, there were *at least forty shillings, brass !* " Again, (*ibid.*, p. 122,) " I expect L.50 in *good silver*, not such as I have had formerly. I am not obliged to take gold, neither will I ; nor stay for it beyond four-and-twenty hours after it is due. You always intended I should get nothing by the second subscriptions, as I found from first to last." And again, (*ibid.*, p. 125,) " upon trial, I find all your trade are sharpers ; and you not more than others, therefore I have not wholly left you."

hand, that when Dryden neglected his stipulated labour, Tonson possessed powers of animadversion, which, though exercised in plain prose, were not a little dreaded by the poet. Lord Bolingbroke, already a votary of the muses, and admitted to visit their high priest, was wont to relate, that one day he heard another person enter the house. " This," said Dryden, " is Tonson : you will take care not to depart before he goes away; for I have not completed the sheet which I promised him; and if you leave me unprotected, I shall suffer all the rudeness to which his resentment can prompt his tongue." [1]

But whatever occasional subjects of dissension arose between Dryden and his bookseller, mutual interest, the strongest of ties, appears always to have brought them together, after the first ebullition of displeasure had subsided. There might, on such occasions, be room for acknowledging faults on both sides ; for, if we admit that the bookseller was penurious and churlish, we cannot deny that Dryden seems often to have been abundantly captious, and irascible. Indeed, as the poet placed, and justly, more than a mercantile value upon what he sold, the trader, on his part, was necessarily cautious not to afford a price which his returns could not pay; so that while, in one point of view, the author sold at an inadequate price, the purchaser, in another, really got no more than value for his money. That literature is ill recompensed, is usually rather the fault of the

[1] Johnson's " Life of Dryden."

public than the bookseller, whose trade can only exist by buying that which can be sold to advantage. The trader, who purchased the " Paradise Lost" for ten pounds, had probably no very good bargain.

However fretted by these teazing and almost humiliating discussions, Dryden continued steadily advancing in his great labour; and about three years after it had been undertaken, the translation of Virgil, " the most noble and spirited," said Pope, " which I know in any language," was given to the public in July, 1697.[1] So eager was the general expectation, that the first edition was exhausted in a few months, and a second published early in the next year. " It satisfied," says Johnson, " his friends, and, for the most part, silenced his enemies." But, although this was generally the case, there wanted not some to exercise the invidious task of criticism, or rather of malevolent detraction. Among those, the highest name is that of Swift; the most distinguished for venomous and persevering malignity, that of Milbourne.

In his Epistle to Prince Posterity, prefixed to the " Tale of a Tub," Swift, in the character of the dedicator, declares, " upon the word of a sincere man, that there is now actually in being a

---

[1] [" I began translating the Iliad," says Pope, " in my twenty-fifth year, and it took up that and five more to finish it. Dryden, though they always talk of his being hurried so much, was as long in translating Virgil. Indeed, he wrote plays and other things in the same period."—*Spence's Anecdotes*, (Malone,) p. 16.]

certain poet, called John Dryden, whose translation of Virgil was lately printed in a large folio, well-bound, and, if diligent search were made, for aught I know, is yet to be seen." In his " Battle of the Books," he tells us,

" That Dryden, who encountered Virgil, soothed the good ancient by the endearing title of ' father,' and, by a large deduction of genealogies, made it appear, that they were nearly related, and humbly proposed an exchange of armour; as a mark of hospitality, Virgil consented, though his was of gold, and cost an hundred beeves, the other's but of rusty iron. However, this glittering armour became the modern still worse than his own. Then they agreed to exchange horses; but, when it came to the trial, Dryden was afraid, and utterly unable to mount."

A yet more bitter reproach is levelled by the wit against the poet, for his triple dedication of the Pastorals, Georgics, and Æneid, to three several patrons, Clifford, Chesterfield, and Mulgrave.

1 " I confess to have been somewhat liberal in the business of titles, having observed the humour of multiplying them, to bear great vogue among certain writers, whom I exceedingly reverence. And indeed it seems not unreasonable, that books, the children of the brain, should have the honour to be christened with variety of names, as well as other infants of quality. Our famous Dryden has ventured to proceed a point farther, endeavouring to introduce also a multiplicity of god-fathers; which is an improvement of much more advantage, upon a very obvious account. It is a pity this admirable invention has not been better cultivated, so as to grow by this time into general imitation, when such an authority serves it for a precedent. Nor have my endeavours been wanting to second so useful an example: but, it seems, there is an unhappy expense usually annexed to the calling of a god-father, which was clearly out of my head, as it is very reasonable to believe. Where the pinch lay, I cannot certainly affirm; but, having employed a world of thoughts and pains to split my treatise into forty sections, and having entreated

But, though the recollection of the contemned Odes, like the *spretæ injuria formæ* of Juno, still continued to prompt these overflowings of Swift's satire, he had too much taste and perception of poetry to attempt, gravely, to undermine, by a formal criticism, the merits of Dryden's Virgil.

This was reserved for Luke Milbourne, a clergyman, who, by that assurance, has consigned his name to no very honourable immortality. This person appears to have had a living at Great Yarmouth,[1] which, Dryden hints, he forfeited by writing libels on his parishioners ; and from another testimony, he seems to have been a person of no very strict morals.[2] Milbourne was once an admirer of our poet, as appears from his letter concerning "Amphitryon."[3] But either poetical rivalry, for he had also thought of translating Virgil himself,[4] or political animosity, for he seems to

forty lords of my acquaintance, that they would do me the honour to stand, they all made it a matter of conscience, and sent me their excuses."

[1] Besides the notes on Virgil, he wrote many single sermons, and a metrical version of the Psalms, and died in 1720.

[2] He is described as a rake, in "The Pacificator," a poem bought by Mr Luttrel, 15th Feb. 1699-1700, which gives an account of a supposed battle between the men of wit, and men of sense, as the poet calls them :

> " M————ne, a renegade from wit, came on,
> And made a false attack, and next to none ;
> The priest, the rake, the wit, strove all in vain,
> For there, alas! he lies among the slain.
> *Memento mori ;* see the consequence,
> When rakes and wits set up for men of sense."

[3] [See Dryden's Works, vol. viii., p. 5.]

[4] This Mr Malone has proved by the following extract from Motteux's "Gentleman's Journal:"—"That best of poets," says

have held revolution principles, or deep resentment for Dryden's sarcasms against the clergy, or, most probably, all these united, impelled Milbourne to publish a most furious criticism, entitled, " Notes on Dryden's Virgil, in a Letter to a Friend."

" And here," said he, " in the first place, I must needs own Jacob Tonson's ingenuity to be greater than the translator's, who, in the inscription of his fine gay (title) in the front of the book, calls it very honestly Dryden's Virgil, to let the reader know, that this is not that Virgil so much admired in the Augustæan age, an author whom Mr Dryden once thought untranslatable, but a Virgil of another stamp, of a coarser allay; a silly, impertinent, nonsensical writer, of a various and uncertain style, a mere Alexander Ross, or somebody inferior to him; who could never have been known again in the translation, if the name of Virgil had not been bestowed upon him in large characters in the frontispiece, and in the running title. Indeed, there is scarce the *magni nominis umbra* to be met with in this translation, which being fairly intimated by Jacob, he needs add no more, but *si populus vult decipi, decipiatur.*"

With an assurance which induced Pope to call him the fairest of critics, not content with criticising the production of Dryden, Milbourne was so ill advised as to produce, and place in opposition to it, a rickety translation of his own, probably the

---

Motteux, " having so long continued a stranger to tolerable English, Mr Milbourne pitied his hard fate; and seeing that several great men had undertaken some episodes of his Æneïs, without any design of Englishing the whole, he gave us the first book of it some years ago, with a design to go through the poem. It was the misfortune of that first attempt to appear just about the time of the late Revolution, when few had leisure to mind such books; yet, though by reason of his absence, it was printed with a world of faults, those that are sufficient judges have done it the justice to esteem it a very successful attempt, and cannot but wish that he would complete the entire translation."—*Gent. Journ.* for August, 1692.

fragments of that which had been suppressed by Dryden's version. A short specimen, both of his criticism and poetry, will convince the reader, that the powers of the critic were, as has been often the case, neutralized by the insipidity of the poet; for who can rely on the judgment of one so ill qualified to illustrate his own precepts? I take the remarks on the tenth Eclogue, as a specimen, at hazard.

" This eclogue is translated in a strain too luscious and effeminate for Virgil, who might bemoan his friend, but does it in a noble and a manly style, which Mr Ogilby answers better than Mr D., whose paraphrase looks like one of Mrs Behn's, when somebody had turned the original into English prose before.

" Where Virgil says,

> *Lauri et myricæ flevêre,*

the figure's beautiful; where Mr D. says,

> —————— *the laurel stands in tears,*
> *And hung with humid pearls, the lowly shrub appears,*

the figure is lost, and a foolish and impertinent representation comes in its place; an ordinary dewy morning might fill the laurels and shrubs with Mr D.'s tears, though Gallus had not been concerned in it.

> *And yet the queen of beauty blest his bed—*

" Here Mr D. comes with his ugly patch upon a beautiful face : what had the queen of beauty to do here? Lycoris did not despise her lover for his meanness, but because she had a mind to be a Catholic whore. Gallus was of quality, but her spark a poor inferior fellow. And yet the queen of beauty, &c. would have followed there very well, but not where wanton Mr D. has fixt her.

> *Flush'd were his cheeks, and glowing were his eyes.*

" This character is fitter for one that is drunk, than one in an amazement, and is a thought unbecoming Virgil.

> *And for thy rival, tempts the raging sea,*
> *The forms of horrid war, and heaven's inclemency.*

" Lycoris, doubtless, was a jilting baggage, but why should Mr D. belie her ?　Virgil talks nothing of her going to sea, and perhaps she had a mind to be only a camp laundress, which office she might be advanced to without going to sea : the forms of horrid war, for *horrida castra,* is incomparable.

> ———————— *his brows, a country crown*
> *Of fennel, and of nodding lilies drown,*

is a very odd figure : Sylvanus had swinging brows to drown such a crown as that, *i. e.* to make it invisible, to swallow it up ; if it be a country crown, drown his brows, it is false English.

> *The meads are sooner drunk with morning dews.*

" *Rivi* signifies no such thing ; but then, that bees should be drunk with flowery shrubs, or goats be drunk with brouze, for drunk's the verb, is a very quaint thought."

After much more to the same purpose, Milbourne thus introduces his own version of the first Eclogue, with a confidence worthy of a better cause :—

" That Mr Dryden might be satisfied that I'd offer no foul play, nor find faults in him, without giving him an opportunity of retaliation, I have subjoined another metaphrase or translation of the First and Fourth Pastoral, which I desire may be read with his by the original.

TITYRUS.

ECLOGUE I.

Mel. Beneath a spreading beech you, Tityrus, lie,
And country songs to humble reeds apply ;
We our sweet fields, our native country fly,
We leave our country ; you in shades may lie,
And Amaryllis fair and blythe proclaim,
And make the woods repeat her buxom name.
　Tit. O Melibæus ! 'twas a bounteous God,
These peaceful play-days on our muse bestow'd ;
At least, he'st alway be a God to me ;
My lambs shall oft his grateful offerings be.
Thou seest, he lets my herds securely stray,
And me at pleasure on my pipe to play.
　Mel. Your peace I don't with looks of envy view,
But I admire your happy state, and you.

In all our farms severe distraction reigns,
No ancient owner there in peace remains.
Sick, I, with much ado, my goats can drive,
This, Tityrus, I scarce can lead alive ;
On the bare stones, among yon hazels past,
Just now, alas ! her hopeful twins she cast.
Yet had not all on's dull and senseless been,
We'd long agon this coming stroke foreseen.
Oft did the blasted oaks our fate unfold,
And boding choughs from hollow trees foretold.
But say, good Tityrus ! tell me who's the God,
Who peace, so lost to us, on you bestow'd ? "

Some critics there were, though but few, who joined Milbourne in his abortive attempt to degrade our poet's translation. Oldmixon, celebrated for his share in the games of the Dunciad,[1] and Samuel

[1] See the Preface to " A Funeral Idyll, sacred to the glorious Memory of King William III.," by Mr Oldmixon. " In the Idyll on the peace, I made the first essay to throw off rhymes, and the kind reception that poem met with, has encouraged me to attempt it again. I have not been persuaded by my friends to change the title of Idyll into Idyllium ; for having an English word set me by Mr Dryden, which he uses indifferently with the Greek, I thought it might be as proper in an English poem. I shall not be solicitous to justify myself to those who except against his authority, till they produce me a better : I have heard him blamed for his innovations and coining of words, even by persons who have already been sufficiently guilty of the fault they lay to his charge; and shown us what we are to expect from them, were their names as well settled as his. If I had qualifications enough to do it successfully, I should advise them to write more naturally, delicately, and reasonably themselves, before they attack Mr Dryden's reputation : and to think there is something more necessary to make a man write well, than the favour of the great, or the success of a faction. We have every year seen how fickle Fortune has been to her declared favourites; and men of merit, as well as he who has none, have suffered by her inconstancy, as much as they got by her smiles. This should alarm such as are eminently indebted to her, and may be of use to them in their future reflections on

Parker,[1] a yet more obscure name, have informed
us of this, by volunteering in Dryden's defence.
But Dryden needed not their assistance.   The
real excellences of his version were before the

---

others' productions, not to assume too much to themselves
from her partiality to them, lest, when they are left like their
predecessor, it should only serve to render them the more
ridiculous."

[1] Preface to "Homer in a Nutshell," (16 Feb.) 1700-9, by
Samuel Parker, Gent.—" Ever since I caught some termagant
ones in a club, undervaluing our new translation of Virgil,
I've known both what opinion I ought to harbour, and what
use to make of them ; and since the opportunity of a digression so luckily presents itself, I shall make bold to ask the
gentlemen their sentiments of two or three lines (to pass over
a thousand other instances) which they may meet with in that
work.   The Fourth Æneid says of Dido, after certain effects
of her taking shelter with Æneas in the cave appear,

Conjugium vocat, hoc prætexit nomine culpam,   v. 172.

which Mr Dryden renders thus :

> *She called it marriage, by that specious name*
> *To veil the crime, and sanctify the shame.*

Nor had he before less happily rendered the 39th verse of the
second Æneid :

> *Scinditur incertum studia in contraria vulgus.*
> The giddy vulgar, as their fancies guide,
> With noise, say nothing, and in parts divide.

" If these are the lines which they call flat and spiritless, I
wish mine could be flat and spiritless too !   And, therefore,
to make short work, I shall only beg Mr Dryden's leave to
congratulate him upon his admirable flatness, and dulness, in
a rapture of poetical indignation :

> " So Parian columns, raised with costly care,
> Vile snails and worms may daub, yet not impair ;
> While the tough titles, and obdurate rhyme,
> Fatigue the busy grinders of old Time.
> Not but your Maro justly may complain,
> Since your translation ends his ancient reign,
> And but by your officious muse outvied,
> That vast immortal name had never died."

public, and it was rather to clear himself from the malignant charges against his moral principles, which Milbourne had mingled with his criticism, than for any other purpose, that the poet deemed his antagonist worthy of the following animadversion:[1]

"Milbourne, who is in orders, pretends amongst the rest this quarrel to me, that I have fallen foul on priestcraft: if I have, I am only to ask pardon of good priests, and am afraid his part of the reparation will come to little. Let him be satisfied, that he shall not be able to force himself upon me for an adversary. I contemn him too much to enter into competition with him. His own translations of Virgil have answered his criticisms on mine. If (as they say, he has declared in print) he prefers the version of Ogilby to mine, the world has made him the same compliment; for it is agreed on all hands, that he writes even below Ogilby. That, you will say, is not easily to be done; but what cannot Milbourne bring about? I am satisfied, however, that while he and I live together, I shall not be thought the worst poet of the age. It looks as if I had desired him underhand to write so ill against me; but, upon my honest word, I have not bribed him to do me this service, and am wholly guiltless of his pamphlet. It is true, I should be glad if I could persuade him to continue his good offices, and write such another critique on any thing of mine; for I find, by experience, he has a great stroke with the reader, when he condemns any of my poems, to make the world have a better opinion of them. He has taken some pains with my poetry; but nobody will be persuaded to take the same with his. If I had taken to the church, (as he affirms, but which was never in my thoughts,) I should have had more sense, if not more grace, than to have turned myself out of my benefice, by writing libels on my parishioners. But his account of my manners, and of my principles, are of a piece with his cavils and his poetry; and so I have done with him for ever."[2]

---

[1] Preface to the Fables, Dryden's Works, vol. xi., p. 235.

[2] [Mr D'Israeli, in his Preface to the "Quarells of Authors," says: "I am inclined to think, that what induced me to select this topic, were the literary quarrels which JOHNSON has given between *Dryden*

While Dryden was engaged with his great translation, he found two months' leisure to execute a prose version of "Fresnoy's Art of Painting," to which he added an ingenious preface, the work of twelve mornings, containing a parallel between that art and poetry; of which Mason has said, that though too superficial to stand the test of strict criticism, yet it will always give pleasure to readers of taste, even when it fails to convince their judgment. This version appeared in 1695. Mr Malone conjectures that our author was engaged in this task by his friends Closterman, and Sir Godfrey Kneller, artists, who had been active in procuring subscriptions for his Virgil. He also wrote a "Life of Lucian," for a translation of his works, by Mr Walter Moyle, Sir Henry Shere, and other gentlemen of pretension to learning. This version, although it did not appear till after his death, and although he executed no part of the translation, still retains the title of "Dryden's Lucian."

There was one event of political importance which occurred in December 1695, and which the public seem to have expected should have employed the pen of Dryden ;—this was the death of Mary, wife of William the Third. It is difficult to conceive in what manner the poet laureat of the unfortunate James could have treated the memory of his daughter. Satire was dangerous, and had indeed been renounced by the poet ; and panegyric

and *Settle*, *Dennis* and *Addison*, &c., and Mr WALTER SCOTT, who, amidst the fresh creations of fancy can delve for the buried truths of research, in his narrative of the Quarrel of *Dryden* and *Luke Milbourne*."]

was contrary to the principles for which he was suffering.   Yet, among the swarm of rhymers who thrust themselves upon the nation on that mournful occasion, there are few who do not call, with friendly or unfriendly voice, upon our poet to break silence.[1] But the voice of praise and censure was heard in vain, and Dryden's only interference was, in character of the first judge of his time, to award the prize to the Duke of Devonshire, as author of the best poem composed on the occasion of the Queen's death.[2]

Virgil was hardly finished, when our author distinguished himself by the immortal Ode to Saint Cecilia, commonly called " Alexander's Feast." There is some difference of evidence concerning the time occupied in this splendid task.   He had been solicited to undertake it by the stewards of the Musical Meeting, which had for several years met to celebrate the feast of St Cecilia, their

[1] See several extracts from these poems, in the Appendix to Dryden's Works, vol. xvii., p. 22, which I have thrown together to show how much Dryden was considered as sovereign among the poets of the time.

[2] This I learn from *Honori Sacellum*, a Funeral Poem, to the Memory of William, Duke of Devonshire, 1707:

> " 'Twas so, when the destroyer's dreadful dart
> Once pierced through ours, to fair Maria's heart.
> From his state-helm then some short hours he stole,
> T' indulge his melting eyes, and bleeding soul:
> Whilst his bent knees, to those remains divine,
> Paid their last offering to that royal shrine."

On which lines occurs this explanatory note:—" An Ode, composed by His Grace, on the death of the late Queen Mary, *justly adjudged by the ingenious Mr Dryden to have exceeded all that had been written on that occasion.*"

patroness, and whom he had formerly gratified by a similar performance.   In September 1697, Dryden writes to his son :—

"In the meantime, I am writing a song for St Cecilia's feast; who, you know, is the patroness of music.   This is troublesome, and no way beneficial; but I could not deny the stewards, who came in a body to my house to desire that kindness, one of them being Mr Bridgeman, whose parents are your mother's friends."

This account seems to imply, that the Ode was a work of some time; which is countenanced by Dr Birch's expression, that Dryden himself "observes, in an original letter of his, that he was employed for almost a fortnight in composing and correcting it."[1]   On the other hand, the following anecdote is told upon very respectable authority.

"Mr St John, afterwards Lord Bolingbroke, happening to pay a morning visit to Dryden, whom he always respected, found him in an unusual agitation of spirits, even to a trembling.   On enquiring the cause, 'I have been up all night,' replied the old bard : 'my musical friends made me promise to write them an Ode for their feast of St Cecilia : I have been so struck with the subject which occurred to me, that I could not leave it till I had *completed* it ; here it is, *finished* at one sitting.'   And immediately he showed him *this* Ode, which places the British lyric poetry above that of any other nation."

These accounts are not, however, so contradictory as they may at first sight appear.   It is possible that Dryden may have completed, at one sitting the whole Ode, and yet have employed a fortnight, or much more, in correction.[2]   There

---

[1] Dr Birch refers to the authority of Richard Graham, junior; but no such letter has been recovered.

[2] [Mr Hallam, in the Edinburgh Review, 1808, quotes these observations, and says,—" They are, we think, highly judi-

is strong internal evidence to show, that the poem was, speaking with reference to its general structure, wrought off at once. A halt or pause, even of a day, would perhaps have injured that continuous flow of poetical language and description, which argues the whole scene to have arisen at once upon the author's imagination. It seems possible more especially in lyrical poetry, to discover where the author has paused for any length of time ; for the union of the parts is rarely so perfect as not to show a different strain of thought and feeling. There may be something fanciful, however, in this reasoning, which I therefore abandon to the reader's mercy ; only begging him to observe, that we have no mode of estimating the exertions of a quality so capricious as a poetic imagination ; so that it is very possible, that the Ode to St Cecilia may have been the work of twenty-four hours, whilst corrections and emendations, perhaps of no very great consequence, occupied the author as many days. Derrick, in his " Life of Dryden," tells us, upon the authority of Walter Moyle, that the society paid Dryden L.40, for this sublime Ode, which, from the passage in his letter above quoted, seems to have been more than the bard expected at commencing his labour. The music for this celebrated poem was originally composed by Jeremiah Clarke,[1] one of the stewards of the festival,

---

cious and acute in themselves, and of decisive authority, when it is considered from what quarter they proceed."]

[1] This discovery was made by the researches of Mr Malone. Dr Burney describes Clarke as excelling in the tender and plaintive, to which he was prompted by a temperament of

whose productions were more remarkable for deep
pathos, and delicacy, than for fire and energy. It
is probable, that, with such a turn of mind and
taste, he may have failed in setting the sublime,
lofty, and daring flights of the Ode to St Cecilia.
Indeed his composition was not judged worthy of
publication. The Ode, after some impertinent
alterations, made by Hughes, at the request of Sir
Richard Steele, was set to music by Clayton, who,
with Steele, managed a public concert in 1711;
but neither was this a successful essay to connect
the poem with the art it celebrated. At length, in
1736, "Alexander's Feast" was set by Handel,
and performed in the Theatre Royal, Covent Garden, with the full success which the combined
talents of the poet and the musician seemed to
ensure.[1] Indeed, although the music was at first
less successful, the poetry received, even in the

---

natural melancholy. In the agonies which arose from an
unfortunate attachment, he committed suicide, in July, 1707.
See a full account of the catastrophe, in Malone's " Life of
Dryden," p. 299.

[1] It was first performed on February 19, 1735-6, at opera
prices. " The public expectations and the effects of the representation (says Dr Burney,) seem to have been correspondent,
for the next day we are told in the public papers, [London
Daily Post, and General Advertiser, Feb. 20,] that ' there
never was, upon the like occasion, so numerous and splendid
an audience at any theatre in London, there being at least
thirteen hundred persons present; and it is judged, that the
receipts of the house could not amount to less than L.450. It
met with general applause, though attended with the incon-
venience of having the performers placed at too great a distance from the audience, which we hear will be rectified the
next time of performance.' "—*Hist. of Music*, vol. iv., p. 391.

author's time, all the applause which its unrivalled excellence demanded. " I am glad to hear from all hands," says Dryden, in a letter to Tonson, " that my Ode is esteemed the best of all my poetry, by all the town. I thought so myself when I writ it; but, being old, I mistrusted my own judgment." Mr Malone has preserved a tradition, that the father of Lord Chief Justice Marlay, then a Templar, and frequenter of Will's Coffee-house, took an opportunity to pay his court to Dryden, on the publication of " Alexander's Feast;" and, happening to sit next him, congratulated him on having produced the finest and noblest Ode that had ever been written in any language. " You are right, young gentleman, (replied Dryden,) a nobler Ode never *was* produced, nor ever *will.*" This singularly strong expression cannot be placed to the score of vanity. It was an inward consciousness of merit, which burst forth, probably almost involuntarily, and I fear must be admitted as prophetic. [1]

The preparation of a new edition of the Virgil, which appeared in 1698, occupied nine days only, after which Dryden began seriously to consider to

[1] [" Every one places this Ode among the first of its class, and many allow it no rival. In what does this superiority consist? Not in the sublimity of its conceptions, or the richness of its language, the passage about Jupiter and Olympia alone excepted. Some lines are little better than a common drinking song, and few of them have singly any great merit. It must be the rapid transitions, the mastery of language, the springiness of the whole manner, which hurries us away, and leaves so little room for minute criticism, that no one has ever qualified his admiration of this noble poem."—HALLAM.]

what he should next address his pen. The state
of his circumstances rendered constant literary
labour indispensable to the support of his family,
although the exertion, and particularly the confinement, occasioned by his studies, considerably
impaired his health. His son Charles had met
with an accident at Rome, which was attended
with a train of consequences perilous to his health;
and Dryden, anxious to recall him to Britain, was
obliged to make extraordinary exertions to provide
against this additional expense. " If it please God,"
he writes to Tonson, " that I must die of over-
study, I cannot spend my life better than in preserving his." It is affecting to read such a passage
in the life of such a man ; yet the necessities of the
poet, like the afflictions of the virtuous, smooth the
road to immortality. While Milton and Dryden
were favoured by the rulers of the day, they were
involved in the religious and political controversies
which raged around them; it is to hours of seclu-
sion, neglect, and even penury, that we owe the
Paradise Lost, the Virgil, and the Fables.

Among other projects, Dryden seems to have
had thoughts of altering and revising a tragedy
called the " Conquest of China by the Tartars,"
written by his ancient friend and brother-in-law,
Sir Robert Howard. The unkindness which had
arisen between them upon the subject of blank verse
and rhyme, seems to have been long since past
away ; and we observe, with pleasure, that Dryden, in the course of the pecuniary transactions
about Virgil, reckons upon the assistance of Sir

Robert Howard, and consults his taste also in the revisal of the version. [1] But Dryden never altered the " Conquest of China," being first interrupted by the necessity of revising Virgil, and afterwards, perhaps, by a sort of quarrel which took place between him and the players, of whom he speaks most resentfully in his " Epistle to Granville," upon his tragedy of " Heroic Love," acted in the beginning of 1698. [2]

The success of Virgil encouraged Dryden about this time to turn his eyes upon Homer; and the general voice of the literary world called upon him to do the venerable Grecian the same service which the Roman had received from him. It was even believed that he had fixed upon the mode of translation, and that he was, as he elsewhere expresses it, to "fight unarmed, without his rhyme."[3]   A

[1] See Dryden's Works, vol. xviii., pp. 123, 126.

[2] " Thine be the laurel, then; thy blooming age
Can best, if any can, support the stage;
Which so declines, that shortly we may see
Players and plays reduced to second infancy.
Sharp to the world, but thoughtless of renown,
They plot not on the stage, but on the town;
And in despair their empty pit to fill,
Set up some foreign monster in a bill:
Thus they jog on, still tricking, never thriving,
And murth'ring plays, which they miscall—reviving.
Our sense is nonsense, through their pipes convey'd;
Scarce can a poet know the play he made,
'Tis so disguised in death; nor thinks 'tis he
That suffers in the mangled tragedy;
Thus Itys first was kill'd, and after dress'd
For his own sire, the chief invited guest."

This gave great offence to the players; one of whom (Powell) made a petulant retort, which the reader will find in a note upon the Epistle itself. Dryden's Works, vol. xi., p. 65.

[3] Moubrenli, in a note on that passage in the dedication to

dubious anecdote bears, that he even regretted he had not rendered Virgil into blank verse, and shows at the same time, if genuine, how far he must now have disapproved of his own attempt to turn into rhyme the Paradise Lost.   The story is told by the elder Richardson, in his remarks on the tardy progress of Milton's great work in the public opinion. [1]   When Dryden did translate the First Book of Homer, which he published with the Fables, he rendered it into rhyme; nor have we sufficient ground to believe that he ever seriously intended, in so large a work, to renounce the advantages which he possessed, by his unequalled command of versification.   That in other respects the task was consonant to his temper, as well as talents, he has himself informed us. " My thoughts," he says, in a letter to Halifax, in 1699, " are at present fixed on Homer; and by my translation of the first Iliad, I find him a poet more according to my genius than Virgil, and consequently hope I may do him more justice, in his fiery way of writing;

the Æneid—" *He who can write well in rhyme, may write better in blank verse*," says,—" We shall know that, when we see how much better Dryden's Homer will be than his Virgil."

[1] " Much the same character he gave of it (*i. e.* Paradise Lost) to a north-country gentleman, to whom I mentioned the book, he being a great reader, but not in a right train, coming to town seldom, and keeping little company. Dryden amazed him with speaking so loftily of it. ' Why, Mr Dryden,' says he, (Sir W. L. told me the thing himself,) ' 'tis not in rhyme.' ' No [replied Dryden]; *nor would I have done my Virgil in rhyme, if I was to begin it again.*' "—This conversation is supposed by Mr Malone to have been held with Sir Wilfred Lawson, of Isell, in Cumberland.

which, as it is liable to more faults, so it is capable of more beauties, than the exactness and sobriety of Virgil. Since it is for my country's honour, as well as for my own, that I am willing to undertake this task, I despair not of being encouraged in it by your favour." But this task Dryden was not destined to accomplish, although he had it so much at heart as to speak of resuming it only three months before his death.[1]

In the meanwhile, our author had engaged himself in the composition of those imitations of Boccacio and Chaucer, which have been since called the " Fables ;" and in spring, 1699, he was in such forwardness, as to put into Tonson's hands " seven thousand five hundred verses, more or less," as the contract bears, being a partial delivery to account of ten thousand verses, which by that deed he agreed to furnish, for the sum of two hundred and fifty guineas, to be made up three hundred pounds upon publication of the second edition. This second payment Dryden lived not to receive. With the contents of this miscellaneous volume we are to suppose him engaged, from the revisal of the Virgil, in 1697, to the publication of the Fables, in March, 1699–1700. This was the last period of

---

[1] [" You take more care of my health than it deserves; that of an old man is always crazy, and, at present, mine is worse than usual, by a St Anthony's fire in one of my legs; though the swelling is much abated, yet the pain is not wholly gone, and I am too weak to stand upon it. If I recover, it is possible I may attempt Homer's Iliad. A specimen of it (the first book) is now in the press."—*Dryden to Mrs Thomas.*— *Works*, vol. xviii., p. 173.]

his labours, and of his life; and, like all the others, it did not pass undisturbed by acrimonious criticism, and bitter controversy. The dispute with Milbourne we noticed before dismissing the subject of Virgil; but there were two other persons who, in their zeal for morality and religion, chose to disturb the last years of the life of Dryden.

The indelicacy of the stage, being, in its earliest period, merely the coarse gross raillery of a barbarous age, was probably of no greater injury to the morals of the audience, than it is to those of the lower ranks of society, with whom similar language is everywhere admitted as wit and humour. During the reigns of James I. and Charles I., this license was gradually disappearing. In the domination of the fanatics, which succeeded, matters were so much changed, that, far from permitting the use of indelicate or profane allusions, they wrapped up not only their most common temporal affairs, but even their very crimes and vices, in the language of their spiritual concerns. Luxury was *using the creature;* avarice was *seeking experiences;* insurrection was *putting the hand to the plough;* actual rebellion, *fighting the good fight;* and regicide, *doing the great work of the Lord.* This vocabulary became grievously unfashionable at the Restoration, and was at once swept away by the torrent of irreligion, blasphemy, and indecency, which were at that period deemed necessary to secure conversation against the imputation of disloyalty and fanaticism. The court of Cromwell, if lampoons can be believed, was not much less vicious than that of Charles II., but it was less scandalous, and, as Dryden himself expresses it,

> " The sin was of our native growth, 'tis true ;
> The scandal of the sin was wholly new.
> Misses there were, but modestly conceal'd,
> Whitehall the naked Goddess first reveal'd ;
> Who standing, as at Cyprus, in her shrine,
> The strumpet was adored with rites divine."

This torrent of licentiousness had begun in some degree to abate even upon the accession of James II., whose manners did not encourage the same general license as those of Charles. But after the Revolution, when an affectation of profligacy was no longer deemed a necessary attribute of loyalty, and when it began to be thought possible that a man might have some respect for religion without being a republican, or even a fanatic, the license of the stage was generally esteemed a nuisance. It then happened, as is not uncommon, that those, most bustling and active to correct public abuses, were men whose intentions may, without doing them injury, be estimated more highly than their talents. Thus, Sir Richard Blackmore, a grave physician, residing and practising on the sober side of Temple-Bar, was the first who professed to reform the spreading pest of poetical licentiousness, and to correct such men as Dryden, Congreve, and Wycherly. This worthy person, compassionating the state to which poetry was reduced by his contemporaries, who used their wit " in opposition to religion, and to the destruction of virtue and good manners in the world," resolved to rescue the Muses from this unworthy thraldom, " to restore them to their sweet and chaste mansions, and to engage them in an employment suited to their dignity." With this laudable view, he wrote " Prince Arthur, an Epic Poem," published in 1695. The preface contained a furious, though just, diatribe against the license of modern comedy, with some personal reflections aimed at Dryden directly.[1] This the poet felt more unkindly, as

---

[1] " Some of these poets, to excuse their guilt, allege for themselves, that the degeneracy of the age makes their lewd way of writing necessary : they pretend the auditors will not be pleased, unless they are thus entertained from the stage; and to please, they say, is the chief business of the poet. But this is by no means a just apology : it is not true, as was said before, that the poet's chief business is to please. His chief business is to instruct, to make mankind wiser and better; and in order to this, his care should be to please and entertain the audience with all the wit and art he is master of. Aristotle and Horace, and all their critics and commentators, all men of wit and sense agree, that this is the end of poetry. But they say, it is their profession to write for the stage ; and that poets must starve, if they will not in this way humour the audience : the theatre will be as unfrequented as the churches, and the poet and the parson equally neglected. Let the poet then abandon his profession, and take up some honest lawful calling, where, joining industry to his great wit, he may soon get above the complaints of poverty, so common among these ingenious men, and lie under no necessity of prostituting his wit to any such vile purposes as are here censured. This will be a course of life more profitable and honourable to himself, and more useful to others. And there are among these writers *some, who think they might have risen to the highest dignities in other professions, had they employed their wit in those ways.* It is a mighty dishonour and reproach to any man that is capable of being useful to the world in any *liberal and virtuous* profession, *to lavish out* his *life and wit in propagating vice and corruption of manners,* and in battering from the stage the strongest entrenchments and best works of religion and vir-

Sir Richard had, without acknowledgment, availed himself of the hints he had thrown out in the " Essay upon Satire," for the management of an epic poem on the subject of King Arthur. He bore, however, the attack without resenting it, until he was again assailed by Sir Richard in his " Satire upon Wit," written expressly to correct the dissolute and immoral performances of the writers of his time. With a ponderous attempt at humour, the good knight proposes, that a *bank for wit* should be established, and that all which had hitherto passed as current, should be called in, purified in the mint, recoined, and issued forth anew, freed from alloy.

This satire was published in 1700, as the title-page bears; but Mr Luttrell marks his copy 23d November, 1699.[1]   It contains more than one attack upon our author.   Thus, we are told, (wit being previously described as a malady,)

> " Vanine, that look'd on all the danger past,
> Because he 'scaped so long, is seized at last;
> By p—, by hunger, and by Dryden bit,
> He grins and snarls, and, in his dogged fit,
> Froths at the mouth, a certain sign of wit."

Elsewhere the poet complains, that the universities,

> " —— debauch'd by Dryden and his crew,
> Turn bawds to vice, and wicked aims pursue."

---

tues. Whoever makes this his choice, when the other was in his power, may he go off the stage unpitied, *complaining of neglect and poverty, the just punishments of his irreligion and folly.*"

[1] Mr Malone conceives, that the Fables were published before the "Satire upon Wit;" but he had not this evidence of the contrary before him.   It is therefore clear, that Dryden endured a second attack from Blackmore, before making any reply.

Again, p. 14,

> " Dryden condemn, who taught men how to make,
> Of dunces wits, an angel of a rake."

But the main offence lies in the following passage :

> " Set forth your edict; let it be enjoin'd,
> That all defective species be recoin'd ;
> St E—m—t and R—r both are fit
> To oversee the coining of our wit.
> Let these be made the masters of essay,
> They'll every piece of metal touch and weigh,
> And tell which is too light, which has too much allay.
> 'Tis true, that when the coarse and worthless dross
> Is purged away, there will be mighty loss.
> E'en Congreve, Southerne, manly Wycherly,
> When thus refined, will grievous sufferers be.
> Into the melting pot when Dryden comes,
> What horrid stench will rise, what noisome fumes !
> How will he shrink, when all his lewd allay,
> And wicked mixture, shall be purged away?
> When once his boasted heaps are melted down,
> A chest-full scarce will yield one sterling crown.
> Those who will D—n's melt, and think to find
> A goodly mass of bullion left behind,
> Do, as the Hibernian wit, who, as 'tis told,
> Burnt his gilt feather, to collect the gold.
>
> But what remains will be so pure, 'twill bear
> The examination of the most severe ;
> 'Twill S—r's scales, and Talbot's test abide,
> And with their mark please all the world beside."

These repeated attacks at length called down the vengeance of Dryden, who thus retorted upon him in the preface to the Fables :

" As for the City Bard, or Knight Physician, I hear his quarrel to me is, that I was the author of ' Absalom and Achitophel,' which, he thinks, is a little hard on his fanatic patrons in London.

" But I will deal the more civilly with his two poems, because nothing ill is to be spoken of the dead ; and, therefore,
peace be to the manes of his ' Arthurs.' I will only say, that
it was not for this noble knight that I drew the plan of an
epic poem on King Arthur, in my preface to the translation of
Juvenal. The guardian angels of kingdoms were machines
too ponderous for him to manage ; and therefore he rejected
them, as Dares did the whirl-bats of Eryx, when they were
thrown before him by Entellus : yet from that preface, he
plainly took his hint ; for he began immediately upon the
story, though he had the baseness not to acknowledge his
benefactor, but, instead of it, to traduce me in a libel."

Blackmore, who had perhaps thought the praise
contained in his two last couplets ought to have
allayed Dryden's resentment, finding that they
failed in producing this effect, very unhandsomely
omitted them in his next edition, and received, as
will presently be noticed, another flagellation in the
last verses Dryden ever wrote.

But a more formidable champion than Blackmore had arisen, to scourge the profligacy of the
theatre. This was no other than the celebrated
Jeremy Collier, a nonjuring clergyman, who published, in 1698, " A Short View of the Immorality
and Profaneness of the Stage." His qualities as a
reformer are described by Dr Johnson in language
never to be amended.

" He was formed for a controvertist ; with sufficient learning ; with diction vehement and pointed, though often vulgar
and incorrect ; with unconquerable pertinacity ; with wit in
the highest degree keen and sarcastic ; and with all those
powers exalted and invigorated by the just confidence in his
cause. Thus qualified, and thus incited, he walked out to
battle, and assailed at once most of the living writers, from
Dryden to Durfey. His onset was violent : those passages,
which, while they stood single had passed with little notice,

when they were accumulated and exposed together, excited horror; the wise and the pious caught the alarm, and the nation wondered why it had so long suffered irreligion and licentiousness to be openly taught at the public charge."

Notwithstanding the justice of this description, there is a strange mixture of sense and nonsense in Collier's celebrated treatise. Not contented with resting his objections to dramatic immorality upon the substantial grounds of virtue and religion, Jeremy labours to confute the poets of the 17th century, by drawing them into comparison with Plautus and Aristophanes, which is certainly judging of one crooked line by another. Neither does he omit, like his predecessor Prynne, to marshal against the British stage those fulminations directed by the fathers of the church against the Pagan theatres; although Collier could not but know, that it was the performance of the heathen ritual, and not merely the scenic action of the drama, which rendered it sinful for the early Christians to attend the theatre. The book was, however, of great service to dramatic poetry, which, from that time, was less degraded by license and indelicacy.

Dryden, it may be believed, had, as his comedies well deserved, a liberal share of the general censure; but, however he might have felt the smart of Collier's severity, he had the magnanimity to acknowledge its justice. In the preface to the Fables, he makes the *amende honorable*.

" I shall say the less of Mr Collier, because in many things he has taxed me justly; and I have pleaded guilty to all thoughts and expressions of mine, which can be truly argued of obscenity, profaneness, or immorality, and retract them.

If he be my enemy, let him triumph; if he be my friend, as
I have given him no personal occasion to be otherwise, he will
be glad of my repentance. It becomes me not to draw my
pen in the defence of a bad cause, when I have so often drawn
it for a good one."

To this manly and liberal admission, he has
indeed tacked a complaint, that Collier had sometimes, by a strained interpretation, made the evil
sense of which he complained; that he had too
much " horse-play in his raillery;" and that, " if
the zeal for God's house had not eaten him up,
it had at least devoured some part of his good
manners and civility." Collier seems to have been
somewhat pacified by this qualified acknowledgment; and, during the rest of the controversy,
turned his arms chiefly against Congreve, who
resisted, and spared, comparatively at least, the
sullen submission of Dryden.

While these controversies were raging, Dryden's time was occupied with the translations or
imitations of Chaucer and Boccacio. Among these,
the "Character of the Good Parson" is introduced,
probably to confute Milbourne, Blackmore, and
Collier, who had severally charged our author with
the wilful and premeditated contumely thrown upon
the clergy in many passages of his satirical writings. This too seems to have inflamed the hatred
of Swift, who, with all his levities, was strictly
attached to his order, and keenly jealous of its
honours.[1] Dryden himself seems to have been

---

[1] In his apology for " The Tale of a Tub," he points out to
the resentment of the clergy, " those heavy illiterate scribblers, prostitute in their reputations, vicious in their lives,

conscious of his propensity to assail churchmen. " I remember," he writes to his sons, " the counsel you gave me in your letter ; but dissembling, although lawful in some cases, is not my talent ; yet, for your sake, I will struggle with the plain openness of my nature, and keep in my just resentments against that *degenerate order.*"[1] Milbourne, and other enemies of our author, imputed this resentment against the clergy, to his being refused orders when he wished to take them, in the reign of Charles, with a view to the provostship of Eaton, or some Irish preferment.[2] But Dryden assures us, that he never had any thoughts of entering the

and ruined in their fortunes, who, to the shame of good sense, as well as piety, are greedily read, merely upon the strength of bold, false, impious assertions, mixed with unmannerly reflections on the priesthood." And, after no great interval, he mentions the passage quoted, p. 317, " in which Dryden, L'Estrange, and some others I shall not name, are levelled at ; who, having spent their lives in faction, and apostasies, and all manner of vice, pretended to be sufferers for loyalty and religion. So Dryden tells us, in one of his prefaces, of his merits and sufferings, and thanks God that he possesses his soul in patience. In other places he talks at the same rate."

[1] Dryden's Works, vol. xviii., p. 133.

[2] Thus, in a lampoon already quoted :

> " Quitting my duller hopes, the poor renown
> Of Eaton College, or a Dublin gown."

Tom Brown makes the charge more directly. " But, prithee, why so severe always on the priesthood, Mr Bayes ? What have they merited to pull down your indignation ? I thought the ridiculing men of that character upon the stage, was by this time a topic as much worn out with you, as love and honour in the play, or good fulsome flattery in the dedication. But you, I find, still continue your old humour, to date from the year of Hegira, the loss of Eaton, or since orders were refused you. Whatever hangs out either black or green

church.   Indeed, his original offences of this kind
may be safely ascribed to the fashionable practice
after the Restoration, of laughing at all that was
accounted serious before that period.   And when
Dryden became a convert to the Catholic faith,
he was, we have seen, involved in an immediate
and furious controversy with the clergy of the
church of England.   Thus, an unbeseeming strain
of raillery, adopted in wantonness, became aggravated, by controversy, into real dislike and
animosity.   But Dryden, in the " Character of a
Good Parson," seems determined to show, that
he could estimate the virtue of the clerical order.
He undertook the task at the instigation of Mr
Pepys, the founder of the library in Magdalen
College, which bears his name ;[1] and has accomplished it with equal spirit and elegance ; not for-
getting, however, to make his pattern of clerical
merit of his own jacobitical principles.

Another very pleasing performance, which entered the Miscellany called " The Fables," is the
Epistle to John Driden of Chesterton, the poet's
cousin.   The letters to Mrs Stewart show the
friendly intimacy in which the relations had lived,

colours is presently your prize : and you would, by your good
will, be as mortifying a vexation to the whole tribe, as an
unbegetting year, a concatenation of briefs, or a voracious
visitor ; so that I am of opinion, you had much better have
written in your titlepage,

—— Manet alta mente repostum
Judicium *Cleri*, spretæque injuria *Musæ*."

The same reproach is urged by Settle. See Dryden's Works,
vol. ix., p. 377-8.

[1] Dryden's Works, vol. xviii., p. 155.

since the opposition of the Whigs to King William's government in some degree united that party in conduct, though not in motive, with the favourers of King James. Yet our author's strain of politics, as at first expressed in the epistle, was too severe for his cousin's digestion. Some reflections upon the Dutch allies, and their behaviour in the war, were omitted, as tending to reflect upon King William; and the whole piece, to avoid the least chance of giving offence, was subjected to the revision of Montague, with a deprecation of his displeasure, an entreaty of his patronage, and the humiliating offer, that, although repeated correction had already purged the spirit out of the poem, nothing should stand in it relating to public affairs, without Mr Montague's permission. What answer "full-blown Bufo" returned to Dryden's petition, does not appear; but the author's opposition principles were so deeply woven in with the piece, that they could not be obliterated without tearing it to pieces. His model of an English member of parliament votes in opposition, as his Good Parson is a nonjuror, and the Fox in the fable of Old Chaucer is translated into a puritan.[1]

[1] There was, to be sure, in the provoking scruples of that rigid sect, something peculiarly tempting to a satirist. How is it possible to forgive Baxter, for the affectation with which he records the enormities of his childhood?—" Though my conscience," says he, " would trouble me when I sinned, yet divers sins I was addicted to, and oft committed against my conscience, which, for the warning of others, I will here confess to my shame. I was much addicted to the *excessive gluttonous eating of apples and pears*, which I think laid the foundation of the imbecility and flatulency of my stomach,

The *epistle* was highly acceptable to Mr Driden of Chesterton, who acknowledged the immortality conferred on him, by " a noble present," which family tradition states to have amounted to L.500.[1] Neither did Dryden neglect so fair an opportunity to avenge himself on his personal, as well as his political adversaries. Milbourne and Blackmore receive in the *epistle* severe chastisement for their assaults upon his poetry and private character :—

" What help from art's endeavours can we have ?
Guibbons but guesses, nor is sure to save ;
But Maurus sweeps whole parishes, and peoples every grave ;
And no more mercy to mankind will use,
Than when he robb'd and murder'd Maro's muse.
Wouldst thou be soon despatch'd, and perish whole,
Trust Maurus with thy life, and Milbourne with thy soul."

Referring to another place, what occurs upon the style and execution of the Fables, I have only to add, that they were published early in spring 1700, in a large folio, and with the " Ode to Saint Cecilia." The Epistle to Driden of Chesterton,

which caused the bodily calamities of my life. To this end, and to concur with naughty boys that gloried in evil, I have oft gone into other men's orchards, and stolen the fruit, when I had enough at home." There are six other retractations of similar enormities, when he concludes :—" These were my sins in my childhood, as to which, conscience troubled me for a great while before they were overcome." Baxter was a pious and worthy man ; but can any one read this confession without thinking of Tartuffe, who subjected himself to penance for killing a flea, with too much anger ?

[1] See Dryden's Works, vol. xviii., p. 180. Mr Malone thinks tradition has confounded a present made to the poet himself, probably of L.100, with a legacy bequeathed to his son Charles, which last did amount to L.500, but which Charles lived not to receive.

and a translation of the first Iliad, must have more than satisfied the mercantile calculations of Tonson, since they contained seventeen hundred verses above the quantity which Dryden had contracted to deliver. In the preface the author vindicates himself with great spirit against his literary adversaries ; makes his usual strong and forcible remarks on the genius of the authors whom he had imitated ; and, in this his last critical work, shows all the acumen which had so long distinguished his powers. The Fables were dedicated to the last Duke of Ormond, the grandson of the Barzillai of " Absalom and Achitophel," and the son of the heroic Earl of Ossory ; friends both, and patrons of Dryden's earlier essays. There is something affecting in a connexion so honourably maintained ; and the sentiment, as touched by Dryden, is simply pathetic.

" I am not vain enough to boast, that I have deserved the value of so illustrious a line ; but my fortune is the greater, that for three descents they have been pleased to distinguish my poems from those of other men ; and have accordingly made me their peculiar care. May it be permitted me to say, that as your grandfather and father were cherished and adorned with honours by two successive monarchs, so I have been esteemed and patronised by the grandfather, the father, and the son, descended from one of the most ancient, most conspicuous, and most deserving families in Europe."

There were also prefixed to the " Fables," those introductory verses addressed to the beautiful Duchess of Ormond,[1] which have all the easy, felici-

[1] She is distinguished for beauty and virtue, by the author of " The Court at Kensington." 1699-1700.
    " So Ormond's graceful mien attracts all eyes,
    And nature needs not ask from art supplies ;

tous, and sprightly gallantry, demanded on such occasions. The incense, it is said, was acknowledged by a present of L.500; a donation worthy of the splendid house of Ormond. The sale of the "Fables" was surprisingly slow: even the death of the author, which has often sped away a lingering impression, does not seem to have increased the demand; and the second edition was not printed till 1713, when Dryden and all his immediate descendants being no more, the sum stipulated upon that event was paid by Tonson to Lady Sylvius, daughter of one of Lady Elizabeth Dryden's brothers, for the benefit of his widow, then in a state of lunacy.

The end of Dryden's labours was now fast approaching; and as his career began upon the stage, it was in some degree doomed to terminate there. It is true, he never recalled his resolution to write no more plays; but Vanburgh having about this time revised and altered for the Drury-lane theatre, Fletcher's lively comedy of "The Pilgrim," it was agreed that Dryden, or, as one account says, his son Charles,[1] should have the profits of a third night, on condition of adding to

---

An air of grandeur shines through every part,
And in her beauteous form is placed the noblest heart:
In vain mankind adore, unless she were
By Heaven made less virtuous, or less fair."

[1] Gildon, in his "Comparison between the Stages."—"Nay then," says the whole party at Drury-lane, "we'll even put 'The Pilgrim' upon him."—"Ay, 'faith, so we will," says Dryden: "and if you'll let my son have the profits of the third night, I'll give you a Secular Masque."—"Done," says the House; "and so the bargain was struck."

the piece a Secular Masque, adapted to the supposed termination of the seventeenth century;[1] a Dialogue in the Madhouse between two Distracted Lovers; and a Prologue and Epilogue. The Secular Masque contains a beautiful and spirited delineation of the reigns of James I. Charles I. and Charles II., in which the influence of Diana, Mars, and Venus, are supposed to have respectively predominated. Our author did not venture to assign a patron to the last years of the century, though the expulsion of Saturn might have given a hint for it. The music of the Masque is said to have been good; at least it is admired by the eccentric author of John Buncle.[2] The Prologue and Epilogue to " The Pilgrim," were written within twenty days of Dryden's death;[3] and their spirit equals that of any of his satirical compositions. They afford us the less pleasing conviction, that even the last fortnight of Dryden's life was occupied in repelling or retorting the venomed attacks of his literary foes. In the Prologue, he gives Blackmore a drubbing which would have annihilated

---

[1] *i. e.* Upon the 25th March, 1700; it being supposed, (as by many in our own time) that the century was concluded so soon as the hundredth year commenced;—as if a play was ended at the *beginning of the fifth act.*

[2] It was again set by Dr Boyce, and in 1749 performed in the Drury-lane theatre, with great success.

[3] By a letter to Mrs Stuart, dated the 11th April, 1700, it appears they were then only in his contemplation, and the poet died upon the first of the succeeding month. Dryden's Works, vol. xviii., p. 182.

any author of ordinary modesty ; but the knight [1]
was as remarkable for his powers of endurance, as
some modern pugilists are said to be for the quality
technically called *bottom*. After having been " bray-
ed in a mortar," as Solomon expresses it, by every
wit of his time, Sir Richard not only survived to

[1] " Quack Maurus, though he never took degrees
  In either of our universities,
  Yet to be shown by some kind wit he looks,
  Because he played the fool, and writ three books.
  But if he would be worth a poet's pen,
  He must be more a fool, and write again ;
  For all the former fustian stuff he wrote
  Was dead-born doggrel, or is quite forgot ;
  His man of Uz, stript of his Hebrew robe,
  Is just the proverb, and ' As poor as Job.'
  One would have thought he could no longer jog ;
  But Arthur was a level, Job's a bog.
  There though he crept, yet still he kept in sight ;
  But *here* he founders in, and sinks downright.
  Had he prepared us, and been dull by rule,
  Tobit had first been turned to ridicule ;
  But our bold Briton, without fear or awe,
  O'erleaps at once the whole Apocrypha;
  Invades the Psalms with rhymes, and leaves no room
  For any Vandal Hopkins yet to come.
  But when, if, after all, this godly gear
  Is not so senseless as it would appear,
  Our mountebank has laid a deeper train ;
  His cant, like Merry Andrew's noble vein,
  Cat-calls the sects to draw them in again."
  At leisure hours in epic song he deals,
  Writes to the rumbling of his coach's wheels ;
  Prescribes in haste, and seldom kills by rule,
  But rides triumphant between stool and stool.
  Well, let him go,—'tis yet too early day
  To get himself a place in farce or play ;
  We know not by what name we should arraign him,
  For no one category can contain him.
  A pedant,—canting preacher,—and a quack,
  Are load enough to break an ass's back.
  At last, grown wanton, he presumed to write,
  Traduced two kings, their kindness to requite ;
  One made the doctor, and one dubb'd the knight."

commit new offences against ink and paper, but had
his faction, his admirers, and his panegyrists, among
that numerous and sober class of readers, who
think that genius consists in good intention. [1]   In

[1] One of these well-meaning persons insulted the ashes of
Dryden while they were still warm, in " An Epistle to Sir
Richard Blackmore, occasioned by the New Session of the
Poets." Marked by Mr Luttrell, 1st November, 1700.

> " His mighty Dryden to the shades is gone,
> And Congreve leaves successor of his throne:
> Though long before his final exit hence,
> He was himself an abdicated Prince;
> Disrobed of all regalities of state,
> Drawn by a hind and panther from his seat.
> Heir to his plays, his fables, and his tales,
> Congreve is the poetic prince of Wales;
> Not at St Germains, but at Will's, his court,
> Whither the subjects of his dad resort;
> Where plots are hatch'd, and councils yet unknown,
> How young Ascanius may ascend the throne,
> That in despite of all the muses' laws,
> He may revenge his injured father's cause.
> Go, nauseous rhymers, into darkness go,
> And view your monarch in the shades below,
> Who takes not now from Helicon his drink,
> But sips from Styx a liquor black as ink;
> Like Sisyphus, a restless stone he turns,
> And in a pile of his own labours burns;
> Whose curling flames most ghastly fiends do raise,
> Supplied with fuel from his impious plays;
> And when he fain would puff away the flame,
> One stops his mouth with bawdy Limberham;
> There, to augment the terrors of the place,
> His Hind and Panther stare him in the face;
> They grin like devils at the cursed toad,
> Who made them draw on earth so vile a load.
> Could some infernal painter draw the sight,   }
> And once transmit it to the realms of light,   }
> It might our poets from their sins affright: }
> Or could they hear, how there the sons of verse
> In dismal yells their tortures do express;
> How scorch'd with ballads on the Stygian shore,
> They horrors in a dismal chorus roar;
> Or see how the laureat does his grandeur bear,
> Crown'd with a wreath of flaming sulphur there,

the Epilogue, Dryden attacks Collier, but with
more courteous weapons: it is rather a palliation
than a defence of dramatic immorality, and contains
nothing personally offensive to Collier.—Thus so
dearly was Dryden's preeminent reputation purchased, that even his last hours were embittered
with controversy; and nature, over-watched and
worn out, was, like a besieged garrison, forced to
obey the call to arms, and defend reputation even
with the very last exertion of the vital spirit.

The approach of death was not, however, so
gradual as might have been expected from the
poet's chronic diseases. He had long suffered
both by the gout and gravel, and more lately the
erysipelas seized one of his legs. To a shattered
frame and a corpulent habit, the most trifling accident is often fatal. A slight inflammation in one
of his toes, became, from neglect, a gangrene. Mr
Hobbes, an eminent surgeon, to prevent mortification, proposed to amputate the limb; but Dryden,
who had no reason to be in love with life, refused
the chance of prolonging it by a doubtful and
painful operation.[1] After a short interval, the
catastrophe expected by Mr Hobbes took place,

> This, sir, 's your fate, cursed critics you oppose,
> The most tyrannical and cruel foes;
> Dryden, their huntsman dead, no more he wounds,
> But now you must engage his pack of hounds."

[1] According to Ward, his expressions were, "that he was
an old man, and had not long to live by course of nature, and
therefore did not care to part with one limb, at such an age,
to preserve an uncomfortable life on the rest."—*London Spy*,
part xviii.

and Dryden, not long surviving the consequences, left life on Wednesday morning, 1st May, 1700, at three o'clock. He seems to have been sensible till nearly his last moments, and died in the Roman Catholic faith, with submission and entire resignation to the divine will; "taking of his friends," says Mrs Creed, one of the sorrowful number, " so tender and obliging a farewell, as none but he himself could have expressed."

The death of a man like Dryden, especially in narrow and neglected circumstances, is usually an alarum-bell to the public. Unavailing and mutual reproaches, for unthankful and pitiless negligence, waste themselves in newspaper paragraphs, elegies, and funeral processions ; the debt to genius is then deemed discharged, and a new account of neglect and commemoration is opened between the public and the next who rises to supply his room. It was thus with Dryden: His family were preparing to bury him with the decency becoming their limited circumstances, when Charles Montague, Lord Jefferies, and other men of quality, made a subscription for a public funeral. The body of the poet was then removed to the Physicians' Hall, where it was embalmed, and lay in state till the 13th day of May, twelve days after the decease. On that day, the celebrated Dr Garth pronounced a Latin oration over the remains of his departed friend ; which were then, with considerable state, preceded by a band of music, and attended by a numerous procession of carriages, transported to

Westminster Abbey, and deposited between the graves of Chaucer and Cowley.

The malice of Dryden's contemporaries, which he had experienced through life, attempted to turn into burlesque these funeral honours. Farquhar, the comic dramatist, wrote a letter containing a ludicrous account of the funeral;[1] in which, as Mr Malone most justly remarks, he only sought to amuse his fair correspondent by an assemblage of ludicrous and antithetical expressions and ideas, which, when accurately examined, express little more than the bustle and confusion which attends every funeral procession of uncommon splendour. Upon this ground-work, Mrs Thomas (the Corinna of Pope and Cromwell) raised, at the distance of thirty years, the marvellous structure of fable, which has been copied by all Dryden's biographers, till the industry of Mr Malone has sent it, with other figments of the same lady, to " the grave of

[1] " I come now from Mr Dryden's funeral, where we had an Ode in Horace sung, instead of David's Psalms; whence you may find, that we don't think a poet worth Christian burial. The pomp of the ceremony was a kind of rhapsody, and fitter, I think, for Hudibras, than him; because the cavalcade was mostly burlesque: but he was an extraordinary man, and buried after an extraordinary fashion; for I do believe there was never such another burial seen. The oration, indeed, was great and ingenious, worthy the subject, and like the author; whose prescriptions can restore the living, and his pen embalm the dead. And so much for Mr Dryden; whose burial was the same as his life,—variety, and not of a piece:—the quality and mob, farce and heroics; the sublime and ridicule mixed in a piece;—great Cleopatra in a hackney coach."

all the Capulets."[1] She appears to have been
something assisted by a burlesque account of the
funeral, imputed by Mr Malone to Tom Brown,
who certainly continued to insult Dryden's memory
whenever an opportunity offered.[2] Indeed, Mrs

[1] Those who wish to peruse this memorable romance, may
find it in (Dryden's Works) vol. xviii. p. 200. It was first
published in "Wilson's Life of Congreve," 1730. Mr Malone
has successfully shown, that it is false in almost all its parts;
for, independently of the extreme improbability of the whole
story, it is clear, from Ward's account, written at the time,
that Lord Jefferies, who, it is pretended, interrupted the funeral, did, in fact, largely contribute to it. This also appears
from a paragraph, in a letter from Doctor, afterwards Bishop
Tanner, dated May 6th, 1700, and thus given by Mr Malone:
—" Mr Dryden died a papist, if at all a Christian. Mr Montague had given orders to bury him; but some lords (my
Lord Dorset, Jefferies, &c.) thinking it would not be splendid enough, ordered him to be carried to Russel's: there he
was embalmed; and now lies in state at the Physicians' College, and is to be buried with Chaucer, Cowley, &c., at Westminster Abbey, on Monday next."—*MSS. Ballard. in Bibl.
Bodl.* vol. iv., p. 29.

[2] The following lines are given by Mr Malone as a specimen:

" Before the hearse the mourning hautboys go,
And screech a dismal sound of grief and woe:
More dismal notes from bogtrotters may fall,
More dismal plaints at Irish funeral;
But no such floods of tears e'er stopp'd our tide,
Since Charles, the martyr and the monarch, died.
The decency and order first describe,
Without regard to either sex or tribe.
The sable coaches led the dismal van,
But by their side, I think, few footmen ran;
Nor needed these; the rabble fill the streets,
And mob with mob in great disorder meets.
See next the coaches, how they are accouter'd
Both in the inside, eke and on the outward:
One p—y spark, one sound as any roach,
One poet and two fiddlers in a coach:

Thomas herself quotes this last respectable authority. It must be a well-conducted and uncommon public ceremony, where the philosopher can find nothing to condemn, nor the satirist to ridicule; yet, to our imagination, what can be more striking, than the procession of talent and rank, which escorted the remains of DRYDEN to the tomb of CHAUCER!

The private character of the individual, his personal appearance, and rank in society, are the circumstances which generally interest the public most immediately upon his decease.

We are enabled, from the various paintings and engravings of Dryden, as well as from the less flattering delineations of the satirists of his time, to form a tolerable idea of his face and person. In youth, he appears to have been handsome,[1] and of a pleasing countenance; when his age was more advanced, he was corpulent and florid, which procured him the nickname attached to him by Rochester.[2] In his latter days, distress and disappointment probably chilled the fire of his eye, and the advance of age destroyed the animation of his countenance.[3] Still, however, his portraits bespeak

---

The playhouse drab, that beats the beggar's bush,
— — — — — — —
By every body kiss'd, good troth,—but such is
Now her good fate, to ride with mistress Duchess.
Was e'er immortal poet thus buffoon'd!
In a long line of coaches thus lampoon'd!"

[1] *Ante*, p. 74.
[2] " Poet Squab." *Ante*, p. 168-9.
[3] From " Epigrams on the Paintings of the most eminent

the look and features of genius; especially that in which he is drawn with his waving grey hairs.

In disposition and moral character, Dryden is represented as most amiable, by all who had access to know him; and his works, as well as letters, bear evidence to the justice of their panegyric. Congreve's character of the poet was drawn doubtless favourably, yet it contains points which demonstrate its fidelity.

" Whoever shall censure me, I dare be confident, you, my lord, will excuse me for any thing that I shall say with due regard to a gentleman, for whose person I had as just an affection as I have an admiration of his writings. And indeed Mr Dryden had personal qualities to challenge both love and esteem from all who were truly acquainted with him.

" He was of a nature exceedingly humane and compassionate; easily forgiving injuries, and capable of a prompt and sincere reconciliation with them who had offended him.

" Such a temperament is the only solid foundation of all moral virtues and social endowments. His friendship, where he professed it, went much beyond his professions; and I have been told of strong and generous instances of it by the persons

---

Masters," by J. E. (John Elsum), Esq., 8vo, 1700, Mr Malone gives the following lines :

The Effigies of Mr DRYDEN, by Closterman,
Epig. clxiv.

" A sleepy eye he shows, and no sweet feature,
Yet was indeed a favourite of nature :
Endow'd and graced with an exalted mind,
With store of wit, and that of every kind.
Juvenal's tartness, Horace's sweet air,
With Virgil's force, in him concenter'd were.
But though the painter's art can never show it,
That his exemplar was so great a poet,
Yet are the lines and tints so subtly wrought,
You may perceive he was a man of thought.
Closterman, 'tis confess'd, has drawn him well,
But short of Absalom and Achitophel."

themselves who received them, though his hereditary income was little more than a bare competency.

"As his reading had been very extensive, so was he very happy in a memory, tenacious of every thing that he had read. He was not more possessed of knowledge, than he was communicative of it. But then his communication of it was by no means pedantic, or imposed upon the conversation; but just such, and went so far, as, by the natural turns of the discourse in which he was engaged, it was necessarily promoted or required. He was extreme ready and gentle in his correction of the errors of any writer, who thought fit to consult him; and full as ready and patient to admit of the reprehension of others, in respect of his own oversight or mistakes. He was of very easy, I may say, of very pleasing access; but something slow, and, as it were, diffident in his advances to others. He had something in his nature, that abhorred intrusion into any society whatsoever. Indeed, it is to be regretted, that he was rather blameable in the other extreme; for, by that means, he was personally less known, and, consequently, his character might become liable both to misapprehensions and misrepresentations.

"To the best of my knowledge and observation, he was, of all the men that ever I knew, one of the most modest, and the most easily to be discountenanced in his approaches either to his superiors or his equals."

This portrait is from the pen of friendship; yet, if we consider all the circumstances of Dryden's life, we cannot deem it much exaggerated. For about forty years, his character, personal and literary, was the object of assault by every subaltern scribbler, titled or untitled, laureated or pilloried. "My morals," he himself has said, "have been sufficiently aspersed; that only sort of reputation, which ought to be dear to every honest man, and is to me." In such an assault, no weapon would remain unhandled, no charge, true or false, unpreferred, providing it was but plausible. Such

qualities, therefore, as we do not, in such circumstances, find excepted against, must surely be
admitted to pass to the credit of Dryden. His
change of political opinion, from the time he entered
life under the protection of a favourite of Cromwell, might have argued instability, if he had
changed a second time, when the current of power
and popular opinion set against the doctrines of the
Reformation. As it is, we must hold Dryden to
have acted from conviction, since personal interest,
had that been the ruling motive of his political
conduct, would have operated as strongly in 1688
as in 1660. The change of his religion we have
elsewhere discussed; and endeavoured to show,
that, although Dryden was unfortunate in adopting
the more corrupted form of our religion, yet considered relatively, it was a fortunate and laudable
conviction which led him from the mazes of scepti-
cism to become a catholic of the communion of
Rome.[1] It would be vain to maintain, that in his
early career he was free from the follies and vices
of a dissolute period; but the absence of every
positive charge, and the silence of numerous accusers, may be admitted to prove, that he partook in
them more from general example than inclination,
and with a moderate, rather than voracious or
undistinguishing appetite. It must be admitted,
that he sacrificed to the Belial or Asmodeus of the
age, in his writings; and that he formed his taste
upon the licentious and gay society with which he

[1] See *ante*, p. 260.

mingled.   But we have the testimony of one who
knew him well, that, however loose his comedies,
the temper of the author was modest;[1] his indelicacy was like the forced impudence of a bashful
man; and Rochester has accordingly upbraided
him, that his licentiousness was neither natural nor
seductive.   Dryden had unfortunately conformed
enough to the taste of his age, to attempt that
" hice mode of wit," as it is termed by the said
noble author, whose name has become inseparably
connected with it; but it sate awkwardly upon his
natural modesty, and in general sounds impertinent,
as well as disgusting.   The clumsy phraseology of
Burnet, in passing censure on the immorality of
the stage, after the Restoration, terms " Dryden,
the greatest master of dramatic poesy, a monster
of immodesty and of impurity of all sorts."   The
expression called forth the animated defence of
Granville, Lord Lansdowne, our author's noble
friend.

" All who knew him," said Lansdowne, " can testify this
was not his character.   He was so much a stranger to immodesty, that modesty in too great a degree was his failing : he
hurt his fortune by it, he complained of it, and never could
overcome it.   He was," adds he, " esteemed, courted, and
admired, by all the great men of the age in which he lived,
who would certainly not have received into friendship a monster, abandoned to all sorts of vice and impurity.   His writings

[1] A correspondent of the Gentleman's Magazine, in 1745, already
quoted, says of him as a personal acquaintance : " Posterity is absolutely mistaken as to that great man : though forced to be a satirist,
he was the mildest creature breathing, and the readiest to help the
young and deserving.   Though his comedies are horribly full of
double entendre, yet 'twas owing to a false complaisance.   He was,
in company, the modestest man that ever conversed."

will do immortal honour to his name and country, and his poems last as long, if I may have leave to say it, as the Bishop's sermons, supposing them to be equally excellent in their kind." [1]

The Bishop's youngest son, Thomas Burnet, in replying to Lord Lansdowne, explained his father's last expressions as limited to Dryden's plays, and showed, by doing so, that there was no foundation for fixing this gross and dubious charge upon his private moral character.

Dryden's conduct as a father, husband, and master of a family, seems to have been affectionate, faithful, and, so far as his circumstances admitted, liberal and benevolent. The whole tenor of his correspondence bears witness to his paternal feelings; and even when he was obliged to have recourse to Tonson's immediate assistance to pay for the presents he sent them, his affection vented itself in that manner. As a husband, if Lady Elizabeth's peculiarities of temper precluded the idea of a warm attachment, he is not upbraided with neglect or infidelity by any of his thousand assailants. As a landlord, Mr Malone has informed us, on the authority of Lady Dryden, that "his little estate at Blakesley is at this day occupied by one Harriots, grandson of the tenant who held it in Dryden's time; and he relates, that his grandfather was used to take great pleasure in talking of our poet. He was, he said, the easiest and the kindest landlord in the world, and never raised

---

[1] Letter to the author of "Reflections Historical and Political." 4to, 1732.

the rent during the whole time he possessed the estate."

Some circumstances, however, may seem to degrade so amiable a private, so sublime a poetical character. The license of his comedy, as we have seen, had for it only the apology of universal example, and must be lamented, though not excused.[1] Let us, however, remember, that if in the hey-day of the merry monarch's reign, Dryden ventured to maintain, that, the prime end of poetry

[1] [" Our editor evinces in behalf of Dryden's moral character, a bias excusable enough in him, but by which we are not so forcibly swayed. The meekness and modesty which Congreve and others largely ascribe to him, must be taken, we conceive, with some allowance. Neither of these qualities is easily discoverable in his writings. The best part of his character seems to have been his gratitude, which, though servile, was sincere. In other respects, there is little enough to praise. The indelicacy of his dramatic writings is ingeniously shifted upon the age in which he lived; but we fear this apology leaves something wanting. He has not left this fault at the doors of the theatre; it runs through almost all his poems; and indicates, not so much a voluptuous fancy, as a radical depravation and coarseness of feeling. It is indeed this moral apathy, this ignorance of virtuous emotions, which is the cardinal defect of his poetry. He seems not to plead that excuse which men of genius ordinarily make for the errors of their lives; *video meliora proboque, deteriora sequor.* There is rarely any thing refined, any thing ennobled in his sentiments; for surely the insipid love of Palamon is as far from the one, as the fustian of Almanzor is from the other. In practical virtue, we would not rate the character of Pope very high; but with what dignified feelings must he have been invested for the moment, when he wrote the epistle to Lord Oxford! This tone was quite unknown to Dryden; it was a strain of a higher mood: and he could as easily have reached the pathos of Eloisa, as the moral sublime of this epistle."—HALLAM, *Edin. Rev.* 1808.]

being pleasure, the muses ought not to be fettered by the chains of strict decorum; yet in his more advanced and sober mood, he evinced sincere repentance for his trespass, by patient and unresisting submission to the coarse and rigorous chastisement of Collier. If it is alleged, that, in the fury of his loyal satire, he was not always solicitous concerning its justice, let us make allowance for the prejudice of party, and consider at what advantage, after the lapse of more than a century, and through the medium of impartial history, we now view characters, who were only known to their contemporaries as zealous partisans of an opposite and detested faction. The moderation of Dryden's reprisals, when provoked by the grossest calumny and personal insult, ought also to plead in his favour. Of the hundreds who thus assailed, not only his literary, but his moral reputation, he has distinguished Settle and Shadwell alone by an elaborate retort. Those who look into Mr Luttrel's collections, will at once see the extent of Dryden's sufferance, and the limited degree of his retaliation.

The extreme flattery of Dryden's dedications has been objected to him, as a fault of an opposite description; and perhaps no writer has equalled him in the profusion and elegance of his adulation. "Of this kind of meanness," says Johnson, "he never seems to decline the practice, or lament the necessity. He considers the great as entitled to encomiastic homage, and brings praise rather as a tribute than a gift; more delighted with the fertility of his invention, than mortified by the prostitu-

tion of his judgment." It may be noticed, in palliation of this heavy charge, that the form of address to superiors must be judged of by the manners
of the times; and that the adulation contained in
dedications was then as much a matter of course,
as the words of submissive style which still precede
the subscription of an ordinary letter. It is probable, that Dryden considered his panegyrics as
merely conforming with the fashion of the day, and
rendering unto Cæsar the things which were Cæsar's,
—attended with no more degradation than the payment of any other tribute to the forms of politeness
and usage of the world.

Of Dryden's general habits of life we can form a
distinct idea, from the evidence assembled by Mr
Malone. His mornings were spent in study; he
dined with his family, probably about two o'clock.
After dinner he went usually to Will's Coffee-
house, the famous rendezvous of the wits of the
time, where he had his established chair by the
chimney in winter, and near the balcony in summer,
whence he pronounced, *ex cathedra*, his opinion
upon new publications, and, in general, upon all
matters of dubious criticism.[1] Latterly, all who

---

[1] See Dryden's Works, vol. xi., p. 52, note; vol. xviii.,
p. 224. From the poem in the passage last quoted, it seems
that the original sign of Will's Coffee-house had been a *cow*.
It was changed, however, to a *rose*, in Dryden's time. This
wits' coffee-house was situated at the end of Bow-street, on the
north side of Russel-street, and frequented by all who made
any pretence to literature, or criticism. Their company, it
would seem, was attended with more honour than profit;
for Dennis describes William Erwin, or Urwin, who kept the

had occasion to ridicule or attack him, represent
him as presiding in this little senate.   His opinions,
however, were not maintained with dogmatism;
and we have an instance, in a pleasing anecdote
told by Dr Lockier,[1] that Dryden readily listened
to criticism, provided it was just, from whatever
unexpected and undignified quarter it happened to

house, as taking refuge in Whitefriars, then a place of asylum,
to escape the clutches of his creditors.   " For since the law,"
says the critic, " thought it just to put Will out of its protection, Will thought it but prudent to put himself out of its
power."

[1] The Dean of Peterborough—" I was," says he, " about
seventeen, when I first came to town; an odd-looking boy,
with short rough hair, and that sort of awkwardness which
one always brings out of the country with one: however, in
spite of my bashfulness and appearance, I used now and then
to thrust myself into Will's, to have the pleasure of seeing the
most celebrated wits of that time, who used to resort thither.
The second time that ever I was there, Mr Dryden was speaking of his own things, as he frequently did, especially of such
as had been lately published.   ' If any thing of mine is good,'
says he, ' 'tis my Mac-Flecknoe; and I value myself the more
on it, because it is the first piece of ridicule written in heroics.'
Lockier overhearing this, plucked up his spirit so far, as to say,
in a voice just loud enough to be heard, that Mac-Flecknoe was
a very fine poem, but that he had not imagined it to be the
first that ever was wrote that way.   On this Dryden turned
short upon him, as surprised at his interposing; asked him
how long he had been a dealer in poetry; and added, with a
smile,—' But pray, sir, what is it, that you did imagine to
have been writ so before?' Lockier named Boileau's *Lutrin*,
and Tassoni's *Secchia Rapita*; which he had read, and knew
Dryden had borrowed some strokes from each.   ' 'Tis true,'
says Dryden;—' I had forgot them.'   A little after, Dryden
went out, and in going spoke to Lockier again, and desired
him to come to him the next day. Lockier was highly delighted with the invitation, and was well acquainted with him as
long as he lived."—MALONE, vol. i., p. 481.

come. In general, however, it may be supposed,
that few ventured to dispute his opinion, or place
themselves in the gap between him and the object
of his censure. He was most falsely accused of
carrying literary jealousy to such a length, as felo-
niously to encourage Creech to venture on a translation of Horace, that he might lose the character
he had gained by a version of Lucretius. But this
is positively contradicted, upon the authority of
Southerne.[1]

We have so often stopped in our narrative of
Dryden's life, to notice the respectability of his
general society, that little need here be said on the
subject. A contemporary authority, the reference

[1] " I have often heard," says Mr George Russell, " that Mr
Dryden, dissatisfied and envious at the reputation Creech
obtained by his translation of Lucretius, purposely advised
him to undertake Horace, to which he knew him unequal,
that he might by his ill performance lose the fame he had
acquired. Mr Southerne, author of ' Oroonoko,' set me right
as to the conduct of Mr Dryden in this affair ; affirming, that,
being one evening at Mr Dryden's lodgings, in company with
Mr Creech, and some other ingenious men, Mr Creech told
the company of his design to translate Horace; from which
Mr Dryden, with many arguments, dissuaded him, as an attempt which his genius was not adapted to, and which would
risk his losing the good opinion the world had of him, by his
successful translation of Lucretius. I thought it proper to
acquaint you with this circumstance, since it rescues the fame
of one of our greatest poets from the imputation of envy and
malevolence." (See also, upon this subject, a note on page 200
of Dryden's Works, vol. viii.) Yet Jacob Tonson told Spence,
" that Dryden would compliment Crowne when a play of his
failed, but was cold to him if he met with success. He used
sometimes to say, that Crowne had some genius ; but then he
always added, that his father and Crowne's mother were very
well acquainted."—MALONE, vol. i., p. 500.

to which I have mislaid, says, that Dryden was
shy and silent in society, till a moderate circulation
of the bottle had removed his natural reserve, and
that he frequently justified this degree of conviviality by saying, " there was no deceit in a brim-
mer." But although no enemy to conviviality,
Dryden is pronounced by Pope to have been regular
in his hours, in comparison with Addison, who,
otherwise, lived the same coffeehouse course of life.
He has himself told us, that he was " saturnine and
reserved, and not one of those who endeavour to
entertain company by lively sallies of merriment
and wit ;" and an adversary has put into his mouth
this couplet:

> Nor wine nor love could ever see me gay;
> To writing bred, I knew not what to say.
> *Dryden's Satire to his Muse.*

But the admission of the author, and the censure
of the satirist, must be received with some limita-
tion. Dryden was thirty years old before he was
freed from the fetters of puritanism ; and if the
habits of lively expression in society are not acquired
before that age, they are seldom gained afterward.
But this applies only to the deficiency of repartee,
in the sharp encounter of wit which was fashionable
at the court of Charles, and cannot be understood
to exclude Dryden's possessing the more solid qualities of agreeable conversation, arising from a
memory profoundly stocked with knowledge, and
a fancy which supplied modes of illustration faster

than the author could use them.[1]   Some few say-
ings of Dryden have been, however, preserved;
which, if not witty, are at least jocose.   He is said
to have been the original author of the repartee to
the Duke of Buckingham, who, in bowling, offered
to lay "his soul to a turnip," or something still
more vile.   " Give me the odds," said Dryden,
" and I take the bet."   When his wife wished to be
a book, that she might enjoy more of his company,
" Be an almanac then, my dear," said the poet,
" that I may change you once a-year."   Another
time, a friend expressing his astonishment that even
Durfey could write such stuff as a play they had
just witnessed, " Ah, sir," replied Dryden, " you
do not know my friend Tom so well as I do; I'll
answer for him, he can write worse yet."   None
of these anecdotes intimate great brilliancy of repartee; but that Dryden, possessed of such a fund
of imagination, and acquired learning, should be
dull in conversation, is impossible.   He is known
frequently to have regaled his friends, by communicating to them a part of his labours; but his

---

[1] His conversation is thus characterised by a contemporary
writer:

" O, sir, there's a medium in all things.   Silence and chat
are distant enough, to have a convenient discourse come between them; and thus far I agree with you, that the company
of the author of ' Absalom and Achitophel' is more valuable,
though not so talkative, than that of the modern men of
banter; for what he says is like what he writes, much to the
purpose, and full of mighty sense; and if the town were for
any thing desirable, it were for the conversation of him, and
one or two more of the same character."—The Humours and
Conversation of the Town exposed, in two Dialogues, 1693, p. 73.

poetry suffered by his recitation.   He read his productions very ill;[1] owing, perhaps, to the modest
reserve of his temper, which prevented his showing
an animation in which he feared his audience might
not participate.   The same circumstance may have
repressed the liveliness of his conversation.   I
know not, however, whether we are, with Mr
Malone, to impute to diffidence his general habit of
consulting his literary friends upon his poems, before
they became public, since it might as well arise from
a wish to anticipate and soften criticism.[2]

Of Dryden's learning, his works form the best
proof.   He had read Polybius before he was ten
years of age;[3] and was doubtless well acquainted
with the Greek and Roman classics.   But from

[1] " When Dryden, our first great master of verse and harmony, brought his play of ' Amphitryon' to the stage, I heard
him give it his first reading to the actors ; in which, though it
is true he delivered the plain sense of every period, yet the
whole was in so cold, so flat, and unaffecting a manner, that
I am afraid of not being believed, when I affirm it."—*Cibber's
Apology*, 4to.

[2] See *ante*, p. 113.

[3] [" I had read Polybius in English, with the pleasure of a
boy, before I was ten years of age; and yet, even then, had
some dark notions of the prudence with which he conducted
his design, particularly in making me know, and almost see,
the places where such and such actions were performed. This
was the first distinction which I was then capable of making
betwixt him and other historians which I read early. But
when, being of a riper age, I took him again into my hands, I
must needs say I have profited more by reading him than by
Thucydides, Appian, Dion Cassius, and all the rest of the
Greek historians together; and amongst all the Romans,
none have reached him in this particular, but Tacitus, who is
equal with him."—*Dryden's Works*, vol. xviii., p. 31.]

these studies he could descend to read romances; and the present editor records with pride, that Dryden was a decided admirer of old ballads, and popular tales.[1] His researches sometimes extended into the vain province of judicial astrology, in which he was a firm believer; and there is reason to think that he also credited divination by dreams. In the country, he delighted in the pastime of fishing, and used, says Mr Malone, to spend some time with Mr Jones of Ramsden, in Wiltshire. Durfey was sometimes of this party; but Dryden appears to have undervalued his skill in fishing, as much as his attempts at poetry. Hence Fenton, in his epistle to Mr Lambard:

> " By long experience, Durfey may no doubt
> Ensnare a gudgeon, or sometimes a trout;
> Yet Dryden once exclaim'd in partial spite,
> ' He *fish!* '—because the man attempts to write."

I may conclude this notice of Dryden's habits, which I have been enabled to give chiefly by the researches of Mr Malone, with two notices of a minute nature. Dryden was a great taker of snuff, which he prepared himself. Moreover, as a prepa-

---

[1] " I find," says Gildon, " Mr Bayes, the younger, [Rowe,] has two qualities, like Mr Bayes, the elder; his admiration of some odd books, as ' Reynard the Fox,' and the old ballads of ' Jane Shore,'" &c.—*Remarks on Mr Rowe's Plays.* " Reynard the Fox," is also mentioned in " The Town and Country Mouse," as a favourite book of Dryden's. And Addison, in the 85th number of the Spectator, informs us, that Dorset and Dryden delighted in perusing the collection of old ballads which the latter possessed.

ration to a course of study, he usually took medi-
cine, and observed a cooling diet.[1]

Dryden's house, which he appears to have resided
in from the period of his marriage till his death,
was in Gerard Street, the fifth on the left hand
coming from Little Newport Street.[2]   The back
windows looked upon the gardens of Leicester
House, of which circumstance our poet availed
himself to pay a handsome compliment to the noble
owner.[3]   His excursions to the country seem to
have been frequent; perhaps the more so, as Lady
Elizabeth always remained in town.   In his latter

[1] [—— " I have translated six hundred lines of Ovid ; but
I believe I shall not compass his 772 lines under nine hundred
or more of mine. This time I cannot write to my wife, because
he who is to carry my letter to Oundle will not stay till I can
write another.   Pray, sir, let her know that I am well ; and
for feare the damsins should be all gone, desire her to buy me
a sieve-full, to preserve whole, and not in mash."—*Dryden to
Jacob Tonson, Aug.* 30, 1693.   This commission will probably
remind the reader of the poetic diet recommended by Bayes.
" If I am to write familiar things, as sonnets to Armida, and
the like, I make use of *stewed prunes* only ; but when I have
a grand design in hand, I ever take physic, and let blood :
for, when you would have pure swiftness of thought, and fiery
flights of fancy, you must have a care of the pensive part. In
fine, you must purge the belly.

" *Smith.* By my troth, sir, this is a most admirable receipt
for writing.

" *Bayes.* Ay, 'tis my secret ; and, in good earnest, I think one
of the best I have."—*Rehearsal,* Act I. This is an instance
of the minute and malicious diligence with which the most
trivial habits and tastes of our author were ridiculed in the
" Rehearsal."—*Note,* (*Sir W . S.*)—*Dryden's Works,* vol. xviii.,
p. 109-10.]

[2] It is now No. 43.

[3] Dryden's Works, vol. vii., p. 288.—See also the Rehearsal.

days, the friendship of his relations, John Driden of Chesterton, and Mrs Steward of Cotterstock, rendered their houses agreeable places of abode to the aged poet. They appear also to have had a kind solicitude about his little comforts, of value infinitely beyond the contributions which they made towards aiding them. And thus concludes all that we have learned of the private life of Dryden.

The fate of Dryden's family must necessarily interest the admirers of English literature. It consisted of his wife, Lady Elizabeth Dryden, and three sons, John, Charles, and Erasmus-Henry. Upon the poet's death, it may be believed, they felt themselves slenderly provided for, since all his efforts, while alive, were necessary to secure them from the gripe of penury. Yet their situation was not very distressing. John and Erasmus-Henry were abroad; and each had an office at Rome, by which he was able to support himself. Charles had for some time been entirely dependent on his father, and administered to his effects, as he died without a will. The liberality of the Duchess of Ormond, and of Driden of Chesterton, had been lately received, and probably was not expended. There was, besides, the poet's little patrimonial estate, and a small property in Wiltshire, which the Earl of Berkshire settled upon Lady Elizabeth at her marriage, and which yielded L.50 or L.60 annually. There was therefore an income of about L.100 a-year, to maintain the poet's widow and children; enough in those times to support them in decent frugality.

Lady Elizabeth Dryden's temper had long disturbed her husband's domestic happiness. " His invectives," says Mr Malone, " against the married state, are frequent and bitter, and were continued to the latest period of his life ;" and he adds, from most respectable authority, that the family of the poet held no intimacy with his lady, confining their intercourse to mere visits of ceremony. A similar alienation seems to have taken place between her and her own relations, Sir Robert Howard, perhaps, being excepted ; for her brother, the Honourable Edward Howard, talks of Dryden's being engaged in a translation of Virgil, as a thing he had learned merely by common report.[1] Her wayward disposition was, however, the effect of a disordered imagination, which, shortly after Dryden's death, degenerated into absolute insanity, in which state she remained until her death in summer 1714, probably, says Mr Malone, in the seventy-ninth year of her life.[2]

---

[1] *Ante*, p. 84.

[2] [" No authentic account has been transmitted of her person, nor has any portrait of her been discovered. I am afraid her personal attractions were not superior to her mental endowments, that her temper was wayward, and that the purity of her character was sullied by some early indiscretions. A letter from Lady Elizabeth to her son at Rome is preserved, as remarkable for the elegance of the style, as the correctness of the orthography. She says, ' Your father is much at woon as to his health, and his defnese is not wosce, but much as he was when he was heare ; give me a true account how my deare sonn Charlles is head dus.'—Can this be the lady who had formerly held captive in her chains the gallant Earl of Chesterfield ?"—*Mitford's Life of Dryden*, p. 135.]

Dryden's three sons, says the inscription by Mrs
Creed, were ingenious and accomplished gentlemen. Charles, the eldest, and favourite son of the
poet, was born at Charlton, Wiltshire, in 1666.
He received a classical education under Dr Busby,
his father's preceptor, and was chosen King's
Scholar in 1680. Being elected to Trinity College in Cambridge, he was admitted a member in
1683. It would have been difficult for the son of
Dryden to refrain from attempting poetry; but
though Charles escaped the fate of Icarus, he was
very, very far from emulating his father's soaring
flight. Mr Malone has furnished a list of his
compositions in Latin and English.[1] About 1692,
he went to Italy, and through the interest of
Cardinal Howard, to whom he was related by the
mother's side, he became Chamberlain of the Household; not, as Corinna pretends, " to that *remarkably fine gentleman*, Pope Clement XI.," but to
Pope Innocent XII. His way to this preferment
was smoothed by a pedigree drawn up in Latin
by his father, of the families of Dryden and
Howard, which is said to have been deposited in
the Vatican. Dryden, whose turn for judicial

[1] These are, 1, Latin verses, prefixed to Lord Roscommon's
Essay on Translated Verse. 2, Latin verses on the Death
of Charles II., published in the Cambridge collection of Elegies on that occasion. 3, A poem in the same language, upon
Lord Arlington's Gardens, published in the Second Miscellany. 4, A translation of the seventh Satire of Juvenal,
mentioned in the text. 5, An English poem, on the Happiness of a Retired Life. 6, A pretty song, printed by Mr
Malone, to which Charles Dryden also composed music.

astrology we have noticed, had calculated the nativity of his son Charles; and it would seem, that a part of his predictions were fortuitously fulfilled. Charles, however, having suffered, while at Rome, by a fall, and his health, in consequence, being much injured, his father prognosticated he would begin to recover in the month of September, 1697. The issue did no great credit to the prediction; for young Dryden returned to England, in 1698, in the same indifferent state of health, as is obvious from the anxious solicitude with which his father always mentions Charles in his correspondence. Upon the poet's death, Charles, we have seen, administered to his effects on 10th June, 1700, Lady Elizabeth, his mother, renouncing the succession. In the next year, Granville conferred on him the profits arising from the author's night of an alteration of Shakspeare's "Merchant of Venice;" and his liberality to the son of one great bard may be admitted to balance his presumption, in manufacturing a new drama out of the labours of another.[1] Upon the 20th August, 1704, Charles Dryden was drowned, in an attempt to swim across the Thames, at Datchet, near Windsor. I have

---

[1] The prologue was spoken by the ghosts of Shakspeare and Dryden; from which Mr Malone selects the following curious quotation:—" Mr Bevil Higgons, the writer of it, *ventured* to make the representative of our great dramatic poet speak these lines!

' These scenes in their rough native dress were mine;
But now, improved, with nobler lustre shine :
The first rude sketches Shakspeare's pencil drew,
But all the shining master-strokes are new.

degraded into the Appendix,[1] the romantic narrative of Corinna, concerning his father's prediction, already mentioned. It contains, like her account of the funeral of the poet, much positive falsehood, and gross improbability, with some slight scantling of foundation in fact.

John Dryden, the poet's second son, was born in 1667, or 1668, was admitted a King's Scholar in Westminster in 1682, and elected to Oxford in 1685. Here he became a private pupil of the celebrated Obadiah Walker, Master of University College, a Roman Catholic. It seems probable that young Dryden became a convert to that faith before his father. His religion making it impossible for him to succeed in England, he followed his brother Charles to Rome, where he officiated as his deputy in the Pope's household. John Dryden translated the fourteenth Satire of Juvenal, published in his father's version, and wrote a comedy, entitled, " The Husband his own Cuckold," acted in Lincoln's-Inn Fields in 1696; Dryden, the father, furnishing a prologue, and Congreve an epilogue. In 1700–1, he made a

---

This play, ye critics, shall your fury stand,
Adorned and rescued by a faultless hand.'

" To which our author replies,

' I long endeavour'd to support the stage,
With the faint copies of thy nobler rage,
But toil'd in vain for an ungenerous age.
They starved me living; nay, denied me fame,
And scarce, now dead, do justice to my name.
Would you repent? Be to my ashes kind;
Indulge the pledges I have left behind.' "

[1] Dryden's Works, vol. xviii.

tour through Sicily and Malta, and his journal
was published in 1706. It seems odd, that, in the
whole course of his journal, he never mentions his
father's name, nor makes the least allusion to his
very recent death. John Dryden, the younger,
died at Rome soon after this excursion.

Erasmus-Henry, Dryden's third son, was born
2d May, 1669, and educated in the Charter-House,
to which he was nominated by Charles II., shortly
after the publication of " Absalom and Achitophel."
He does not appear to have been at any university; probably his religion was the obstacle. Like
his brothers, he went to Rome; and as both his
father and mother request his prayers, we are to
suppose he was originally destined for the church.
But he became a Captain in the Pope's guards,
and remained at Rome till John Dryden, his elder
brother's death. After this event, he seems to
have returned to England, and in 1708 succeeded
to the title of Baronet, as representative of Sir
Erasmus Driden, the author's grandfather. But
the estate of Canons-Ashby, which should have
accompanied and supported the title, had been
devised by Sir Robert Driden, the poet's first
cousin, to Edward Dryden, the eldest son of Erasmus, the younger brother of the poet. Thus, if
the author had lived a few years longer, his pecuniary embarrassments would have been embittered
by his succeeding to the honours of his family,
without any means of sustaining the rank they
gave him. With this Edward Dryden, Sir Erasmus-Henry seems to have resided until his death,

which took place at the family mansion of Canons-Ashby in 1710. Edward acted as a manager of his cousin's affairs; and Mr Malone sees reason to think, from their mode of accounting, that Sir Erasmus-Henry had, like his mother, been visited with mental derangement before his death, and had resigned into Edward's hands the whole management of his concerns. Thus ended the poet's family, none of his sons surviving him above ten years. The estate of Canons-Ashby became again united to the title, in the person of John Dryden, the surviving brother.[1]

[1] Mr Malone says, " Edward Dryden, the eldest son of the last Sir Erasmus Dryden, left by his wife, Elizabeth Allen, who died in London in 1761, five sons; the youngest of whom, Bevil, was father of the present Lady Dryden. Sir John, the eldest, survived all his brothers, and died without issue, at Canons-Ashby, March 20, 1770."

SECTION VIII.

The State of Dryden's Reputation at his Death, and after-
wards—The general Character of his Mind—His Merit
as a Dramatist—As a Lyrical Poet—As a Satirist—As
a Narrative Poet—As a Philosophical and Miscella-
neous Poet—As a Translator—As a Prose Author—As
a Critic.

IF Dryden received but a slender share of the
gifts of fortune, it was amply made up to him in
reputation.   Even while a poet-militant upon earth,
he received no ordinary portion of that applause,
which is too often reserved for the " dull cold ear
of death."   He combated, it is true, but he con-
quered ; and, in despite of faction, civil and religious, of penury, and the contempt which follows
it, of degrading patronage, and rejected solicitation, from 1666 to the year of his death, the name
of Dryden was first in English literature.   Nor
was his fame limited to Britain.   Of the French
literati, although Boileau,[1] with unworthy affectation, when he heard of the honours paid to the
poet's remains, pretended ignorance even of his
name, yet Rapin, the famous critic, learned the
English language on purpose to read the works of

[1] Life and Works of Arthur Maynwaring, 1715, p. 17.

Dryden.[1] Sir John Shadwell, the son of our author's ancient adversary, bore an honourable and manly testimony to the general regret among the men of letters at Paris for the death of Dryden:— " The men of letters here lament the loss of Mr Dryden very much. The honours paid to him have done our countrymen no small service ; for, next to having so considerable a man of our own growth, 'tis a reputation to have known how to value him; as patrons very often pass for wits, by esteeming those that are so." And from another authority we learn, that the engraved copies of Dryden's portrait were bought up with avidity on the Continent.[2]

But in England the loss of Dryden was as a national deprivation. It is seldom the extent of such a loss is understood, till it has taken place ; as the size of an object is best estimated, when we see the space void which it has long occupied. The men of literature, starting as it were from a dream, began to heap commemorations, panegyrics, and elegies : the great were as much astonished at their own neglect of such an object of bounty, as if the same omission had never been practised before ; and expressed as much compunction, as if it were never to occur again. The poets were not silent; but their strains only evinced their woeful

[1] So says Charles Blount, in the dedication to the *Religio Laici*. He is contradicted by Tom Brown.

[2] In a poem published on Dryden's death, by Brome, written, as Mr Malone conjectures, by Captain Gibbon, son of the physician.

degeneracy from him whom they mourned. Henry Playford, a publisher of music, collected their effusions into a compilation, entitled, " Luctus Britannici, or the Tears of the British Muses, for the death of John Dryden;" which he published about two months after Dryden's death.[1]   Nine ladies, assuming each the character of a Muse, and clubbing a funeral ode, or elegy, produced " The Nine Muses;" of which very rare (and very worthless) collection, I have given a short account in the Appendix;[2] where the reader will also find an ode on the same subject, by Oldys, which may serve for ample specimen of the poetical lamentations over Dryden.

The more costly, though equally unsubstantial, honour of a monument, was projected by Montague; and loud were the acclamations of the poets on his

[1] In " The Postboy," for Tuesday, May 7, 1700, Playford inserted the following advertisement :

" The death of the famous John Dryden, Esq., Poet Laureat to their two late Majesties, King Charles, and King James the Second, being a subject capable of employing the best pens ; and several persons of quality, and others, having put a stop to his interment, which is designed to be in Chaucer's grave, in Westminster-Abbey ; this is to desire the gentlemen of the two famous Universities, and others, who have a respect for the memory of the deceased, and are inclinable to such performances, to send what copies they please, as Epigrams, &c. to Henry Playford, at his shop at the Temple 'Change, in Fleet-street, and they shall be inserted in a Collection, which is designed after the same nature, and in the same method, (in what language they shall please,) as is usual in the composures which are printed on solemn occasions, at the two Universities aforesaid." This advertisement, (with some alterations,) was continued for a month in the same paper.

[2] Dryden's Works, vol. xviii.

generous forgiveness of past discords with Dryden, and the munificence of this universal patron. But Montague never accomplished his purpose, if he seriously entertained it. Pelham, Duke of Newcastle, announced the same intention; received the panegyric of Congreve for having done so; and, having thus pocketed the applause, proceeded no further than Montague had done. At length Pope, in some lines which were rather an epitaph on Dryden, who lay in the vicinity, than on Rowe, over whose tomb they were to be placed,[1] roused Dryden's original patron, Sheffield, formerly Earl of Mulgrave, and now Duke of Buckingham, to erect over the grave of his friend the present simple monument which distinguishes it. The inscription was comprised in the following words:—
J. Dryden. Natus 1632. *Mortuus* 1 *Maii*, 1700. *Joannes Sheffield Dux Buckinghamiensis posuit,* 1720.[2]

[1] " Thy reliques, Rowe, to this fair urn we trust,
And sacred place by Dryden's awful dust:
Beneath a rude and nameless stone he lies,
To which thy tomb shall guide enquiring eyes:
Peace to thy gentle shade, and endless rest!
Blest in thy genius, in thy love too, blest!
One grateful woman to thy fame supplies,
What a whole thankless land to his denies."

[2] The epitaph at first intended by Pope for this monument, was,
" This Sheffield rais'd; the sacred dust below
Was Dryden once:—the rest, who does not know?"

Atterbury had thus written to him on this subject, in 1720: " What I said to you in mine, about the monument, was intended only to quicken, not to alarm you. It is not worth your while to know what I meant by it; but when I see you, you shall. I hope you may be at the Deanery towards the end of October, by which time I think of settling there for the

In the school of reformed English poetry, of which Dryden must be acknowledged as the founder, there soon arose disciples not unwilling to be considered as the rivals of their master. Addison had his partisans, who were desirous to hold him up in this point of view; and he himself is said to have taken pleasure, with the assistance of Steele, to

---

winter. What do you think of some such short inscription as this in Latin, which may, in a few words, say all that is to be said of Dryden, and yet nothing more than he deserves?

> " JOHANNI DRYDENO,
> CUI POESIS ANGLICANA
> VIM SUAM AC VENERES DEBET ;
> ET SI QUA IN POSTERUM AUGEBITUR LAUDE,
> EST ADHUC DEBITURA.
> HONORIS ERGO P. ETC.

" To show you that I am as much in earnest in the affair as you yourself, something I will send you of this kind in English. If your design holds, of fixing Dryden's name only below, and his busto above, may not lines like these be graved just under the name?

> " This Sheffield raised, to Dryden's ashes just;
> Here fix'd his name, and there his laurell'd bust:
> What else the Muse in marble might express,
> Is known already : praise would make him less.

Or thus :

> " More needs not; when acknowledged merits reign,
> Praise is impertinent, and censure vain."

The thought, as Mr Malone observes, is nearly the same as in the following lines in " Luctus Britannici," by William Marston, of Trinity College, Cambridge :

" *In* JOANNEM DRYDEN, *poetarum facile principem.*

> Si quis in has ædes intret fortasse viator,
> Busta poetarum dum veneranda notet,
> Cernat et exuvias Drydeni,—plura referre
> Haud opus : ad laudes *vox ea* sola satis."

depreciate Dryden, whose fame was defended by Pope and Congreve.[1] No serious invasion of Dryden's preeminence can be said, however, to have taken place, till Pope himself, refining upon that structure of versification which our author had first introduced, and attending with sedulous diligence to improve every passage to the highest pitch of point and harmony, exhibited a new style of composition, and claimed at least to share with Dryden the sovereignty of Parnassus. I will not attempt to concentrate what Johnson has said upon this interesting comparison.

" In acquired knowledge, the superiority must be allowed to Dryden, whose education was more scholastic, and who, before he became an author, had been allowed more time for study, with better means of information. His mind has a larger range, and he collects his images and illustrations from a more extensive circumference of science. Dryden knew more of man in his general nature, and Pope in his local manners. The notions of Dryden were formed by comprehensive speculation, and those of Pope by minute attention. There is more dignity in the knowledge of Dryden, and more certainty in that of Pope.

" Poetry was not the sole praise of either ; for both excelled likewise in prose ; but Pope did not borrow his prose from his predecessor. The style of Dryden is capricious and varied, that of Pope is cautious and uniform. Dryden obeys the motions of his own mind, Pope constrains his mind to his own rules of composition. Dryden is sometimes vehement and rapid ; Pope is always smooth, uniform, and gentle. Dryden's page is a natural field, rising into inequalities, and diversified by the varied exuberance of abundant vegetation ; Pope's is a velvet lawn, shaven by the scythe, and levelled by the roller.

[1] [" Addison was so eager to be the first name, that he and his friend Sir Richard Steele used to run down Dryden's character as far as they could. Pope and Congreve used to support it."—TONSON—*Spence's Anecdotes*, (Malone,) p. 114.]

" Of genius, that power which constitutes a poet; that quality, without which judgment is cold, and knowledge is inert; that energy, which collects, combines, amplifies, and animates; the superiority must, with some hesitation, be allowed to Dryden. It is not to be inferred, that of this poetical vigour Pope had only a little, because Dryden had more; for every other writer, since Milton, must give place to Pope: and even of Dryden it must be said, that if he has brighter paragraphs, he has not better poems. Dryden's performances were always hasty, either excited by some external occasion, or extorted by domestic necessity; he composed without consideration, and published without correction. What his mind could supply at call, or gather in one excursion, was all that he sought, and all that he gave. The dilatory caution of Pope enabled him to condense his sentiments, to multiply his images, and to accumulate all that study might produce, or chance might supply. If the flights of Dryden, therefore, are higher, Pope continues longer on the wing. If of Dryden's fire the blaze is brighter, of Pope the heat is more regular and constant. Dryden often surpasses expectation, and Pope never falls below it. Dryden is read with frequent astonishment, and Pope with perpetual delight." [1]

[1] ["I told Moore, not very long ago, ' we are all wrong, except Rogers, Crabbe, and Campbell.' In the meantime, the best sign of amendment will be repentance, and new and frequent editions of Pope and Dryden.

" There will be found as comfortable metaphysics, and ten times more poetry in the ' Essay on Man,' than in the ' Excursion.' Where is it to be found stronger than in the epistle from Eloisa to Abelard, or in Palamon and Arcite ? Do you wish for invention, imagination, sublimity, character ? Seek them in the Rape of the Lock, the Fables of Dryden, the Ode of Saint Cecilia's day, and Absalom and Achitophel. You will discover in these two poets only, *all* for which you must ransack innumerable metres, and God only knows how many *writers* of the day, without finding a tittle of the same qualities,—with the addition, too, of wit, of which the latter have none. I have not, however, forgotten Thomas Brown the Younger, nor the Fudge Family, nor Whistlecraft; but that is not wit—it is humour. I will say nothing of the harmony of Pope and Dryden in comparison, for there is not a living poet (except Rogers, Gifford, Campbell, and Crabbe) who can write an heroic couplet. The fact is, that the exquisite beauty of their versification has withdrawn the public attention from their other excellences, as the vulgar eye will rest more upon the splendour of the uniform than the quality of the troops."— BYRON, vol. xv., p. 87.]

As the eighteenth century advanced, the difference between the styles of these celebrated authors became yet more manifest. It was then obvious, that though Pope's felicity of expression, his beautiful polish of sentiment, and the occasional brilliancy of his wit, were not easily imitated, yet many authors, by dint of a good ear, and a fluent expression, learned to command the unaltered sweetness of his melody, which, like a favourite tune, which has descended to hawkers and ballad-singers, became appalling and even disgusting as it became common. The admirers of poetry then reverted to the brave negligence of Dryden's versification, as, to use Johnson's simile, the eye, fatigued with the uniformity of a lawn, seeks variety in the uncultivated glade or swelling mountain. The preference for which Dennis, asserting the cause of Dryden, had raved and thundered in vain, began, by degrees, to be assigned to the elder bard; and many a poet sheltered his harsh verses and inequalities under an assertion that he belonged to the school of Dryden.[1] Churchill—

" Who, born for the universe, narrow'd his mind,
And to party gave up what was meant for mankind,"[2]—

Churchill was one of the first to seek in the " Mac-

[1] ["I learned versification wholly from the works of Dryden, who had improved it much beyond any of our former poets, and would probably have brought it to its perfection, had he not been unhappily obliged to write so often in haste. . . . Dryden always uses proper language, lively, natural, and fitted to the subject: it is scarce ever too high or too low; never, perhaps, except in his plays." —POPE— Spence's Anecdotes, p. 114.]

[2] [From Goldsmith's lines on Burke in " Retaliation."]

Flecknoe," the " Absalom," and the " Hind and Panther," authority for bitter and personal sarcasm, couched in masculine, though irregular versification, dashed from the pen without revision, and admitting occasional rude and flat passages, to afford the author a spring to comparative elevation. But imitation always approaches to caricature; and the powers of Churchill have been unable to protect him from the oblivion into which his poems are daily sinking, owing to the ephemeral interest of political subjects, and his indolent negligence of severe study and regularity. To imitate Dryden, it were well to study his merits, without venturing to adopt the negligences and harshness, which the hurry of his composition, and the comparative rudeness of his age, rendered in him excusable. At least, those who venture to sink as low, should be confident of the power of soaring as high; for surely it is a rash attempt to dive, unless in one conscious of ability to swim.

While the beauties of Dryden may be fairly pointed out as an object of emulation, it is the less pleasing, but not less necessary, duty of his biographer and editor, to notice those deficiencies, which his high and venerable name may excuse, but cannot render proper objects of applause or imitation.

So much occasional criticism has been scattered in various places through these volumes,[1] that, while attempting the consideration of one or two of his distinguishing and preeminent compositions, which

[1] Dryden's Works.

have been intentionally reserved to illustrate a few pages of general criticism, I feel myself free from the difficult, and almost contradictory task, of drawing my maxims and examples from the extended course of his literary career. My present task is limited to deducing his poetic character from those works which he formed on his last and most approved model. The general tone of his genius, however, influenced the whole course of his publications; and upon that, however modified and varied by the improvement of his taste, a few preliminary notices may not be misplaced.

The distinguishing characteristic of Dryden's genius seems to have been, the power of reasoning, and of expressing the result in appropriate language. This may seem slender praise; yet these were the talents that led Bacon into the recesses of philosophy, and conducted Newton to the cabinet of nature.[1] The prose works of Dryden bear

[1] [" There is nothing very happy in these allusions. Neither Bacon nor Newton were poets; and it is of poets alone that such praise could possibly appear slender. To us, we own, it appears both slender in itself, and defective with respect to Dryden: in a character of Sir John Davis, no better terms could have been chosen. The leading feature of this great poet's mind was its rapidity of conception, combined with that, which is the excellence of some great painters,—a readiness of expressing every idea, without losing any thing by the way. Whatever he does, whether he reasons, relates, or describes, he is never, to use his own phrase, *cursedly confined;* never loiters about a single thought or image, or seems to labour about the turn of a phrase. Though he has many slovenly and feeble lines, perhaps scarce any poet has so few which have failed for want of power to make them better. He never, like Pope, forces an awkward rhyme, or spins out a

repeated evidence to his philosophical powers. His philosophy was not indeed of a formed and systematic character; for he is often contented to leave the path of argument which must have conducted him to the fountain of truth, and to resort with indolence or indifference to the leaky cisterns which had been hewn out by former critics. But where his pride or his taste are interested, he shows evidently, that it was not deficiency in the power of systematizing, but want of the time and patience necessary to form a system, which occasioned the discrepancy that we often notice in his critical and philological disquisitions. This power of ratiocination, of investigating, discovering, and appreciating that which is really excellent, if accompanied with the necessary command of fanciful illustration, and elegant expression, is the most interesting quality which can be possessed by a poet. It must indeed have a share in the composition of every thing that is truly estimable in the fine arts, as well as in philosophy. Nothing is so easily attained as the power of presenting the extrinsic qualities of fine painting, fine music, or fine poetry; the beauty of colour and outline, the combination of notes, the melody of versification, may be imitated by artists of mediocrity; and many will view, hear, or peruse their performances, without being able positively to discover why they should not,

---

couplet for the sake of a pointed conclusion. His thoughts, his language, his versification, have all a certain animation and elasticity which no one else has ever equally possessed."— HALLAM, 1808.]

since composed according to all the rules, afford
pleasure equal to those of Raphael, Handel, or
Dryden. The deficiency lies in the vivifying spirit,
which, like *alcohol*, may be reduced to the same
principle in all the fine arts, though it assumes such
varied qualities from the mode in which it is exerted
or combined.   Of this power of intellect, Dryden
seems to have possessed almost an exuberant share,
combined, as usual, with the faculty of correcting
his own conceptions, by observing human nature,
the practical and experimental philosophy as well
of poetry as of ethics or physics. The early habits
of Dryden's education and poetical studies gave
his researches somewhat too much of a metaphysical character; and it was a consequence of his
mental acuteness, that his dramatic personages
often philosophized or reasoned, when they ought
only to have felt.   The more lofty, the fiercer, the
more ambitious feelings, seem also to have been
his favourite studies. Perhaps the analytical mode
in which he exercised his studies of human life,
tended to confine his observation to the more
energetic feelings of pride, anger, ambition, and
other high-toned passions. He that mixes in public
life must see enough of these stormy convulsions;
but the finer and more imperceptible operations of
love in its sentimental modifications, if the heart
of the author does not supply an example from
its own feelings, cannot easily be studied at the
expense of others. Dryden's bosom, it must be
owned, seems to have afforded him no such means
of information; the license of his age, and perhaps

the advanced period at which he commenced his
literary career, had probably armed him against
this more exalted strain of passion. The love of
the senses he has in many places expressed, in as
forcible and dignified colouring as the subject
could admit; but of a mere moral and sentimental
passion he seems to have had little idea, since he
frequently substitutes in its place the absurd, unnatural, and fictitious refinements of romance. In
short, his love is always in indecorous nakedness,
or sheathed in the stiff panoply of chivalry. The
most pathetic verses which Dryden has composed,
are unquestionably contained in the epistle to Congreve, where he recommends his laurels, in such
moving terms, to the care of his surviving friend.[1]
The quarrel and reconciliation of Sebastian and
Dorax, is also full of the noblest emotion. In both
cases, however, the interest is excited by means
of masculine and exalted passion, not of those
which arise from the mere delicate sensibilities of
our nature; and, to use a Scottish phrase, "bearded men" weep at them, rather than Horace's
audience of youths and maidens.

But if Dryden fails in expressing the milder
and more tender passions, not only did the stronger
feelings of the heart, in all its dark or violent work-
ings, but the face of natural objects, and their
operation upon the human mind, pass promptly in

---

[1] [The reader who wishes to see the most remarkable instances of Dryden's deficiency in *the pathetic*, is requested to
compare him with Chaucer in the death-bed scene of *Palamon
and Arcite.*]

review at his command. External pictures, and their corresponding influence on the spectator, are equally ready at his summons; and though his poetry, from the nature of his subjects, is in general rather ethic and didactic, than narrative, yet no sooner does he adopt the latter style of composition, than his figures and his landscapes are presented to the mind with the same vivacity as the flow of his reasoning, or the acute metaphysical discrimination of his characters.

Still the powers of observation and of deduction are not the only qualities essential to the poetical character. The philosopher may indeed prosecute his experimental researches into the *arcana* of nature, and announce them to the public through the medium of a friendly *redacteur*, as the legislator of Israel obtained permission to speak to the people by the voice of Aaron: but the poet has no such privilege; nay, his doom is so far capricious, that, though he may be possessed of the primary quality of poetical conception to the highest possible extent, it is but like a lute without its strings, unless he has the subordinate, though equally essential, power of expressing what he feels and conceives, in appropriate and harmonious language. With this power Dryden's poetry was gifted, in a degree surpassing in modulated harmony that of all who had preceded him, and inferior to none that has since written English verse. He first showed that the English language was capable of uniting smoothness and strength. The hobbling verses of his predecessors were abandoned

even by the lowest versifiers; and by the force of
his precept and example, the meanest lampooners
of the year seventeen hundred wrote smoother
lines than Donne and Cowley, the chief poets of
the earlier half of the seventeenth century. What
was said of Rome adorned by Augustus, has been,
by Johnson, applied to English poetry improved
by Dryden; that he found it of brick, and left it
of marble. This reformation was not merely the
effect of an excellent ear, and a superlative command of gratifying it by sounding language; it
was, we have seen, the effect of close, accurate, and
continued study of the power of the English
tongue. Upon what principles he adopted and
continued his system of versification, he long meditated to communicate in his projected prosody of
English poetry. The work, however, might have
been more curious than useful, as there would have
been some danger of its diverting the attention,
and misguiding the efforts of poetical adventurers;
for as it is more easy to be masons than architects,
we may deprecate an art which might teach the
world to value those who can build rhymes, without attending to the more essential qualities of
poetry. Strict attention might no doubt discover
the principle of Dryden's versification; but it
seems no more essential to the analyzing his poetry,
than the principles of mathematics to understanding
music, although the art necessarily depends on
them. The extent in which Dryden reformed
our poetry, is most readily proved by an appeal
to the ear; and Dr Johnson has forcibly stated,

that "he knew how to choose the flowing and the sonorous words; to vary the pauses and adjust the accents; to diversify the cadence, and yet preserve the smoothness of the metre." To vary the English hexameter, he established the use of the triplet and Alexandrine. Though ridiculed by Swift, who vainly thought he had exploded them for ever, their force is still acknowledged in classical poetry.

Of the various kinds of poetry which Dryden occasionally practised, the drama was that which, until the last six years of his life, he chiefly relied on for support. His style of tragedy, we have seen, varied with his improving taste, perhaps with the change of manners. Although the heroic drama, as we have described it at length in the preceding pages, presented the strongest temptation to the exercise of argumentative poetry in sounding rhyme, Dryden was at length contented to abandon it for the more pure and chaste style of tragedy, which professes rather the representation of human beings, than the creation of ideal perfection, or fantastic and anomalous characters. The best of Dryden's performances in this latter style are unquestionably "Don Sebastian," and "All for Love." Of these, the former is in the poet's very best manner; exhibiting dramatic persons, consisting of such bold and impetuous characters as he delighted to draw, well contrasted, forcibly marked, and engaged in an interesting succession of events. To many tempers, the scene between Sebastian and Dorax, already noticed,

must appear one of the most moving that ever
adorned the British stage.   Of " All for Love,"
we may say, that it is successful in a softer style of
painting ; and that, so far as sweet and beautiful
versification, elegant language, and occasional tenderness, can make amends for Dryden's deficiencies
in describing the delicacies of sentimental passion,
they are to be found in abundance in that piece.
But on these, and on the poet's other tragedies, we
have enlarged in our preliminary notices prefixed
to each piece.[1]

Dryden's comedies, besides being stained with
the license of the age (a license which he seems to
use as much from necessity as choice), have, generally speaking, a certain heaviness of character.
There are many flashes of wit ; but the author has
beaten his flint hard ere he struck them out.   It is

[1] [Dryden's Works, *passim.*—" I don't think Dryden so
bad a dramatic writer as you seem to do.   There are many
things finely said in his plays as almost by any body.   Beside
his three best (' All for Love,' ' Don Sebastian,' and the ' Spanish Fryar,') there are others that are good ; as ' Cleomenes,'
' Sir Martin Mar-all,' ' Limberham,' and the ' Conquest of
Mexico.'   His ' Wild Gallant ' was written while he was a boy,
and is very bad.   All his plays are printed in the order that they
were written."—POPE—*Spence's Anecdotes*, (Malone,) p. 111.

" Of all the tragedies of Dryden, two only rise above the
level of mediocrity.   Had the last four acts of ' All for Love '
been equal to the first, it would have been surpassed by very
few theatrical productions.   The reconciliation between Don
Sebastian and Dorax approaches very nearly to perfection.
But his Montezumas and Almanzors, which he seems to consider as prototypes of heroical excellence, would be better placed
among the monsters of the opera stage, than among the personages of a drama, that at least affects to be rational."—
Quarterly Review, Oct. 1814.]

almost essential to the success of a jest, that it should at least seem to be extemporaneous. If we espy the joke at a distance, nay, if without seeing it we have the least reason to suspect we are travelling towards one, it is astonishing how the perverse obstinacy of our nature delights to refuse its currency. When, therefore, as is often the case in Dryden's comedies, two persons remain on the stage for no obvious purpose but to say good things, it is no wonder they receive but little thanks from an ungrateful audience. The incidents, therefore, and the characters, ought to be comic; but actual jests, or *bon mots*, should be rarely introduced, and then naturally, easily, without an appearance of premeditation, and bearing a strict conformity to the character of the person who utters them.[1] Comic situation Dryden did not greatly study; indeed I hardly recollect any scene, unless the closing one of " The Spanish Friar," which indicates any pecu-

---

1 [" In one of Dryden's plays there was this line, which the actress endeavoured to speak in as moving and affecting a tone as she could :

' My wound is great—because it is so small,'

and then she paused and looked very distressed. The Duke of Buckingham, who was in one of the boxes, rose immediately from his seat, and added in a loud ridiculing tone of voice—

' Then 'twould be greater were it none at all,'

which had such an effect on the audience, who before were not very well pleased with the play, that they hissed the poor woman off the stage, would never bear her appearance in the rest of her part, and as this was the second time only of its appearance, made Dryden lose his benefit night."—LOCKIER —*Spence's Anecdotes*, (Malone,) p. 103.]

liar felicity of invention. For comic character, he is usually contented to paint a generic representative of a certain class of men or women; a Father Dominic, for example, or a Melantha, with all the attributes of their calling and manners, strongly and divertingly pourtrayed, but without any individuality of character. It is probable that, with these deficiencies, he felt the truth of his own acknowledgment, and that he was forced upon composing comedies to gratify the taste of the age, while the bent of his genius was otherwise directed.[1]

In lyrical poetry, Dryden must be allowed to have no equal. "Alexander's Feast" is sufficient to show his supremacy in that brilliant department.[2] In this exquisite production, he flung from him all the trappings with which his contemporaries had embarrassed the ode. The language, lofty and striking as the ideas are, is equally simple and har-

[1] ["Dryden, strong and nervous as was his muse in other walks, had no talent for dramatic poetry. He described nature to make passion declamatory; and, prostituting his facility at rhyming, shackled the free measures of our tragic verse with an imitation French jingle, more insupportable, if possible, when recurring at every tenth, than at every fourteenth syllable. He preserved no likeness to human creatures in painting their hearts; but throwing aside the sock and buskin, mounted both tragedy and comedy upon stilts; and he was the less able to resist the bad taste of his times, because he wrote for bread."—*Quarterly Review*, July, 1823.]

[2] ["Many people would like my Ode on Music better, if Dryden had never written on that subject. It was at the request of Mr Steele that I wrote mine; and not with any thought of rivalling that great man, whose memory I do, and have always reverenced!"—POPE—*Spence's Anecdotes*, (Malone,) p. 12.]

monious; without farfetched allusions, or epithets, or metaphors, the story is told as intelligibly as if it had been in the most humble prose. The change of tone in the harp of Timotheus, regulates the measure and the melody, and the language of every stanza. The hearer, while he is led on by the successive changes, experiences almost the feelings of the Macedonian and his peers; nor is the splendid poem disgraced by one word or line unworthy of it, unless we join in the severe criticism of Dr Johnson, on the concluding stanzas. It is true, that the praise of St Cecilia is rather abruptly introduced as a conclusion to the account of the Feast of Alexander; and it is also true, that the comparison,

> " He raised a mortal to the sky,
> She drew an angel down,"—

is inaccurate, since the fate of Timotheus was metaphorical, and that of Cecilia literal. But while we stoop to such criticism, we seek for blots in the sun.

Of Dryden's other pindarics, some, as the celebrated " Ode to the Memory of Mrs Killigrew," are mixed with the leaven of Cowley; others, like the " *Threnodia Augustalis*," are occasionally flat and heavy. All contain passages of brilliancy, and all are thrown into a versification, melodious amidst its irregularity. We listen for the completion of Dryden's stanza, as for the explication of a difficult passage in music; and wild and lost as the sound appears, the ear is proportionally gratified by the unexpected ease with which harmony is extracted from discord and confusion.

The satirical powers of Dryden were of the highest order. He draws his arrow to the head, and dismisses it straight upon his object of aim. In this walk he wrought almost as great a reformation as upon versification in general; as will plainly appear, if we consider, that the satire, before Dryden's time, bore the same reference to " Absalom and Achitophel," which an ode of Cowley bears to " Alexander's Feast." Butler, and his imitators, had adopted a metaphysical satire, as the poets in the earlier part of the century had created a metaphysical vein of serious poetry.[1] Both required store of learning to supply the perpetual expenditure of extraordinary and farfetched illustration; the object of both was to combine and hunt down the strangest and most fanciful analogies; and both held the attention of the reader perpetually on the stretch, to keep up with the meaning of the author. There can be no doubt, that this metaphysical vein was much better fitted for the burlesque than the sublime. Yet the perpetual scintillation of Butler's wit is too dazzling to be delightful; and we can seldom read far in " Hudibras " without feeling more fatigue than pleasure. His fancy is employed with the profusion of a spendthrift, by whose eternal round of banqueting his guests are at length rather wearied out than regaled. Dryden was destined to

[1] See *ante*, p. 37.

correct this among other errors of his age ; to show the difference between burlesque and satire ; and to teach his successors in that species of assault, rather to thrust than to flourish with their weapon. For this purpose he avoided the unvaried and unrelieved style of grotesque description and combination, which had been fashionable since the satires of Cleveland and Butler. To render the objects of his satire hateful and contemptible, he thought it necessary to preserve the lighter shades of character, if not for the purpose of softening the portrait, at least for that of preserving the likeness. While Dryden seized, and dwelt upon, and aggravated, all the evil features of his subject, he carefully retained just as much of its laudable traits as preserved him from the charge of want of candour, and fixed down the resemblance upon the party. And thus, instead of unmeaning caricatures, he presents portraits which cannot be mistaken, however unfavourable ideas they may convey of the originals. The character of Shaftesbury, both as Achitophel, and as drawn in " The Medal," bears peculiar witness to this assertion. While other court poets endeavoured to turn the obnoxious statesman into ridicule, on account of his personal infirmities and extravagances, Dryden boldly confers upon him all the praise for talent and for genius that his friends could have claimed, and trusts to the force of his satirical expression for working up even these admirable attributes with such a mixture of evil propensities and dangerous qualities, that the whole character shall appear dreadful, and even

hateful, but not contemptible. But where a character of less note, a Shadwell or a Settle, crossed
his path, the satirist did not lay himself under
these restraints, but wrote in the language of
bitter irony and unmeasurable contempt: even
then, however, we are less called on to admire the
wit of the author, than the force and energy of his
poetical philippic. These are the verses which are
made by indignation, and, no more than theatrical
scenes of real passion, admit of refined and protracted turns of wit, or even the lighter sallies of
humour. These last ornaments are proper in that
Horatian satire, which rather ridicules the follies of
the age, than stigmatizes the vices of individuals ;
but in this style Dryden has made few essays. He
entered the field as champion of a political party,
or as defender of his own reputation; discriminated
his antagonists, and applied the scourge with all
the vehemence of Juvenal. As he has himself
said of that satirist, " his provocations were great,
and he has revenged them tragically." This is
the more worthy of notice, as, in the " Essay on
Satire," Dryden gives a decided preference to
those nicer and more delicate touches of satire,
which consist in fine raillery. But whatever was
the opinion of his cooler moments, the poet's practice was dictated by the furious party-spirit of the
times, and the no less keen stimulative of personal
resentment. It is perhaps to be regretted, that so
much energy of thought, and so much force of expression, should have been wasted in anatomizing
such criminals as Shadwell and Settle ; yet we

cannot account the amber less precious, because
they are grubs and flies that are enclosed within it.[1]

The "Fables" of Dryden are the best examples
of his talents as a narrative poet ; those powers of
composition, description, and narration, which must
have been called into exercise by the Epic Muse,
had his fate allowed him to enlist among her votaries.   The "Knight's Tale," the longest and most
laboured of Chaucer's stories, possesses a degree of
regularity which might satisfy the most severe critic.   It is true, that the honour arising from thence
must be assigned to the more ancient bard, who
had himself drawn his subject from an Italian model ; but the high and decided preference which
Dryden has given to this story, although somewhat
censured by Trapp, enables us to judge how much
the poet held an accurate combination of parts, and
coherence of narrative, essentials of epic poetry.[2]

---

[1] ["Perhaps the annals of poetry do not furnish an instance
of a more general enlistment of the Muses under the banners
of party—certainly none when satire became more coarse,
personal, and malignant. Whether the gall flowed from a pen
of lead or gold, it was equally undiluted. The denizens of
Grub-street employed the scourge with the vulgar ferocity of
a parish beadle. Dryden and Pope wielded the imperial knout
of the Czar Peter, and the sufferers had only the consolation
that they were flogged by no common hands."—*Quarterly Review*, October, 1814.]

[2] "*Novimus judicium Drydeni de poemate quodam Chauceri,
pulchro sane illo, et admodum laudando, nimirum quod non modo
vere epicum sit, sed Iliada etiam atque Æneada æquet, imo supe-
ret.   Sed novimus eodem tempore viri illius maximi non semper
accuratissimas esse censuras, nec ad severissimam critices normam
exactas : illo judice id plerumque optimum est, quod nunc præ
manibus habet, et in quo nunc occupatur.*"

That a classic scholar like Trapp should think the plan of the " Knight's Tale" equal to that of the Iliad, is a degree of candour not to be hoped for ; but surely to an unprejudiced reader, a story which exhausts in its conclusion all the interest which it has excited in its progress, which, when terminated, leaves no question to be asked, no personage undisposed of, and no curiosity unsatisfied, is, abstractedly considered, more gratifying than the history of a few weeks of a ten years' war, commencing long after the siege had begun, and ending long before the city was taken. Of the other tales, it can hardly be said that their texture is more ingenious or closely woven than that of ordinary novels or fables : but in each of them Dryden has displayed the superiority of his genius, in selecting for amplification and ornament those passages most susceptible of poetical description. The account of the procession of the Fairy Chivalry in the " Flower and the Leaf ;" the splendid description of the champions who came to assist at the tournament in the " Knight's Tale ;" the account of the battle itself, its alternations and issue,—if they cannot be called improvements on Chaucer, are nevertheless so spirited a transfusion of his ideas into modern verse, as almost to claim the merit of originality. Many passages might be shown in which this praise may be carried still higher, and the merit of invention added to that of imitation. Such is the description of the commencement of the tourney, which is almost entirely original, and most of the ornaments in the translations from Boccacio, whose prose fictions demanded more additions from the poet than the exuberant imagery of Chaucer. To select instances would be endless; but every reader of poetry has by heart the description of Iphigenia asleep, nor are the lines in " Theodore and Honoria," which describe the approach of the apparition, and its effects upon animated and inanimated nature, even before it becomes visible, less eminent for beauties of the terrific order :

" While listening to the murmuring leaves he stood,
More than a mile immersed within the wood,
At once the wind was laid; the whispering sound
Was dumb; a rising earthquake rocked the ground;
With deeper brown the grove was overspread,
A sudden horror seized his giddy head,
And his ears tingled, and his colour fled.
Nature was in alarm; some danger nigh
Seem'd threaten'd, though unseen to mortal eye."

It may be doubted, however, whether the simplicity of Boccacio's narrative has not sometimes suffered by the additional decorations of Dryden. The retort of Guiscard to Tancred's charge of ingratitude is more sublime in the Italian original,[1] than as diluted by the English poet into five hexameters. A worse fault occurs in the whole colouring of Sigismonda's passion, to which Dryden has given a coarse and indelicate character, which he did not derive from Boccacio, though the Italian

[1] " *Amor puo troppo più, che ne voi ne io possiamo.*" This sentiment loses its dignity amid the " levelling of mountains and raising plains," with which Dryden has chosen to illustrate it.

be apt enough to sin in that particular. In like manner, the plea used by Palamon in his prayer to Venus, is more nakedly expressed by Dryden than by Chaucer. The former, indeed, would probably have sheltered himself under the mantle of Lucretius; but he should have recollected, that Palamon speaks the language of chivalry, and ought not, to use an expression of Lord Herbert, to have spoken like a *paillard*, but a *cavalier*. Indeed, we have before noticed it as the most obvious and most degrading imperfection of Dryden's poetical imagination, that he could not refine that passion, which, of all others, is susceptible either of the purest refinement, or of admitting the basest alloy. With Chaucer, Dryden's task was more easy than with Boccacio. Barrenness was not the fault of the Father of English poetry; and amid the profusion of images which he presented, his imitator had only the task of rejecting or selecting. In the sublime description of the temple of Mars, painted around with all the misfortunes ascribed to the influence of his planet, it would be difficult to point out a single idea, which is not found in the older poem. But Dryden has judiciously omitted or softened some degrading and some disgusting circumstances; as the " cook scalded in spite of his long ladle," the " swine devouring the cradled infant," the " pickpurse," and other circumstances too grotesque or ludicrous, to harmonize with the dreadful group around them. Some points, also, of sublimity, have escaped the modern poet. Such is the appropriate and picturesque accompaniment of the statue of Mars :

> " A wolf stood before him at his feet,
> With eyen red, and of a man he eat." [1]

In the dialogue, or argumentative parts of the poem, Dryden has frequently improved on his original, while he falls something short of him in simple description, or in pathetic effect. Thus, the quarrel between Arcite and Palamon is wrought up with greater energy by Dryden than Chaucer, particularly by the addition of the following lines, describing the enmity of the captives against each other :

> " Now friends no more, nor walking hand in hand,
> But when they met, they made a surly stand,
> And glared like angry lions as they pass'd,
> And wish'd that every look might be their last."

But the modern must yield the palm, despite the beauty of his versification, to the description of Emily by Chaucer ; and may be justly accused of loading the dying speech of Arcite with conceits for which his original gave no authority. [2]

[1] An emblem of a similar kind (a tiger devouring a man) was found in the palace of Tippoo Sultan.

[2] As " Near bliss, and yet not blessed." Dryden's Works, vol. xi., p. 315, and this merciless quibble, where Arcite complains of the flames he endures for Emily :

> " Of such a goddess no time leaves record,
> Who burnt the temple where she was adored."

Yet Dryden, in the preface, declaims against the " *inopem me copia fecit*," and similar jingles of Ovid.

[" The *Theseide* of Boccacio possesses a yet higher claim to

When the story is of a light and ludicrous kind, as the Fable of the Cock and Fox, and the Wife of Bath's Tale, Dryden displays all the humorous expression of his satirical poetry, without its personality. There is indeed a quaint Cervantic gravity in his mode of expressing himself, that often glances forth, and enlivens what otherwise would be mere dry narrative. Thus, he details certain things which past,

" While Cymon was *endeavouring* to be wise:"

the force of which single word contains both a ludicrous and appropriate picture of the revolution which the force of love was gradually creating in the mind of the poor clown. The tone of expression he perhaps borrowed from Ariosto, and other poets of Italian chivalry, who are wont ever and anon to raise the mask, and smile even at the romantic tale they are themselves telling.

Leaving these desultory reflections on Dryden's powers of narrative, I cannot but notice, that, from haste or negligence, he has sometimes mistaken the sense of his author. Into the hands of the champions in the " Flower and the Leaf," he has placed *bows* instead of *boughs*, because the word is in the original spelled *bowes;* and, having made the error,

---

distinction, as the first modern poem in which the author, abandoning the dull repetition of dreams and visions, imagined a regular action or fable, and conducted it, through different stages of adventure, to its close. To the English reader it presents the additional interest, of being the model of the ' Knight's Tale' of Chaucer, and the origin therefore of one of the noblest poems in our language, the ' Palamon and Arcite' of Dryden."—*Quarterly Review*, April, 1814.]

he immediately devises an explanation of the device which he had mistaken :

> " For bows the strength of brawny arms imply,
> Emblems of valour, and of victory."

He has, in like manner, accused Chaucer of introducing Gallicisms into the English language ; not aware that French was the language of the court of England not long before Chaucer's time, and that, far from introducing French phrases into the English tongue, the ancient bard was successfully active in introducing the English as a fashionable dialect, instead of the French, which had, before his time, been the only language of polite literature in England. Other instances might be given of similar oversights, which, in the situation of Dryden, are sufficiently pardonable.

Upon the whole, in introducing these romances of Boccacio and Chaucer to modern readers, Dryden has necessarily deprived them of some of the charms which they possess for those who have perused them in their original state. With a tale or poem, by which we have been sincerely interested, we connect many feelings independent of those arising from actual poetical merit. The delight, arising from the whole, sanctions, nay sanctifies, the faulty passages ; and even actual improvements, like supplements to a mutilated statue of antiquity, injure our preconceived associations, and hurt, by their incongruity with our feelings, more than they give pleasure by their own excellence. But to antiquaries Dryden has sufficiently justified himself, by declaring his version made for the sake of modern readers, who understand sense and poetry, as well as the old Saxon admirers of Chaucer, when that poetry and sense are put into words which they can understand. Let us also grant him, that, for the beauties which are lost, he has substituted many which the original did not afford; that, in passages of gorgeous description, he has added even to the chivalrous splendour of Chaucer, and has graced with poetical ornament the simplicity of Boccacio; that, if he has failed in tenderness, he is never deficient in majesty; and that, if the heart be sometimes untouched, the understanding and fancy are always exercised and delighted.

The philosophy of Dryden, we have already said, was that of original and penetrating genius; imperfect only, when, from want of time and of industry, he adopted the ideas of others, when he should have communed at leisure with his own mind. The proofs of his philosophical powers are not to be sought for in any particular poem or disquisition. Even the " *Religio Laici,*" written expressly as a philosophical poem, only shows how easily the most powerful mind may entangle itself in sophistical toils of its own weaving; for the train of argument there pursued was completed by Dryden's conversion to the Roman Catholic faith.[1] It is therefore in the discussion of incidental subjects, in his mode of treating points of controversy, in the new lights which he seldom fails to throw upon a controversial subject, in his talent of argumenta-

[1] See *ante,* p. 263.

tive discussion, that we are to look for the character of Dryden's moral powers. His opinions, doubtless, are often inconsistent, and sometimes absolutely contradictory; for, pressed by the necessity of discussing the object before him, he seldom looked back to what he said formerly, or forward to what he might be obliged to say in future. His sole subject of consideration was to maintain his present point; and that by authority, by declamation, by argument, by every means. But his philosophical powers are not the less to be estimated, because thus irregularly and unphilosophically employed. His arguments, even in the worst cause, bear witness to the energy of his mental conceptions; and the skill with which they are stated, elucidated, enforced, and exemplified, ever commands our admiration, though, in the result, our reason may reject their influence. It must be remembered also, to Dryden's honour, that he was the first to hail the dawn of experimental philosophy in physics; to gratulate his country on possessing Bacon, Harvey, and Boyle; and to exult over the downfall of the Aristotelian tyranny.[1] Had he lived to see a similar revolution commenced in ethics, there can be little doubt he would have welcomed it with the same delight; or had his

---

[1] " The longest tyranny that ever sway'd,
Was that wherein our ancestors betray'd
Their free-born reason to the Stagyrite,
And made his torch their universal light.
So truth, while only once supplied the state,
Grew scarce, and dear, and yet sophisticate.
Still it was bought, like emp'ric wares, or charms,
Hard words seal'd up with Aristotle's arms."

leisure and situation permitted him to dedicate his
time to investigating moral problems, he might
himself have led the way to deliverance from error
and uncertainty.   But the dawn of reformation
must ever be gradual, and the acquisitions even of
those calculated to advance it must therefore frequently appear desultory and imperfect.   The
author of the *Novum Organum* believed in charms
and occult sympathy; and Dryden in the chimeras
of judicial astrology, and probably in the jargon of
alchymy.   When these subjects occur in his poetry,
he dwells on them with a pleasure, which shows
the command they maintained over his mind.
Much of the astrological knowledge displayed in
the Knight's Tale is introduced, or at least amplified, by Dryden; and while, in the fable of the
Cock and the Fox, he ridicules the doctrine of
prediction from dreams, the inherent qualities of
the four complexions,[1] and other abstruse doctrines
of Paracelsus and his followers, we have good
reason to suspect, that, like many other scoffers,
he believed in the efficacy and truth of the subject
of his ridicule.   However this shade of credulity
may injure Dryden's character as a philosopher,
we cannot regret its influence on his poetry.
Collins has thus celebrated Fairfax :

> " Prevailing poet, whose undoubting mind
>   Believed the magic wonders which he sung."

[1] These I found quaintly summed up in an old rhyme :—
> " With a red man read thy rede,
>   With a brown man break thy bread,
>   On a pale man draw thy knife,
>   From a black man keep thy wife."

Nor can there be a doubt, that, as every work of imagination is tinged with the author's passions and prejudices, it must be deep and energetic in proportion to the character of these impressions. Those superstitious sciences and pursuits, which would, by mystic rites, doctrines, and inferences, connect us with the invisible world of spirits, or guide our daring researches to a knowledge of future events, are indeed usually found to cow, crush, and utterly stupify, understandings of a lower rank; but if the mind of a man of acute powers, and of warm fancy, becomes slightly imbued with the visionary feelings excited by such studies, their obscure and undefined influence is ever found to aid the sublimity of his ideas, and to give that sombre and serious effect, which he can never produce, who does not himself feel the awe which it is his object to excite. The influence of such a mystic creed is often felt where the cause is concealed; for the habits thus acquired are not confined to their own sphere of belief, but gradually extend themselves over every adjacent province: and perhaps we may not go too far in believing, that he who has felt their impression, though only in one branch of faith, becomes fitted to describe, with an air of reality and interest, not only kindred subjects, but superstitions altogether opposite to his own. The religion, which Dryden finally adopted, lent its occasional aid to the solemn colouring of some of his later productions, upon which subject we have elsewhere enlarged at some length.[1]

[1] See the introduction to Britannia Rediviva, Dryden's Works, vol. x., p. 287.

The occasional poetry of Dryden is marked strongly by masculine character. The Epistles vary with the subject; and are light, humorous, and satirical, or grave, argumentative, and philosophical, as the case required. In his Elegies, although they contain touches of true feeling, especially where the stronger passions are to be illustrated, the poet is often content to substitute reasoning for passion, and rather to show us cause why we ought to grieve, than to set us the example by grieving himself. The inherent defect in Dryden's composition becomes here peculiarly conspicuous; yet we should consider, that, in composing elegies for the Countess of Abingdon, whom he never saw, and for Charles II., by whom he had been cruelly neglected, and doubtless on many similar occasions, Dryden could not even pretend to be interested in the mournful subject of his verse; but attended, with his poem, as much in the way of trade, as the undertaker, on the same occasion, came with his sables and his scutcheon. The poet may interest himself and his reader, even to tears, in the fate of a being altogether the creation of his own fancy, but hardly by a hired panegyric on a real subject, in whom his heart acknowledges no other interest than a fee can give him. Few of Dryden's elegiac effusions, therefore, seem prompted by sincere sorrow. That to Oldham may be an exception; but, even there, he rather strives to do honour to the talents of his departed friend, than to pour out lamentations for his loss. Of the Prologues and

Epilogues we have spoken fully elsewhere.[1] Some of them are coarsely satirical, and others grossly

[1] [" The collection of these pieces is far from being the least valuable part of our author's labours. The variety and richness of fancy which they indicate, is one of Dryden's most remarkable poetical attributes. Whether the theme be, the youth and inexperience, or the age and past services, of the author; the plainness or magnificence of a new theatre; the superiority of ancient authors, or the exaltation of the moderns; the censure of political faction, or of fashionable follies; the praise of the monarch, or the ridicule of the administration; the poet never fails to treat it with the liveliness appropriate to verses intended to be spoken, and spoken before a numerous assembly. The manner which Dryden assumes, varies also with the nature of his audience. The prologues and epilogues intended for the London stage, are written in a tone of superiority, as if the poet, conscious of the justice of his own laws of criticism, rather imposed them upon the public as absolute and undeniable, than as standing in need of their ratification. And if he sometimes condescends to solicit, in a more humble style, the approbation of the audience, and to state circumstances of apology, and pleas of favour, it is only in the case of other poets; for, in the prologues of his own plays, he always rather demands than begs their applause; and if he acknowledges any defects in the piece, he takes care to intimate, that they are introduced in compliance with the evil taste of the age; and that the audience must take blame to themselves, instead of throwing it upon the writer. This bold style of address, although it occasionally drew upon the author the charge of presumption, was, nevertheless, so well supported by his perception of what was just in criticism, and his powers of defending even what was actually wrong, that a miscellaneous audience was, in general, fain to submit to a domination as successfully supported as boldly claimed. In the Oxford prologues, on the other hand, the audience furnished by that seat of the Muses, as of more competent judgment, are addressed with more respectful deference by the poet. He seems, in these, to lay down his rules of criticism, as it were under correction of

indelicate. Those spoken at Oxford are the most valuable, and contain much good criticism and beautiful poetry. But the worst of them was probably well worth the petty recompense which the poet received.[1] The songs and smaller pieces of Dryden have smoothness, wit, and, when addressed to ladies, gallantry in profusion, but are deficient in tenderness. They seem to have been composed with great ease ; thrown together hastily and occasionally ; nor can we doubt, that many of them are now irrecoverably lost. Mr Malone gives us an instance of Dryden's fluency in extempore composition, which was communicated to him by Mr Walcott. " Conversation, one day after dinner, at Mrs Creed's, running upon the origin of names, Mr Dryden bowed to the good old lady, and spoke extempore the following verses :

> ' So much religion in *your* name doth dwell,
> Your soul must needs with piety excell.
> Thus names, like [well-wrought] pictures drawn of old,
> Their owners' nature and their story told.—
> Your name but half expresses ; for in you
> Belief and practice do together go.
> My prayers shall be, while this short life endures,
> These may go hand in hand with you and yours ;
> Till faith hereafter is in vision drown'd,
> And practice is with endless glory crown'd.' "

---

superior judges ; and intermingles them with such compliments to the taste and learning of the members of the university, as he disdains to bestow upon the motley audience of the metropolis."—SCOTT'S *Dryden*, vol. x., p. 312.]

[1] It has been stated on the authority of the " Life of Southerne," that Dryden had originally five guineas for each prologue, and raised the sum to ten guineas on occasion of Southerne's requiring such a favour for his first play. But I am convinced the sum is exaggerated ; and incline now to believe, with Dr Johnson, that the advance was from *two* to *three* guineas only.

The *Translations* of Dryden form a distinguished part of his poetical labours. No author, excepting Pope, has done so much to endenizen the eminent poets of antiquity. In this sphere also, it was the fate of Dryden to become a leading example to future poets, and to abrogate laws which had been generally received, although they imposed such trammels on translation as to render it hardly intelligible. Before his distinguished success showed that the object of the translator should be to transfuse the spirit, not to copy servilely the very words of his original, it had been required, that line should be rendered for line, and, almost, word for word. It may easily be imagined, that, by the constraint and inversion which this cramping statute required, a poem was barely rendered *not Latin*, instead of being made English, and that, to the mere native reader, as the connoisseur complains in " The Critic," the interpreter was sometimes " the harder to be understood of the two." Those who seek examples, may find them in the jaw-breaking translations of Ben Jonson and Holyday. Cowley and Denham had indeed rebelled against this mode of translation, which conveys pretty much the same idea of an original, as an imitator would do of the gait of another, by studiously stepping after him into every trace which his feet had left upon the sand. But they assumed a license equally faulty, and claimed the privilege of writing what might be more properly termed imitations, than versions of the classics. It was reserved to Dryden manfully to claim and vindicate the freedom of a just translation; more limited than paraphrase, but free from the metaphrastic severity exacted from his predecessors.[1]

With these free, yet unlicentious principles, Dryden brought to the task of translation a competent knowledge of the language of the originals, with an unbounded command of his own. The latter

[1] [" Dryden may be considered as the first popular attempter in English of the system of free translation, as it is supposed to be recommended by Horace; we say *supposed to be*, because we do not think that his words admit the wide inferences which have been drawn from them; and what is much more important, Ben Jonson, the translator of his ' Art of Poetry,' did not; and well justified in his own practice his different opinion of Horace's meaning. Even Dryden, however, had as strict theoretical notions of the duties of a translator as *he* could entertain who would follow his author—

' Non ita certandi cupidus quam propter amorem.'

' A translator,' says he, ' is to be like his author : it is not his business to excel him.' This was his theory; but though he may occasionally catch the graces of his author, (besides exhibiting many rare qualities of his own,) can he be said to resemble the poet whom he translates, when he renders Horace's

——————— ' si celeres quatit
Pennas, *resigno quæ dedit,*'

by

' But if she dances in the wind,
And shake her wings, and will not stay,
I puff the prostitute away,'

recollecting always that Horace is speaking of a recognised and severe deity? or, when designating the priests of Cybele as *clumsy clergymen*, does he convey to us Juvenal's picture of those painted, mitred, and effeminate fanatics? Does he not rather conjure up a vision of portly gentlemen in black worsted stockings, thick shoes, and shovel hats? And yet how full is every translation by him, even his noble Æneid, of faults such as these, produced partly by the ambition of excelling his original, and partly by his indulging in the vicious use of equivalents."—*Quarterly Review,* June, 1826.]

is, however, by far the most marked characteristic of his Translations. Dryden was not indeed deficient in Greek and Roman learning; but he paused not to weigh and sift those difficult and obscure passages, at which the most learned will doubt and hesitate for the correct meaning. The same rapidity which marked his own poetry, seems to have attended his study of the classics. He seldom waited to analyze the sentence he was about to render, far less scrupulously to weigh the precise purport and value of every word it contained. If he caught the general spirit and meaning of the author, and could express it with equal force in English verse, he cared not if minute elegances were lost, or the beauties of accurate proportion destroyed, or a dubious interpretation hastily adopted on the credit of a *scholium*. He used abundantly the license he has claimed for a translator, to be deficient rather in the language out of which he renders, than that into which he translates. If such be but master of the sense of his author, Dryden argues, he may express that sense with eloquence in his own tongue, though he understand not the nice turns of the original. " But without the latter quality he can never arrive at the useful and the delightful, without which reading is a penance and fatigue."[1] With the same spirit of haste, Dryden is often contented to present to the English reader some modern image, which he may at once fully comprehend,

[1] Life of Lucian, Dryden's Works, vol. xviii., p. 81.

instead of rendering precisely a classic expression, which might require explanation or paraphrase. Thus the *pulchra Sicyonia*, or buskins of Sicyon, are rendered,

> " Diamond-buckles sparkling in their shoes."

By a yet more unfortunate adaptation of modern technical phraseology, the simple direction of Helenus,

> " *Læva tibi tellus, et longo læva petantur .*
> *Æquora circuitu : dextrum fuge littus et undas,*"

is translated,

> " Tack to the larboard, and stand off to sea,
> Veer starboard sea and land."———

A counsel which, I shrewdly suspect, would have been unintelligible, not only to Palinurus, but to the best pilot in the British navy. In the same tone, but with more intelligibility, if not felicity, Dryden translates *palatia cœli* in Ovid, " *the Louvre of the sky;*" and, in the version of the First Book of Homer, talks of the court of Jupiter in the phrases used at that of Whitehall. These expressions, proper to modern manners, often produce an unfortunate confusion between the age in which the scene is laid, and the date of the translation. No judicious poet is willing to break the interest of a tale of ancient times, by allusions peculiar to his own period ; but when the translator, instead of identifying himself as closely as possible with the original author, pretends to such liberty, he removes us a third step from the time of action, and so confounds the manners of no less than three distinct eras,—that in which the scene is laid, that in which the poem was written, and that, finally, in which the translation was executed. There are passages in Dryden's Æneid, which, in the revolution of a few pages, transport our ideas from the time of Troy's siege to that of the court of Augustus, and thence downward to the reign of William the Third of Britain.

It must be owned, at the same time, that when the translator places before you, not the exact words, but the image of the original, as the classic author would probably have himself expressed it in English, the license, when moderately employed, has an infinite charm for those readers for whose use translations are properly written. Pope's Homer and Dryden's Virgil can never indeed give exquisite satisfaction to scholars, accustomed to study the Greek and Latin originals. The minds of such readers have acquired a classic tone; and not merely the ideas and poetical imagery, but the manners and habits of the actors, have become intimately familiar to them. They will not, therefore, be satisfied with any translation in which these are violated, whether for the sake of indolence in the translator, or ease to the unlettered reader; and perhaps they will be more pleased that a favourite bard should move with less ease and spirit in his new habiliments, than that his garments should be cut upon the model of the country to which the stranger is introduced. In the former case, they will readily make allowance for the imperfection of modern language; in the latter, they will hardly pardon the sophistication of ancient manners. But the mere English reader, who finds rigid adherence to antique costume rather embarrassing than pleasing, who is prepared to make no sacrifices in order to preserve the true manners of antiquity, shocking perhaps to his feelings and prejudices, is satisfied that the Iliad and Æneid shall lose their antiquarian merit, provided they retain that vital spirit and energy, which is the soul of poetry in all languages, and countries, and ages whatsoever. He who sits down to Dryden's translation of Virgil, with the original text spread before him, will be at no loss to point out many passages that are faulty, many indifferently understood, many imperfectly translated, some in which dignity is lost, others in which bombast is substituted in its stead. But the unabated vigour and spirit of the version more than overbalances these and all its other deficiencies. A sedulous scholar might often approach more nearly to the dead letter of Virgil, and give an exact, distinct, sober-minded idea of the meaning and scope of particular passages. Trapp, Pitt, and others have done so. But the essential spirit of poetry is so volatile, that it escapes during such an operation, like the life of the poor criminal, whom the ancient anatomist is said to have dissected alive, in order to ascertain the seat of the soul. The carcass indeed is presented to the English reader, but the animating vigour is no more. It is in this art, of communicating the ancient poet's ideas with force and energy equal to his own, that Dryden has so completely surpassed

all who have gone before, and all who have succeeded him.　The beautiful and unequalled version
of the Tale of Myrrha in the " Metamorphoses,"
the whole of the Sixth Æneid, and many other
parts of Dryden's translations, are sufficient, had
he never written one line of original poetry, to
vindicate the well-known panegyric of Churchill:

> " Here let me bend, great Dryden, at thy shrine,
> Thou dearest name to all the tuneful Nine!
> What if some dull lines in cold order creep,
> And with his theme the poet seems to sleep?
> Still, when his subject rises proud to view,
> With equal strength the poet rises too:
> With strong invention, noblest vigour fraught,
> Thought still springs up, and rises out of thought;
> Numbers ennobling numbers in the course,
> In varied sweetness flow, in varied force;
> The powers of genius and of judgment join,
> And the whole art of poetry is thine."

We are in this disquisition naturally tempted to
enquire, whether Dryden would have succeeded in
his proposed design to translate Homer, as happily
as in his Virgil?　And although he himself has
declared the genius of the Grecian to be more fiery,
and therefore better suited to his own than that of
the Roman poet, there may be room to question,
whether in this case, he rightly estimated his own
talents, or rather, whether, being fully conscious of
their extent, he was aware of labouring under certain deficiencies of taste, which must have been
more apparent in a version of the Iliad than of the
Æneid.　If a translator has any characteristic and
peculiar foible, it is surely unfortunate to choose an
original, who may give peculiar facilities to exhibit

them.   Thus, even Dryden's repeated disclamation
of puns, points, and quibbles, and all the repentance
of his more sober hours, was unable, so soon as he
began to translate Ovid, to prevent his sliding back
into the practice of that false wit with which his
earlier productions are imbued.   Hence he has
been seduced, by the similarity of style, to add to
the offences of his original, and introduce, though
it needed not, points of wit and antithetical pretti-
nesses, for which he cannot plead Ovid's authority.
For example, he makes Ajax say of Ulysses, when
surrounded by the Trojans,

" No wonder if he roar'd that all might hear,
His elocution was increased by fear."

The Latin only bears, *conclamat socios*.   A little
lower,

" *Opposui molem clypei, texique jacentem,*"

is amplified by a similar witticism,

——" My broad buckler hid him from the foe,
Even the shield trembled as he lay below."

If, in translating Ovid, Dryden was tempted
by the manner of his original to relapse into a
youthful fault, which he had solemnly repented of
and abjured, there is surely room to believe, that
the simple and almost rude manners described by
Homer, might have seduced him into coarseness
both of ideas and expression, for which the studied,
composed, and dignified style of the Æneid gave
neither opening nor apology.   That this was a
fault which Dryden, with all his taste, never was
able to discard, might easily be proved from various

passages in his translations, where the transgression
is on his own part altogether gratuitous. Such is
the well-known version of

> ———————" *Ut possessor agelli*
> *Diceret, hæc mea sunt, veteres migrate coloni,*
> *Nunc victi,*" &c.

> " When the grim captain, with a surly tone,
> Cries out, Pack up, ye rascals, and be gone !
> Kick'd out, we set the best face on't we could," &c.

In translating the most indelicate passage of
Lucretius, Dryden has rather enhanced than veiled
its indecency. The story of Iphis in the Metamorphoses is much more bluntly told by the English
poet than by Ovid. In short, where there was a
latitude given for coarseness of description and
expression, Dryden has always too readily laid
hold of it. The very specimen which he has given
us of a version of Homer, contains many passages
in which the antique Grecian simplicity is vulgarly
and inelegantly rendered. The Thunderer terms
Juno

> " My household curse, my lawful plague, the spy
> Of Jove's designs, his other squinting eye."

The ambrosial feast of Olympus concludes like
a tavern revel :

> " Drunken at last, and drowsy, they depart
> Each to his house, adorn'd with labour'd art
> Of the lame architect. The thundering God,
> Even he, withdrew to rest, and had his load ;
> His swimming head to needful sleep applied,
> And Juno lay unheeded by his side."

There is reason indeed to think, that, after the
Revolution, Dryden's taste was improved in this,

as in some other respects. In his translation of
Juvenal, for example, the satire against women,
coarse as it is, is considerably refined and softened
from the grossness of the Latin poet ; who has,
however, been lately favoured by a still more elegant, and (excepting perhaps one or two passages)
an equally spirited translation, by Mr Gifford of
London. Yet, admitting this apology for Dryden
as fully as we dare, from the numerous specimens
of indelicacy even in his later translations, we are
induced to judge it fortunate that Homer was
reserved for a poet who had not known the age of
Charles II. ; and whose inaccuracies and injudicious decorations may be pardoned, even by the
scholar, when he considers the probability, that
Dryden might have slipped into the opposite
extreme, by converting rude simplicity into indecency or vulgarity. The Æneid, on the other
hand, if it restrained Dryden's poetry to a correct,
steady, and even flight, if it damped his energy
by its regularity, and fettered his excursive imagination by the sobriety of its decorum, had the
corresponding advantage of holding forth to the
translator no temptation to license, and no apology
for negligence. Where the fervency of genius is
required, Dryden has usually equalled his original ;
where peculiar elegance and exact propriety are
demanded, his version may be sometimes found
flat and inaccurate, but the mastering spirit of
Virgil prevails, and it is never disgusting or indelicate. Of all the classical translations we can
boast, none is so acceptable to the class of readers,

to whom the learned languages are a clasped book and a sealed fountain. And surely it is no moderate praise to say, that a work is universally pleasing to those for whose use it is principally intended, and to whom only it is absolutely indispensable.

The prose of Dryden may rank with the best in the English language. It is no less of his own formation than his versification, is equally spirited, and equally harmonious. Without the lengthened and pedantic sentences of Clarendon, it is dignified where dignity is becoming, and is lively without the accumulation of strained and absurd allusions and metaphors, which were unfortunately mistaken for wit by many of the author's contemporaries. Dryden has been accused of unnecessarily larding his style with Gallicisms. It must be owned, that, to comply probably with the humour of Charles, or from an affectation of the fashionable court dialect, the poet laureat employed such words as *fougue, fraîcheur,* &c., instead of the corresponding expressions in English; an affectation which does not appear in our author's later writings. But even the learned and excellent Sir David Dalrymple was led to carry this idea greatly too far.

" Nothing," says that admirable antiquary, " distinguishes the genius of the English language so much as its general naturalization of foreigners. Dryden, in the reign of Charles II., printed the following words as pure French newly imported : *amour, billet-doux, caprice, chagrin, conversation, double entendre, embarrassed, fatigue, figure, foible, gallant, good graces, grimace, incendiary, levée, maltreated, rallied, repartée, ridicule, tender, tour ;* with several others which are now considered as natives.—' Marriage a-la-Mode.' " [1]

[1] Poems from the Bannatyne Manuscript, p. 228.

But of these words many had been long naturalized in England, and, with the adjectives derived from them, are used by Shakspeare and the dramatists of his age.[1]   By their being printed in italics in the play of " Marriage a-la-Mode," Dryden only meant to mark, that Melantha, the affected coquette in whose mouth they are placed, was to use the *French*, not the vernacular pronunciation.   It will admit of question, whether any single French word has been naturalized upon the sole authority of Dryden.

Although Dryden's style has nothing obsolete, we can occasionally trace a reluctance to abandon an old word or idiom; the consequence, doubtless, of his latter studies in ancient poetry.   In other respects, nothing can be more elegant than the diction of the praises heaped upon his patrons, for which he might himself plead the apology he uses for Maimbourg, " who, having enemies, made himself friends by panegyrics. "   Of these lively critical prefaces, which, when we commence, we can never lay aside till we have finished, Dr Johnson has said, with equal force and beauty:

" They have not the formality of a settled style, in which the first half of the sentence betrays the other.   The clauses are never balanced, nor the periods modelled; every word seems to drop by chance, though it falls into its proper place. Nothing is cold or languid ; the whole is airy, animated, and

[1] Shakspeare has *capricious, conversation*, fatigate (if not *fatigue*), *figure, gallant, good graces ; incendiary* is in Minshew's " Guide to the Tongues," ed. 1627.   *Tender* often occurs in Shakspeare, both as a substantive and verb.   And many other of the above words may be detected by those who have time and inclination to search for them, in authors prior to Dryden's time.

vigorous; what is little is gay, what is great is splendid. He may be thought to mention himself too frequently; but while he forces himself upon our esteem, we cannot refuse him to stand high in his own. Every thing is excused by the play of images and the sprightliness of expression. Though all is easy, nothing is feeble; though all seems careless, there is nothing harsh; and though, since his earlier works, more than a century has passed, they have nothing yet uncouth or obsolete. * * * He, who writes much, will not easily escape a manner, such a recurrence of particular modes as may be easily noted. Dryden is always *another and the same.* He does not exhibit a second time the same elegancies in the same form, nor appears to have any art other than that of expressing with clearness what he thinks with vigour. His style could not easily be imitated, either seriously or ludicrously; for, being always equable and always varied, it has no prominent or discriminative characters. The beauty, who is totally free from disproportion of parts and features, cannot be ridiculed by an overcharged resemblance."

The last paragraph is not to be understood too literally; for although Dryden never so far copied himself as to fall into what has been quaintly called *mannerism;* yet accurate observation may trace in his works, the repetition of some sentiments and illustrations from prose to verse, and back again to prose.[1] In his preface to the Æneid, he has en-

---

[1] The remarkable phrase, "to possess the soul in patience," occurs in the "Hind and Panther;" and in the Essay on Satire, Dryden's Works, vol. xiii., p. 80, we have nearly the same expression. The image of a bird's wing flagging in a damp atmosphere, occurs in Don Sebastian, and in prose elsewhere, though I have lost the reference. The same thought is found in the "Hind and Panther," but is not there used metaphorically:

"Nor need they fear the dampness of the sky
Should flag their wings, and hinder them to fly."

Dryden is ridiculed by an imitator of Rabelais, for the recurrence of the phrase by which he usually prefaces his own de-

larged on the difficulty of varying phrases, when
the same sense returned on the author; and surely
we must allow full praise to his fluency and command of language, when, during so long a literary
career, and in the course of such a variety of miscellaneous productions, we can detect in his style so
few instances of repetition, or self-imitation.

The prose of Dryden, excepting his translations,
and one or two controversial tracts, is entirely
dedicated to criticism, either general and didactic,
or defensive and exculpatory.   There, as in other
branches of polite learning, it was his lot to be a
light to his people.   About the time of the Restoration, the cultivation of letters was prosecuted in
France with some energy.   But the genius of that
lively nation being more fitted for criticism than
poetry; for drawing rules from what others have
done, than for writing works which might be themselves standards ; they were sooner able to produce
an accurate table of laws for those intending to
write epic poems and tragedies, according to the

---

fensive criticism.   " *If it be allowed me to speak so much in my
own commendation ;*—see Dryden's preface to his Fables, or
any other of his works that you please."   The full title of
this whimsical tract, from which Sterne borrowed several
hints, is " An Essay towards the theory of the intelligible
world intuitively considered.   Designed for forty-nine parts.
Part Third, consisting of a preface, a postscript, and a little
something between, by Gabriel Johnson ; enriched by a faithful account of his ideal voyages, and illustrated with poems
by several hands, as likewise with other strange things not
insufferably clever, nor furiously to the purpose ; printed in
the year 17, &c."

best Greek and Roman authorities, than to exhibit distinguished specimens of success in either department; just as they are said to possess the best possible rules for building ships of war, although not equally remarkable for their power of fighting them. When criticism becomes a pursuit separate from poetry, those who follow it are apt to forget, that the legitimate ends of the art for which they lay down rules, are instruction or delight, and that these points being attained, by what road soever, entitles a poet to claim the prize of successful merit. Neither did the learned authors of these disquisitions sufficiently attend to the general disposition of mankind, which cannot be contented even with the happiest imitations of former excellence, but demands novelty as a necessary ingredient for amusement. To insist that every epic poem shall have the plan of the Iliad and Æneid, and every tragedy be fettered by the rules of Aristotle, resembles the principle of an architect, who should build all his houses with the same number of windows, and of stories. It happened, too, inevitably, that the critics in the plenipotential authority which they exercised, often assumed as indispensable requisites of the drama, or epopeia, circumstances, which, in the great authorities they quoted, were altogether accidental and indifferent. These they erected into laws, and handed down as essentials to be observed by all succeeding poets; although the forms prescribed have often as little to do with the merit and success of the originals from which they are taken, as the shape of the drinking-glass with the flavour of the wine which it contains.

" To these encroachments," says Fielding, after some observations to the same purpose, " time and ignorance, the two great supporters of imposture, gave authority; and thus many rules for good writing have been established, which have not the least foundation in truth or nature; and which commonly serve for no other purpose than to curb and restrain genius, in the same manner as it would have restrained the dancing-master, had the many excellent treatises on that art laid it down as an essential rule, that every man must dance in chains." [1]

It is probable, that the tyranny of the French critics, fashionable as the literature of that country was with Charles and his courtiers, would have extended itself over England at the Restoration, had not a champion so powerful as Dryden placed himself in the gap. We have mentioned, in its place, his " Essay of Dramatic Poesy," the first systematic piece of criticism which our literature has to exhibit. In this Essay, he was accused of entertaining private views, of defending some of his own pieces, at least of opening the door of the theatre wider, and rendering its access more easy, for his own selfish convenience. Allowing this to be true in whole, as it may be in part, we are as much obliged to Dryden for resisting the domination of Gallic criticism, as we are to the fanatics who repressed the despotism of the crown, although they buckled on their armour against white surplices, and the cross in baptism. The character which Dryden

[1] Introduction to Book Fifth of " Tom Jones."

has drawn of our English dramatists in the Essay, and the various prefaces connected with it, have unequalled spirit and precision. The contrast of Ben Jonson with Shakspeare is peculiarly and strikingly felicitous. Of the latter portrait, Dr Johnson has said, that " the editors and admirers of Shakspeare, in all their emulation of reverence, cannot boast of much more than of having diffused and paraphrased this epitome of excellence, of having changed Dryden's gold for baser metal, of lower value, though of greater bulk." While Dryden examined, discussed, admitted, or rejected the rules proposed by others, he forbore, from prudence, indolence, or a regard for the freedom of Parnassus, to erect himself into a legislator. His doctrines, which chiefly respect the intrinsic qualities necessary in poetry, are scattered, without system or pretence to it, over the numerous pages of prefatory and didactic essays, with which he enriched his publications. It is impossible to read far in any of them, without finding some maxim for doing or forbearing, which every student of poetry will do well to engrave upon the tablets of his memory. But the author's mode of instruction is neither harsh nor dictatorial. When his opinion changed, as in the case of rhyming tragedies, he avows the change with candour, and we are enabled the more courageously to follow his guidance, when we perceive the readiness with which he retraces his path, if he strays into error. The gleams of philosophical spirit which so frequently illumine these pages of criticism ; the lively and appropriate grace of illustration; the true and correct expression of the general propositions; the simple and unaffected passages, in which, when led to allude to his personal labours and situation, he mingles the feelings of the man with the instructions of the critic,—unite to render Dryden's Essays the most delightful prose in the English language.

The didactic criticism of Dryden is necessarily, at least naturally, mingled with that which he was obliged to pour forth in his own defence; and this may be one main cause of its irregular and miscellaneous form. What might otherwise have resembled the extended and elevated front of a regular palace, is deformed by barriers, ramparts, and bastions of defence; by cottages, mean additions, and offices necessary for personal accommodation. The poet, always most in earnest about his immediate task, used, without ceremony, those arguments which suited his present purpose, and thereby sometimes supplied his foes with weapons to assail another quarter. It also happens frequently, if the same allusion may be continued, that Dryden defends with obstinate despair, against the assaults of his foemen, a post which, in his cooler moments, he has condemned as untenable. However easily he may yield to internal conviction, and to the progress of his own improving taste, even these concessions, he sedulously informs us, are not wrung from him by the assault of his enemies; and he often goes out of his road to show, that, though conscious he was in the wrong, he did not stand legally convicted by their arguments. To the chequered and inconsistent appearance which these circumstances have given to the criticism of Dryden, it is an additional objection, that through the same cause his studies were partial, temporary, and irregular. His mind was amply stored with acquired knowledge,—much of it perhaps the fruits of early reading and application. But, while engaged in the hurry of composition, or overcome by the lassitude of continued literary labour, he seems frequently to have trusted to the tenacity of his memory, and so drawn upon this fund with injudicious liberality, without being sufficiently anxious as to accuracy of quotation, or even of assertion. If, on the other hand, he felt himself obliged to resort to more profound learning than his own, he was at little pains to arrange or digest it, or even to examine minutely the information he acquired, from hasty perusal of the books he consulted; and thus but too often poured it forth in the crude form in which he had himself received it, from the French critic, or Dutch schoolman. The scholarship, for example, displayed in the Essay on Satire, has this raw and ill-arranged appearance; and stuck, as it awkwardly is, among some of Dryden's own beautiful and original writing, gives, like a borrowed and unbecoming garment, a mean and inconsistent appearance to the whole disquisition. But these occasional imperfections and inaccuracies are marks of the haste with which Dryden was compelled to give his productions to the world, and cannot deprive him of the praise due to the earliest and most entertaining of English critics.

I have thus detailed the life, and offered some remarks on the literary character of JOHN DRYDEN: who, educated in a pedantic taste, and a fanatical religion, was destined, if not to give laws to the stage of England, at least to defend its liberties; to improve burlesque into satire; to free translation from the fetters of verbal metaphrase, and exclude from it the license of paraphrase; to teach posterity the powerful and varied poetical harmony of which their language was capable; to give an example of the lyric ode of unapproached excellence; and to leave to English literature a name, second only to those of Milton and of Shakspeare.

ABBREVIATIONS USED IN EDITOR'S NOTES

Macdonald   Hugh Macdonald, *John Dryden: A Bibliography of Early Editions and of Drydeniana* (Oxford: Clarendon Press, 1939).

Noyes   George R. Noyes (ed.), *The Poetical Works of Dryden* (new ed. rev.; Boston: Houghton Mifflin, 1950).

Osborn   James M. Osborn, *John Dryden: Some Biographical Facts and Problems* (New York: Columbia University Press, 1940).

Saintsbury   George Saintsbury, *Dryden* (London: Macmillan, 1881).

Ward   Charles E. Ward, *The Life of Dryden* (Chapel Hill: University of North Carolina Press, 1961).

EDITOR'S NOTES

p. 3, ll. 14–15
and n. 2:   The two-theatre monopoly still held in London at the time Scott wrote. For his views on the relationship of morality to the drama, see his "Essay on the Drama."

p. 5, ll. 3–4:   John Lyly, *Euphues: The Anatomy of Wit* (London: 1578 [not 1581]).

p. 6, l. 12:   "Bacon sat on the woolsack." The Lord Chancellor of England presides over the House of Lords while seated on a woolsack.

p. 11, n. 1:   John Cleveland, *Clevelandi Vindiciae; or Cleveland's Genuine Poems . . . with an Account of the Author's Life* (London: 1677).

pp. 16 ff.:   Corrections to Dryden's genealogy may be found in Osborn, pp. 235–252; and Ward, pp. 6–13.

pp. 17–18:   The Gunpowder Plot. A conspiracy by certain Roman-Catholics, notably Guy Fawkes and Robert Catesby, to blow up King James I and the members of Parliament on November 5, 1605, as a reply to the anti-Catholic laws which were being enforced by the king after a period of relaxation. The plot was discovered and most of the conspirators executed. Guy Fawkes Day (November 5) is still celebrated in England.

p. 20, l. 17:   Dryden's birth date is no longer uncertain. He was born August 9 (August 19, N.S.), 1631, at 5:33:16 P.M. For a discussion of this detailed nativity, see Roswell G. Ham, "The Date of Dryden's Birth," *Times Literary Supplement*, August 20, 1931, p. 633.

p. 21, ll. 1–2:   The records do exist and Dryden was baptized on August 14, 1631. See P. D. Mundy, "The Baptism of John Dryden," *Notes and Queries*, CLXXXIV (1943), 286, 352; and Osborn, p. 270.

p. 22, ll. 8–9:   Richard Brome, comp., *Lachrymae Musarum* (London: 1649).

p. 22, l. 20:   The "obscure libeller," as the note indicates, was Thomas Shadwell, who succeeded Dryden as poet laureate in 1688.

p. 24, l. 1:   The original inheritance, Noyes estimates (p. xviii), came to "about £40 a year."

p. 24, ll. 7–8:   An entry in the Trinity College records for April 23, 1655, indicates that Dryden was to forfeit a scholarship if he did not continue to reside at the College, and there is no evidence that he did remain at Trinity until 1657.

p. 26, n. 1:   Richard Corbet, Bishop of Norwich, *Poems,* ed. Octavius Gilchrist (London: 1807).

p. 29, ll. 2–4:   Osborn, pp. 168–170, agrees with Scott that Dryden was employed by his relative Sir Gilbert Pickering, Cromwell's Lord Chamberlain. However, accounts of Dryden's life between 1654 and 1659 are speculative.

p. 29, l. 6:   Noll, short for Oliver, is a nickname of Oliver Cromwell.

p. 29, l. 24:   "A flaming and bigoted puritan." In Scott's political and social essays, which occasionally touch on religion, he makes no personal evaluation between the Anglican and Presbyterian establishments, but he is generally severe on the sects.

p. 31, ll. 1–2
and 19–20:   "Heroique Stanzas Consecrated to the Glorious Memory of his Most Serene and Renowned Highnesse Oliver, Late Lord Protector of this Common-Wealth" in *Three Poems Upon the Death of his Late Highness Oliver Lord Protector of England, Scotland, and Ireland* (London: 1659). The first edition noted by Scott actually appeared "circa 1692," Macdonald, p. 7.

p. 31, ll. 8–12:   Scott's political prejudices are again obvious in these lines. He is strongly anti-Cromwellian in his historical writings.

p. 31, l. 13:   Richard is, of course, Richard Cromwell, son and successor of the Lord Protector.

p. 43, l. 10
and n. 1:   Scott derived these and subsequent comments on the spelling of Dryden's name from Edmond Malone (ed.), *The Critical and Miscellaneous Prose Works of John Dryden* (3 vols., London: Cadell, 1780), I, 3, n. 3; and 322, n. 7. Malone evidently decided that the matter was questionable, for he planned to drop the note on p. 322 from the second edition of his biography. But the second edition never appeared, and Scott accepted comments which apparently are without foundation. See Osborn, pp. 136–137; and p. 243, n. 33.

p. 43, l. 14
and n. 2:   Thomas Brown, *The Reasons of Mr. Bays Changing His Religion* (London: 1691); Thomas Shadwell, *The Medal of John Bayes* (London: 1682).

p. 43, ll. 16–17:   Herringman's employment of Dryden is studied by Osborn, pp. 168–183, who feels that the evidence for such employment is inconclusive.

p. 44, l. 11:   *Berkeley* should read *Berkshire.*

p. 44, l. 13:   *Cropley* should read *Cropredy.*

pp. 45–46:   The "Satire on the Dutch" was not a 1662 poem which Dryden later "wove into the prologue and epilogue of the tragedy of Amboyna," but a piece concocted by a bookseller in 1704 from the material in *Amboyna.*

p. 47, n. 1:   Footnotes by Henry Hallam are taken from his review "Scott's Edition of Dryden," *Edinburgh Review,* XIII (1808), 116–135.

pp. 58–59:   Scott is generally antipathetic to the French stage. For a fuller presentation of his views, see his "Essay on the Drama."

p. 59, n. 1:   Hester Chapone, 1727–1801, and Elizabeth Carter, 1717–1806, both prominent Blue Stockings.

p. 67, l. 14:   *Artificial* is a term Scott used consistently in its accepted nineteenth-century meaning of *artful.*

p. 67, ll. 22–25:   The scene is from Act IV Scene 1.

p. 68, l. 1:   *The Wild Gallant,* first acted on February 5, 1663, Macdonald, p. 100.

p. 69, l. 3:   Macdonald, p. 88, says *The Rival Ladies* was first acted "c. May 1684."

p. 71, l. 6:   *The Indian Emperour,* first performance "in the Spring of 1665 at the Theatre Royal," according to Macdonald, p. 92.

p. 72, ll. 5–6:   Monmouth was the illegitimate son of Charles II.

p. 74, ll. 6–9:   She became a nun sometime before July, 1675. See Thorn-Drury's comments in *Covent Garden Drollery* (London: 1928), pp. 135–137.

p. 74, l. 19:   The marriage took place on December 1, 1663.

p. 75, l. 8:   What Scott says of the Howard family attitude toward the marriage probably reflects his own class attitudes. There is no evidence that the Howards were in any way opposed to the marriage.

p. 79, ll. 8–10:   "Crites" is generally thought to represent Sir Robert Howard, but Noyes suggests the Earl of Roscommon as a more appropriate choice. See "Crites in Dryden's Essay of Dramatic Poesie," *Modern Language Notes,* XXXVIII (1923), 333–337. Sir Charles Sedley is represented by "Lisideius"; Charles Sackville, Lord Buckhurst, 6th Earl of Dorset by "Eugenius"; and Dryden by "Neander."

p. 79, ll. 22–30:   Dryden's preference for Shakespeare over Jonson was not characteristic of most seventeenth-century critics, but it was of decisive influence in the growth of Shakespeare's reputation. See Gerald E. Bentley, *Shakespeare and Ben Jonson: Their Reputations in the Seventeenth Century Compared* (Chicago: University of Chicago Press, 1945), I, 101–102.

p. 82, ll. 5–6:   *The Great Favourite, or the Duke of Lerma.*

p. 85, ll. 1–3:   Copies of the second edition of *The Indian Emperour* containing the " 'Defence' are very rare," Macdonald, p. 94; and it was not reprinted until well after Dryden's death.

p. 85, l. 20:   "in the course of the year": that is, every year.

p. 86, n. 1:   Osborn, pp. 184–191, has a full examination of the contract.

p. 88, ll. 1–2:   Scott is mistaken about the date. "First performance: 2 March 1667," Macdonald, p. 95, note. The note adds that "this may not have been the actual first performance." The play's full title is *Secret Love: or the Maiden Queen.*

p. 91, ll. 7–10:   Dryden's name appears on the title-page of the 1691 edition of *Sir Martin Mar-All*, which was first performed on August 15, 1667, and first published in 1668. *The Tempest* was first performed on November 7, 1667, Macdonald, pp. 97, 98, and 101.

p. 92, ll. 10–12:   *An Evening's Love* was first performed on June 12, 1668, and published in 1671, Macdonald, p. 106.

p. 93, l. 15:   *Tyrannick Love; or The Royal Martyr,* first acted in June, 1669. See Leslie Hotson, *The Commonwealth and Restoration Stage* (Cambridge: Cambridge University Press, 1928), pp. 250–253.

p. 95, l. 12:   *The Conquest of Granada,* Part I, first performed December, 1670; Part II, January, 1671.

p. 98, ll. 21–28:   Dryden was created Poet Laureate by a warrant dated April 13, 1668 (Davenant died April 7), and was sworn to the post on April 22. The Patent of August 18, 1670, conferred the post of Historiographer Royal on Dryden and confirmed his previous appointment as Laureate. Dryden's pension of £200 began on June 24, 1668, and was raised to £300 on July 2, 1677. See Edmund Kemper Broadus, *The Laureateship* (Oxford: Oxford University Press, 1921) pp. 59–74; and Louis I. Bredvold, "Notes on Dryden's Pension," *Modern Philology,* XXX (1933), 267–274.

p. 108, n. 1:   *The Censure of the Rota* (Oxford: 1673) was an anonymous attack on Dryden's heroic plays, particularly *The Conquest of Granada*.

p. 114, l. 25:   George Villiers 2nd Duke of Buckingham, *The Rehearsal* (London: 1672). A farce by Buckingham and others satirizing heroic plays, with particular reference to Dryden's work.

p. 116, n. 1:   Samuel Briscoe, *A Key to the Rehearsal* (London: 1704). Briscoe tried to pass it off as the work of Buckingham, and it appears as part of volume II of the *Miscellaneous Works of Buckingham* (London: 1704–1705).

p. 120, ll. 20–23:   Ward says *Marriage-à-la-Mode* was acted before *The Rehearsal*. See "The Dates of Two Dryden Plays," PMLA, LI (1936), 786–792. On the other hand, Macdonald, p. 110, suggests that there is no clear reference to *Marriage-à-la-Mode* in *The Rehearsal*.

p. 121, l. 12:   "Smith and Johnson" are characters in *The Rehearsal*.

p. 122, l. 3 and n. 2:   "Zimri" is a character portrait of Buckingham. The quotation in the note is from Dryden's "Discourse Concerning Satire."

p. 122, ll. 7–8:   Saintsbury, p. 52, makes essentially the same statement that *The Rehearsal* had the effect of a good advertisement for heroic dramas. Noyes, p. xxviii, also agrees with Scott.

p. 124, ll. 1–2:   The Theatre Royal was burned on January 25, 1672, and the King's Company occupied the former theatre of the Duke's Company in Lincoln's Inn Fields until their own house was ready in March, 1674.

p. 131, l. 21:   "Matthew," more properly "Martin," as Scott names him on page 116. In *A Key to the Rehearsal* he is called "Matt." Macdonald, p. 256, does not think that the four letters were published prior to 1687, despite the date.

p. 133, ll. 10–13:   Scott is mistaken. *A Description of the Academy of the Athenian Virtuosi* is a defense of Dryden and an attack on *The Censure of the Rota*.

p. 140, ll. 4–5:   Charles E. Ward, "The Dates of Two Dryden Plays," *PMLA*, LI (1931), 786–792, believes that *Amboyna* was designed as a piece of political propaganda, and that "we should place the date of the presentation some time before June 1672."

p. 149, ll. 20–22:   *The State of Innocence,* says A. W. Verrall in *Lectures on Dryden* (Cambridge: Cambridge University Press, 1914), p. 225, *was* intended for the stage.

p. 152, l. 10: Charles Blount, 1654–1693, wrote a defense of Dryden, *Mr. Dryden Vindicated*. Blount committed suicide.

p. 153, l. 1: Macdonald, p. 115, dates the first publication of *The State of Innocence* as 1677.

pp. 154 ff.: For an opposing view of Dryden's relations with Rochester, see V. de Sola Pinto, *Enthusiast in Wit: A Portrait of John Wilmot Earl of Rochester, 1647–1680* (Lincoln: University of Nebraska Press, 1962).

p. 158, l. 7: Scott follows Malone in attributing Settle's introduction at court to Rochester. The assumption is questionable, since Dryden at this time dedicated *Marriage-à-la-Mode* to Rochester. The Earl of Norwich probably was Settle's court patron.

p. 164, l. 16: Properly entitled *Notes and Observations on the Empress of Morocco*.

pp. 165–166: Macdonald, pp. 210–211, like Scott, sees Rochester's hand in the Calisto affair, but Pinto, *Enthusiast in Wit*, pp. 97–98, and Saintsbury in his edition of Scott's *Life of Dryden*, p. 162, disagree.

p. 168, ll. 10–13: The lines refer to a story that upon receiving a challenge to a duel from Otway, Settle admitted writing *A Session of the Poets*. He was not the author, and the story is probably false.

p. 171, ll. 5–9: Dryden's use of the word *zany*, which Rochester had previously used in an attack, is now thought to be a direct reference by Dryden to Rochester.

p. 172, ll. 3-5: Macdonald, p. 217, agrees that Dryden had no hand in the *Essay on Satire*; but Noyes, p. xxxix, believes Dryden may have had a hand in polishing the verse.

pp. 174–175: Current scholarship links the Duchess of Portsmouth rather than Rochester with the Rose Alley ambuscade. See J. Harold Wilson, "Rochester, Dryden, and the Rose Street Affair," *Review of English Studies*, XV (1939), 294–301; and V. de Sola Pinto, "Rochester, Dryden, and the Duchess of Portsmouth," *Review of English Studies*, XVI (1940), 177–178.

p. 176, n. 1: Coincidentally, Dryden may also have commented in verse, in the "barbarous assassination" of Thomas Thynne. See Osborn, pp. 253–254.

p. 178, ll. 17–18: Dryden may not have considered Rochester responsible for the ambuscade.

p. 181, l. 6: On the "Prosodia," see R. D. Jameson, "Notes on Dryden's Lost Prosodia," *Modern Philology*, XX (1923), 241–253.

p. 186, l. 6:	First performance of *All For Love*, "c. 12 December 1677," according to Macdonald, p. 117.
p. 188, ll. 29–30:	*The Kind Keeper; or Mr. Limberham.*
p. 198, n. 1:	*Chrononhotonthologus* by Henry Carey, produced in 1734, was a burlesque of the drama of the period.
p. 199, ll. 18–20:	Macdonald, p. 123, says of *The Spanish Friar*, "first performance: 8 March 1680." The "Popish Plot" was an anti-Catholic conspiracy based on evidence forged by Titus Oates, which purported to disclose a Jesuit plot to assassinate Charles II and crown the Duke of York, his Catholic brother.
p. 203, n. 2:	The translator is not Jonathan Dryden, but John Davies, 1627–1693. See the *D.N.B.*, V, 595.
pp. 204 ff.:	Since Charles II had no legitimate issue, the Duke of York was heir to the throne. The Duke of Monmouth was the son of Charles by Lucy Walter, his mistress during his exile in Holland. In order to exclude the Catholic Duke of York, Shaftesbury's party sought Monmouth's accession to the throne.
p. 205, ll. 28–29:	Robert Ferguson, d. 1714, called the "Plotter"; Edmund Witheringill, 1651–1708; Thomas Hunt, 1627(?)–1688.
pp. 209–210:	On the point of the "twelve additional lines" in the second edition of *Absalom and Achitophel*, Macdonald, p. 21, and Noyes, p. 959, suggest that these lines were present in the original draft of the poem.
p. 214, last line:	*1681* should read *1682*.
p. 218, ll. 8–9:	Macdonald, p. 224, doubts that Buckingham is the author of *Poetical Reflections . . . On Absalom and Achitophel*.
p. 218, ll. 11–18:	Both poems are attributed to Christopher Nesse, Macdonald, p. 225.
p. 226, l. 18:	*The Medal of John Bayes*, according to Osborn and Macdonald, was published in 1682.
p. 230, l. 12:	*Green-Dragon Club* should read *Green-Ribbon Club*. It is an allusion to the King's Head Club, whose Whig adherents wore a green ribbon in their hats.
pp. 242–243:	The political plot of *The Duke of Guise* centers about a conflict between Henry IV of France and the Holy League headed by the House of Guise, an obvious parallel to Charles I of England and his conflict with the Covenanters. The play had many other contemporary political parallels.
p. 244, l. 14:	The first performance of *The Duke of Guise*, Malone says, was on November 30, 1682.

p. 246, ll. 27–30: Macdonald, p. 243, doubts that Shadwell is the author of *A Lenten Prologue*.

p. 250, ll. 8–9: Rye House Plot. A plot to assassinate Charles II and the Duke of York in April, 1683, as they passed Rumbold's Rye House on the London road. The plot was discovered and some of the conspirators were executed.

p. 254, n. 2: Not *Religio Laici*, but Maimbourg's *History of the League*.

p. 259, l. 1: Scott is overly kind to Lewis Grabu's reputation.

p. 261, ll. 23–30: Dryden's reward for his religious conversion has been a subject of much investigation, and modern scholarship now maintains that he did not receive any such reward. See Louis I. Bredvold, "Notes on John Dryden's Pension," *Modern Philology*, XXX (1933), 267–274.

p. 276, ll. 3–7: This is now known to be an error; see the note for page 261. The additional £100 was conferred prior to James's accession to the throne and prior to Dryden's conversion.

p. 283, ll. 8–11: Charles Montague and Matthew Prior, *The Hind and the Panther Transvers'd to the Story of the Country-Mouse and the City-Mouse* (London: 1687).

p. 294, ll. 6–10: Contemporary scholarship denies that Dryden ever translated any hymn but *Veni, Creator Spiritus*. See George R. Noyes and George R. Potter (eds.), *Hymns Attributed to Dryden* (Berkeley: University of California Press, 1937).

p. 296, n. 2: "Hounslow Heath" appeared in a series of collections referred to as "Poems on Affairs of State." See Macdonald, pp. 316–318, for an account of these collections.

p. 310, l. 6: *Love Triumphant*, "first performance: c. January 1694," Macdonald, p. 134.

p. 312: Malone's list of plays must be checked against modern bibliographies and essays for corrections.

p. 314, n. 1: Osborn, pp. 261–265, accounts for three letters from Dryden to Dorset.

p. 319, l. 9: *1692* should read *1693*.

p. 320, ll. 3–6: William Walsh, *A Dialogue Concerning Women* (London: 1691); Sir Henry Sheeres, trans., *The History of Polybius* (London: 1693).

p. 327, ll. 1–3: For a corrected statement of Dryden's receipts from these translations, see Charles E. Ward, "The Publications and Profits of Dryden's Virgil," *PMLA*, LIII (1938), 807–812. Ward says Dryden made £590 8s. 8d. exclusive of gifts.

p. 343, l. 3: Charles Alphonse Du Fresnoy, *De Arte Graphica: The Art of Painting* (London: 1695).

p. 343, ll. 17–20: Dryden's part in this translation venture is given by Hardin Craig in "Dryden's Lucian," *Classical Philology*, XVI (1921), 150–163.

p. 345, ll. 15–27: The story of Lord Bolingbroke's visit to Dryden was first published by Joseph Warton in his *Essay on the Genius and Writings of Pope*, II, 19. Malone was skeptical of the anecdote; see Osborn, p. 136.

p. 350, ll. 7–8: Dryden wrote the poem "To Mr. Granville," which was prefixed to the 1698 publication of Granville's *Heroick Love*.

p. 355, l. 4: Richard Blackmore, *Prince Arthur, An Heroick Poem* (London: 1659).

p. 356, l. 7: Richard Blackmore, *A Satyre Against Wit* (London: 1700).

p. 358, ll. 13–17: Regarding the omission of the commendatory couplet, Macdonald, p. 291, notes that it "is not omitted in the next editions (2nd and 3rd, 1700), as Scott says it is; but it is omitted in Blackmore's Poems, 1718."

p. 359, l. 14: William Prynne, 1600–1669, a Puritan pamphleteer who wrote about two hundred books and pamphlets in an effort to reform the manners of his period.

p. 361, l. 11: Dryden was alleged to have designs not only on the Provostship of Eton, but on several other academic offices, particularly the Wardenship of All Souls College. See Macdonald, p. 138, n. 2; and Samuel Holt Monk, "Dryden Studies, A Survey," *ELH*, XIV (1947), p. 51.

p. 362, l. 22: "To My Honoured Kinsman John Driden."

p. 367, l. 14: Thomas Amory, 1691–1788, published the eccentric novel *The Life of John Buncle, Esq.* in two volumes, 1758 and 1766.

p. 368, l. 4: "Bottom = Physical resources; staying power, power of endurance; said esp. of pugilists, wrestlers, race-horses, etc.," *OED*, II, 1016.

p. 370, ll. 17–23: On the story of Dryden's death, see Ward, pp. 369–370, n. 8.

p. 381, l. 20: Narcissus Luttrell, 1657–1732, formed a large and valuable collection of fugitive poetical pieces. Though the collection was partially dispersed after his death, the British Museum later acquired the bulk of the collection.

pp. 384–385: Osborn, p. 147, notes that he cannot locate the source of the anecdote on Dryden's drinking habits.

p. 386, ll. 8–11: The almanac story is probably apocryphal, as it has many antecedents and variations.

p. 391, l. 17:   Ward, p. 370, n. 4, questions the account of Lady Dryden's insanity.

p. 392, ll. 1–2:   Mrs. Elizabeth Creed, Dryden's kinswoman, erected a tablet to his memory in Titchmarsh Church.

p. 394, l. 2:   "Corinna," Mrs. Elizabeth Thomas, who wrote an extravagant account of Dryden's funeral.

p. 395, ll. 2–6:   *1706* should read *1776*. He died in 1703.

p. 395, l. 19:   Erasmus-Henry succeeded to the baronetcy in 1710, not 1708.

p. 421, l. 1:   Joseph Trapp, 1679–1747, poet and academician, translated Virgil into blank verse.

Index